Violence and Subjectivity

Sponsored by the Culture, Health, and Human Development Program of the Social Science Research Council.

Violence
and
Subjectivity

EDITED BY
Veena Das,
Arthur Kleinman,
Mamphela Ramphele,
AND
Pamela Reynolds

UNIVERSITY OF CALIFORNIA PRESS
Berkeley   Los Angeles   London

University of California Press
Berkeley and Los Angeles, California
University of California Press, Ltd.
London, England

© 2000 by
The Regents of the University of California

Library of Congress Cataloging-in-Publication Data

Violence and subjectivity / edited by Veena Das . . . [et al.].
    p.   cm.
    Includes bibliographical references and index.
    ISBN 0-520-21607-5 (cloth) — ISBN 0-520-21608-3 (paper)
    1. Violence.   2. Political Violence.   3. International relations.
    4. Ethnic relations.   5. Subjectivity.   6. Context effects (Psychology).
    I. Das, Veena.
    HM886.V56   2000
    303.6—dc21   99055800

Printed in Canada

09 08 07 06 05 04 03 02 01 00
    10 9 8 7 6 5 4 3 2 1

To the memory of Neelan Tiruchelvam,
assassinated in Colombo in July 1999.
Neelan, in his life and work, exemplified the vision
and the courage to work for peace and democracy.

CONTENTS

ACKNOWLEDGMENTS

In 1993 the editors, who are members of the Committee on Culture, Health, and Human Development of the Social Science Research Council (New York), planned a series of volumes to examine anthropological questions on the relation of violence to states, local communities, and individuals. The first book, *Social Suffering*, explored the different ways in which social force inflicts harm on individuals and collectivities. In this, the second book in this series, we offer fourteen essays that explore the relation between violence and subjectivity from an off-the-center position. While the major part of the discussion is dedicated to what may be described as extreme situations, we include explorations into the more subtle violences of science and the state. All the essays address how violence shapes subjectivity and affects the capacity to engage everyday life. Together they contest a geography that makes a sharp division between "violence-prone areas" and "peaceful areas," and suggest that such shorthand descriptions might themselves have contributed to the shaping of violence in the present global context.

We are grateful to the Social Science Research Council (SSRC) for its support of this project and especially to Frank Kessel for his generously offered help in the different phases of the project. We thank Diana Colbert and Carrie Nitka for their assistance in organizational matters, and both D. Scott Giampetruzzi and Julie Lake for overseeing the final preparation of the manuscript. The John D. and Catherine T. MacArthur Foundation gave generous support for the SSRC Committee effort as a whole.

The essays in this volume were first discussed in a seminar entitled "Violence, Political Agency, and Self" in Delhi in April 1995, which was supported by the Rajiv Gandhi Foundation. Abid Hussain's enthusiasm for the project and the marvelous hospitality of the Foundation made it a memorable occasion. We are grateful to Shalini Joshi for the logistic help she provided. Above all we are indebted to the participants for the stimulating discussions. Unfortunately, for various reasons, the papers by Elizabeth Kiss, Achille Mbembe, Gyanendra Pandey, and Löic Wacquant could not be included. We take this opportunity to express our gratitude to them for their marvelous contributions to those discussions. Comments by two anonymous reviewers of the University of California Press were very helpful in revising the manuscript. Most important has been the patience of the authors, for which we are truly grateful. Stanley Holwitz at the University of California Press provided the right kind of impetus to bring the project to completion.

Veena Das
Arthur Kleinman
Mamphela Ramphele
Pamela Reynolds

Introduction

Veena Das and Arthur Kleinman

A new political geography of the world has emerged in the last two decades, in which whole areas are marked off as "violence-prone areas," suggesting that the more traditional spatial divisions, comprising metropolitan centers and peripheral colonies, or superpowers and satellite states, are now linguistically obsolete. The violence in these areas seems to belong to a new moment in history: it certainly cannot be understood through earlier theories of contractual violence or a classification of just and unjust wars, for its most disturbing feature is that it has occurred between social actors who lived in the same local worlds and knew or thought they knew each other. While some see this violence as a remnant of long-standing primordial conflicts, others see it as a sign of the distortion of local moral worlds by forces (national and global) which originate outside those worlds and over which local communities can exercise little control. In either case it becomes necessary to consider how subjectivity—the felt interior experience of the person that includes his or her positions in a field of relational power—is produced through the experience of violence and the manner in which global flows involving images, capital, and people become entangled with local logics in identity formation. Our notions of normality and pathology seem to be at stake as we explore the connections between the different forms of violence that pervade our contemporary world.

In 1993, the editors, who are members of the Committee on Culture, Health, and Human Development of the Social Science Research Council (New York), planned a series of volumes to examine anthropological questions on the relation of violence to states, local communities, and individuals. The first volume, *Social Suffering* (Kleinman, Das, and Lock 1997), dealt with sources and major forms of social adversity, with an emphasis on political violence. It gave illustrations of how transformations in cultural representations and collective experiences of suffering reshape interpersonal responses to catastrophe and terror. It also charted the effects of bureaucratic responses to human problems and found that these institutional actions can (and often do) deepen and make more intractable the problems they seek to ameliorate.

The present volume, the second in our series on social danger, examines the processes through which violence is actualized—in the sense that it is both produced and consumed. The comparative ethnographies provide graphic accounts of the manner in which everyday life is transformed in the engagement with violence, but in doing so the essays also interrogate the notion of the everyday as the site of the ordinary. Because most of the essays are located in spaces in which ongoing violence has blurred boundaries between violence, conflict, and peaceful resolution, they look at these issues from an off-the-center position in two senses. First, they ask how people engage in the tasks of daily living, rehabiting the world in the full recognition that perpetrators, victims, and witnesses come from the same social space. Second, they seek to analyze not only the explicit acts of bodily harm that occur in violent conflict but also the more subtle forms of violence perpetrated by institutions of science and the state. The traditional appeal of ethnography has been the ability to see the social world in terms of a scale that is commensurable with face-to-face inquiry. Yet these ethnographies reveal that larger social actors such as the state, international organizations, and the global media, as well as transnational flows in finances and people, are all implicated in the actualization of the violence that transforms the everyday life of local communities. In order to portray this heterogeneity of contexts, authors were invited to describe forms of violence that are widely dispersed—taking in ethnic riots, civil war, and the subtle technological violence of organized science and state policies and programs.

The strength of the ethnographies in this volume lies in their careful attention to detail and the long-term engagement of the ethnographers with the places and people they describe: they demonstrate that there is no straightforward translation of social scripts into social action. The continuous creation of new contexts and the sudden removal of the access to established contexts frame the manner in which violence and subjectivity tend to become mutually implicated in the contemporary world. Without presuming to summarize the rich descriptions in the essays, we indicate some of the themes which bind these ethnographies together.

GLOBAL FLOWS AND LOCAL LOGICS

Taking a close look at contemporary ethnic violence and wars, many scholars discern a bewildering loss of context as collective identities forged through practices of the nation-state, or through images that cascade through global media, invade the local worlds of face-to-face relations. Arjun Appadurai states it as follows: "The worst kinds of violence in these wars appear to have something to do with the distorted relationship between daily, face-to-face relations and the large-scale identities produced by modern nation-states and complicated by large-scale diasporas" (Appadurai 1996: 154). While there is much merit in this argument, it treats the actual processes through which such distortion happens as a black box; it also seems relatively silent on the ethnography of transnational institutions through which the pressure on locally defined identities is generated. The essays in this volume propose a tighter integration in the analysis of institutional failures and the phenomenology of affect in the analysis of collective violence through attention focused on the specificity of their interrelations.

The first chapter, "Violence-Prone Area or International Transition? Adding the Role of Outsiders in Balkan Violence," by Susan Woodward, can be read as a contribution to the ethnography of international organizations and to local-level forces in the large-scale violence in the case of former Yugoslavia. In terms of a story of local events, nostalgia for an ethnic identity led to an attempt to recover that identity through the process of war, and there was a longing to right the wrongs of history at one stroke through a violent confrontation with the "other." These longings came to form the rhetoric of the inter-ethnic violence in this region. While such longings for a lost home cannot be regarded as *causes* for the conflict—they do seem to have provided the local context within which the violence witnessed at the breakup of Yugoslavia may be said to have been actualized. In order to understand this actualization, though, we need to understand how the perception of international organizations concerned with international relations interacts with the vector of forces described above to change local worlds and the world at large in distinctive ways.

Woodward traces the outbreak of internal violence in Yugoslavia to the last decade of the Cold War, when the state in Yugoslavia was faced with a series of dilemmas, which eventually overcame it. Bringing the vision of a political scientist and security expert to these issues, Woodward shows first how the state broke down and then how communal violence emerged out of "the demand for majority rights in a land of minorities." Yet her argument is that these local failures, dangerously disturbing as they were, were ultimately of less significance for generating civil violence then the responses of the international community. The European community undermined Yugoslavia's political order. The IMF, NATO, and other international agencies, in the name of mediation, pressed the situation toward its violent denouement. The UN, individual European nations, and the United States all contributed to the Balkan debacle. What is tragic is that such concepts as "the culture of violence" and "violence-prone area" seem to have

served as a shorthand for international agencies to define away their own
role in the dissolution of the country by attributing a form of dangerous
subjectivity to the inhabitants of these regions. Woodward's acute analysis
shows that, rather than culture as a cause of violent peoples and places, it
was the politics of international relations and agencies that enabled the
internal disintegration to reach the point of complete breakup. This international politics of violence complements views from within settings of violence, suggesting that for each of the cases of local violence described in this
book, the level of nation-states and international agencies must be engaged
if we are to understand the powerful sources and consequences of internal
conflict.

The former Yugoslavia, Bosnia, Kosovo, Sri Lanka, and Rwanda loom
large in the popular imagination as places caught within a spiral of violence.
A theory of transnational flows needs to address not only how the representation of people and places as "inherently violent" distorts identity in
face-to-face relations, but also how the circulation of such images in the
global media seeps into the relatively peaceful and affluent homes in countries like the United States and alters the experience of social suffering. In
an impressive description of the "dismay of images," Arthur Kleinman
("The Violences of Everyday Life: The Multiple Forms and Dynamics of
Social Violence") offers an example of the way in which images of disaster
circulate and connect not only distant spaces but also different kinds of
events through analogy. Icons of Nazi savagery, which stand for extreme violation and horror, are offered in newspaper advertisements along with
more recent examples of the savagery of war in Bosnia or Rwanda. But what
does such a mediatization of violence do to the moral sensibilities of the vast
number of people who consume such images on television or in the press?
They may be moved to help by offering financial assistance while remaining
relatively secure that they risk nothing, for nothing very tangible is at stake
for them. Or they may tune out with the morally troubling excuse of fatigue
with victim accounts or even criticism of a culture of victimhood. Thus the
appeal of the perceived experience of suffering to mobilize social action
and create solidarity with the victims is transformed via the media into what
Kleinman calls "a dismay of images." If this dismay becomes overwhelming,
we are always free to switch the TV channel or turn the page of the newspaper to something more palatable for the moment. Thus the consumer of
these images may require ever more detail in words and images of hurt and
suffering to authenticate reality. This, in turn, alters the social situation of
the people on whose suffering this authentication is to be produced by making their interiority ever more present, as if their experiences were commodities that were being advertised. A transnational analysis of violence
must focus on the junction where the forms in which violence is produced
can be linked to the forms in which its images are consumed. If we have a

sense that such images of violence are displaced from their local contexts in the process of their circulation, we cannot yet ignore the fact that the media itself may be seen as generative of the contexts that produce authoritative versions of the different spatial mappings upon which we base our visions of global conditions.

In Kleinman's essay cultural representations also contribute to collective experience and the shaping of subjectivity. One cannot draw a sharp line between collective and individual experiences of social violence. These are so thoroughly interwoven that *moral* processes (i.e., social engagements centered on what is at stake in relationships) and *emotional* conditions are inseparable. Violence creates, sustains, and transforms their interaction, and thereby it actualizes the inner worlds of lived values as well as the outer world of contested meanings. Neither are social violence and its consequences only of one kind. Multiple forms and dynamics of social violence animate local worlds and the individual lives in them. From this perspective, the social violences of day-to-day living are central to the moral order: they orient norms and normality.

The relation between global flows and local logics raises powerfully the question of the struggle over the real. One of the important claims of modernity is that the forces that shape the world can be represented as totalities, which can, in turn, be verified. The genealogy of realism would point, however, to the *multiple* realisms through which legal, penological, and economic disciplines are instituted under the constitution of modernity. Several essays show how these realisms are experienced in both zones and times of terror. Allen Feldman, for instance, in his powerful analysis of the dangers of photography in Northern Ireland ("Violence and Vision: The Prosthetics and Aesthetics of Terror"), asks how realisms are experienced in zones of terror, where to be seen is to become hypervisible to the apparatuses of the state. The capacity to survive in such zones of terror consists not in optical clarity but in the ability to hide, dissimulate, and defuse one's presence. Photographs, documents, or numbers through which the real is authorized may circulate in many contradictory contexts and become the subject of micro-exchanges, which bear traces of the apparatuses of the state.

TRACES OF THE STATE: END OF MASTER NARRATIVES?

Although many have theorized that this is the era of declining states, the chapters that follow point to the contradictory aspects in which the state is encountered in the context of violence. In some cases it is the agency through which brutal violence is perpetrated, as in the hateful regime of apartheid in South Africa or in the violent civil wars in Sri Lanka and Northern Ireland. In other cases it ensnares the poor and the disadvantaged to work for it even in their own repression, as was the case of the national emergency in India; in still others it redefines violation through bureaucratic procedure to produce its own legitimacy by normalizing trauma in terms of business as usual, as in the case of hemophilic patients infected by the HIV virus in the United States. Finally, in cases such as that of former Yugoslavia, the absence of the state was the prelude to the desperate civil violence that followed.

The ambivalent role of the state invites us to focus attention on the processes through which the state works in everyday life in both the "emergency zones," as Feldman calls them, and in the relatively more peaceful situations when violence is muted. Behind, or rather in the neighborhood of, the official rationality and the rule of law to which the modern state is officially committed, lies the secret life of the state. Feldman shows how stories of photographs displayed in the briefing room of security officials become part of the rumors through which notions of the secret rituals of the state's repressive apparatus circulate. The rumors derive their authenticity from the everyday ecology of fear, mistrust, and anxiety in which life is lived in the zones of emergency.

These issues are further explored in several essays and show how the secret life of the state has its corresponding affect in the everyday ecology of fear and greed. Emma Tarlo, in her contribution ("Body and Space in a Time of Crisis: Sterilization and Resettlement during the Emergency in Delhi"), demonstrates how two administrative schemes, the Resettlement Scheme and the Family Planning Scheme, were implemented during the National Emergency declared in India in 1975. Though ostensibly formulated to provide housing for the poor and to control the burgeoning population, their mode of implementation ended up by making the poor into partners in the coercive programs of the state. Given the atmosphere of fear in this period when all fundamental rights were suspended, the lower echelons of the bureaucracy were under tremendous compulsion to meet targets and produce results. As part of bureaucratic procedures, claims to housing were made dependent upon the production of certificates of sterilization, though this connection was never officially acknowledged. This translated at local levels into a structure of co-victimhood—people searched for poorer relatives or neighbors who could be induced to undergo sterilization for money. An informal market in certificates arose in which the poor migrants, beggars, or other homeless people could be induced to undergo sterilization, and the certificates were sold to those who needed to show that they had motivated others, so that they could keep their jobs or their houses. By portraying the poor as active participants in the implementation of state policies of repression, rather than passive victims or noble resisters, Tarlo is able to show how the political regime of the National Emergency was able to draw different sections of people through fear or greed into its implementation.

Compelling cases for further understanding how the pathologies of the state get folded into everyday life are provided in the accounts of the destruction of the family under the long, unremitting violence of the regime of apartheid in South Africa and the terror of populations caught between the violence of the state and the terrorist organizations in Sri Lanka. But if the pathologies of the state acquire a life in the everyday, then we need to interrogate our idea of the ordinary. Is the ordinary a site of the uneventful, or does it have the nature of something *recovered* in the face of terrible tragedies?

INTERROGATING THE ORDINARY

The two essays dealing with the themes of family, kinship, and the shaping of masculinity in South Africa by Pamela Reynolds ("The Ground of All Making: State Violence, the Family, and Political Activists") and Mamphela Ramphele ("Teach Me How to Be a Man: An Exploration of the Definition of Masculinity") show how institutions of family and kinship which were singled out for destruction during the apartheid regime were bent, shaped, and deformed by the policies and programs of the state. There is an important difference in the cohorts of young men described by these two authors. Reynolds is narrativizing the lives of the young who were active participants in the Soweto rebellions, who could forge meaningful models of masculinity through engagement with the political process. Ramphele, on the other hand, is dealing with the ruinous consequences of apartheid on local communities. One of the most poignant points made by Ramphele is that the relations between the sexes and the intergenerational connections on which the flow of everyday life is premised were themselves destroyed under the policies of apartheid. There is a high prevalence of sexual abuse in the localities she studied. Intergenerational connections were broken as young boys were forced to do battle with "fathers" who controlled the squatter camps with the help of South African police. Thus, while there is an adherence *in form* to traditional norms of male initiation, the affirmation of maleness promised through intergenerational connections within the community of men has been completely broken down by the wars between fathers and comrades, among other wars. The definition of what it is to be a child is forcefully shaped by the experience of the ongoing violence in which children have played major roles. As one woman said to the researchers, "What is worse—letting children handle corpses and preside over funerals or getting them to settle family disputes?" Ramphele's engagement with the youth she describes is not only to show why it becomes so difficult under such conditions of violence to fulfill life projects that tradition enjoins, but also to ask how a young generation brought up under a brutal regime may be taught to take up fresh responsibilities as a new regime is brought into being. Her insights have much to offer on questions of what responsibilities toward the young need to be addressed as societies such as that of South Africa make a transition to democratic regimes and responsible governance.

Ethnography of this kind makes many of the concepts offered in recent years to explain brutal violence of civil society appear too mechanical. There is a slow erosion through which connections between generations, as in this case, or loss of trust in one's known world happen in the shadow of violence. Without a sense of people's unremitting engagement with violence in their everyday lives, through which their subjectivity is produced, it would be difficult to understand the manner in which their access to established contexts and trusted categories disappears. Patricia Lawrence, in her contribution ("Violence, Suffering, Amman: The Work of Oracles in Sri Lanka's Eastern War Zone"), puts it with devastating simplicity: "In Eastern Sri Lanka there is a pervasive sense of living out life without the possibility of extrication from the unrelenting political violation pressing upon daily life." Lawrence's essay provides one of the most powerful ethnographies on how the old maps and charts that guided people in their relation to the ordinary have disappeared. People have to "unlearn" normal reactions— for instance, they learn how *not* to respond to cries from a neighboring house in case their reactions are being watched by the security police or one of the terrorist organizations and are interpreted as sympathy for one or the other political cause. The grounds on which trust in everyday life is built seem to disappear, revealing the ordinary as *uncanny* and in need of being recovered rather than something having the quality of a taken-for-granted world in which trust can be unhesitantly placed.

We see this particular quality of everyday life as the loss of *context* even in face-to-face relations, as these are bent and distorted by the powerful social forces emanating from the state as well as terrorist, insurgency, or resistance movements. As faith in trusted categories disappears, there is a feeling of extreme contingency and vulnerability in carrying out everyday activities, a feeling to which all the essays provide testimony in one way or another. As Daniel points out in his essay, yesterday's terrorist could be today's prime minister. Everyday life is then something that has to be recovered in the face of a skepticism that surrounds it like a ditch. One is not safe simply because one never left home.

The relation between local structures of feeling and the large events that work their way into local communities is not easy to describe. Commenting on the diachronic dimension of this linkage, Appadurai (1996) suggests that local readings of macro events or cascades become shot through with local imaginings of broader regional, national, or international events. He goes on to state, however, that "the trouble with such local readings is that they are often silent or literally unobservable, except in the smallest of passing comments. . . . They are part of the incessant murmur of urban political discourse and its constant undramatic cadences. But people and groups at this most local level generate those structures of feeling that over time provide the discursive field within which the explosive rumors, dramas, and speeches of the riot can take hold" (153).

Deepak Mehta's essay in this volume ("Circumcision, Body, Masculinity: The Ritual Wound and Collective Violence") discusses precisely this question—how do local structures of feeling provide the discursive field within which the speech of riots takes place? The transitions he suggests are much subtler than even such a sensitive thinker as Appadurai can imagine. Mehta starts with a classical, thick description of the ritual of circumcision in an Indian Muslim community to show how this ritual encodes masculinity on the body and simultaneously marks the transition in the life of a child from having a "Hindu" uncircumcised body to the circumcised body appropriate to a Muslim male. But what Mehta is further interested in is to show how the notion of the Muslim as a circumcised body travels from the context of the ritual to that of exegesis in male conversations in everyday life. In everyday discursive talk, he argues, circumcision becomes a *verbal* rather than a *corporeal sign,* designated as *musalmani* (the making of a Muslim), through which men articulate the differences between Hindu and Muslim male identity. In his fascinating account of the circulation of these signs, Mehta reveals the slippage between the ideas of circumcision, the making of a Muslim, and castration—slippage which transforms the Muslim body, in the eyes of the Hindu, into a bestial body. The movement and slippage between the verbal signs leads to the reconstitution of the Muslim as one who is unable to respect boundaries necessary for the maintenance of social life: those between pure and impure, sexual abandon and control, man and animal. This magma of significations crystallizes during communal riots when the discourse of *musalmani* and *khatna,* both referring to rituals of circumcision and the dense encoding of maleness on the body, are completely effaced and replaced by the notions of *katua* (castration; lit., one who is cut), a kind of lack, circumcision becoming castration.

Examples of similar linguistic transformation, and especially the theme of animalizing a victim through verbal slippage, draw upon a rich cosmology in many cultures (see, for instance, Gilsenan 1996). Mehta's essay is a salutary reminder that face-to-face relations in local communities are fraught with the potential for violence and that the shifting of contexts as signaled in the use of different terms shows the impregnation of everyday life by the potential for violence. The point is that while nationalist or separatist projects might have further complicated the question of how identities are defined, the potential for effacing the concreteness of relationships and replacing them by imagined identities such as that of "the castrated ones" or "the sacrificial beasts" is equally embedded in the logic of everyday life. It is true that these are not the imagined identities created by nationalist or global discourses, but they are as removed from face-to-face relations as identities created by such processes as enumeration and classification of census reports.

REMAKING THE WORLD IN THE SHADOW OF VIOLENCE

Interestingly, while everyday life is fraught with the potential of danger, as many of these essays show, it is in the institutions of everyday life itself that we find the making of hope. Thus, despite the fact that under the regime of apartheid the black family was singled out for destruction, it was in the family that the youth who led and participated in the struggle against apartheid found shelter and solace. Reynolds's essay gives a moving description of the capacity of mothers to hold and support their children in times of terror, forming a counterpoint to the dominant ecology of fear and hatred. Reynolds offers an important methodology for looking at family in times of stress. She isolates co-residence as a factor, which provides an index to the political turmoil of the period. Thus the residential configurations, she suggests, cannot be analyzed as phases of the developmental cycle of domestic groups formed only by the gentle rhythms of births, marriages, and deaths. Rather, they indicate the processes of fleeing and hiding as children and youth faced and struggled with the brutality of the political regimes.

Veena Das's essay in this volume, "The Act of Witnessing: Violence, Poisonous Knowledge, and Subjectivity," similarly addresses the way in which the gruesome and terrifying brutalities of the Partition of India left a legacy of relationships marked by suspicion, bitterness, and betrayal not only between the Hindus and Muslims but also between men and women of the same community and even the same kinship groups. The violence that is folded into intimate, interpersonal relationships comes to constitute what Das, following Martha Nussbaum (1992), calls "poisonous knowledge." She shows that the way out of this knowledge for many women was not an ascent into some kind of godliness but a descent into everyday life. Through the life of one woman, Asha, Das shows how women engaged in the patient repair of relationships, establishing continuity between the estranged generations and the estranged sexes. The cultural memory of the Partition of India is made up of stories of women who chose to sacrifice their lives and thus were valorized in family narratives and popular culture in the Punjab. The trajectories of many female lives did not correspond to this culturally sanctioned memory: such women were often erased from familial accounts of the past. Yet the case of Asha shows that even the most injurious signs of violation could be taken up as part of one's own being to radically redefine the self and one's place in the world. The events of the Partition became points of origin of a new configuration of the self and the social world for Asha. Her case shows that subjectivity, understood as the lived and imaginary experience of the subject, creates both resistance to the expected norms through which women were expected to perform their gender identity and an elaborate subjection to these norms. These women "performed" their gender identities in a manner that made them the castaways of the official culture. Yet it seems to Das that they transformed the social death handed over to them into the birth of culture through acts of forgiveness.

Many who write about so-called violence-prone areas or a culture of violence often assume that powerful social scripts of vengeance and hatred get mechanically translated into social action. Such are the assumptions behind models of violence contained, for instance, in the genealogical models of the feud, in which agency is displaced from the person to a structural position. Collective violence particularly presents the temptation to homogenize a collectivity through languages of patriotism and betrayal in popular representations, which is then mimicked in anthropological accounts of this violence. Jonathan Spencer's essay ("On Not Becoming a 'Terrorist': Problems of Memory, Agency, and Community in the Sri Lankan Conflict") reformulates the question to ask: How do some individuals manage to *resist* the collective trance created through social pressures to join the violence? The figure of Piyasena, the villager who rejects the idea of community created through violence but can express his own subject position only through acts of avoidance, indicates that within the dominant ecology of fear, it is not easy to find individuals who actively resist the violence. But acts such as running from the scene of violence may not express consent; rather, these may be the only ways available to individuals to express their distance or even their disapproval of violence. Spencer's essay further shows that there are different ways of imaging violence which anchor the individual to the community. Thus the figure of the martyr provided the central trope through which the discourse of the Tamil militants sought to both demand sacrifices from individuals and give meaning to the deaths that have occurred in this movement. Piyasena's resistance to the seduction of this trope shows that nonviolence requires as much effort within this climate of alternating affects of fear and euphoria as does the capacity to engage in violent acts.

If Mehta's essay showed how local structures of feeling are generated to sustain the potential for violence, Lawrence, Spencer, Reynolds, and Das show the heterogeneity of these local structures of feeling and the potential for a different stance toward violence contained in them. Clearly the anthropological text must take into account these varied subject positions as well as the temporal realignments that prolonged engagement with violence seems to create at the level of local society. The identity of the individual cannot be seen as subsumed by the identity of the group, despite pressures toward totalization and clear demarcation of groups in times of terror. To the image of the consumption of violence through its mediatization we can now add the image of its consumption within local structures of feeling.

While the potential of dramatic stories relayed in rumors or in tea shop conversations to generate violence is important, as shown by Feldman and Mehta, there are also the counterimages of digesting, containing, and sealing through which local societies deal with this violence. These are especially important in the narratives of women (but not exclusively so) as they describe their work of protecting the future generations from the spirals of continuing violence.

MEMORY AND RENARRATIVIZING: THE CALL OF STORIES

How is the act of writing (on) violence to be conceptualized? This question haunts many of the authors of these essays and in fact mirrors the struggle with representation in the accounts of survivors and witnesses of violence. Valentine Daniel, for instance, takes us to the fieldwork context of Sri Lanka ("Mood, Moment, and Mind"), where a daughter who had witnessed her father's murdered body being dragged away, tied to an army jeep, in the midst of the applause and cheering of soldiers, asks him at one moment to write about the way her father was made to meet his brutal death and, at another moment, never to write about her father because the way he was made to die was a direct negation of all he had lived by. How is the writing to be commensurate to this kind of divided responsibility?

The survivor's tale or the sufferer's lament may be seen as examples of stories called forth out of what Lawrence Langer (1991, 1997) calls the "ruins of memory." But do the voices that speak through the wounded call victims to say something that is not theirs to possess? For a story to count as memory it must have a feeling of pastness about it, yet violence distorts the sense of time so that it becomes difficult to say when the past enters the present. In Daniel's words, "When the past facts return in memory and experience only to reactualize themselves, the past does not enter the flow of time in the full sense." Thus victims of violence as narrators appear as those who have already lost the means to author their stories. Perhaps for this reason one of the struggles of survivors is to find the means of reestablishing authorship over their stories.

Two opposite ways of responding to the loss are evident in the accounts given in these ethnographies: both relate to the collective authorization of individual experience. In the first case a culturally authorized form draws out a story of terror to return the subject to her everyday life. The stories that are made present by Saktirani's enactment of terror in Lawrence's telling; or those that have taken the form of poisonous knowledge in the life of Asha, the protagonist of Das's essay; or the accounts related to the researchers in South Africa do not become part of the official public memory. In the case of South Africa some of these stories are now part of the public memory through the work of the Truth and Reconciliation Commission, but others continue to be circulated only in small private circles away from the eyes of the judicial work being performed by the Commission. Take the poignant example of the young boy who is in a demonstration, arrested by the police, and imprisoned. Reynolds describes how—hungry, alone, and afraid—he suddenly hears his name being called by his mother, who, unable to get any information about him, had simply trudged along from one prison to another, calling out his name. The feel of this cadence is registered only on the walls of the child's memory, though many would have read accounts of the brutal torture and imprisonment of young children in South Africa. When we ask how the subject is produced under such conditions of violence, we have to recognize that much work on the production of the subject is invisible to public commissions and judicial inquiries. Such repertoires of sensory memories call for authorization in culturally recognized forms but paradoxically also exceed these forms. In this sense the various lines of connection and exclusion established between these forms complicate the relation between cultural memory, public memory, and the sensory memory of individuals.

An opposite direction may be discerned in the relation between collective hurts and public recognition of these hurts in some of the other essays, as in the cases of Guatemala and Nigeria described respectively by Kay Warren and Murray Last. How a society deals with the violence of memories as it moves from active warfare to low-intensity peace is demonstrated in the pan-Mayan movement in Guatemala. Kay Warren's analysis of Mayan multiculturalism and the violence of memories shows how Mayan intellectuals dismantle the *authoritativeness* of accounts of sixteenth-century Spanish chronicles that recorded the initial contacts with indigenous peoples in the New World and are still seen as neutral windows to the national past. Reading the texts against the grain, as many subaltern historians have done with other colonial records, the Mayan intellectual Enrique Sam Colop is able to authorize a new account of the past in which the reverberation of terror through centuries is mastered and molded. Connective flashes that are attuned to the reverberations of signals that have to do with torture, confession, and punishment from the sixteenth to the twentieth centuries are not one-way temporal insights, Warren suggests. These flashes represent the reflection of present violence and racism in a past of which the present is a part.

Thus the question of memory and representation is not only a question of the authenticity of memories, as if these were written in stone, but the struggle to author one's stories in relation to representations that seek to impose a different kind of truth on them. The pressure to create a different kind of past for oneself is related to how one deals with the violence of memories in the present. The notion of memory as text may be complemented perhaps by the idea that work is required to forge a future in relation to a violent past. In our contemporary political context, with its emphasis on the "politics of recognition," such work is oriented toward creating a public sphere in which the hurts of the victims may be voiced: dramatic gestures in which representatives of the state have offered "regrets" or "apologies" for historical wrongs committed on behalf of the state come to mind.[1] At one level such gestures are important because they signify an acknowledgment of the "crimes" of the state even when it has acted within the "law." As per-formative gestures, however, the "apologies" acquire force only if notions of "sincerity" and "authenticity" can be read in these gestures and if there can be an agreement on the identification of communities as perpetrators and victims as these are crafted through such gestures. On this point Murray Last's essay ("Reconciliation and Memory in Postwar Nigeria") offers impor-tant and novel insights. Taking us back to the Nigerian civil war and Biafra's attempted secession in the tumultuous period of 1966 to 1970, Last argues that the policy of reconciliation was a move made by the government mid-way through the war as an inducement to bring the fighting to an early end. Thus reconciliation was not coupled with "truth" and was oriented toward different kinds of ends—those that had to do with resumption of everyday life rather than with justice or healing. As Last states it, "Hurt was shifted out of the public domain and became a dimension of private memory . . . there was no public judgment on what had been suffered, no reparations, no apology; almost no one was held to be accountable for what they had done. Nor were any medals awarded."

Last's essay then addresses the issues of memory and recovery that arose in local communities away from public debate. He points to the divisions within the category of victims—the Biafrans who could re-create commu-nity on the basis of the solidarity born of "heroic failure" are distinguished from the communities on the margins that were divided by their differential support of Biafra or Nigeria. Further, not all communities had the same resources to benefit from the state policies of reconciliation, rehabilitation, and reconstruction. Thus, while dramatic gestures of apology construct the victims as singular communities, the work of rehabilitation sees survivors as having very different capacities to reengage with everyday life. Recon-ciliation therefore is a complex process of reestablishing sociality, in which the differential stakes of not only the perpetrators and victims (different from the vanquished), but also of witnesses and bystanders, must be under-stood in order for a return to everyday life to become possible.

The major part of this volume is dedicated to the understanding of vio-lence in extreme situations, but the organizing tropes are not those of hor-ror and mesmerizing brutality—instead there is a turn toward the everyday, within which the authors have engaged questions of violence and subjectiv-ity.[2] Thus, whether the context is that of the ecology of fear or the redefinition of family, violence is seen in these ethnographies as having a temporal depth that influences the patterns of sociality. The stake in the everyday takes us further into an exploration of how violence is embedded in the "normal" patterns of sociality in Western industrialized societies.

Describing what he calls "the *violences* of everyday life," Arthur Kleinman makes a case for understanding the variety of ways in which structural violence affects people throughout the social order. He argues that the lion's share of ethnographic description has dealt with the violence of everyday life almost as if that form of violence were equivalent to the social experience in shanty towns and slums in poor countries or in the poorest inner-city ghettos of wealthy nations. Yet violence that is multiple and mundane may be all the more fundamental, because it is out of such hidden or secret violence that images of people are shaped and experiences of groups are coerced. One telling example is the manner in which the experiences of hemophilia patients in North America who were exposed to infected blood products has been "normalized" through routine bureaucratic procedures. Is there an insight here regarding how disaster is absorbed through bureaucratic procedures and is made to appear as part of a world engaged in "business as usual"? It seems to us that to understand the cases of extreme violence described in many of the essays in this volume, another generation of ethnographers must describe further the routinization and domestication of the experiences of violence. On the other hand, it is imperative to see how the violences which may have become buried in the routines of the everyday may acquire life—how unfinished social stories may be resumed at different times to animate feelings of hate and anger.

The essay by Margaret Lock on the world of transplant technology ("The Quest for Human Organs and the Violence of Zeal") seems far removed from the scenes of violence and death described in most of these essays. Its importance lies in the new directions in which it takes the discussion on violence. Lock argues that the rhetoric of progress within which scientific experimentation takes place masks a violence of zeal. In the world of transplant technology which she scrutinizes, bodies of donors and recipients of organs are brought into intimate relations. This coupling is, however, elided in the success stories of this technology by silencing the plight of those from whom organs are taken. The protocols through which death is defined and ethical rules for procurement of organs formulated have to be interpreted in specific institutional contexts where subtle distinctions between deserving recipients and nondeserving ones are put into place. Thus, while the *rhetoric* of transplant surgery focuses on its success in saving lives, the *practices* show a far greater ambivalence. Lock suggests that until the practices on which the progress of science is based can be named as violence and the ramifications of these practices in the lives of communities and individuals are documented, the language of these discourses will continue to mask this violence as progress. We must note here that Lock does not take an essentialist antitechnology position. In fact she concedes that the inherent tension between the experimental and the therapeutic in the pursuit of medical knowledge cannot be avoided. But she argues that it is only through the recognition of this tension that a more informed public discussion on the manner in which transplant technology affects the lives of both recipients and sources ("donors" in ordinary parlance) of organs can take place. Even the language which renames "sources" as "donors" needs to be examined in order for the hidden face of this violence to be revealed.

Taken together, these essays question any established distinctions between war and civil violence on the one hand, and times of violence and times of peace on the other. The dividing line between the different forms of violence, as these essays show, has become extremely thin in empirical situations. Further, the distinction between war and civil violence has been called into question, since it reproduces the distinction between contractual and noncontractual violence based on the presumed monopoly of the state over the use of violence. Once we add to this the manner in which the violence of extreme situations is carried into everyday life, we realize that a radical reconceptualization of everyday life seems necessary. The reverse movement is suggested by Kleinman and Lock, in which we study and name the embedded violences of everyday practices of the state and institutionalized science in order to understand and delineate the varieties of social suffering. Only thus may it be possible to dismantle the social geography by which violence is sought to be localized in "violence-prone areas."

One can sense an exasperation among the international elite of policy makers and bureaucrats who demand that social scientists should be able to suggest solutions rather than go into the minutiae of the lived experiences of people caught up in such violence. Daniel's account in this volume suggests that such demands for clarity often produce habits of description that tempt one into "premature acceptance of meanings that culture has to offer, or the ready-made solutions the social scientist comes up with."

Anthropological framings of how violence relates to individual agency, no less than the framings of policy makers, carry with them prepotent moral and political implications. The conundrum of how to square collective and individual responsibility for social violence is not readily resolvable in most cases and often returns us to the cul-de-sac of agency/structure debates in social theory. Thus, conceptual framings have to be examined with respect to their potential uses. On this issue there is no avoiding moral and political entailments. There are no neutral framings. If we understand individuals in civil disturbances running amok in deadly trances—their subjectivity dominated and commandeered for crowd violence by master puppeteers and enigmatic political engineers who work behind the scenes on behalf of dark forces, their agency motivated and focused by a nucleus of commodities, thugs, and criminals, their targets the result of atavistic religious or ethnic hatreds, or their actions a kind of protective adaptation to the most dangerous of circumstances, then the issue of responsibility for atrocity or failure of witnessing is too easily side-stepped, and the potential for refusal or resistance denied. But if the language of such framings is instead that of individual choice, then the powerful effects of deep structure, social process, relationships, and collective action are obscured, while the determination of victims and victimizers is made too absolute. If we constrain agency in an explanatory framing so fully that no individual persons are to blame, then ethical responsibility cannot be assigned. Make everything agency, and local moral worlds lose the sense of powerful social constraints that organize collective experience. As a number of the contributions to this collection make clear, both moral processes and ethical judgments must be taken into account and understood within the context of politics and social history. This is the source of a crucial uncertainty and indeterminacy in social analysis that is perhaps as adequately set out in ethnography as it is in biography. This is Primo Lévi's "gray zone," where the drowned and saved commingle (Lévi 1989). There is no new answer. But there is also no turning away from the search for reducing the tension by making framings attentive to the lineaments of interaction of collective and individual experience. The theoretical moves in contemporary anthropology in reconceptualizing violence need to have a companionship with new practices of ethnographic work and textual production. We offer this book as a step in that direction.

NOTES

1. Examples include the apology offered on behalf of Germany to Polish Jews and regrets on behalf of Japan to the Korean "comfort" women. Demands for such apologies have been made recently by representatives of several groups, including indigenous populations. Notions of guilt, remorse, and apology as these inform public action offer a rich field for exploration; see Cox (1999).

2. The way in which the use of such tropes signaled the emergence of "violence" as a new kind of object in anthropological discourse is masterfully analyzed by Jeganathan (1998) for Sri Lanka. In his words, "In the rhetorical economy of these texts horror remains an untheorized trope."

REFERENCES

Appadurai, Arjun. 1996. *Modernity at Large: Cultural Dimensions of Modernization.* Minneapolis: University of Minnesota Press.

Cox, Murray. 1999. *Remorse and Reparation.* London: Jessica Kingsley.

Gilsenan, Michael. 1996. *Lords of the Lebanese Marches: Violence and Narrative in an Arab Society.* Berkeley: University of California Press.

Jeganathan, Pradeep. 1998. "'Violence' as an Analytical Problem: Sri Lankanist

Anthropology after July 1983." *Nethra: Journal of the International Centre for Ethnic Studies* 2 (4): 7–47.

Kleinman, Arthur, Veena Das, and Margaret Lock, eds. 1997. *Social Suffering.* Berkeley: University of California Press.

Langer, Lawrence. 1991. *Holocaust Testimonies: The Ruins of Memory.* New Haven: Yale University Press.

———. 1997. "The Alarmed Vision: Social Suffering and Holocaust Atrocity." In Kleinman, Das, and Lock, 1997.

Lévi, Primo. 1989. *The Drowned and the Saved.* Trans. Raymond Rosenthall. London: Michael Joseph.

Nussbaum, Martha C. 1992. *The Fragility of Goodness: Luck and Ethics in Greek Tragedy and Philosophy.* London: Cambridge University Press.

Violence-Prone Area
or International Transition?

Adding the Role of Outsiders in Balkan Violence

Susan L. Woodward

The end of the Cold War left the West without markers to identify potential threats to its way of life or reasons to be prepared. With the collapse of communist regimes in Eastern Europe, followed spectacularly by the dissolution of the Soviet Union itself, the global ideological confrontation that had served so well to identify friend and foe vanished. Behind the euphoria of people in the West that they had "won" the war and that everywhere peoples were conceding their superiority by liberalizing trade, reducing governmental powers, and privatizing banks, postal services, transport, health care, and public sector firms, there was a growing disquiet (in some corners even nostalgia for the Cold War) over the loss of clarifying categories. The world had become an undifferentiable mass of friends. Where was the threat to national security? What potential dangers justified expenditures on armed forces and intelligence, and told national and collective security organizations how to adjust?

The violent collapse of Yugoslavia, followed by communal violence in many parts of Africa, the Caucasus, and the Middle East, provided an answer. The world was clearly divided into violence-prone areas and zones of peace and stability. The zone of peace was at risk from the zone of violence. The West, as a peaceable area, must build a buffer between it and these areas to protect it from infection and spillover of violence and refugees.

The Balkan peninsula is the quintessential "violence-prone area" in this new understanding of threats to global peace and security. This concept of violence-proneness contains two elements: *inevitability* and *otherness*. According to the first, people who live in such areas are inclined, almost genetically, as a result of centuries of antagonism and combat, to manage social relations by reaching for a gun and resorting to violence; and this tendency is buttressed by a cultural climate of ethnic hatred and traditional justice executed through blood feud. According to the second element, their violent nature distinguishes the Balkans from the West. They are violent, we are not.

The location of the Balkan peninsula on the edge of Europe heightened receptivity to this new classification, for the wars in the disintegrating Yugoslavia did clearly appear, over time, to represent a new type of security threat to the core area of stable, civilized (an essential term in the new differentiating discourse), normally peaceable areas and peoples. So close to home, the real violence during 1988–99 in Slovenia, Croatia, Kosovo, and especially Bosnia and Herzegovina required some response, thus giving policy momentum to this classification. Pressures to intervene and stop the violence, the flow of refugees, and the televised pictures of horrendous atrocities and massive columns of displaced persons moving shell-shocked away from their homes raised a fundamental policy challenge to an international community and its leading powers, who were still thinking in Cold War terms. What principles should the major powers of the world defend in the post–Cold War era? What were the new threats to their security? What principles legitimize intervention against such threats? Under what conditions should they intervene? What were the limits to intervention?

At the same time, the perception that violence was inevitable in the Balkans—that despite geographical propinquity, they were not real Europeans—programmed a nearly automatic distancing. Even before the wars began and disturbing events had provoked early warnings that a breakup of Yugoslavia was imminent and that it would be profoundly violent, policy makers in Washington adopted a stance of sorrowful resignation. This was the Balkans, where violence is common, and if it erupts, outsiders can do little to stop it until the opponents exhaust their bloody urges. The proper policy response of outsiders, western Europeans also concluded, was containment: keep the people and their wars *in* the Balkans.

The Balkans, it is true, have an ancient reputation for instability and internal conflict that had even spawned its own classification in the Western term *Balkanization*.[1] In explaining why the area should be prone to *violence,* pundits and politicians cited a history of ethnic hatred and political fragmentation. With the disappearance of the Second World and its ideological alternative, this idea of ethnic conflict provided a distinct analytical advantage regarding an environment that was still too undefined and in transition to generate its own ideological category.[2] An immense literature on the Third World could simply be transplanted. Analysts of the Yugoslav wars that begin in 1991 were classified into one of only two schools borrowed from studies of postcolonial regimes in the Third World: the primordialists, who believed that ethnicity was inherent and tribalistic, and that ethnic conflict was by definition violence-prone; and the instrumentalists, who attempted to demonstrate the tendency of power-hungry politicians to incite ethnic conflict and nationalism as a way of resisting change and loss of power.[3]

The end of the Cold War added fuel to this way of thinking because of the Western equation between anticommunism and a yearning for freedom. Anticommunist ideology viewed communist rule as an alien imposition, whereas nationalism was a reasserted pride in cultural distinctiveness and national history. If nationalism was separatist, it was only an extension of this yearning for freedom to the nation itself, a natural development favoring national liberation and independence. Violence revealed forces of reaction, which opposed the historical development favoring nation-states and, if necessary, wars of independence.

VIOLENCE IN FORMER YUGOSLAVIA

The Axis occupation of pre-socialist Yugoslavia in World War II (when Germany, Italy, Hungary, and Bulgaria each took a piece of the country, and puppet fascist regimes were set up in Croatia and in Serbia) was extremely violent.[4] Debates continue fifty years later over the number of deaths from combat between occupying and liberating armies, from civil war among competing domestic armies, from concentration camps and nationalist pogroms of extermination, and from individual opportunities to avenge past grievances. Three years after the end of war in Europe and the liberation of Belgrade in October 1944, moreover, a conflict between the new Yugoslav President, Marshal Josip Broz Tito, and the official head of the world Communist movement, Joseph Stalin, provoked a second civil war combining ideological and fratricidal elements.

Except for the highly unusual attempts in the early 1970s by bands of anticommunist émigrés from Austria and Germany to provoke popular uprisings in Bosnia and Croatia, however, everyday life in the Yugoslavia of 1949–80 was remarkably peaceful, stable, and increasingly prosperous. Communal disturbances did occur in Croatia in a wave of political nationalism in 1967–71. Periodic tensions between the ethnic Albanians of Kosovo, an autonomous region of the Serbian republic, and either the Yugoslav federal government or Serbian internal security forces had been a part of the landscape ever since the Balkan Wars of 1912–13. But on the scale of communal violence in other parts of the world, both instances were remarkably low in physical violence.

Beginning in August 1990, the story changes, with armed confrontations in the republic of Croatia between internal security (militarized) police and local police of Serb ethnicity in an area that once formed the military border (*krajina*) between the Habsburg and Ottoman empires. By the spring of 1991, confrontations between Croatian officials and Serb locals and between ethnic Croat and ethnic Serb paramilitaries had become common. At the end of June 1991, a ten-day war erupted in Slovenia between the federal army and Slovene territorial defense forces after the republic's government declared independence from Yugoslavia. That war left about sixty-eight dead, nearly all of them conscripted soldiers of the Yugoslav army, and more than three hundred injured, including foreign truck drivers used as hostages. By late July, the civil disturbances in Croatia were also evolving into a war of Croatian secession (Croatia had joined Slovenia in declaring its independence, on June 25). By mid-August, the population expulsions on the basis of national (ethnic) affiliation, fratricidal atrocities, and the shelling of cities that later came to be associated with Balkan violence were in full view.

Despite the signing on November 23, 1991, of a cease-fire agreement between the Croatian and federal armies, negotiated by a special envoy of the United Nations secretary general, civil disturbances in the neighboring republic of Bosnia and Herzegovina also exploded into horrendous war in April 1992. The regularly televised violence between political parties representing Bosnia's three national groups (Bosnian Muslims, Bosnian Serbs, and Bosnian Croats)—cities under siege; terrorized prison camps; massive forced marches and expulsions of civilians; destruction by fire, bombs, and mortars of homes, religious institutions, and cultural monuments amounting to cultural genocide—which outside intervention brought to a halt only in October 1995 seemed to confirm beyond a doubt that the Balkans were a violence-prone area.

The explanation for this outbreak of civil violence and wars of independence, however, lies in quite specific events and political disputes during the preceding ten years. What is now called the end of the Cold War was a drawn-out process of transformation within socialist countries in Europe and between the two ideological blocs of East and West that accelerated during 1982–85. Although Yugoslavia was not a member of either bloc, the consequences of economic and political reform to adjust to a balance-of-payments crisis, on the one hand, and the growing incompatibility between the assumptions of economic development policy and the society that such policy had transformed in preceding decades (including urbanization, industrialization, rising levels of education, health, and professionalization), on the other, were bringing the political and social order to the brink of collapse. Popular disgruntlement at a sharp decline in living standards and the loss of expected status and jobs gave rise to youthful rebellions and to bolder critiques of the system by anticommunist intellectuals, but there was no countrywide social movement to overthrow the regime comparable to those that occurred in the eastern bloc countries. Yugoslav communism had provided a relatively high and growing standard of living until the economic crisis (albeit on the false bottom of borrowed funds and long-term, structural unemployment). Instead, each social group and federal republic began to fight to keep what it had and preserve its socialist property rights against the onslaught of fiscal crisis and liberalization. The road to war, however, lay with the crucial role of the state as prime mover *and object* of reform, lightning rod for dissatisfaction, and guarantor of peace and security.

The Yugoslav state had three functions. Like any modern state, it held a monopoly in the legitimate use of violence, although as states go, this authority over coercive power was dispersed across a large number of actors. The armed forces were composed of two parts: a standing federal army, and territorial defense forces (TDF) under republican authority comprising locally based, all-citizen militia and local stockpiles of weapons and defense supplies. The internal security forces of each republic also had militarized police units, and each locality had local police forces. As a part of Yugoslavia's national security policy of self-reliance, the army had become the fifth largest in Europe, with a substantial economic role through contracts for domestic supplies and defense goods resulting from the requirement that a minimum of one-third of all its military needs be produced at home. By 1983, however, domestic defense industries were producing 80 percent of the army's needs, and the export of arms and engineering services exceeded imports at an ever higher rate, up to four times in value terms by 1985 (Gow 1992: 103). Moreover, repeated reductions in the scope of federal expenditures, due to successive fiscal decentralizations aimed at currency stabilization, had made veterans' benefits and pensions one of the largest remaining federal expenditures, while veterans' housing programs were a substantial local expenditure.

The second function of the state, also common to other modern states, was to confer and enforce rights. These rights included civil rights regarding the equality of citizens, as individuals and as members of national communities, and also economic and social rights, such as the right of individuals in public sector employment to a guaranteed income and a share of enterprise profits, the right of men and women to equal pay for equal work, the right of property owners (local and republican governments, in fact) to a share in enterprise profits, the right of firms to retain a specified proportion of earned income (including foreign exchange, which was essential to foreign trade and more often referred to as *rights* to import on the basis of export earnings), and the right of individuals in the private sector to subsistence.

The third function of the state was protection. As the creation of a political movement that organized in response to the consequences of agrarian and industrial depression in the 1920s and 1930s, with an ideology based on protecting the weak and propertyless against exploitation, the socialist state defined its raison d'être in terms of preventing exploitation and ensuring the survival—minimum material subsistence—of all its citizens. The

Yugoslav system of self-managing market socialism differed greatly from the Soviet model of central planning. After Tito's quarrel with Stalin, the system went through almost continuous reform of the kind introduced in the Soviet Union under Gorbachev in the mid-1980s, intended to make firms ever more autonomous, run by managers and workers in consultation, to give market signals an ever greater role in production and marketing decisions, and to decentralize planning decisions to the republics. The economy was managed by indicative planning, export subsidies, income policies, and fiscal redistribution. But its goals remained full employment, rising standards of living based on highly egalitarian foundations, including federal transfers to the budgets of below-average localities, and regional development.

In the course of the 1980s, all three functions of the state began to break down. A fiscal crisis and budget-cutting austerity program of debt repayment signed with the International Monetary Fund undermined the government's ability to provide protections and guarantee minimum welfare. Hyperinflation and mass unemployment (affecting 70 percent of the generation aged fifteen to twenty-five) spread uncertainty about survival itself to an ever larger part of the population. The authority of the federal government was severely challenged by liberalizing economic and political reforms and by republican politicians who opposed any loss of economic rights they had obtained during the decentralizing reforms in the 1970s. The result was a serious decline in the federal government's capacity to enforce rights. By 1988–89, two of the six republics (Slovenia and Croatia) began secretly to build separate armies, and this together with the growth of paramilitary groups aligned with emerging, right-wing political parties in many parts of the country indisputably ended the state's monopoly on the legitimate use of violence by early 1991.[5]

There is no need for any history of ethnic animosity or civil war to predict growing uncertainty, social chaos, and potential violence under such circumstances. The violence that later ensued was not a revival of historical patterns or cultural traits, although historical memories were recalled (or invented) by political leaders to justify the claims they were making against the federal government or each other. Instead, the violence reflected the incapacity of political institutions and political leaders to manage the severe conflicts of economic crisis and constitutional reform peacefully. Moreover, the pattern of conflict, looting, and violence that occurred after mid-1991 reflected the specific class, regional, urban-rural, generational, ideological, and national divisions on which the socialist order and system of rights had been built after 1945. Only within rural areas were earlier patterns of conflict apparent, and those were not ethnic but ideological—fascist versus antifascist—and not of tribal origin but from the conflict in World War II.

The escalating collapse of the legal and social order was in part a result of, and in part a stimulus to, rising political conflict within the political class over taxes, governmental powers, and economic policies. This political class comprised many layers—a single ruling party composed of eight autonomous parties; federal government officials and an elected parliament; republican authorities and elected parliaments; directors of firms (most of whom were nominally members of the party but managing autonomous firms according to their own interests); and alongside this managerial class, a large middle class of professionals in public employment and on "guaranteed salary" (to be head of any organization, such as a local police chief or school principal, one had to have a university degree, and salaries were indexed to level of formal education as well as to industrial wages, giving an incentive to obtain an advanced degree as a way of increasing income). Therefore, the political competition over increasingly scarce resources, particularly jobs and public expenditures, was played out at many levels and on many issues.

The unifying thread of these many conflicts, however, was the program of economic and political reform required by the international financial institutions to service the debt. Therefore, the dominant conflict was over reform of monetary and financial institutions and of the federal constitution. And although the actors were largely officials, their methods of competing and winning were in disarray. Long-ruling patriarch Tito died in 1980. The decentralization of the preceding thirty years had eroded beyond repair the command and control of the ruling party. The reforms required to make the government more effective in managing the currency and foreign trade ignored or ended, one by one, the rules of proportional representation and consensual decision making built up over decades to fulfill the commitment to national equality and to symbolize the inclusiveness of the regime. The austerity of the economic program made the gap between the rhetoric and reality of the ruling party acutely visible. Still rhetorically committed to full employment and economic equality but composed of a narrow managerial stratum responsible for guarding access to elite positions and privilege, the party engendered open resentment in the face of rapidly rising urban unemployment among unskilled workers and youth seeking their first jobs. The ensuing contest over states' rights and federal authority included outright defiance of constituted authorities, party decisions, and enacted legislation.

By January 1990, the Yugoslav Communist party dissolved after the Slovene delegation (followed by the Croats) walked out of an extraordinary congress convened to address the crisis. In the decade-long contest over federal policy, reform, and resources, leaders in the republics had already by 1985–86 started to violate the political taboo against seeking popular support directly, rather than working through the party organization. The Slovene Communist leadership, for example, quietly funded alternative youth groups that were waging a campaign against conscription, the defense budget, arms exports, and the federal army in general, including a call to replace the army with "national armies" of the republics, as well as those publishing irreverent magazines that aimed to shock public opinion into oppositional activity on issues ranging from educational reform to environmental issues and national rights (Benderly and Kraft 1994; Ramet 1985: 3–26). The Serbian Communist leadership yielded to demands by Serb minority groups in its autonomous southern province of Kosovo for attention to their claims of discrimination at the hands of the Albanian majority government, but it did so as a means to reduce the extensive provincial autonomy that had made governance in the republic nearly impossible. The Albanians' campaign to convert that autonomy into a separate republic was an excuse that might be acceptable to the other republic party leaderships who would have to concur with any constitutional change in Serbia. Serbian party leaders also instigated mass demonstrations of Serbs (called "meetings of truth") to provoke the resignations of uncooperative provincial leaders in Vojvodina and Kosovo and in the republic of Montenegro in hopes of gaining allies in federal voting bodies. The Croatian Communist party was more reticent in seeking popular support because the political reaction against the use of this appeal for mass support to bargain over states' rights in an earlier period of economic reform, in 1967–71, still colored public life and leaders in the republic.[6] But in 1989, when events in Eastern Europe demonstrated that party leaders had to take initiative in managing change or be drowned by it, the Croatian leadership also entered the fray and allowed intellectuals to register a political association (the Association for a Yugoslav Democratic Initiative) and discuss competitive elections.

Increasingly backed by popular support and emotion, but without the political restraints that a functioning democracy, an effective central government, or a strong party leader might have imposed, leaders in the republics (particularly Slovenia and Serbia) took ever greater risks in boldly asserting *their* rights and interests against others. The rules regulating elite interaction and decision making on the basis of parity representation and consensus could not function. In place of negotiated compromise, stalemate and confrontation ruled the day.

Because the republics were supposed to represent the states' rights of the six constituent south Slav nations recognized by the federal constitution of 1945, any fight over the rights of the republics in that federation or over the institutions of federal power was vulnerable to expression in a rhetoric of "national rights" and "national interest." Similarly, a policy to cut public expenditures and transfer the burden to the republics and localities, when the republics' economic ability to make good their legal commitments to guaranteed subsistence and promises of rising living standards for all citizens was on the decline, provoked calls for "national preferences" in jobs and housing. Public discontent over rising unemployment, declining consumption, and growing insecurity found an outlet in scapegoating, attacking federal taxes that "deprived them of their national rights," and imagining discrimination as a national group against the privileges of others. At the same time, those activities that were not expressed as national rights, such as the increased union activity in defense of workers' interests or the pro-democracy groups of liberal or left-of-center intellectuals, could not escape the federal structure and republican arena of active politics. Cross-republic alliances were particularly difficult to form on the very issues of most concern to the average citizen, because policy on employment, education, conscription, and taxes was under republican jurisdiction, and the need to cut under economic stagnation made choices increasingly zero-sum. By contrast, right-wing groups of anticommunist or antisystem persuasion could play on cultural—and therefore ethnonational and ethno-religious—bonds, which did not confine their mobilizing activities to single republics or republican-based delegations to the federal center. Trying to influence issues of government policy required working within the governmental structure, which was defined in terms of national rights, while trying to mobilize for radical change did not require attention to those structures and could be done in terms of national sentiments.

In an atmosphere moving toward democracy (whether it would be mass or representative democracy remained unclear), there were additional advantages to politicians who appealed for popular support on nationalist grounds rather than on interests and beliefs that were independent of national identity. The urban, middle-class constituency for liberal or pro-regime (Yugoslav and socialist) ideas was rapidly diminishing under the onslaught of economic crisis. Neither market advocates nor supporters of redistribution and equality were likely to be as popular under conditions of austerity and rising inequality as were states' rights advocates who claimed that individuals had *rights*—national rights—to their earnings and employment. The authority of states in conferring rights and legitimizing privileged access to declining resources makes state power a far more desirable objective than the uncertainties of a market or the solidarity of social justice. The declining legitimacy and power of communist institutions also created a vacuum of partisan identity which the only other officially recognized political identity—that of national identity—was ready-made to fill, giving anticommunists a cover during the transition in the mobilization of popular support on the basis of national sentiment (regardless of republic).

Majoritarianism in each republic—the rights of members of the majority national group as against the constitutionally equal rights of members of all national groups—was a perfect vehicle for the exclusionary politics of austerity and for republic-level politicians (officially still communist) to build winning coalitions on the right under the guise of democratic principle. But it was only a matter of two or three years before grumbling over questions like, "Why did he get that job when I am better qualified?" became ethnicized into questions like, "Why do Serbs have most of the police, army, and government jobs in Croatia when Croats are in the majority and this should be their state?" or "Why do Albanians get all the credit when we Serbs are just as poor?" or "Why do we Slovenes who work so hard and efficiently but see our incomes stagnating have to pay for those lazy Albanians or Bosnians?" By December 1990, when a referendum in Slovenia won 90 percent in favor of independence if the rest of the country did not adopt the Slovene government proposal on political reform (transforming Yugoslavia into a confederation of independent states with a common currency until European Community [EC] membership was obtained), the slippery slope toward the country's disintegration was greased with inchoate individual fears. The reaction took the general form, "Why should I be a minority in your state when you can be a minority in mine?"

"Bestial words, bestial war," writes a Serbian intellectual in exile in Slovenia in 1993 (Slapšak 1993). The ensuing violence was foreseeable, some argue, in the political rhetoric of nationalism (Thompson 1994). In fact, three deadly components combined to create the political context in which politicians, their aspiring opponents, and cultural leaders would use such rhetoric, and people would listen.

First, the Slovene program to enhance the republic's "sovereignty" and then move toward full independence was a revolutionary act, challenging the territorial integrity of the country, subverting its constitutional order, and ignoring the fate of all non-Slovenes. Its leaders knew they were risking violence when they began secretly to import arms to replace the weapons confiscated in spring 1990 by the federal army after it became convinced of Slovene plans to leave. But this program was far less part of an overall plan than an accumulation of steps putting Slovene republican interests first, and many would argue that the first shot at territorial integrity was fired by a small group of radical Albanians in Kosovo province in 1981. Their demand for a separate republic sent tremors throughout the country, for if internal borders might be up for revision, then the country itself was at risk from within, and republics might view ethnic minorities as a threat to be controlled. But the influence of the Slovene defense of republican rights and challenge to federal authority over many years was far greater because of its inordinate economic influence over federal policy and because of the consequence of its challenge—a substantial weakening of the federal government.

Despite efforts by economic and political reformers (including the IMF advisors and many Slovene economists and politicians) to restore the federal capacity to govern by reducing some of the republics' autonomy from earlier reforms, the effect of their liberalizing, market reforms, anti-inflationary policies, and budget cuts actually left the prime minister with few powers and fewer resources, short of calling out the troops. Nor was that resource readily available to those (led by Serb politicians in Serbia) who wanted the army to exercise its constitutional mandate to defend the country's borders and constitutional (socialist) order. The minister of defense and commander of the armed forces at the time, Veljko Kadijević, proved maddeningly indecisive and insisted repeatedly on prior constitutional authority and political direction before the army would act. And such direction or policy of common interest would not emerge from political authorities—the federal party, the collective presidency (as commander-in-chief of the armed forces), the parliament, and the executive council (cabinet)—who could not agree.

Communal violence required a second deadly component: the demand for majority rights in a land of minorities. Once political, cultural, and economic elites called on Yugoslavs to think in terms of their ethnic identity and as members of a national (instead of Yugoslav) community and claimed that their very survival was threatened by other Yugoslav nations and that protection in insecure times lay with their own nation and its leaders, the gravity of the loss of an overarching Yugoslav state became crystal clear. All national groups in Yugoslavia, whether rich or poor, advantaged or at risk, were numerical minorities. They could therefore imagine themselves at risk from some larger group and thus as acting legitimately in self-defense, however aggressive their actions might appear to another group that was viewing the situation from the same, apprehensive perspective. Politicians succeeded who used a discourse of the weak. The circumstances of economic crisis and the habits of forty years of socialist rhetoric made it easy, in fact, to reach for a language of exploitation and victimization.

Serbian president Slobodan Milošević told the nationalist Serb minority in Albanian-majority Kosovo, "Nobody must ever again dare to beat this people!" (Čuruvija and Torov 1995: 82) when he received reports that police were using batons against demonstrators. But non-Serbs heard this as a threat to them. Slovenia's government began in the early 1980s to restrict the number of non-Slovene workers in the republic, sending Bosnians and ethnic Albanians back to their home republics and limiting entry of new labor migrants, because of the economic costs in social infrastructure and a policy to reverse the exodus of Slovenes (such as to neighboring Austria) by reserving wage increases and jobs for them. But they justified this policy on the grounds that their "national distinctiveness" and cultural identity were "threatened." Within ever smaller circles of interaction, local majorities took advantage of local minorities in the economic crisis. The spiraling behavior that is produced by the security dilemma (Jervis 1976: 62–68) and has no automatic brakes led people to arm with words, and then with discriminatory legislation, guns, and finally preemptive secession.

When the Slovene drive for independence moved to Croatia, its drive for a state for the Croatian nation met resistance from Serbs in border regions who feared or directly opposed becoming a minority in such a state. With Serbs willing to defend their lives and homes with arms in order to remain in a rump Yugoslavia, or to join an eventual Serbian nation-state if events so developed, the constitutional niceties of Minister Kadijević could not be sustained. Worse, once Slovenia and Croatia seceded and Yugoslavia dissolved without third-party assistance in negotiating the process peacefully, there was no obvious outcome for the multinational republic of Bosnia and Herzegovina. The Yugoslav federal system had provided the only sure protection against claims from Croatia and from Serbia that Bosnian territory was theirs, while an independent nation-state based on majoritarian principles provided no protection for the Serbs and Croats in Bosnia who would become minorities. As a result of the multiparty elections in November 1990, moreover, Bosnia was being governed by three nationalist parties, each asserting the *national rights* of one of the three constituent nations of the republic. The choice of independent states in place of Yugoslavia was a claim for national rights over territory, and despite the thorough intermixing of the members of the three Bosnian national communities in families, apartment buildings, and local communities, such claims would engage them in a fight over land and therefore the danger of armed struggle.

The third, essential, deadly component was the breakdown of legal order. Eventually the army took sides and used force, first to prevent secession and, failing that, then to create a smaller Yugoslavia, with borders that could include defense industries, strategic routes, and those people who wanted to remain (with their land) in such a Yugoslavia. Long before 1991, however, the governmental capacity to provide justice, protection, and a fair hearing was succumbing to political revolution, unlimited partial interests, and chaos. Out of pecuniary interest or political loyalty to local leaders, many in the police forces had even switched to protecting political parties, as paramilitary formations or criminal networks. Many judges attempted to remain professional and independent, but multiparty elections were the beginning of a political revolution, and newly elected political parties sought consolidation by appointing loyalists to the bench. And as the possibility of armed confrontation grew, local authorities began to distribute their cache of TDF weapons, aided in some cases by the federal army and its stocks, and citizens in rural areas pulled rusty rifles from barns.

OUTSIDE INTERVENTION

By the time that full-scale war was raging in border areas of Croatia, in the autumn of 1991, the fact of violence and predictions of its spread to Bosnia and Herzegovina appear overdetermined. Any suggestion that the violence was not inevitable—was even preventable—was relegated to the realm of counterfactual analysis. The image of the Balkans as steeped in a history of bloodshed and as "an intractable 'problem from hell' that no one can be expected to solve . . . less a moral tragedy . . . and more a tribal feud that no outsider could hope to settle" (U.S. Secretary of State Warren Christopher, cited in Friedman 1993) was confirmed in the minds of all who had already suspected as much in 1990, obliterating any second thoughts.[7] Nonetheless, the nationalist path of state dissolution and forced population movements to create homogeneous nation-states out of Yugoslavia was only one of several paths which the country might have taken from the vantage of trends in the late 1980s. That this path was the only one imaginable five years later, in 1996, cannot be explained without adding the role played by outsiders and the fundamental changes taking place in the external environment of Yugoslavia. But such an addition does damage to the concept of violence-prone areas. Classifying the world into zones of stability and zones of violence creates a false sense of separation between local and foreign events that cannot be sustained in an era of increasing interdependence and in areas where countries (such as Yugoslavia) had provided a buffer in the East-West confrontation that was no longer needed and was thus no longer financed.

In the events leading to war in 1991–92, for example, the economic crisis cannot be explained without external economic shocks (such as the two oil price increases in the 1970s, the abrupt halt in 1979 of commercial bank lending and the sharp rise in interest rates for the American dollar the same year, the sudden stiffening of terms for IMF loans in 1982, the declining trade revenues resulting from European protection, the Iran-Iraq war, and the Western market shifts of the reforming Soviet Union and collapsing eastern bloc). The constitutional crisis was generated by requirements of political reform from the IMF and the World Bank. And the success of nationalist causes in 1989–90 against other domestic political trends cannot be separated from the financial support and physical return of émigrés and workers who had been living abroad to participate directly in support of anticommunist and nationalist forces (the most striking example is the $8 million raised in support of Franjo Tudjman's victorious campaign for president of Croatia in April 1990, but a number of Yugoslav national groups of guest workers in Germany were mobilizing to fight in Yugoslavia during 1989–90).

Of far greater consequence than these Yugoslav specifics, however, is the way in which normal actions by the international community actually made violence more likely. Both through the normal interactions of states in a world system and through specific interventions to manage the crisis, foreign actors strengthened the causes of violence in at least three ways: by contributing to the weakness of the federal government and state capacity, by legitimizing the people and ideas that would win, and by failing to do (or even understand the need for) the hard work required to make peace when they accepted the peacemakers' role.

Undermining Political Capacity

Episodes of violence in modern Balkan history are limited to periods of external disjuncture. Whether they resulted from the retreat of a stabilizing power or regional system into domestic troubles or reforms (as with the Habsburg and Ottoman empires in the early to mid-nineteenth century, or with the Cold War system of bipolar, superpower governance and balance-of-terror in the late 1980s), or from altered foreign policies in neighboring powers that threatened the peace (as with World Wars I and II), these changes in the external environment required locals to respond—to the uncertainty, threat, occupation, or opportunity. In each regional system, moreover, military power played a central role. For example, in the late Habsburg period, the Ministry of War in Vienna directly governed the mid-section of the Balkans and restricted residence in this military border (*vojna krajina*) to settlers willing to bear arms and defend the border for the Empire; under the Ottomans, the Janissaries and *spahis* ruled the Balkan province for the Porte; and in World War II, the invading Axis armies divided up the territory and occupied it directly or through local collaborators, the Ustashi and Chetniks. In much of their modern history, locals thinking of political action under such circumstances had had to entertain the risk, at least, of war.

The transformation taking place in European and global order in the course of the 1980s, and particularly after 1985, was profoundly destabilizing to Yugoslavia. Under the Communist party leadership of president-for-life Josip Broz Tito, the country had created a sovereign identity and a socialist order in relation to its position in the Cold War international system, including an independent defense that was crucial to NATO's eastern policy, a nonalignment movement that gave the country and many of its citizens working abroad alternatives in third world markets and outside the East-West security blocs, and independence from Moscow in exchange for special access to American aid and the international financial institutions. It prospered by maneuvering domestic and foreign policies in relation to shifts in superpower relations and, like South Korea or Mexico, by accumulating a substantial foreign debt. But in 1979–82, the international financial institutions adopted harsher policies toward debtors, and the European Union and European Free Trade Association (EFTA) both substantially toughened their bargaining over the renewal of association agreements with Yugoslavia, including uncertainty-generating delays. In the mid-1980s, when talks resumed between the two Cold War blocs over conventional force reductions and economic rapprochement, neutral states, including Yugoslavia, were excluded.

Developments in the Western alliances at the same time, in 1985, rein-forced this exclusion. The European Community decided to advance by 1992 to full financial integration of its member states, including a parallel deepening of political integration among western European states, and NATO took a more aggressive posture toward the eastern Mediterranean, so that the Yugoslav defense establishment perceived the West as a growing security threat. In the same year, Soviet reform was looking westward under Mikhail Gorbachev's new foreign policy of a "European home"; a Vatican campaign began (under a Polish pope) for new converts and the end of communism in eastern Europe; and economic and cultural contacts between Slovenes and Croats and their neighbors in Italy and Austria began to take on institutional form (as in the association Alpe-Adria). By April 1989, in this atmosphere of East-West détente and deepening European integration, the Yugoslav government was told by a new United States ambassador presenting his credentials that Yugoslavia was no longer of strategic significance to the United States.

All these developments were diminishing the economic resources and political power on which the Yugoslav federal government depended for independent revenues and for leverage over the republican governments. While the intent of the IMF conditionality programs was to reverse the hyper-decentralization that had resulted from more than three decades of IMF and World Bank advice so as to strengthen the federal government's administrative and economic capacity within the country, the effect was to provoke massive resistance from republican governments which had inde-pendent sources of revenue through export earnings and foreign support (such as from the Vatican, Austria, Italian provinces, and eventually Germany). The protective role of the federal government collapsed as a result of IMF-mandated liberalizing reforms and austerity policies. And the international role of the federal armed forces was rapidly becoming irrele-vant because of the renewal of European détente and Soviet reforms; they needed a new role, at the very time when Slovene youth were on a campaign against the federal army, when NATO maneuvers seemed to pose a rising threat, and when the IMF stabilization program required substantial cuts in the defense budget *and* new imports to modernize weapons systems and increase exports.

More than six months before the republican governments in Slovenia and Croatia declared independence, in late 1990, when the prime minis-ter's anti-inflationary program of economic reform appeared to be working to bring the country out of economic crisis and to create an enthusiastic domestic constituency for the federal (as opposed to their republican) gov-ernment—the United States moved to abandon the federal government a second time. As David Gompert, special assistant to President Bush for national security affairs at the time, recounts, "The Bush administration could not justify putting the dying Yugoslav federal authority on life-support systems." He continues, "The United States declared its sympathy for the teetering Yugoslav federal government of Ante Marković, who was committed to democracy, a civil society, and a market economy. But the prime minister wanted debt relief and a public signal of unreserved American political backing—commitments that seemed unwarranted in view of his government's apparent terminal condition" (Gompert 1996: 123).

At the same time, the Slovene and Croatian governments were receiving increasingly open support from Austria, Switzerland, Hungary, and Germany for their plans to secede, including weapons assistance in their illegal buildup of independent republican armies. The United States actually cut off all economic aid to the federal government (about $5 million) by May 1991 because of human rights abuses against Albanians in Kosovo (mandated by the Nickles Amendment to the foreign operations appropriations act passed in November 1990). When the federal presidency ordered the army in January 1991 to restore the state's legitimate authority over the use of violence by overseeing the disarming and disbandment of paramilitary formations, the United States warned the army that it would brook no use of force inside the country. On March 13, 1991, after Slovenia and Croatia declared that federal laws no longer applied in their republics, the European parliament passed a resolution declaring "that the constituent republics and autonomous provinces of Yugoslavia must have the right freely to determine their own future in a peaceful and democratic manner and on the basis of recognized international and internal borders." By the spring of 1991, when the federal government turned to European powers for aid in support of its economic program to replace American retreat, aid necessary to navigate the market and democratic transition successfully, delegations from the EC and from neighboring countries such as Italy and Austria began to deal directly, instead, with leaders from the republics (starting with Slovenia and Croatia). In some cases, they bypassed the federal government altogether.

Mediation and Its Language

A striking aspect of the explosion of popular engagement in Yugoslav public life that republican politicians used so skillfully to support their political aims during the 1980s was the almost childlike yearning to be heard. Slovene adolescents and young adults screamed obscenities and attacked the army and other sacred cows in their music, magazines, posters, and clothing, clearly aiming to provoke a reaction from inattentive adults. Serbs in Kosovo, joined by small-town Serbs in Serbia, organized demonstrations they called "meetings of truth," pleading to have their grievances heard by Belgrade officialdom and parliament and then to "tell their story" in other republics. Traveling throughout the country in 1990 and 1991, Brian Hall was told over and over again by individuals he met, "Tell the truth," as if their truth was the only one and was "obvious" (Hall 1994: 5–6). But because they spoke in the language of the underdog, the chance that others would hear them was small. At the political level, politicians and activists were clearly talking past each other. And the absence of democratic institutions meant there were no regularized ways to listen and be heard.

The primary role of a mediator is to provide that neutral forum: to listen and to translate so that all parties can hear. The EC and the Commission on Security and Cooperation in Europe (CSCE) responded to the declarations of independence by the republics of Slovenia and Croatia on June 25, 1991, with the weakest form of mediation: offering their "good offices" to the parties. From the Brioni Agreement of July 7, 1991, which established a cease-fire in Slovenia and terms that enabled Slovene independence by the end of the year, to the Dayton Accord of November 21, 1995, which affirmed an October cease-fire in Bosnia and Herzegovina and enabled a NATO-led military intervention to help implement the agreement, western Europeans and Americans became increasingly involved, through mediation, in ending the violence and preventing its spread. But the more they listened, the more they disenfranchised whole categories of complaints and people. The prospects for political agency by those not chosen for a hearing by Western diplomats declined dramatically. And the more violence there was, the less neutral outsiders became. But in efforts to assist, they cut off an independent sphere of domestic politics, and in choosing sides, they left those whom they refused to hear or protect to rely on force to make themselves heard and to protect themselves.

The process of hearing and mediating was guided by two factors: the strategies of the various Yugoslav parties, and outsiders' criteria for legitimate intervention. As Yugoslavia headed for collapse, and particularly as Slovenia headed for secession, political leaders chose different strategies. First the Slovene and Croat, then the Bosnian Muslim and Macedonian republican politicians, along with the Albanian provincial leaders in Kosovo, chose a strategy of internationalization. They saw their best hope for success in external intervention, and they directed substantial resources and tactical choices into shaping foreign perceptions in their favor. This culminated successfully in the German policy to recognize Slovene and Croatian independence so as to *internationalize* the conflict. By declaring Slovenia and Croatia sovereign states, the Germans reasoned, they could define the actions of the federal army in Slovenia and Croatia and of Serb resisters in Croatia as illegitimate violations of Slovene or Croatian sovereignty. In short, they could lump all Serbian and federal actors into one category of "Serbs" and accuse them of aggression—and thereby have legitimate grounds for external intervention. The strategy of politicians in Serbia, Montenegro, and Serbian communities in Croatia, Bosnia, and

Herzegovina was instead to claim that the Yugoslav conflict was an internal matter, to address their attempts at persuasion to leaders in the other republics rather than to the international community, and to insist that the Bosnian conflict was a civil war.

The strategy of the federal government fell between these two camps, for its prime minister and foreign minister worked hard during the 1980s to gain association agreements with the EC, EFTA, and the Council of Europe and to obtain financial assistance for their economic reform and debt repayment program. As a part of that objective, they invited the EC in to mediate. But federal leaders also insisted that their conflict over constitutional reform and human rights was an internal matter, protected by the rules of sovereignty. Only in September 1991 at the United Nations did they concede to vote for interference, but as a means of *regaining* international acknowledgment of *Yugoslav* sovereignty as a member state of the United Nations and of shoring up their domestic authority by proposing and voting for a United Nations Security Council Resolution to place an arms embargo on the country.

International intervention in the internal affairs of countries does occur, but it must be legitimated by claims that do not abrogate the country's formal sovereignty. Thus, military intervention short of declaring war can only occur at the *consent* of the legitimate government. This was obtained when Macedonian president Gligorov requested UN peacekeeping troops to guard his country's border against external aggression (in fact, Gligorov's goal was to gain international recognition of Macedonian sovereignty over Greek objections), but the meaning of consent in the Bosnian case was too unclear to satisfy Europeans or the UN when President Izetbegović requested the same in the fall of 1991. Yugoslavia had not yet dissolved *de jure*, and Izetbegović represented only one of three parties in a ruling coalition and a seven-person collective presidency that were bound constitutionally to rule by consensus. Similarly, foreign troops would not deploy to the country until a cease-fire had been negotiated and signed—by the Croatian government and federal army in the case of UN peacekeepers in Croatia, and by Croatia, Serbia, and three Bosnian parties in the case of NATO-led troops to Bosnia and Herzegovina. The one exception to the rule of explicit consent—UN peacekeepers sent to protect humanitarian workers in Bosnia and Herzegovina during its war—allows intervention in defense of principles accepted by states as higher law—fundamental human rights and humanitarian principles or direct threats to international peace and security. The claims made by the Yugoslav parties who chose internationalization to support independence were, in fact, made in terms of such principles—especially the principle of human rights.

The intersection of these two factors—the strategies of domestic elites and the principles of legitimate intervention—had disastrous consequences. By choosing to talk only to elected leaders as representatives of a people's sovereignty, outsiders accepted without question that the conflict was as the republican leaders and their nationalist rhetoric portrayed it. By seeking to speak with people capable of giving consent and exercising sovereignty, mediators privileged the assertion of national rights and ethnic community over those who claimed civic rights and multiethnic tolerance within or across the republican boundaries. By "mediating" between the Slovene authorities and federal authorities, moreover, the EC transformed the constitutional conflict over federal-republic relations into a border conflict, one that was more likely to lead to violence. EC mediators thereby eliminated the federal government as the legitimate sovereign actor and violated the EC's and CSCE's own principle of territorial integrity, which should have denied to Slovenia the right to secede.

Although Western mediators insisted that all parties demonstrate a commitment to democracy in order to be heard, they never proposed a referendum of all Yugoslav citizens on the country's dissolution, nor even required the Slovene government to withdraw its veto of its earlier commitment to a federal referendum on the constitution, in 1989, and of federal elections in 1990. In that context, both federal and republican leaders in Belgrade who opposed the breakup of the country heard Western calls for democracy as biased support for Slovenes and Croats, such as when United States Secretary of State James Baker declared in a last-minute visit to the capital on June 21, 1991, that if the United States had to choose between unity and democracy, it would insist on democracy. Such views were interpreted in the armed forces and Serbian leaderships, instead, as a continuation of Western anticommunism aimed at destroying the country, which they felt obliged to prevent and justified in preventing with force.[8] This judgment was only reinforced when outsiders accepted the right to self-determination of Slovenes and Croats, based on popular referendums in the two republics, but denied the same right to Serbs in Croatia (who had also held a referendum) and to two of three parties in Bosnia and Herzegovina (Serbs boycotted the EC-mandated referendum on independence, while both Serbs and Croats, for the most part, fought against the sovereignty of the republic and for national rights through secession).

In addition to partial listening, outsiders tended to hear their view of the conflict, not that of the parties. In the two years preceding the outbreak of violence, the U.S. Ambassador to Yugoslavia, Warren Zimmermann, actively condemned the Serbian government for its violation of the human rights of Albanians in Kosovo. But by 1989, when this American policy began, the nature of the conflict between the Serbian government and Kosovo Albanians was over territorial governance—Belgrade changed its constitution to reduce substantially the autonomy of its two provinces (Vojvodina and Kosovo), with the necessary approval of the other republics required by the federal constitution, and Albanian activists had been attempting to transform that extensive autonomy into full republic status (redefining the right of national self-determination to a republic on majoritarian rather than constitutional grounds).[9] The Slovene government did argue that human rights could only find full expression in a national community and be protected by a national state, but this joining of national and human principles was an argument for secession, not constitutional reform within Yugoslavia.

Nonetheless, the elision worked. Outside mediators accepted this nationalist view and equated human rights with self-governance for the majority and minority rights for those not in the majority—confirming the very fear of becoming a minority that was motivating many to fight. Croatia was required to adapt its constitution to grant "minority rights" to Serbs before recognition.[10] The CSCE/OSCE Commissioner on National Minorities went frequently to Macedonia on the grounds that insufficient protections for the rights of the Albanian minority posed the greatest threat of violence in Macedonia. Economic sanctions on Serbia and Montenegro (which formed a new federal republic of Yugoslavia after Bosnia was granted recognition) for their role in the war in Bosnia and Herzegovina were extended until Albanians in Kosovo were restored full human rights and autonomy. While the fear of being demoted to the status of a minority in someone else's national state was the motive for violence, the Western decision to dissolve the country into national states redefined their national rights—for example, Serbs in Croatia, Albanians in Serbia and in Macedonia, and Serbs and Croats in Bosnia and Herzegovina—as the *internal affairs* of the new sovereign states, not subject to international protection beyond declarations in support of minority and human rights.[11]

Once violence began in earnest, however, negotiators narrowed further the circle of interlocutors. Giving priority to ending the violence, they talked to those in control of armies (but not of the paramilitary groups that were responsible for much of the early violence and terror in Croatia, Bosnia and Herzegovina, and Kosovo). Thus, they denied a voice to anyone who had done as outsiders demanded—eschewed violence and fought through peaceful means to reform the system, prevent war, oppose the nationalists, and write constitutions for the new states. These peaceful, civic-oriented, and democratic forces were not sovereign actors, nor, as they did not resort to violence, were they threats to international peace and stability with whom one had to deal. Among armed groups, moreover, diplomats from states or regional and international organizations privileged leaders whom outsiders viewed as legitimate representatives of sovereignty—for example, treating the nationalist Croat president as the only legitimate representative of Croatia and treating Serbs as rebels, or in Bosnia and Herzegovina, treating the man who held the chair of the seven-person collective presidency at the time of recognition in 1992 as the only legitimate representative of the country, even though that position was supposed to rotate annually.

Intervention remains a decision of states and their calculation of national interest—either on grounds of vital national interest or national commitments of collective security alliances. With the end of the Cold War, Yugoslavia ceased to be a strategic asset for the West; although European states had national interests in the Balkans, there was no compelling strategic interest to mobilize troops. Human rights were not enough. Humanitarian principles outlawing genocide and providing a strong international mandate to protect refugees and civilian victims of war, however, were. Beginning in June 1992, nearly one hundred UN Security Council Resolutions mandated international organizations—including UN peacekeeping troops deployed to protect refugee and relief organizations—to provide humanitarian assistance to Bosnians at war and—here national interests were clearer—to contain the fighting and the refugee outflow from spilling over Bosnian borders. One year later, enclaves of Muslim-majority towns in Serb-controlled areas were declared "safe areas," under UN protection. But just as humanitarian assistance also fed armies and provided a cover for arms deliveries, so peacekeepers could not provide protection in the midst of war.

Humanitarianism, however, is a language of rights which defines the claims that people can make on the international community. It thus fed back into the discourse on national rights that had come to dominate the political contest in Yugoslavia by the late 1980s and that led to war. Now the claim was not constitutional rights to self-determination or particular economic assets but to protection against genocide. Already in the mid-1980s, Serbs in Kosovo sought support from Serbia proper and Belgrade authorities by claiming that the pressures against them were tantamount to genocide; and Serb nationalists attempted to mobilize supporters and sympathy within Croatia by reviving fears that a second genocide against Serbs would occur if Croatian nationalists claiming the legacy of the wartime fascist state came to power. The Bosnian Muslim leadership claimed international intervention in Bosnia on the ground that Muslims were victims of genocide. And the language of national victimization within the country was easily translated by those leaders who chose an internationalization strategy into the international language of aggressors and victims. All sides used their perception of victimization to legitimize violence, but those who used the argument to obtain outside assistance—as if a new strategy of resource acquisition was replacing the ideological categories of the Cold War—had to act as victims, even to the point of delaying military preparations and inviting violence to make the case convincing. The strategy worked in the case of Croatia and Bosnia-Herzegovina, but not without cost. In Bosnia, eight peace plans were rejected by American patrons of the Bosnian Muslim leadership between March 1992 and October 1994 on the grounds that none provided sufficient justice to the victims, but "appeased" the "aggressor" Serbs instead. Apart from the fact that Bosnian citizens were never asked their view of these plans, the price of sovereignty was a land partitioned into three nationally controlled territories and at least three more years of death and destruction than might have been necessary.

Making Peace

The failure of international mediation and diplomacy to prevent or stop the violence in Croatia and in Bosnia and Herzegovina is generally attributed to the failure to intervene with force. Interposition forces proposed for Croatia in July 1991 were rejected, as were calls to bomb federal forces besieging Vukovar and Dubrovnik in the fall of 1991. Diplomats negotiating peace plans lamented their lack of influence over the parties without a credible threat of force to wield. United Nations peacekeeping forces were vilified as appeasers, and worse, because their mandate required impartiality and rules of engagement that limited them to the use of force in proportionate response and self-defense. Critics called for lifting the arms embargo for the Bosnian government and bombing the Serbs. "The only language they understand is the language of force," was the repeated refrain throughout the war, always directed at Serbs. And indeed, the Bosnian war was brought to a halt in October 1995 by a policy of force. The American policy aimed to end the war by altering control of land as a prelude, rather than outcome, of a political settlement: first in March 1994 by creating a military alliance between enemies, the Bosnian government forces and the Bosnian Croats, and sending them arms (despite the embargo), and then in the summer of 1995, by assisting the Croatian government to overrun three of the four UN-protected areas with force, bombing fleeing Serbs and burning their homes to oblivion as a means to "reintegrate the territory" of sovereign Croatia, and to sweep through Serb-held territory in western Bosnia— aided by a massive NATO bombing campaign against Bosnian Serb targets. And to undergird the peace agreement negotiated in November—the Dayton accords—it insisted on a program to train and equip these allied Bosnian Muslim (government) and Bosnian Croat forces (ostensibly in a federated army) to defend against any renewed threat of Bosnian Serb aggression, even though the accord declared an autonomous Bosnian Serb republic to be one of two equal entities in a single Bosnian state.

In fact, there would have been little cause for violence if the state had not dissolved and borders of the new states not been contested—not only between parties in Yugoslavia but also between those who wanted borders redrawn more in conformity with national borders and representatives of the Western and international powers who insisted that the borders of the republics (treated as surrogates for existing borders once Slovenia and Croatia chose to secede) were inviolable. Neither the Europeans nor regional and international organizations had a procedure for negotiating the dissolution of a multinational state or contested borders. Those who contested the internal borders were accused of aggression, and international intervention only came *in response* to violence. If this had not been obvious in 1991, then it was clearly so by 1998, when the contest over the province of Kosovo turned violent: the unwillingness to intervene in the interests of prevention, acting only when violence occurred, sent a signal that one had to go to war to get attention. Moreover, the initial causes of the conflict that turned deadly were first the state's inability to provide its constitutionally mandated protections under the budgetary demands of debt repayment and liberalization, then uncertainty about the country's international position, and finally the breakdown of the constitutional and legal order as a result of political quarrels over rights to economic resources and the competition to enter Europe. Yet outsiders sought to control the conflict by imposing economic sanctions (first on the federal government, then on Serbia and Montenegro, and then also on Serbs in Croatia and in Bosnia and Herzegovina), and the primary task of the new states (including the framework for peace in Bosnia) was to resume the same economic and political reforms in order to become eligible for membership in the international financial institutions and the European Union.

The international capacity to assist the process of restoring peace is no less confined by the rules of sovereignty than its approach to prevention and war. Counterparts must be found who will implement agreements made— to withdraw armies, to approve loans for economic reconstruction and be responsible for their implementation and repayment, and to begin to govern. Anything more than assistance to consenting sovereign actors is derided as inappropriate, if not illegitimate, "nation-building." In peacemaking, as in peace negotiations, leaders of the nationalist political parties claiming sovereignty have their position further strengthened by the international community.

Some outsiders did take advantage of the Bosnian war to obtain recognition of the rape of women in wartime as an international crime, and women and children were aided as refugees, displaced persons, and civilians in need of food, shelter, and help in finding missing husbands and sons—in other words, as victims in need of protection. But women who organized antiwar campaigns, civic self-help groups, and reconciliation projects in schools and villages got no hearing. International negotiators for a Bosnian peace emphasized the necessity of justice to reconciliation and healing, but they placed responsibility for that process on an international criminal tribunal in The Hague that would indict and try political and military leaders as war criminals. Just as the disintegration of political authority moved too rapidly for non-nationalists to organize effectively against the tide, and the resort to violence and terror overwhelmed nonviolent forms of political agency, so the impatience of outsiders with the costs of intervention in the Balkans also imposed a short time line (twelve months at first, then eighteen months, and only then, an undetermined stay) on those who would attempt to generate political organization and action in opposition to the ruling nationalist parties who led them to war. To be able to withdraw troops in twelve months, the American negotiators required that elections be held within six to nine months—too soon to organize against those who had used violence to achieve political ends and wielded the means of physical protection (armies, police, and foreign aid) in the minds of voters who still feared war.

CONCLUSION

Outsiders' perceptions of the wars of Yugoslav succession have given a boost to culturalist explanations of violence. Yet their categories for local behavior (victim and aggressor, nation and minority) and for legitimate intervention (interstate aggression or civil war, threat to international peace or internal affairs, humanitarian principles and prohibitions against genocide or human rights) reinforced the incentives within the current state system to organize ethnically and claim sovereign rights. Where is the perspective that addresses the core of the problem leading to violence in Yugoslavia, the widespread phenomenon of retreating or collapsing states?

The current trend, beginning in the early 1980s, of adjustment to global economic interdependence aims at dismantling the regulatory and welfare state. A profound ideological and epistemological shift became perceptible during the decade whereby government was no longer viewed as the source of justice and equal rights, protector of the weak, and guardian against economic crisis. Government was seen as corrupt, an overweening bureaucracy, a force of political repression and an obstacle to freedom, the cause of economic distortion and decline, and the destroyer of community and social values. But under attack were the accommodations, compromises, and methods of economic and group coexistence that had been developed in many parts of the world over the past fifty years to achieve social peace. Policies of economic austerity, balance-of-payments adjustment, cuts in public expenditures, liberalization, and privatization coincide, moreover, with the disruptive consequences for social values and stable communities of the effects of earlier policies of industrialization, foreign trade, and international capital flows for rural-urban migration, land use patterns, and unemployment of both the growing urban underclass and the highly educated, formerly solid middle class. The result was economic inequality and material insecurity, challenging the status achieved by the middle administrative and professional classes, and intensifying individual competition and envy over jobs and privileges.

The political result, however, was not to accept a leaner state, but to use accusations of repression and failing public management of the economy to replace office-holders with new groups and to seek control of state assets for one's own group to the exclusion of others. Those who demanded that bureaucracies be less corrupt and more accountable to the public they are supposed to serve were unprepared for the consequences of their elimination and the need to seek alternative protections outside the state, in private provision of collective goods. Raised in traditions of resistance, activists and social movements find it difficult to organize resistance when the object of their protest crumbles. International organizations, diplomats, and foreign ministers of major powers assume the existence of sovereign actors who can control populations and be accountable to international norms, but seem to have no alternative when governments do not have that capacity, or when political leaders avoid making or keeping commitments if the result would be to expose their lack of power to their followers. Major powers even speak with two voices—demanding that states protect human and minority rights and, simultaneously, cut expenditures on the very programs that guarantee rights. Amidst these contradictory pressures and attitudes toward the state, the current winners are those who use the first-strike option to leave or exclude: opting out by claiming political autonomy or secession, or kicking others out by sending migrants, refugees, and asylum-seekers home, forcing mass population movements, or discriminating with regard to jobs and citizen rights. Clearly, the ordering principles of international organizations and of the foreign policy of the major powers have yet to adjust to the end of the Cold War and to the more profound changes being required in local societies and state orders by liberalization and globalization—if the resort to violence is a concern.

NOTES

1. But on the foreign (to the Balkans) origin of this concept, see Todorova 1997.

2. A representative of this shift can be found in Kaufman 1996, where "Cold War" conflicts are said to have been "ideological," and "post–Cold War" conflicts are "ethnic."

3. In the case of Yugoslavia, see Denitch 1994, Gagnon 1994/1995, and Silber and Little 1997.

4. The analysis and facts of the Yugoslav case are based on Woodward 1995; see that monograph for greater detail and documentary support.

5. The final crisis is vividly portrayed in chapter 8, " 'You've Chosen War': The Arming of Slovenia and Croatia, April 1990–January 1991," in Silber and Little 1997: 105–118.

6. The myriad activities aiming at political change, decentralization, university reform, language rights, and so forth during that period even gained the label MASPOK, shorthand for "mass movement."

7. David Gompert, who served as special assistant to the president for national security affairs in the Bush Administration, 1990–93, expresses the initial American

attitude toward the Yugoslav crisis, almost three years earlier than Christopher's statement: "Those American officials who knew the Balkans best believed that no external power, not even the sole superpower, could prevent Yugoslavs from killing each other and destroying their country, much less impose a fair and lasting peaceful solution" (Gompert 1996: 123).

8. This is made particularly clear in the memoirs of the period of Borisav Jović, Serbian representative to the federal presidency holding the chair in May 1990–May 1991 (Jović 1995).

9. The Yugoslav constitution of 1945 recognized five constituent nations—all speaking south Slavic—with the right to self-determination; it added a sixth, Bosnian Muslims, in 1968; but ethnic groups with a national homeland elsewhere, such as Hungarians or Albanians, and who were not Slavic, did not have that constitutional right.

10. In fact, recognition preceded this requirement as a result of German patronage; the Croatian government adopted a constitutional law, not a change in its constitution; and the law was not implemented.

11. Although NATO states continued to define their intervention of spring 1999 as a defense of Albanian human and minority rights within a sovereign Yugoslavia, their method of a massive bombing campaign was a fundamental shift in a decade of Western policy instruments.

REFERENCES

Benderly, Jill, and Evan Kraft, eds. 1994. *Independent Slovenia: Origins, Movements, Prospects.* New York: St. Martin's Press.

Čuruvija, Slavko, and Ivan Torov. 1995. "The March to War (1980–1990)." In *Yugoslavia's Ethnic Nightmare: The Inside Story of Europe's Unfolding Ordeal,* ed. Jasminka Udovički and James Ridgeway, 73–104. New York: Lawrence Hill Books.

Denitch, Bogdan. 1994. *Ethnic Nationalism: The Tragic Death of Yugoslavia.* Minneapolis: University of Minnesota Press.

Gagnon, V. P. 1994/1995. "Ethnic Nationalism and International Conflict: The Case of Serbia." *International Security* 19, no. 3 (winter): 30–166.

Friedman, Thomas L. 1993. "Bosnia Reconsidered." *New York Times,* April 8, 1993, A1.

Gompert, David C. 1996. "The United States and Yugoslavia's Wars." In *The World and Yugoslavia's Wars,* ed. Richard H. Ullman. New York: Council on Foreign Relations.

Gow, James. 1992. *Legitimacy and the Military: The Yugoslav Crisis.* London: Pinter; New York: St. Martin's Press.

Hall, Brian. 1994. *The Impossible Country: A Journey through the Last Days of Yugoslavia.* Boston: David R. Godine.

Jervis, Robert. 1976. *Perception and Misperception in International Politics.* Princeton, NJ: Princeton University Press, 1976.

Kaufman, Chaim. 1996. "Possible and Impossible Solutions to Ethnic Civil Wars." *International Security* 20, no. 4 (spring): 136–75.

Jović, Borisav. 1995. *Poslednji Dani SFRJ: izvodi iz dnevnika* [The last days of the SFRY: selections from a diary]. Belgrade: Politika.

Ramet, Pedro. 1985. "Apocalypse Culture and Social Change in Yugoslavia." In *Yugoslavia in the 1980s,* ed. Pedro Ramet, 3–26. Boulder and London: Westview Press.

Silber, Laura, and Alan Little. 1997. *Yugoslavia: Death of a Nation.* London: Penguin.

Slapšak, Svetlana. 1993. "Bestial Words, Bestial War." *New York Times,* May 25, A23.

Thompson, Mark. 1994. *Forging War: The Media in Serbia, Croatia, and Bosnia-Herzegovina.* London: Article 19, International Centre against Censorship (May).

Todorova, Maria. 1997. *Imagining the Balkans.* New York: Oxford University Press.

Woodward, Susan L. 1995. *Balkan Tragedy: Chaos and Dissolution after the Cold War.* Washington, DC: Brookings Institution Press.

Violence and Vision

The Prosthetics and Aesthetics of Terror

Allen Feldman

Such the confusion now between the real—how say the contrary? No
matter. That old tandem. Such now the confusion between them once
so twain.

SAMUEL BECKETT,
Id., Ill Seen, Ill Said

SCOPES

One of the few photographs I associate with my fieldwork in Northern
Ireland shows a burly mustached man in a tank top, wearing aviation sun-
glasses. He proudly displays a second photograph of a woman seated at a
desk cluttered with papers, an ashtray, and a telephone. Her eyes smile at
the camera lens; her friendliness is contrasted to the almost ominous dark
background. He is the author of this second image. The picture within the
picture is notable for its high definition; in its expert use of lit foreground
and darkened background creating perspectival depth, it is a competent
example of visual realism. I use the latter term following John Tagg (1988)
as pertaining to the evidentiary, typified, and mimetic dimension of photography: a core attribute which establishes its privileged claim on truth, fac-
ticity, and intelligibility. This picture is a souvenir that I needed to bring
home, for it communicates a visual ideology that permeates the structure
and experience of political violence in Northern Ireland.

Among my raw data from fieldwork in Belfast such firsthand photographic artifacts are rare.[1] Photography in the policed zones of working-
class Belfast has been a dangerous avocation during the course of the conflict. The photo lens is considered equivalent to the gun sight and the
pointed rifle. The British army, the Royal Ulster constabulary, even the
Belfast fire department react angrily and precipitously if they find a camera
pointed at their bodies and activities. The police and army have been
known to rip film out of the cameras of accredited foreign photojournalists

and arrest them. The security apparatus claims that photographs of state personnel doing their duty can find their way to the IRA and other Republican paramilitary groups and serve to identify off-duty soldiers, policemen, and firemen for assassination.

Visual depiction is feared to the extent that it interdicts role distancing, collapses the space between public and private lives, and spreads terror and violence into the everyday recesses of government functionaries. The police and the provincial army reserve particularly fear assassination when they are away from the front line, in mufti, in their homes, and pubs, among family and/or friends, relaxing and recreating.[2] Republican paramilitaries relish such attacks as eloquent inversions of the mutation of their own homes into war zones by these same representatives of the state.[3] Repeated predawn raids of domestic space by the police and army have been commonplace in working-class Catholic neighborhoods for the last two decades. Bereft of any domestic insularity themselves, paramilitaries assume that the war's front line can and should be everywhere as an objective condition of social life.

Republican and Loyalist paramilitaries also fear iconic capture, seeing it as a sure harbinger of sudden death. Both paramilitaries and noncombatants in the communities in which paramilitaries live or operate (particularly Catholic communities) have been subjected to a totalizing optical surveillance by the state; this includes video cameras mounted on street corners and covert photography conducted from behind special slits cut into delivery vans or from the roofs of high-rise buildings, or from helicopter overflights covering political demonstrations and funerals. The visual appearance and dress of many residents in Catholic working-class communities are registered and cross-referenced in extensive computer files that are accessed by police, army patrols, and their respective road blocks. An informant (male, thirty-two, Catholic), who lived in Divis Flats housing project, which lies under the gaze of British Army video cameras mounted on an adjacent high-rise building, declared, "They know the patterns of your wall paper and the color of your underwear!" Here the linkage between the penetration of the domestic space and the penetration of the body directly captures the psychic affect of the surveillance grid—private life is lived on the outside and by inference political activism, which must be kept hidden from the state's gaze, is correlated with privacy. And indeed a good deal of political violence in Northern Ireland is aimed at domestic spaces and is disruptive of the private sphere. Visual surveillance authorizes other forms of bodily invasion. Young males fourteen and older, the group most frequently stopped and searched on the street, have been known to return home and take a shower after being body-frisked in public by the "security forces." Such tactile invasion extends visual surveillance and is experienced as dirtying the self in much the same manner that scopic penetration contaminates private space and lives.[4]

I attended a meeting between activists at Divis Flats and representatives of the British National Mineworkers Union in 1984; the latter were recounting the surveillance/harassment techniques they had been subjected to by police on the British mainland.[5] The housing project activists nodded with quiet recognition until a woman from Divis Flats silenced the miners by pointing to the window behind the union representatives and remarking, "Their cameras are on you even now," as we all followed her gaze out the window and upward to the high-rise with its crown of electronic sensing antennas and video cameras.

In 1986 over a drink in a suburban home located in a residential enclave for policemen, a Loyalist paramilitary, discussing his frequent arrests by the security forces, related the following rumor to me. The persons named below are either well-known IRA or Loyalist paramilitaries and politicians, many of whom had been killed by assassination, fire-fights, and ambushes.

> There was a member of the security branches, and they've seen a board with various photos on it in one of their briefing rooms.[6] The last person who had a face on it was a fellow called Bryson.[7] On one side of the board there were photos of all Republicans and on the other side there was the Paisleys, the Bill Craigs, the Tommy Herrons, and mine.[8] Joe McCann of the Official IRA was up there; he was dead, Bryson was dead, and a few others were still alive. But it appeared that most of them on the other side of the board were Republicans, and they were dead. Red Xs through them like it was something out of the comics or 007.

The dead men's photo-display story was repeated to me by Republican paramilitaries. The tale evokes rituals of the state: arcane rooms, conspiratorial conferences, unforgiving archives where individual deaths are subject to rational planning, and the sympathetic magic of manipulating personhood through visual replicas. Such rumors, true or not, are a necessary complement to the secret knowledge systems that accompany the counterinsurgency campaign; they ascribe to the half-hidden state apparatus an authorial center, a visible place from which its aggressive activity emanates. As such, this ascription is a reaction to the actual, diffuse, capillary threading of state surveillance and power through the warp of everyday life. Resisting this cohabitation of the state and private life takes the form of rumoring. There is a frisson here between the precision optics of the state—the rationalization of political subjects by visual grids and archives—and the imprecise, out-of-focus, and floating quality of rumor. Rumor becomes a vehicle for evading the rationalization of existence under state surveillance. It is the very imprecision of rumor that drives it as a counternarrative against the electronic grid of the state's gaze.

Not only do such fears, insecurities, and rumors about photographic depiction inhibit documentary picture taking, they reveal to what extent visual perception, after more than two decades of clandestine and not-so-clandestine war, is informed by, if not actually modeled on, acts of violence; seeing and killing, being seen and being killed are entangled and exchangeable in the ecology of fear and anxiety. Further, visual appropriation, because it is always pregnant with the potential for violence, has become a metonym for dominance over others: power lies in the totalizing, engorged gaze over the politically prone body, and subjugation is encoded as exposure to this penetration. In the war zones of Northern Ireland vision can be aggressive, and weapons, in turn, become instruments of political image making—weaponry makes ideological objects, objectives, and scenography appear; this is the politically visible, that horizon of actors, objects, and events that constitute the worldview and circumscribed reality of the political emergency-zone—the gathered and linked components of crises.[9] This symbiosis means that political subjects are formed, in part, within a circuit of visual prosthetics: the surveillance camera, the helicopter overflight, the panoptic architecture of the interrogation room and prison,[10] and the aimed gun. These instruments of fatal vision can be divided into hardware and software technologies, and among the latter must be included the human gaze, subject to a high degree of spatial and temporal extension and electronic supplementation. In turn, the fabrication of the politically visible infers the concomitant creation of that which is politically invisible. The circuit formed by vision and violence is itself circumscribed by zones of blindness and inattention.[11]

Foucault conceived of Bentham's Panopticon apparatus within an evolutionary trajectory that progressively distanced punition from the practice of visible, hands-on violence. I find little historical evidence for this sanitized application of ocular aggression either in Northern Ireland or in other neocolonial situations. Foucauldian optical rationality is not "contaminated" by "exceptional" violence in Northern Ireland; compulsory visibility is the rationality of state counterinsurgency, and of neostatist paramilitary violence—this is evident in the visual staging and technological penetration of the body by cameras, high-velocity bullets, or digitized bombs, which unite both seeing and killing, surveillance and violence in a unified scopic regime.[12] By a *scopic regime* I mean the agendas and techniques of political visualization: the regimens that prescribe modes of seeing and visual objects, and which proscribe or render untenable other modes and objects of perception. A scopic regime is an ensemble of practices and discourses that establish the truth claims, typicality, and credibility of visual acts and objects and politically correct modes of seeing. In Northern Ireland each sectarian assassination victim, each detainee interrogated and tortured, each prisoner incarcerated, each army or police patrol ambushed have been subjected to a ritualized gaze, an ex-posture that is an endowment of power to the aggressor. The violent imagination in Northern Ireland is a visual imagination that extends from the surveillance and imaging of bodies living and dead to the public imaging of projected yet nonexistent national entities such as a United Ireland or a British Ulster.

SCOTOLOGY

The particular photograph under discussion, taken indoors and with a subject posing for the camera, seems free of the complicity imposed upon vision by violence.[13] The former Loyalist paramilitary shows the ethnographic camera a picture of a smiling, middle-aged woman sitting at a desk busy with papers. In contrast, the desk he sits at is vacant. The woman in the photograph has accumulated her clutter because she reads, she looks and smiles with her eyes at the lens, her sight is captured by the camera lens. The ex-paramilitary is framed by a desk devoid of papers and files, not because he is idle, but because he is blind. The photograph he holds up to the camera is one he has recently taken. Since he lost his eyesight to sectarian gunfire, photography has become an avidly pursued hobby. When he was sighted and militarily active, he would, with equal enthusiasm, "do snipes," looking through the scope of a 303 Enfield rifle and picking off Catholics across Belfast's Crumlin Road, the sectarian divide that separates his neighborhood, Woodvale, from the predominately Catholic Ardoyne. Even fourteen years after his wounding, he would rhapsodize over the scopic powers of particular rifles. However, he was not blinded while sniping, but during the sectarian rioting of August 15, 1969.[14] His paramilitary career was cut short when an Ardoyne resident fired a shotgun loaded with pellets into his face as the photographer was standing guard by a recently erected neighborhood barricade. The erection of these barricades in working-class neighborhoods transformed these areas into "no-go areas," cutting them off from the outside world and placing them under virtual paramilitary rule until the British army tore the barriers down in 1972. When I met him in the mid-1980s, the blind photographer was working at a community center, a respected figure who has exhibited his work.

Made by a blind former gunman, this photograph is emblematic of crucial dimensions of my ethnographic experience in Belfast; it evokes the perceptual possibilities that emerge during and in the aftermath of violence. This image of vision captured by sightlessness, evokes the words of another paramilitary—in this case, a Republican—who summed up his experience of violence in the city: "An eye for an eye will make the whole world blind." The saying distills the exchangist structure of political aggression identified in my ethnography of violence and the body in Northern Ireland, *Formations of Violence* (Feldman 1991).[15] When I first heard this Gandhian maxim, I envisioned a cosmic darkness, but considering this photograph's juxtaposition of images, of vision and nonvision, its realism both fabricated and objective, I now imagine the sensory alterity of aggressors, the wounded, the maimed, and the terrified. How does one perceive during and after chronic political violence? What knowledge emerges from the terror zones, and at what cultural sites does it appear? Where does violence emerge into visibility, and what visibilities does violence create? What are the *perceptual and somatic* coordinates of political depiction and imagining in Northern Ireland? Within the visual regimes under which the blind former gunman was formed, where does the rifle scope leave off and the camera lens begin? Can we presume that he pursues photography partly in order to remain within an empowering scopic regime, and not simply because it is a medium for rehabilitating the disabled—providing them with therapy or a hobby.

The photo taken by the blind man is fictive; he has seen nothing shown by that photograph, and he has not seen the photograph that repeats these things that he holds up for others to see. It is artifice posing as documentary, the most fabricated aspect being the photo's realist aura, which most of us, educated since childhood in photo-realism, would initially accept as an adequate and intelligible representation of woman seated behind a desk. Yet the image is autonomized; it is solely a product of a prosthetic—the automatic-focus camera. Though the photographer may have used sensory capacities like sound and touch to make it, the picture captures no human vision on the other side of the camera lens. The visual artifact itself gives birth to the optical circuit that makes it intelligible.

The validation of this particular photograph's intelligibility is beyond the blind photographer's optical capacities and dependent on an external witness—a sighted viewer, or in this case a second camera. The photographer poses himself behind the picture and holds his photograph as an emblem of the mimetic adequacy of his nonexistent vision. Positioned behind his creation, he borrows from the metaphor of receding perspective to claim authorship. Since the photographer is sightless, his picture poses the realist gaze, just as much as it poses a woman behind a desk. Thus his blindness foregrounds another ironic and allegorical schema: the elimination of an actual human eye here reinforces the unmediated naturalness of the photograph. Visual realism is created through the defacement of the human eye and through the cultivation of a certain type of nonseeing; for one of the artifacts created by realist representation is the very normative eye that apprehends the image—seeing supposedly does not exist outside the realist frame, or so we are conditioned to assume.

As an artifact of realist conventions, the photograph aesthetically replicates many of the optical values that are deployed in the sensory configuration and aesthetics of the political violence that blinded the photographer in the first place. It is my contention that the photo partakes of past socio-perceptual coordinates of its author when he saw and placed others between the cross hairs of his riflescope. The absence of sight is at the origin of this photograph, and yet it preserves a gaze (here momentarily pacified) that also channels and materializes violence as a sensory ecology. The reified character of that gaze is all the more stark here because it is detached from the eye.

The gaze is ex-orbited, and in this detached state can be more readily appreciated or ex-posed as a potential instrument of technical aggression. For *who* really looks in a panoptic or scopic regime, whether state-sponsored or otherwise? The question is better put as, "What sees in the scopic regime?" We know who and what can be watched, but what sees? It is simply not enough to say the state, or the assassin, or sniper—the former is too general, and the latter too particularistic. Neither response accounts for the political agency of seeing. There is no original and literal eye of the scopic regime. Behind the hegemonic facade of multiple, insectlike, envisioning orifices there is a core of blindness: a dis-association between making the visible and receptive cognitive seeing, in which the latter is simply an imprecise anthropomorphic figure—a fictive terminus for the images created and consumed by the scopic machine. For the ultimate claustrophobic attribute of the scopic regime is that dominant vision is autonomized and requires no singular authorial eye, only the circuit of visibility and the power relation ignited within this circuit between autonomized technical instruments of visualization and those surveilled and objectified by vision and/or violence. Thus in the interrogation rooms of Castlereagh, the prominently displayed video cameras that are meant to monitor interrogation and forestall human rights abuses are either unattended, turned off, or manned by police who turn a *blind eye* to any violence taking place, while the detainees are frequently blindfolded, for being seen and surveilled requires the removal of their vision, and the monopolization of that sense by the state. A scopic regime, like Foucault's panopticon or Lacan's Mirror Stage, is an apparatus behind which lies no one who sees; for *seeing,* no matter how privileged, is but one position internal to, and a function and product of, the total scopic apparatus and is not the mechanism's point of origin. Hence the distinction between the eye and the gaze. The latter is a mechanics of power,[16] the former a sensory organ that can be socially appropriated to channel and materialize normative power in everyday life. Here human vision becomes an adjunct, an instrument, and an automaton of the scopic regime.

ETHNIC LANDSCAPES AS VISUAL CULTURE

Belfast, from the early nineteenth century onwards, has been characterized by the rapid expansion of industrial capitalism, an ethnic/religious division of labor, and residential segregation enforced by populist sectarian violence. In Belfast the reproduction of an ethnic division of labor among the working class rested on (1) kin-based and therefore sectarian labor recruitment, (2) the creation of a predominately Catholic labor reserve through rural-to-urban migration, (3) a segregated or ghettoized settlement pattern, and (4) endogamous marriage practices based on religiously bifurcated descent systems. The urban settlement pattern was also determined by the punctuation of overt crowd violence by the Protestant majority (frequently abetted by the sectarian state), alternating with more silent forms of covert intimidation which enabled the social engineering of ethnic populations and classes into urban reserves that were associated with economic cores and peripheries, that is, to major and minor industries, each with their own confessional, ethnic, and topographic associations. The sectarianization of labor and settlement promoted an ethnicized visual landscape of confessional neighborhoods, Catholic and Protestant commercial and manufacturing zones, and in-place and out-of-place bodies.

Violence and urbanism underwrote the colonial experience in Northeast Ireland. Urban development in Belfast advanced not only through massive industrialization and rural in-migration but through ghettoization. Said has termed geography the imperial methodology, and ghettoization in Northern Ireland implemented imperial and colonial agendas by using geographical control to constrain and rationalize social and therefore bodily and perceptual contact between sundered populations.[17] In Belfast visual experience in everyday life was intimately linked to ethnic contact avoidance as a typified somatic posture in the urban setting. The perceptual organization of working-class Protestants and Catholics was and is organized around the metaphysics of "telling"—discerning who was Protestant or who was Catholic. "Telling" mobilized imaginary and projected images of embodied ethnicity and body politics.[18] Visual imaginaries, once transcribed onto the physiognomy, dress, and body comportment of the encountered ethnic other, played a crucial role in the construction of identity in urban everyday life. In Belfast, the social logic of telling is so encompassing that even the foreign visitor, if there long enough, becomes engulfed in inferential visual classification of ethnicity. Neighborhood segregation of Protestants and Catholics provides an environmental frame for such visual quick-studies of ethnic identity, though telling is more frequently and forcefully applied to potentially out-of-place bodies and to ethnically plural spaces, such as the mass transport system or the downtown commercial center.

Sectarian political violence in Belfast continued many of the ocular strategies of ghettoization. Victim selection in sectarian violence frequently fuses social space, the body, and ethnicity in a visual diagnostic for homicide, and this can directly result in the killing of someone from one's own group in space classified as Other—a consequence that reveals the discrepancy between the visual-spatial imaginary and the real. The ocular character of ethnic classification indicates that contact avoidance is not only the immediate precipitant of sectarian violence, but inhabits the very infra-structure of its enactment. Contact avoidance can be indexed in the way in which visual distancing organizes victims and aggressors into stylized pos-tures and poses, as has been shown in the assassination narrative above.

"Telling" practices are the oldest organizer of the politically visible, but other ideological imaginaries deploy rigid discriminatory and context-bound classification grids in language and discourse to create the politically visible and the politically unseen. Moral discrimination and ethno-historical context are the basic mechanisms for differentiating one act of violence from another. Moral discrimination takes on a particular character in Northern Ireland because the dominant morality is not a matter of choosing nonvio-lence over violence but of morally legitimizing one act of violence in another. Political discourse harbors a visual logic that enhances its credibility. Ideological objects in Northern Irish political culture are subjected to a high-contrast, binary optic based on exclusive and opposing ethnic, confessional, and political categories—Protestant/Catholic, Loyalist/Republican, state/antistate—in which nothing is blurred, thus enabling their polarity to antag-onistic ideological objects. This high-contrast visual figure is also formed of foregrounds and backgrounds or perspectival regression that set the truth claims of any political act or statement. The Northern Irish ideological object is forged through strategies of receding or regressive historical per-spective and typification; contemporary political acts of insult and injury are proposed and popularly received as reenactments, replications, analogies, and echoes of earlier acts in a linear trajectory that eventually recedes toward an elusive historical horizon line of first injury, first assault, and first death dating back to the Cromwellian Plantation if not earlier. Thus all depicted ideological objects (linguistic or visual) possess (1) distinct foregrounds—lit-eral commonsensical presence—and (2) supportive backgrounds or per-spectival depth: spatial origin, historical genealogy, and social causation. Any act of personal destruction and social disfigurement is typified by being immediately absorbed back into this regressive and mimetic temporal schema where each act of violence repeats another and where each act of vio-lence both epitomizes and renews the dualism of the political culture in time and space. Typification is not guaranteed in advance and may always be con-tested, but no act of paramilitary violence is legitimized in support commu-nities without it.[19]

I term this schema the historiography of excuse, where prior acts of vio-lence extenuate the commission of present and future acts. The rationality of excuse depends on recursive time and mimetic resemblance as narra-tivized by political discourse and popular memory. Through temporal mimesis and regression, each act of violence becomes typified insofar as it participates in and takes its validity from a prior aggression. Typification, considered by John Tagg (1988) to be an important attribute of the realist percept, entails the instantaneous transference and extraction of usually stereotypical and fetishized cultural codes, to and from the act of violence. In Northern Ireland these codes are organized around sectarian ethnic classifications, law-and-order imperatives, or antiquated pro– and anti– British Empire discourse. Ernst Bloch (1990) anticipated Tagg's linkage of typification to realism in describing the latter as the *cult of the immediately ascertainable fact.* Rapid fact-setting is dependent on the recognition codes built into any violent enactment, which is the foundation of its typicality. In terms of the sheer materiality of acts of violence, these acts are basically undifferentiated in terms of their concrete human consequences. They are polarized and differentiated through the instantaneous infusion of idealizing nationalist, ethnic, and other cultural codes into the material performance and its debris, rendering the latter excusable. The fusing of realist frame and material act is so overdetermined that the act of violence can be a visualizing apparatus, a lens, and a narrativizing frame all at once. The wrack and ruin of dead, wounded, and maimed bodies and of buildings is already a representational configuration; a created or artificed scene that is prepared in advance for an ex-post-facto second representation by the media, along with various apologetics or condemnations.

Typification and mimesis allow violence to function as collective memory because violence is grounded on the moral aesthetics of reenactment in Northern Ireland. The meaning and memory of any political act is prepared in advance by an accumulation of mimetic moments and reenactments that weave together fate and fatality. As one Republican paramilitary answered in response to my question about why repeated acts of violence were necessary, "Because people forget." Violence, repetition, and memory create the circumscribed and enframed space of the politically real, that is, of political totality in Northern Ireland. While much attention has been paid in the literature on the conflict to official ideological discourse, which can certainly be dissected for its realist narrative, little has been said about the performative infrastructure of acts of violence and of the political iconography they project, even though it is this actual enactment of violence upon the bodies and spaces of others that constitutes the material substrate and the material culture of the conflict. To move to the performative is to ask what does violence visualize in Northern Ireland, and in what forms of seeing are these visions possible?

TARGETS

The weapon in Belfast is a perceptual instrument that organizes urban prospects, frames a historical landscape before itself: a political spectacle of targets as moral objects. The built environment records the effects of this scene making—and not only with literal ruins. The walls of the red brick houses where snipings have occurred are subsequently painted black up to a height of six feet by the British army to block optical acquisition by IRA snipers so that "no profile would come in," as one IRA member put it. Places where previous snipes or bomb attacks have occurred are marked with white paint by the army and police—"Look Here, Look Up"—so violent vision has a history and a geography. Other graphics include numerous wall murals and graffiti dedicated to the neighborhood dead. The gun when it is pointed—not even fired, but pointed—possesses a manifest power to alter the material surround and to temporarily freeze life. The ideological rationality that informs the aiming of a weapon and the final act of assault against the body establishes the weapon as a field of vision, a relationship that can frequently invert, rendering specific acts of perception akin to the infliction or receipt of violence. In Belfast I have felt perceptual assault, like an itch at the back of my head as I sensed the scopes of patrolling British soldiers framing my body as they traced my crossing a street with a movement of their gun barrels.

A blind man makes a picture that gives us the real; previously he shot at Catholics with the aid of a gun-scope to create the political. In its fixation of poses, in framing political targets and objectives, the weapon intersects with the perceptual infrastructure of the camera: they are both prosthetic instruments. The gun translates visual acquisition into tactile destruction. The weapon in Northern Ireland's military-political culture is comprehended by the actors and audience of violence as an icon-making device; it is a prosthetic instrument that extends ideology and visions of history into the depth of the human body, leaving the dead and the depicted in its wake.

The scopic dimension of targeting and weaponry plays at several levels in the following narrative about an attempted *coup d'état* within the Ulster Defense Organization, the largest Loyalist paramilitary organization (10,000 members). The attempted assassination described below halted a split in the organization. The West Belfast component of the Ulster Defense Organization initiated an armed takeover of the organization headquarters on the Shankill Road located in the heart of Loyalist community. The ejected leadership countered this move with a plan to assassinate the coup leader, one Harding Smith.

> There's a fish store in the Shankill Road, Frizell's. . . . Above this fish shop is the UDA headquarters, and on the opposite side of the street there was an optician's, and the Brits go into it because they couldn't go anywhere else in Belfast for their glasses without getting sniped—this man must have had a contract to supply glasses to the army. The optician's across from the headquarters was a vantage point, a spying point. There was this sort of scenario. They placed a kid to sit there in a long black coat and mustache reading the Daily Mirror; under the coat is a machine gun. Next to him there are these two young birds—receptionists—he's the lookout. The lads [two gunmen] move

in and take the optician up the stairs. They stuck the machine gun out: "Any nonsense, you're fucked, you're getting the message. We know the Brits come in here, if youse want to live with these Brits, go up and tell them their gear is not ready—get them out." Now they were sitting there upstairs and downstairs for hours. The receptionists were asking the young buck, "Do you do all this all the time? Are you a professional?" The strategy in the game was you put a kid who doesn't do any thinking. If the kid is young enough, he smells no or knows no danger. And he's sitting with these wee girls. And the Brits come in between: "I'm sorry, you will have to come back in the afternoon, your order is not ready" (imitating a woman's voice). You see, the girls were that fascinated. While the boy downstairs is sitting with a machine gun, the boys are up the stairs, one with some sort of handgun stuck to the optician's ear or up his nose or ass. Wherever it was stuck, it was very impressionable because the optician seemed to respond.

Because the way the windows on the block opposite were set a wee bit lower, they opened the sash at the top, commonly known in Belfast as the fanning light, making a foot square gap. They were leaning on the table, and your man puts a chair on the top table, takes the gun, and sits and watches like Roy Rogers. So he sees the two top men [of the other faction] through the two windows of the office [across the street], Tucker Little and Bucky McCullough. There were these two windows, and they were standing there; one moved over to the other, and the two were standing by the one window waiting on Harding Smith coming [the leader of the coup]. All I'm telling you this was in the police reports, so I am not telling you any tales out of school—because I wasn't there nor was I involved in the conspiracy [laughter], I was in East Belfast [the other side of town] waiting on the other end of the phone line [more laughter].[20]

The next thing it was they [were] titting away at this wee man (the optician): "See you walking down the road every day." "Well, I just get the bus at Oxford street." "Oh, I know where you get the bus all right, don't you dare tell me I know you the bus all right!" [said with exaggerated menace] They had looked at his wallet, found his photo ID, and knew that he lived in Donaghadee, and given it back, but the wee man was so terrified he didn't even realize all that. "We know you get the number 56 [bus] to Donaghadee." "Oh Jesus Christ! You know where I live an all—what sort of people are you?" "We have to do [kill] someone, but we'll not hurt you now, we know all about your family." "Don't hurt my daughter because her man's not well." So they find out all about the wee man's personal business. He starts panicking, and they were winding him up—so the wee man is so wound up like a big spring so he goes blank off their identification. It a whole ploy. While the wee girls down the stairs are fascinated by this professional killer. He was like Lee Marvin—he killed dead ones.

The next thing it was, they lift the phone and ring, and this is what the wee man heard, "We got two men here, McCullough and Little; will we shoot them ones and come back for your man?" [Harding Smith]. The optician said, "He put the phone down and replied to his partner, 'Don't shoot them ones, the man says we can shoot them ones anytime, we're not worried about them ones, we want to shoot Smith and get rid of him now. We can touch them ones any old time and the rest of their family [other members of their faction West Belfast UDA].'"

The first thing Smith does when he arrives, he stands and looks out the window: "Lovely day boys." That was his common thing to do; he done it regular as clockwork and watching the cars go up and down as if he was someone important. They were forty yards across the street—they seen the wee window opened. They hit him with an M-1 carbine, and he spun around like a pirrie about a half dozen times, and the only thing that saved him was that he didn't drink nor smoke and was as fit as a fiddle. He spun around like a pirrie, and every time he spun around they kept banging him, and every time they spun him they hit him on the rebound and actually skimming him. There were just flesh wounds in him; they put a couple through him anyway, but they went right through the stairs . . .

While he was lying in the fucking hospital after the shooting, his men, McCullough and Little, were at a peace conference selling him out. It was psychological: the two men picks up the phone, one says, "Will we do these two wee bastards, and the other one says—we can get them ones any time." Well that scared the shit right out of them ones; that the boys were standing there for two hours waiting on Harding Smith, and they could've been dead; how easy it was for them to die and how determined the other ones who were watching them for two hours. They couldn't believe it; it just blew their minds.

The cinematic aesthetic of the narrative is both sophisticated and self-conscious. The narrator locates the assassination in the midst of the banal particularities of a shopping district. It builds tension with jump cuts between the upstairs, the professional assassins, and the downstairs—the "kid" and the receptionists—a repetitive turn between foreground and background. The optician is repeatedly characterized as "wee," a diminutive indicating smallness and vulnerability; in the narrative he occupies the same visual position as the targets forty yards across the street. It is as if he is being viewed down the barrel of a miniaturizing lens. The convergence of scopic signifiers is almost punlike, and most are borrowed from the aesthetics of visual realism—framing of visual objects, foreground and background action, synoptic action sequences, and the formatting of the killing ground as a proscenium stage. Narrative structure and value can be found as much in the visual values as in the described action or ideological rationale of the attack: consider the choice of the optician's as the staging ground of the killing; the window frames of the target that set up a Hitchcockian mise-en-scène for murder; and the repeated thematic of surveillance as a form of image making that implies prospective death. This motif runs from the manipulation of the optician's photo ID to the deferral of material violence against the targets for the pleasures of watching—"them ones"—who could be made targets at any time in the future. The pleasure of seeing without being seen empowers the act of violence; the invisibility of the killer is crucial to the optical reduction of the victim. Both the optician and the paramilitaries not shot at are devastated by the fact that they have been invisibly surveilled. Scopic power over the target is the source of fear and compliance; the gun as prosthetic vehicle both augments the human eye and materializes vision in physical assault and trauma. In terms of the creation of fear and dominance there is very little differentiation here between physical assault and scopic power; each reinforces and, more important, each simulates the other. Finally, with its cinematic references to Roy Rogers and Lee Marvin films, the tale winds around itself, disclosing the optical metaphors and convergences of the narrative as being not only literal descriptions of the event but pleasure-endowing keys or punctuations where the alchemical substances of dominance are stored, tapped, and remembered.

THE GENEALOGY AND GENDER OF THE REAL

I mean to show that realist strategies of depiction can be found, not only in discourse and conventional practices of visualization like photography, but also in the perceptual infrastructure of acts of domination and violence. To link visual realism to postcolonial violence in Northern Ireland is to remove the former from a purely expressive domain and to uncover the uses of visual realism: what it does to situations and persons, what it makes, alters, and transforms. These issues explicitly challenge visual realism as passive reflection, or naturalized mimesis. The ethic of the correctness of the gaze, the concept of *homoiosis*—the resembling gaze that matches perception to what *should be sighted*—is the ground of realist aesthetics and should be placed under question in any inquiry into politicized vision. I seek to reverse the conventions of photojournalism, the cinematized eye, and legal representation.[21] Rather than solely treating realism as the privileged depictive vehicle for the expression of violence as advanced by the aforementioned cultural institutions, I am interested in approaching violence as the depictive blade that inscribes realist aesthetics onto a social landscape and uses these aesthetics to uphold truth claims about the power and efficacy of political violence.

Emily Apter (1995) has identified a plurality of realisms in colonial and postcolonial societies. Alongside the synoptic realism associated with nineteenth-century literature and twentieth-century cinema, she locates a related but distinct colonial visual realism akin to tourist and ethnological depiction that is exemplified by the tourist postcard. To this can be added the mathematical imagery of colonial census taking—the multiplication and division tables of ethnic, caste, and tribal counts—that Arjun Appadurai (1996) identifies as essential to the surveillance technology and governmental imagination of imperial administration. John Tagg (1988), in his archeology of nineteenth-century criminal and phrenological photography, identifies visual realism with various legal, penological/disciplinary regimes, while Anson Rabinbach (1990) links the realism of nineteenth-century scientific kinesthetic photography to Fordist labor discipline applied to the body of the worker on the factory floor.

To recognize a multiplicity of realisms, visual or literary, and to map a genealogy of visual realism historically rooted in diverse sociocultural locales and media infers that the political agenda of realist modes of depiction and perception must be established in specific historical circumstances and institutional contexts on a case-by-case basis—there can be no general theodicy of visual realism which would amount to indiscriminate iconoclasm. Different utilities have been found for visual realism in various sociohistorical circumstances. I could not describe seventeenth-century Dutch still life and interior painting or the photography of Eugene Atget as politically invested in domination, as is the surveillance system or ocular aggression in Northern Ireland. The molding of realist modes of depiction into a hierarchy of credibility and fact-setting and as a public form of truth-claiming and depictive legitimation was a long and fragmented historical labor that emerged in a variety of discontinuous but overlapping social sites—and not all at one time if we consider the respective development of state archiving, juridical rules of evidence, popular media, optical experimentation, art movements, and the commodification of visual experience.

Terry Eagleton (1995) has recently characterized "literary" realism as the dominant narrative genre of external and internal colonialism in nineteenth-century Ireland and the United Kingdom respectively. Realism for Eagleton is suited for nation-building projects and expansionist and centralizing bureaucracies. It is "the form par excellence of settlement and stability gathering individual lives into a whole . . . realism depends on the assumption that the world is story-shaped—that there is a well-formed narrative implicit in reality itself" (1995: 147). For Eagleton, narratological realism harbors a decidedly visual project of totalization:

> It (realism) . . . springs from a characteristically[*sic*] way of seeing.[22] In the complex industrial milieu of nineteenth-century England, social relations are diffuse and opaque, . . . the dense intricate texture of social life is notably hard to totalize, and secreted behind each social persona is some hinterland of inscrutable private experience, which only the *omniscient authorial eye can decipher.* (174–75; emphasis added)

Here realism is identified as a scopic project committed to the domination of space, to the appropriation of bodies that move through space, and to the recuperation of the "hidden" private lives borne by these bodies. The creation of a unified spatial/perceptual field and mastery over that terrain, which animates the realist scopic regime, readily lends itself to nation-building projects, which are grounded on the presumption or desire for spatial/cultural/racial/ethnic homogeneity.

The tableau of a blind male photographer displaying and portraying a woman introduces a pervasive gender dimension that I would contend is also integral to the realist construct, particularly as it pertains to violence and vision in Northern Ireland. I suggest that the militarized gaze and the realist gaze have been historically crossed with the male gaze if not identical with it. The Western male gaze, played out in painting, cinema, pornography, social science, and the network of glances that form daily visual culture, situates femininity in a state of passivity and receptivity: the feminine is something fixed, pictorial, framed, and sculptured. Masculinity and the male gaze are activity in itself; they both rigidify and inform the feminized body as the bearer of sociopolitical values and of imaginary and symbolic networks. In nationalist and ethnic politics the feminine is permitted to be an image, but women are not readily positioned as authors of national imagery, as Partha Chatergee (1993) has pointed out in demonstrating the gendering of development/nation-building ideology.

The moment of iconic capture is the preeminent realist event, whether accomplished by cameras, rifle scopes, or discourse, and it is frequently a gendered and politicized event. As Mary Ann Doane (1981) proposes, the camera/subject nexus mobilizes relations of power, the authority of the distanced observer or the off-screen or out-of-frame voice who commands and frames the scene, staging and molding the depicted: "Smile, don't smile; move here, move there." Contained within this disciplining of the body is a politics of the pose. In the performance culture of the pose, visual subjects, male or female, receive a veneer of iconic femininity in order to become depictable, as though the condition of the feminine were synonymous with the pose. Posing and being posed can be a mortification of the flesh, a freezing and rigidification by way of being submitted to the Medusan gaze of the other.[23] This politics speaks to the "pose" as both a bearer of ideological codes and as a state of embodiment in which social fictions are rendered tangible and literal.

To talk of a "politics" of the pose is to take an aesthetic act and to show how it can be politically magnified, fetishized, and institutionalized, and this is not to mechanically assert that all painting or photography or depiction are automatically political or gendered violence. One must examine what is done to bodies to create these images, to enforce their legitimacy, and to substantiate their typicality. It is not only a question of how an iconography of poses is made to bear normative social codes, but also of how heterogeneous bodies are made to bear desired poses. I suggest that political violence is a crucial medial in transcribing prescriptive poses onto bodies that never volunteered for such portraiture in the first place.

In this framework acts of political violence and the human debris they

leave in their wake engage and enlarge the politics of the pose and its material consequences. For instance, in Belfast acts of political violence can be
linked to the gendering of aggressors and victims as well as to imagery of
rigidification, petrifaction, and mortification—the politically encoded
corpse can be re-read in light of the politics of the pose. In Belfast the noun
and image "stiff" describes the victim of political violence, and the verb "to
stiff" or "stiffing" refers to the actual act of homicide and gives the latter a
dynamic visual contour. The term *stiff* is vernacular for a corpse, but in the
last two decades the term has narrowed, and the noun and verb forms
largely refer to those corpses created by political and sectarian violence. In
Belfast the stiff and the act of stiffing are related to other body imagery that
metaphorizes bodily harm and political punishment. In paramilitary vernacular a targeted male victim prior to being stiffed is "a cunt," which is a
targeting phrase. To "knock his cunt in" refers to killing or a beating. To stiff
someone is also to "give him the message." Violence is a transfer of political
signs from self to other. In the working-class vernacular "giving the message"
predates the civil violence and was slang for the male role in heterosexual
intercourse. Bearing in mind its prepolitical nuances, "giving the message"
now implies the feminization of the object of political violence as a "cunt."
In turn the "cunt" is understood as a passive recipient prior to and during
the infliction of violence. The stiff is not only given the message, but is
meant to display these messages of visceral intimidation and manifest power
to prescribed audiences.[24] The petrified dead are first posed by acts of violence and then by justifying narratives that excuse or condemn these acts.
The "stiff" created by political violence is statuary—a frozen bearer of
unyielding ideological agendas and an unavoidable spectacle for a community of witness. And the montaging of a female sex organ onto male victims
is a prescription for how one should see and consider the enemy dead.
Gendered inflections of aggression and victimage distribute male and feminine essences between agents and recipients of political violence—the
posers and the posed. And it is no coincidence that the domestic space,
which has explicit gendered connotations in Northern Ireland, has been
the social unit most frequently violated by the surveillance apparatus and
sectarian assassination.

The male gaze, like the realist percept, is blind to itself; the eye and the
gaze are split. To the extent that it obliterates its gendered, embodied, and
positioned origins, the male gaze establishes its realist, transparent, and naturalist truth claims. "Realism, so the Formalists instruct us, works by con-
cealing its mechanisms" (Eagleton 1995: 148). Both visual realism and the
male gaze have in common the tendency to obscure the constructed origins
of their perceptual apparatus and advance themselves as natural, unchang-
ing, and ahistorical.[25] Visual realism and the male gaze are in symbiosis in
this strategy of naturalization because they both stand for the correctness of

vision, for a predetermined adequation between the viewer and the viewed, which actually entails the reduction of the viewed to the coordinates of gaze—a process which I would call posing.

The political nexus between the male gaze, the mortification of the viewed body, and the rigidity of the pose are expounded upon in Lacanian theory (Lacan 1977: 2–3, 16–17, 28). For Lacan, executive organs of the body are detachable objects: through a sensory specialization and hierarchy vision is retooled as an instrument of technical aggression.[26] The visually constructed world must also be intimately connected to the engineering and aggressive encoding of social space. For Lacan, the enclosure of experience within a "self-preserving" fetishized vision in "full forward flight" characterizes the drive for scopic domination as a kind of vertigo displaced onto unmastered, unending space as the preeminent visual object (28). Social space and somatic spaces are both terrains of disorder and desired objects of visual control requiring vectoring and boundaries—the rationality of societal margins and edges that cannot be crossed without being surveilled—borders that can be equally planted on the body or on a social-scape. In a scopic regime, subject formation and spatial command intersect—visual command of the body of the Other is both the command of a unit of space and a reduction of the envisioned subject to a spatial determination. Projects of surveillance regulate movement between spaces and create a spatialized social life mediated by rigid and normative geographies. Lacan's correlation of visual objectification, vertigo, and the drive to spatial domination implicitly connects scopic regimes with the spatialized politics of nationalism and related projects of topographic control.

Lacanian space is not empty, and he returns us to the politics of the pose, for Lacanian social space is punctuated by vertical beings, by ideological statuary—exemplary figurines and emblems of mastery or subjugation, upon which humanity projects itself, generating a world of fetishized identity-objects. The Lacanian social-scape is an assemblage of authoritative and authorizing postures rigidified and supported by vision, mimesis, and desire. This Mirror Stage of the political is a museum peopled with immobile images, petrified hieratic monuments of domination/subjugation: stiffs, or heroes.[27] The gaze of political mastery stands "ex-posed" and mirrored before itself in the form of the postured other. The world is composed of statues "in which man projects himself" and "produces himself in front of himself," creating automata—ideological sculpture, a garden of sexual and political figureheads (Lacan 1977: 2–3; Borch-Jacobsen 1991: 60). Ideological projects throw up statuary which form a continuum of stasis, of things, identities, and substances stabilized by vision and mimesis. Mastery is constructed through forceful bodily projection onto a subordinated posed other who then is consumed or read for the domination codes that can be extracted from the mirror effects of its objectified and petrified embodiment. In Northern Ireland the victim posed in violence and death is the mimetic artifact, the detachable part of the master gaze, and a metonym of spatial domination.

BEING SEEN

Oral testimony about war experience in Belfast usually approaches the scopic regime from the position of being seen, being registered in the politically visible. Some of these narratives trace the symbolic ecology of the scopic regime as it is inserted into the crevices of everyday life and into the body itself. In arrest and interrogation situations the scopic regime is felt at the level of the socially constructed nervous system and in the form of rumor-consciousness.[28]

To the extent that it visually fixes and reduces its victims to manipulatable surfaces, the scopic regime of the state can effectively derealize the body and the self. The state uses visual disinformation to create rumor, disorientation, and fear. When the interrogated are to be released, the police stage photographs showing the interrogated and tortured shaking the hands of their aggressors in order to create the impression of collaboration, and as if to create an institutional memory of the physical intimacy they have shared. These photographs can be used to blackmail the interrogated, or they can be disseminated in the community of the prisoner, thereby discrediting the suspect and possibly setting him up for assassination as an informer by paramilitary organizations. Another staged photograph appears to show the suspect receiving a check from the police. After release, these checks can be publicly delivered by the police to the suspect's home. As in other instances, the photograph and the politics of the pose can kill.

Rumor-consciousness fed by the scopic regime and its fictions seems to cultivate its own special perceptual array that weaves new sensibilities between personhood and the state—vectoring the body in unexpected fashions. The following stories are taken from both Republican and Protestant paramilitaries and concern their experience of "the warning." In these stories the force of being seen and thus targeted by the state is not experienced as a human act of perception, but rather is apprehended as affect within the body that is scripted by the state.

FIRST ARREST NARRATIVE

The police had an occasion to look for me. Their normal thing is to come out at a quarter to six in the morning. That's to disorient ye, so ye don't know what's happening. I'm lying there awake in bed, can't sleep at a quarter past five. You get a gut feeling about this. Sure as God above you know when there's a raid on. And you know there's somebody coming for ye. I'm lying in bed, and I have this terrible gut feeling that they're coming for me. I says to the wife, "I've got to get dressed." I'm just about to put my trousers on . . . Bang!

Bang! Bang! Knock comes to the door. I had a blanket up the previous night behind the front door so the peelers couldn't see me if I came down the front stair past the door. I grabbed my trousers in my hand and my shoes, no socks on scarpers down the stairs out the back, leaps over the top of the back fence, didn't get my trousers on till I was half way down the street. There was me running down the street bollick naked. (Male, Loyalist paramilitary)

SECOND ARREST NARRATIVE

You ask my ma. I would wake up in the middle of the night and tell her, "The house will be hit today, so be expecting." You have that feeling inside you. Things weren't just right. You'd have been picking up bits and pieces of info from other guys that were getting picked up and interviewed. Sometimes it added up, other times it mightn't. But then always at night the feeling would come onto you and you knew you were for it. A load of times out of nowhere I would wake the mother and tell her the house would be hit. I told her a load of times. (Male, Republican paramilitary)

THIRD ARREST NARRATIVE

When they came for me, . . . I was up at half five in the morning. I had been up the same time the Monday and Tuesday before. Though I hadn't been involved for some time, I knew they were coming for me. I'm thinking, "Will I keep the door open?" Here's me, "Sure, when they come I'll rap the window for to let them know I'm expecting them." I went back to sleep for an hour, woke up and told the wife to get up because the house is getting done today. At a quarter past six I hear the Land Rover coming up the street. Before the peelers could get to the door, I jump up and rap the window.

The peeler says to me, "How did you know that we were coming?" Here's me: "I'm psycho." He says, "If you're psycho, you could have saved me from getting out of my bed and coming down to lift you. You could have come down to Castlereagh [interrogation center] yourself." He got me on that one. I says, "You think I'm going to fucking do your job for you?" I was asked again and again in the interrogation, "How did you know we were coming for ye?" (Male, Loyalist Paramilitary)

In these accounts rumor-consciousness functions as a somaticized symptom or specialized organ of sensory perception. The bodily registration of rumor as warning is indexed in such phrases as "terrible gut feeling," or as a nocturnal sensation: "At night the feeling would come onto you." The liminality of the night is crucial to the somatic shift, for it magnifies the encompassing capacities of state vision. This dis-ease of the body records the other and affective side of scopic claustrophobia and penetration: these sensations and apprehensions are seismic traces of visual power and violence at the level of the socially mediated nervous system. The stories encode the subjective experience of the hyper-visibility of the targeted body and the tangible invisibility of scopic aggressors.

The warning tales above come close to describing somaticized rumor/

danger as *nerves,* a term which is not used by these male narrators because it is associated with female disorders in working-class Belfast. The gendered concept of "nerves" is used by working-class women to explain their overuse of barbiturates and other sedatives because of the personal losses and terror many have experienced. "Nerves" is a condition that continues the mourning process stemming from trauma accruing from the arrest, torture, imprisonment, and death of immediate family, kin, and neighbors (mainly males). Self-medication with barbiturates prolongs the numbing effects of trauma stemming from these events and thus perversely extends the mourning process through the alternation between an attack of nerves and chemical sedation. For these women, "nerves" is a political disease come by through the structures of everyday life in Belfast. "Nerves," like rumor, becomes a micro-language of terror that is conveyed by gesture and expression from body to body in everyday muted contact. In working-class Catholic neighborhoods, "nerves" is state terror sunk into the lived body. However, nerves are also recognized as a condition of war that can cut across adversary lines, linking others in a unified field of fear. The following stories emerged from a conversation with two "Catholic" mothers at a day care center in West Belfast. The second story was presented as a commentary on the first.

FIRST NARRATOR

The Brits here are constantly taking nerves and cracking up—being taken away screaming hob nob to the hospital. There was a fairy ring in McCort's fort where the British soldiers are situated. And when they moved into the fort, they ploughed the land up and dug the ring up. Everybody was shouting at him or her, "You'll regret it. You'll regret it." So some of these Brits who had dug the ring up were lying in bed, and red light hovered over them every night. And another cracked up because he kept seeing these wee men around the fort. So they took him away.

SECOND NARRATOR

When the Brits used to come into this area raiding, we would tell the yarns about Riddle's Field [where the ghost of a Protestant factory owner haunts his own property]. An army barrack had been built on the site. We would say, "Old Riddle will come and get you!" This old Brit would be standing at the door of your house while they were tearing it apart and say, "Tell us that again!" Then they would tell us of incidents that happened to them that they couldn't explain. One of them saw a horseless carriage with an old man sitting on it. A couple of them (British soldiers) were supposed to be taken away from that.

The first story connects the contemporary dynamics of military occupation to the violation of pre-Christian sacred space, the faery ring. Such stories have a long history in rural Irish oral culture as commentaries on British colonial occupation in the west of Ireland in the eighteenth and nineteenth centuries. In the Belfast story sequence an equation is tacitly made between the transgression of historicized and/or sacred space and the violation of contemporary domestic space: occupiers are people out-of-place who do you out of your place. This is indexed in the ironic juxtaposition of the second narrative where, as they tear apart the narrator's house, the British soldiers ask her about the legends and rumors attached to the site of *their* domicile. McCort's Fort and its faery ring are remnants of prehistoric Ireland, while Riddle, a classic Dickensian figure, exemplifies an earlier form of colonization from Belfast's age of industrial capitalism. The nonsynchronicity of these places with the present calls into question the unlimited capacity of the counterinsurgency apparatus to domesticate the urban landscape, to control its time and space. These judgments are concentrated in the disordering or de-rationalization of the soldiers' vision, their major vehicle of spatial control and command. I am drawn to the fact that it is the vision of these agents of the state, with all of its potencies and instrumental rationality, that is subjected to a supernatural, that is, antirealist, interruption. These supernatural visitations constitute a blind spot in the military visual apparatus. The soldiers may share these phantasmic apparitions with the locals, but they are ultimately culturally alien and antagonistic to the military gaze, generating nerves and various mental disorders.

These rumors and legends of the colonized speak about unfinished historical experience, unreconciled pasts, precolonial Ireland, and nineteenth-century industrial capital, which, through the uncanny, remain critically contemporaneous with the current experience of foreign domination and social dislocation. The infiltration of the uncanny in the warning and visitation experiences, the former's somaticization of the state's gaze, and the latter's disordering of that gaze, imply that the scopic rationalization can be reframed by a counternarrative which taps into the popular memory of folklore, the supernatural, and rumor.[29]

A BESTIARY

During a night of late drinking, a Loyalist paramilitary described to me a rumor and a legend of his organization, a faceless assassin known as "the Jackal." Jackal stories circulated throughout the Loyalist paramilitary community. The Jackal killed Catholic males by moving in and out of Catholic areas, silently slipping into their bedrooms at night, and slitting their throats while they slept—the body to be discovered by the unsuspecting family members or the wife who had been asleep beside the victim the next morning. His silent intrusions and subsequent surveying of Catholic domestic scenes magnified the Jackal's aura for the narrator. As he described the silent invisibility of the Jackal's movements in and out of people's homes, he invoked an almost dreamlike creature, whom he apparently found to be exotic, frightening, and admirable for his technique. As he talked, I could not shake the realization that the elegiac tone of his discourse, the faraway look in his eyes, and his intimacy with telling details of specific acts of murder indicated that he was relating stories about a double, a secret sharer, who may have been himself—a self who was and was not in the room with us, who was also far away, haunting other rooms and other nights.

The presence of animal imagery in the name "the Jackal" can be considered integral to the phantasmagoria of violence. In Belfast there was the figure of the Blackman, who was associated with the sacrificial death of animals; his rumored appearances and murders congealed accumulated perceptions about the uncanny urban space brought about by kaleidoscopic terror (Feldman 1991: 81–84). There is also the association of the name "the Jackal" with a popular film concerning a professional killer whose elaborately crafted rifle, fitted out with custom-made magnifying scope, was as much a personality in the film as the assassin. Like the Loyalist killer, the film's character was also a master of incognito.

There is a scopic subtext encased in the name of the killer. In Belfast the zoological jackal is not popularly known as a predator or hunter but as an eater of carrion, consuming bodies already dead, already rendered inert. Does this say anything about the practices of the Loyalist killer of the same name? I would suggest that embedded in the animal image and the killing methods of the Jackal is the recognition that the actual physical death of his victims was a secondary act of violence. The Jackal invades and visually commands the nocturnal domestic space, an eminently feminized terrain in Belfast and a fitting stage for the politics of the pose. His victims are first assaulted by ocular aggression when the killer infiltrates their privacy and surveys these sleeping, unknowing bodies. The Jackal indulges in the pleasures of seeing before killing and in seeing as killing and power—therefore his focus on the sleeping, unknowing victim with closed eyes. Sleep observed anticipates petrifaction and mortification; the gaze of the killer imprints these qualities on the body, and the material act of violence leaves a forensic record of these operations. Here vision robs the victim of material subjecthood in transforming the victim into an iconic object. The second theft of the Jackal takes life itself. Physical death is a redundant action after the gaze of the killer has pierced and frozen the victim. The Jackal leaves for others, in the form of "the stiff," the concretion of his invasive vision: the petrified body of his victim. The Jackal's vision is only visible in the displayed corpse, for as the name infers, there is no human source for this sight—its inhumanity is tied to its invisibility.

The body left by the Jackal is both a *materialization and memory of the killer's vision*. These associations continue and transpose many of the motifs of the attempted assassination through the window discussed above and add another element to that zone of mediation where ocular aggression and visual hierarchy transmute into the phantasmic. An important element in both accounts is the invisibility of the observing aggressor. The externality of the spectator/killer to the scene of violence establishes the potency of the latter by removing this figure from perceptual fixation and framing—the gaze in the scopic regime is off-frame; it cannot be posed, for it is that which poses; it has no site because it is the author of sites.[30] And yet this potency requires materialization in the act of physical assault that leaves marks not solely of tactile contact, but of ocular contact on the body. The site-less gaze is located and seen only in the bodies of the viewed, posed and harmed. The victim becomes the reminder, the remainder, and the visual record of the invisible killer.

The rumors of the Jackal exceed any individual act of violence or any individual killer they describe and circumscribe an objective condition, a political and sensory situation by which the killers themselves, among others, narrate the historical fulcrum from which they carve out their political identities with acts of visual and violent acquisition. Such stories evade the neat argumentation and historical logic of formal ideological rationale; they seem to have nothing to do with elevated projects of nation building and ethnic assertion, yet they do capture a spatial substrate: the locus where aggression, vision, and the body covertly come together in the production of power and historical agency which, in turn, colors the experience of violence as an intermediate yet efficacious plateau of dominance. Upon this material geography, hidden in ideological cellars, more grandiose and dematerialized nationalist edifices rest and stake their territory as viable political forces in contemporary and postwar Northern Ireland.

CONCLUSION: PIERCINGS

I

The blind man's photo possesses a disturbing clarity. It appears at once to be the ultimate triumph of realist aesthetics—that realist aesthetics exist independently of human subjectivity. Yet, once contextualized in blindness and war, certitude, hallucination, and rumor, the photo imposes an estrangement effect on visual realism. The "ethnographic photo," which records this scene and which cannot be divorced from the contexts I have rehearsed above, stands at the fulcrum of this bivalent visual nexus. For it seemingly shows someone's sight, yet shows nothing of the sort; rather it *elicits* the viewer's consent to realist conventions such as typification, intelligibility, and perspective. However, the photograph's "realist description" is disfigured by contextual and wider cultural implications to such an extent that the sensory medium of vision falls into ethnographic crisis and serves more as a signpost of the perceptual crisis of both the ethnographer and informants than as an authoritative description of the ethnographic object. In this sense it is a figure of double aspect, what Salvador Dali called the paranoiac image: "The way in which it has been possible to obtain a double image is clearly paranoiac. By a double image is meant such a representation of an object that it is also without the slightest physical or anatomical change, the representation of another entirely different object."[31] Such figures are anamorphic, one image or form arising from or out of another form without the cancellation or disappearance of the first image. If realist fixation fabricates an eternal present of social permanence, the anamorphic percept is the equivalent of historicity in motion and of its indeterminate signification. Merleau-Ponty describes the anamorphic figure in terms of temporality that fractures realist domestication:

> The assumed plenitude of the object and of the moment only appears in the presence of the imperfect nature of the intentional being. A present without future or an eternal present is precisely the definition of death, the living present is torn between a past and a projected future. It is therefore essential for the thing and the world to present themselves as open to project us beyond their predetermined manifestations and constantly to promise us other things to see. (1978: 38)

If critiquing the truth claims of visual realism proceeds by establishing its genealogical linkage to domination and to colonial and postcolonial hegemony in particular contexts, then it is also important to connect this critique to movements of perceptual and depictive decolonization within the imperial metropole as the center of realist cathexis and capital. The exponents of DaDa and Surrealism, such as Dali, may have presented themselves as afflicted by realist closure, but they elaborated a sophisticated iconographic critique of visual realism that connected it to forms of military, technological, and economic domination that bear relevance to the perceptual culture of Belfast today.

At the end of World War I the DaDa and Surrealist movements characterized the depth penetration of modernity as bodily trauma and perceptual shock, thus putting the realist percept into crisis and fragmentation. This judgment largely originated in the complimentary experiences of the World War I battlefield, with its unprecedented mechanized assault on the human body, and in the accelerated commodification and technological refunctioning of culture, of which war technology was a part (see Jay 1993; Silver 1989; Stich 1990). The war created eleven million disabled veterans: bodies patched up with artificial limbs and prosthetics, images of postwar everyday life that informed DaDa and Surrealist aesthetics of the human figure: alterations to human proportions implicated corresponding mutations in human identity and its perceptual coordinates. The confrontation of organic life with mechanized violence was experienced by the exponents of DaDa and Surrealism as a denaturing and derealization of the body. Disfigurement could be abrupt, violent, and dramatic as on the battlefield, or it could be a silent accretion within the structures of everyday, postwar urban life. In this manner the mundane oneiric practices associated with Surrealism transmogrified the everyday into a sensory war zone. The infamous opening scene of the film *Un Chien Andalou* (1929), by Luis Bunuel and Salvador Dali, directly evoked this theme of perception as somatic trauma and as gendered: a razor cuts across a woman's eye, which fills the screen with its orificial wound. This image was both description and manifesto. Under the perceptual razor of modernity, the transformation of executive organs meant their wounding and bifurcation through the encounter with aggressive objecthood. There was an inherent inversion linked to the mutilation of an eye: inasmuch as the eye could be victimized and pierced, it could also aggress against and pierce what it viewed—the camera is the razor in this scene.

The "picture shock" (*Bildshock*) aimed at by the film's imagery was the aesthetic equivalent of the battle or shell shock of war experience. Max Ernst's collages of the 1920s frequently show body parts, particularly hands, pierced by sharp objects and/or amputated from the body whole—the latter act implying not only dismemberment but also the technological detachment, specialization, and consequent autonomization of the perceptual organs, in which they achieve new capabilities and produce new perceptual objects. The violent decontextualization of the sensory organism, the imagery of the body that has lost its organs, was an attempt to apprehend perception within new socio-historical coordinates.

The Surrealist inheritance offers not only a critique of the fetishized integration of realist aesthetics into warfare and the structure of everyday life, but also the possibility of rehabilitating other antirealist perceptual postures within the sensorium of war. The historical and aesthetic record of these perceptual postures points to the historical possibility of a postwar countermemory to the canonical ideological narratives and positivist event histories of Northern Ireland that prescribe the manner in which violence is to be remembered, depicted, and recorded and therefore reproduced as consciousness and agency. Can we preclude the possibility of countermemory arising, not only from artistic and theoretical critique, but also from the marginalized practices of popular imagining and memory grounded in vernacular idioms such as the rumor and the uncanny? The ethnographic encounter with such antimemories may well recuperate the slender narrative of the dehistoricized. Dehistoricization is a perceptual, experiential, and depictive aftereffect of certain practices of violence, of representations of violence and coercive experiences of embodiment. I have proposed elsewhere that dehistoricization is to a large extent the aftereffect of cultural anesthesia, the repression or inadmissibility of multiform, painful sensory experience (see Feldman 1994; see also Koselleck 1985). In turn, counter-memory is also contingent on the recovery of multiform sensory alterity and its re-historicization.

I would suggest that in Belfast the dehistoricized can be partially located in the shifting spaces of the uncanny, the phantasmal, and the rumored, which are not merely external to political-military realism, but can be found within anxieties about the nature of the politically real. Thus the stories I have related are double-edged; they attest to the dominance of visual para-digms in the prosecution of political warfare and in its culture of represen-tation, and yet at the same time, in their very telling, they register the limits of vision and of violence as vehicles for claiming truth.

II

This essay has been an analysis of the decay of realism toward its margins—toward anamorphic fracture that promises us other things to see. I began with the emblematic—a visual souvenir, a postcard from my fieldwork—and proceeded to fashion an ethnography of emblems: of realism as an emblem and of visual, linguistic, and corporeal emblems of realism which seem fixed but are constantly shifting and unstable. In making such an analysis I would suggest that ethnographic inquiry, merely on the basis of its cross-cultural and historical contingency, is constantly confronted with and generating paranoiac and anamorphic figures which bar ethnography from a naive acceptance of visual and other forms of realism and their perceptual coordinates. My position here is not to exorcise visual or synoptic realism from ethnographic depiction but to clarify its constructed, perceptually rel-ative, and historically determined character as an inherited complicity of both ethnographer and informants. To take an iconoclastic posture with realist depiction would be to repeat the very stratifying and hierarchical ges-ture that allows realist representation to monopolize the construction of fac-ticity in modernity: this is the customary strategy of a crude postmodernism. Realism, in its ejection and repression of alternate perceptual postures, in its monopolization of facticity, has been the most successful iconoclasm to date. Indeed I have marshaled realist depictive procedures, the citation of empirical evidence, to incriminate realism in its historical contingency.[32] The critique of realist aesthetics can only take place from within the cultural inheritance of realist depiction; the latter is but one vector of a multiplex dialogical terrain, much of which has been submerged by the realist gaze, which creates invisibility in the very process of describing and inscribing the visible.

In Belfast the political efficacy of violence itself is contingent on norms of visual realism and perceptual circuits of visibility and invisibility. I have shown also that the political efficacy of the act of violence is also an aesthetic efficacy that provides pleasures of consumption and reception, which respectively positions aggressor and victim in an iconic and stylized relationship. Further, I have explored how the rigid geometry of scopic power may be relativized at the margins of experience by the phantasmic, the rumored, and the uncanny.

As opposed to continuing the "postmodernist" tendency of aestheticizing domination, this analysis identifies acts of aestheticization as intrinsic to power, thereby moving the aesthetics of political violence into the center of a political anthropology concerned with war. Aestheticization is the civilizational heritage of all depictions of violence and all empowered discourses. There are counteraesthetic positions that one can take—rehabilitation of historicity against dominant history, and of sensory alterities that problematize the aesthetic continuum of domination—but I doubt one can find a purely pre-aesthetic ground from which to write against domination. The circuitry of scopic domination and violation in Northern Ireland, the visual realism it deploys and elevates, and the sensory alterities it devalues, suppresses, and yet instigates remain the epistemic terrain where the metaphysics of political violence in Belfast and elsewhere will have be demystified. Like rumor, the warning sensation of impending arrest, or tales of ghosts, faeries and banshees, the politics of visual and narrative realism is a hieroglyph that requires its own decipherment and archaeology. This project would aggravate the iconoclastic strictures of realism at work in the public culture of both the ethnographer and the victim of violence. But this endeavor might also return us to the agendas and emblems of the Surrealists, who countered the realist eye that cuts and pierces with an another orb, the eye, neither totally blind nor all-seeing, that weeps with memory in the face of violence.

NOTES

My fieldwork in the war zones of Northern Ireland stems from 1978, when I was writing my first book, *The Northern Fiddler*. This essay, in part, originated in the rich dialogues on violence and aesthetics that took place at the conference entitled "States of Violence" in March 1994, organized and sponsored by the journal *Comparative Studies in Society and History* and the Department of Anthropology at the University of Michigan. A longer version of this paper appeared in *Public Culture* 10, no. 1 (1997), and I would also like to acknowledge my fruitful dialogues with the editorial board of that journal. I owe a debt to the insightful readings of this paper by E. Valentine Daniel, Pamela Reynolds, James Boon, and Kay Warren. In addition I am grateful to the 1995 conference entitled "Violence and Political Agency," organized by Veena Das, Arthur Kleinman, and Mamphela Ramphele at the Rajiv Gandhi Foundation and sponsored by the Social Science Research Council; the conference facilitated the development of the theoretical frameworks presented here. Nadia

Seremetakis and Paul Stoller were instrumental in turning my attention to the anthropology of the senses, and I dedicate this essay to them.

1. Fieldwork was conducted in County Tyrone during the years 1978–80, and in Belfast in 1984–87, 1990, and 1992.

2. Under the current tenuous truce conditions, which at the time of writing the IRA no longer observes, it is difficult to ascertain whether these descriptions of assassination logic should be in the past or present tense.

3. On house raiding by governmental "security forces" in Northern Ireland, see Feldman 1991: 85–105.

4. The state's counterinsurgency program drastically altered civil life, including the civil character of law enforcement through the suspension of common rules of law, enhanced powers of arrest, detention, and interrogation (the latter frequently culminating in torture), altered rules of evidence, and trials without jury. This panoptic apparatus is applied with greater force and violence to the Catholic working-class community than to the Protestant working-class community. Such ethnic imbalance is always considered to be politically motivated in Northern Ireland. The Catholic populations subjected to this surveillance perceive it to be explicitly political and an invasive erosion of their personal lives effectively criminalizing the latter. The majority of people subjected to this surveillance are not engaged in either political or "criminal" activity; this is an intervention system designed by the state to intimidate mass populations.

5. This was during the massive coal mine strike of 1984.

6. There are many covert informational and military linkages between Loyalist paramilitaries and certain sections of the police and army reserves, which are largely composed of Protestants.

7. Bryson was a legendary IRA gunman of the first years of the conflict who was shot to death by the British army.

8. Ian Paisley and William Craig are leading Loyalist politicians, and Tommy Herron was a legendary assassinated leader of the Ulster Defense Association. This is a Loyalist pantheon with which the narrator is associating himself, deservedly or not.

9. I do not distinguish here between the actual use and the theatrical display of weaponry, for both acts create political iconography.

10. See my discussion of the panopticon technology in Northern Ireland (Feldman 1991: 115–38).

11. The thematic of vision circumscribed by or organized around a core of blindness can be found in the works of Merleau-Ponty, Lyotard, and Derrida; it is conspicuously absent in Foucault.

12. Here only the aggressor strives to remain invisible or cultivates a mediated visibility in the material record of bodies wounded, killed, captured, and tortured.

13. The title of this section, "Scotology," comes from the term *scotomization*—a psychosomatic blind spot that appears in vision where something is too threatening to be seen. *Skotos* in Greek means "darkness."

14. See *Sunday Times* Insight Team 1972 for a comprehensive account of these events. The aftermath of this crowd violence precipitated the rapid growth and institutionalization of paramilitary organizations in both Protestant and Catholic working-class communities.

15. For discussion of the exchange structure of violence, see Feldman 1991: 72–74, 100–102, 234–35.

16. Obviously the gaze as a technique of power has its own cultural history that is both continuous and discontinuous with the development of human vision—for we must also allow for resistance to the politicized gaze by vision and other senses. See Buck-Morss 1989; Asendorf 1993; and Crary 1991.

17. On the sectarianization, racialization, and ghettoization of social space, see Smith 1992; Rodman 1992; Goldbery 1993; Massey 1984; and Shields 1991.

18. See my discussion of ethnicity, embodiment, and the practice of "telling" (Feldman 1991: 56–59).

19. State violence is usually legitimized by the Loyalist political culture, though not always. This community embeds state violence in its own local genealogies whether they approve of it or not. Consider the recent rioting over ceremonial marching, in which the police along with Catholics became objects of Loyalist antagonism.

20. In fact the narrator planned the assassination.

21. See my discussion on violence, racism, and visual and legal realism (Feldman 1994).

22. In the nineteenth century, "realism" was associated with modes of narration and visualization that presumed an omniscient observer detached from and external to the scenography being presented. It was linked to formal pictorial perspectivism and narrative linearity with all its assumptions about causality, space, and time (Crary 1991).

23. In modernity the gender reversal in the transfer of Medusan powers to the male gaze is traced back to the demonization of the female in the Medusa myth. Medusa is the radical and monstrous image of the Other who threatens the male self and is defeated when Perseus uses a mirror effect to turn that gaze back upon her— indicating a male channeling and mediation of the powers of vision. A critical mythography of this myth and its cultural replication in modernity is beyond the scope of this paper.

24. I have elsewhere subjected these terms to a more expanded discussion (see Feldman 1991: 68–74); however, the issue of posing compels a different reading of these terms than I originally generated.

25. The gendering of vision here in the phrase "the male gaze" is based on several historical processes—the Western civilizational pattern that associates visual empowerment with dominant elites; monopolized technologies; hierarchies of credibility and truth claiming (Crary 1991); the history of Western painting and sculpture; and the historical formation of vision as a commodity form closely associated with pleasure and mobile consumption, as in Baudelaire's and Benjamin's notion of the *flaneur*—again a male figure whose female counterpart for Benjamin was the prostitute (Buck-Morss 1989). The adjective *male* does not mean that only men "see" in a scopic regime. I am not arguing for an essentialized male gaze but for the male gaze as a mobile cultural form; thus, both men and women and transgendered persons can engage in the male gaze as a mode of objectification. It is to avoid essentialization that I argue that in a scopic regime there are only positions of vision internal to the apparatus and no anthropomorphic vision at the source or as the author of the apparatus. A woman behind the scope of a rifle in Northern Ireland, or

behind the video camera in the torture chamber is engaging the politics of the pose and positioned within the male gaze as a practice of domination as much as any man.

26. The intersection between the historical formation of the senses and the division of labor is first discussed by Marx in *The Economic and Philosophical Manuscripts,* which indicates that there is a dense stratigraphy of modern perceptual techniques that links the economic, aesthetic, and political spheres—a history that has been only partially explored.

27. The theory of the pose is based on Lacan's discussion of the Mirror Stage, in which the child displaces its identity and origin to the posed image of its body in the mirror—the first statue relation so to speak. This pose image is introjected by the child through mimetic play (Lacan 1977: 2–3).

28. "In zones of violence, *the terror of everyday life is risk and rumor felt on the body.* Rumor is somaticized as the dream of the executioner borne within the imputed victim's body. Through rumor and risk-perception, embodiment is doubled: expected victimizer and potential victim are intermingled in the same form. The body becomes transitive and historicized by the conjuncture of chance and finality. Torture and assassination become rumor materially enacted upon other people's bodies, which in turn can be transmuted into rumor as they are first subtracted by violence as living entities and then frequently made to vanish altogether as both persons and corpses by state silence and/or popular incomprehension" (Feldman 1995: 234).

29. Several works on rumor, colonialism, and political culture explore rumor as the opposition between seeing and believing and as resistance to hierarchies of credibility; see Ann Stoler (1992), who refers to the prevalence of hearsay as opposed to visually confirmed facts; Rafael 1991; and Turner 1993. Spivak (1988: 215) and Bhabha (1995: 331–32) relate rumor to the antirealism of the uncanny and the phantasmal.

30. Those who have experienced the "warning" sensation (described above) prior to their arrest can attest to this.

31. For a discussion of his concept of the paranoiac-critical, see Dali 1930: 9–12.

32. I owe this insight to James Boon's insightful critique of an earlier version of this paper, which influenced a more Derridean take on the realist archive.

REFERENCES

Appadurai, Arjun. 1996. *Modernity at Large: Cultural Dimensions of Globalization.* Minneapolis: University of Minnesota Press.

Apter, Emily. 1995. "Ethnographic Travesties: Colonial Realism, French Feminism and the Case of Eliss Rhais." In *After Colonialism: Imperial Histories and Postcolonial Displacements,* ed. Gyan Prakash. Princeton: Princeton University Press.

Asendorf, Christoph. 1993. *Batteries of Life: On the History of Things and Their Perception in Modernity.* Berkeley: University of California Press.

Beckett, Samuel. 1980. *Id., Ill Seen, Ill Said.* New York: Grove Press.

Bhabha, Homi. 1995. "In a Spirit of Calm Violence." In Prakash 1995.

Bloch, Ernst. 1990. *Heritage of Our Times*. Trans. N. Plaice and S. Plaice. Cambridge: MIT Press.

Borch-Jacobsen, Mikkel. 1991. *Lacan: The Absolute Master*. Trans. Douglas Brick. Stanford: Stanford University Press.

Buck-Morss, Susan. 1989. *The Dialectics of Seeing: Walter Benjamin and the Arcades Project*. Cambridge: MIT Press.

Chatergee, Partha. 1993. *The Nation and Its Fragments: Colonial and Post-Colonial Histories*. Princeton: Princeton University Press.

Crary, Jonathan. 1991. *Techniques of the Observer*. Cambridge: MIT Press.

Dali, Salvador. 1930. "L'ane pourri." In *Le Surrealisme au service de la Revolution*, (Paris) no. 1 (1930).

Doane, Mary Ann. 1981. "Women's Stake: Filming the Female Body." *October* 17 (summer).

Eagleton, Terry. 1995. *Heathcliff and the Great Hunger: Studies in Irish Culture*. London: Verso.

Feldman, Allen. 1991. *Formations of Violence: The Narrative of the Body and Political Terror in Northern Ireland*. Chicago: University of Chicago Press.

————. 1994. "On Cultural Anesthesia: From Desert Storm to Rodney King." *American Ethnologist* 21, no. 2.

————. 1995. "Ethnographic States of Emergency." In *Fieldwork Under Fire*, ed. C. Nordstom and T. Robben. Berkeley: University of California Press.

Foucault, Michel. 1998. *Language, Counter Memory, Practice: Selected Essays and Interviews*. Ed. Donald F. Bouchard. Ithaca, NY: Cornell University Press.

Goldbery, David T. 1993. "Polluting the Body Politic: Racist Discourse and Urban Location." In *Racism, the City, and the State*, ed. Malcom Cross and Michael Keith. London: Routledge.

Jay, Martin. 1993. *Downcast Eyes: The Denigration of Vision in Twentieth-Century French Thought*. Berkeley: University of California Press.

Koselleck, Reinhart. 1985. "Terror and Dream: Methodological Remarks on the Experience of Time during the Third Reich." In *Futures Past: On the Semantics of Historical Time*. Cambridge: MIT Press.

Lacan, Jacques. 1977. *Ecrits: A Selection*. Trans. Alan Sheridan. New York: Norton.

Massey, Doreen. 1984. *Spatial Division of Labour: Social Structures and the Geography of Production*. London: Macmillan.

Merleau-Ponty, Maurice. 1978. *Phenomenologie de la Perception*. Paris: Gallimard.

Prakash, Gyan, ed. 1995. *After Colonialism: Imperial Histories and Postcolonial Displacements*. Princeton: Princeton University Press.

Rabinbach, Anson. 1990. *The Human Motor: Energy, Fatigue, and the Origins of Modernity*. New York: Basic Books.

Rafael, Vincente. 1991. "Anticipating Nationhood: Collaboration and Rumor in the Japanese Occupation of Manila." *Diaspora* 1, no. 1 (spring): 67–82.

Rodman, Margeret C. 1992. "Empowering Place: Multilocality and Multivocality." *American Anthropologist* 94, no. 3: 640–56.

Shields, Rob. 1991. *Places on the Margin: Alternative Geographies of Modernity*. London: Routledge.

Silver, Kenneth. 1989. *Esprit de Corps: The Art of the Parisian Avant-Garde and the First World War, 1914–1925*. Princeton: Princeton University Press.

Smith, David. 1992. *Apartheid City and Beyond Urbanizations*. London: Routledge.

Spivak, Gayatri Chakravorty. 1987. "Subaltern Studies: Deconstructing Historiography." In *Other Worlds: Essays in Cultural Politics*. New York: Methuen.

Stich, Sidra. 1990. *Anxious Visions: Surrealist Art*. New York and Berkeley: Abbeville Press.

Stoler, Ann Laura. 1992. "In Cold Blood: Hierarchies of Credibility and the Politics of Colonial Narrative." *Representations* 37 (winter).

Sunday Times Insight Team. 1972. *Ulster*. London: Penguin.

Tagg, John. 1988. *The Burden of Representation: Essays on Photographies and Histories*. Amherst: University of Massachusetts Press.

———. 1993. "Malefacium: State Fetishism." In *Fetishism as Cultural Discourse*, ed. Emily Apter and William Pietz. Ithaca, NY: Cornell University Press.

Turner, Patricia. 1993. *I Heard It through the Grapevine: Rumor in African-American Culture*. Berkeley: University of California Press.

Circumcision, Body, Masculinity

The Ritual Wound and Collective Violence

Deepak Mehta

Circumcision is realized in bodies and inscribed on them. This truism becomes part of a powerful literary imagination once the circumcised body of the Muslim male is located in violent conflicts between Hindus and Muslims in contemporary India. Here the Muslim's body remains at the center of the conflict but is curiously de-animated, and the wrath that it invites points to the intimate violence so characteristic of Hindu-Muslim relations in the Subcontinent. What this imagination does not tell us is the kind of body inhabited by the adult male Muslim and the significance of circumcision in constituting it.

The paper analyzes the inscription of circumcision by seeing how the male body is constituted, eclipsed, and reformulated in three related domains.[1] First, drawing from fieldwork (1985–86) among the Ansaris of Barabanki,[2] I show how the body is constituted through the ritual of circumcision, called *khatna*. The classical term *khitan* is not used. Second, remaining with this fieldwork, I argue that in everyday life the ritual body is effaced under a series of verbal signs, signified by the term *musalmani*. Finally, with reference to fieldwork conducted with a colleague in Bombay (1994 and 1995), I indicate how an alternate imagination of the body emerges from the fact of being circumcised, seen in the significance of the term *katua* (to cut). The thread connecting the three domains is the body of the male Muslim, one that participates in different zones of significance and initiates the processes of signification. By means of *khatna* and *musalmani,* the Muslims of Barabanki make claims to an Islamic heritage and argue that the male body is socialized into a legitimate sexuality. *Katua,* on the other hand, introduces a fissure in the Muslim's conception of a socialized body. Once and for all it constitutes the male body as bestial.

In the ritual of circumcision the body is willed and represented so that it enters the domestic group and the community of Islam at the same time.[3] The ritual conceives of circumcision as an eternal truth individuated on every male body. It thus describes the body's metaphysic.[4] This metaphysic constitutes masculinity and a "correct" sexuality by establishing a unity between the spiritual and the corporeal, male and female. Everyday conversations, too, imagine circumcision as eternal, but for purposes of establishing the limits of the male Ansari community. These conversations do not privilege the bodies of male actors, but of the entire community considered as a singularity. In the process of constituting the male community, such conversations substitute a collective body for the individual one. This substitution is achieved, first, by showing how the pain of the circumcision operation is distributed over every male of the community. Each male must bear this pain and witness it in another. Second, the conversations establish a fundamental difference between Muslims and Hindus. Both the ritual and everyday conversations show the power of circumcision to fabricate individual bodies (the ritual) and communities (everyday conversations). Thus, *khatna* and *musalmani* make and recreate the world in the way that Scarry (1985: 161–326) shows when wounding and pain are conflated.

During collective violence between Hindus and Muslims, *khatna* and *musalmani* are suspended and replaced by another term, *katua*. *Katua*, too, privileges the wound, but as a stigmatized mark of identity of the other.[5] The term *katua* indicates a complex of meanings. As synecdoche, it refers to Muslim males, but also to a movement toward castration since the penis has been cut. In times of collective disorder between Muslims and Hindus it is not uncommon to hear Muslim males being designated by non-Muslims as *katua*. As I see it, *katua* is distinguished from *khatna* since it does not point to the search for a fulfilled sexuality, as does the latter, but to an effect that crystallizes the present through acts of brutality. Both *katua* and *musalmani* indicate Muslim males, but *katua* differs from *musalmani* because it constitutes Muslims as inadequate males. The main difference, however, is that while *khatna* and *musalmani* imagine the body as being located in the time of making, *katua* emphasizes a time of destroying. These two types do not share the same causality, the same linking principles. *Katua* gives the temporal essence of menace a deferred but inevitable aggression. The Muslim is hunted because of the mark he carries on him. Such speech refers to the other, the enemy. It designates a violation, since it indicates from the point of view of the speaker the idea of the Muslim male as less than human. At the heart of the analysis of this paper, then, is a larger question: in which way(s) does circumcision as a mark of identity shape and alter the destiny of individuals and groups? In referring to circumcision as a literal and figurative mark, I suggest that this question may be reformulated to refer to the potential of collective violence (through wounding) to create and destroy. This potential shows how actors' experiences of violence are translated into either a sense of community or the abrogation of what makes them human. The creative capacity of violence, as suggested earlier, is found in the ritual and the everyday.

The ritual, in constituting masculinity, allows the body to simultaneously enter into the life cycle of the domestic group and the community of Islam. This simultaneity is evident when we focus on the gestural and graphic inscription of the ritual on the body. The gestural and graphic unfold in three modes. I understand this unfolding through the term *biunity*.[6] Biunity, the signature of the ritual, confers an identity on the novice and inscribes it on his body. This identity, I will argue, is found in the combination of blood and milk, male and female. The medium is primarily gestural. Second, the signature shows how the physical body is socially posited. I will discuss this issue by detailing the regimen of three types of signs impressed on the novice. The medium is both verbal and gestural. Finally, what is implied in the signature is the appearance of the other. The other is not only the mark of the domestic group, but also the word of God stamped on the novice's body. Biunity, here, establishes a relationship of identity between the spiritual and the corporeal. The medium is primarily verbal. Together, biunity constitutes the masculinity of the body by suffusing it with the word of God, regulating the body's sexuality, and premising a unity between the sexes. Implicit in this ritual is a triadic classification of the male body into a depth, a surface, and a celestial height.

In focusing on everyday speech we find a repressed hostility between Muslims and non-Muslims. The Muslim is separated from the Hindu through the inscription of the wound. In the estimation of Muslim speakers, it is only with circumcision that they become Muslim and masculine at the same time. Here such speech articulates a sense of community found in the association of *musalmani* with other terms, most notably pain *(dard)*. *Khatna*, too, has its own association of signifiers. If *musalmani* is conjoined to pain, belief, and witness, *khatna* is linked to an elaborate hygiene of the body, spelled out through the terms *ghusl* (ritual bath) and *istibra* (cleaning up after the last drop of urine, preferably on a stone), and through the recitation of liturgical prayer. *Katua* intersects both with the ritual and everyday conversations. From the ritual, it elaborates on the theme of the penis that has been cut, while drawing from *musalmani*, it deepens the divide between Muslims and Hindus. In this sense the signification of *katua* loops back on both *khatna* and *musalmani*, but it produces a different system of meanings. *Katua* constitutes the Muslim as less than human and also indicates that he is alien. As an alien, the Muslim is dangerous, threatening the moral world of the attacker. What we have, then, are three different domains of speech: the ritual body, characterized by the discourse of Ansari women and men; the community, elicited from the everyday conversations of Ansari men; and the stigmatized male Muslim, found in speech (among informants, both

Hindus and Muslims, and between them and me) that reflects on collective disorder.

I first discuss the ritual.

THE RITE TO BE MALE

In August 1985, while doing fieldwork in Barabanki, I was staying in the house of Sadiq Ali when he decided to have his young son circumcised.[7] The age at which boys are circumcised varies from two to six years (generally, after they have been weaned). I started taking notes on circumcision a month later after a Hindu *patwari* (village administrative officer) sarcastically mentioned that because of my association with Muslims, commensal and residential, I was an "uncircumcised *mullah*." The conversation reproduced here is instructive because it points both to the body as a referential object and the verbal discourse surrounding circumcision.

Most evenings a few of us would sit around a local tea-stall talking of the day's activities. Toward the end of September 1985 there was a marked difference in the content of our conversations. Some of my friends were agitated over the emerging controversy in Ayodhya,[8] barely thirty kilometers southeast of the villages of this fieldwork. The conversations reflected the fear of violence touching the area. During one of these sessions, I was introduced to the *patwari:*

P: Your name?

DM: Deepak.

P: Deepak what?

DM: Deepak Mehta.

P: Are you a Srivastava?

DM: No, I'm a Punjabi Khatri.[9]

P: That's the same thing. Where do you stay?

DM: Sometime Mawai, sometime Gulharia.

P: Oh! Do you stay in a Pasi household?[10]

DM: No, with a Khan saheb.[11]

P: Is that so! Then you must be eating their food?

DM: Yes.

P: This is the first time I have come across an uncircumcised *mullah.*

The *patwari* met me a few days later. I was advised not to talk to him. "Good day, wise man. Have you been circumcised?" ("*Salam alai kum miyan. Musalmani karva li?*"). On receiving no response he said, "What happened? You can't read the *namaz* without being circumcised?" *Musalmani* is the term most often used in the field to denote circumcision. *Khatna* is employed in the company of *tuhr* (to clean). *Tuhr* is associated with other terms, most notably *ghusl, hajamat* (haircut), and *istibra*. Here, circumcision is a way of experiencing one's body, of apprehending it, of assuming it positively and fully.

The Setting

The Ansaris circumcise their male offspring in the *zanana* (female quarter) of their household.[12] The courtyard of the *zanana* and the quilt room are especially prepared for the ceremony. The western wall of the courtyard, cleared of impedimenta, is made to resemble the blank western wall of the mosque. All ritual connected with circumcision is directed toward the wall. In contrast, the quilt room is decorated with the choicest marriage quilts, the nuptial bed is made with new sheets, and a little flour is sprinkled on it. An earthen pot, placed in one of the corners of the room, is broken after the operation.

Broadly, four types of people are involved in the ceremony: the novice, his mother, the female barber, and those who witness the ceremony. The last includes the father of the novice, his mother's brother and all his father's circumcised agnates, and also the circumcised members of the novice's generation. The mother and the female barber work on the body, while the witnesses authenticate this work by providing verbal legitimacy to the act, and they are the ones who talk of circumcision in the public domain.[13]

The Mother

A day before his circumcision the novice child is placed under the care of his mother. She ensures that his hair is cut, his nails are pared, and he is massaged with mustard oil. Subsequently, the novice is bathed in flowing water by his mother.

In the present instance, Shabnam (Sadiq Ali's wife), after bathing her child, introduced him to all the guests assembled in the *zanana* as if he were a stranger. She used the formal, third-person, honorific *ap* and not the more familiar *yeh:* "*Ap hain Shujat Ahmad. Apki umar teen sal hai. Kal ap Hindu se Musalman honge.*" ("Here is Shujat Ahmad. He is three years old. Tomorrow he will become Musalman from Hindu.") The people gathered responded "*Bismillah-al-Rahim.*" After the introduction the boy was asked to sit at the head of the cot next to his father.

On the day of the ritual, the child is bathed by his mother, dressed in the head-dress of a groom, and led to the compound of the *zanana*. He is handed over to his mother's brother. In direct contrast to the preceding day, the mother's brother introduces the guests to the child by their genealogically appropriate term.

After the prepuce is removed, the child is held up by his mother so that blood from the wound runs down her chest. Mother and child are draped over by a green cloth. It is believed that blood and milk commingle in producing a healthy male. Blood and milk, vital ingredients of the body, must be perfectly balanced. Balance is achieved after the mother relinquishes her bond as it has existed with her child. This interpretation is suggested from my conversations with Shabnam and Miriam. Shabnam, in her mid-thirties (in 1985), had participated in her first son's ceremony. Miriam, in her early seventies, is considered by members of her community to be an authority on traditional matters. Her husband, Muhammad Umar, is the head of a particular lineage and a distinguished weaver.

Describing her son's ceremony, Shabnam began by saying,

> When I was small my father would say, "Don't sit next to your brothers; otherwise you will become like them. Play with other girls. In this lies your honor." When Shujat [referring to her son by his formal name] became Muslim, I had to forget he was my Munna [an affectionate diminutive term], because this is what my father meant. I must pass on this *amanat* (thing held in trust, in this case her son) to his father. Soon enough I will not be able to play with him, to hold him, to caress him, for he will have become male (*mard*).

I asked, "What does becoming a male mean?" I was given a formal answer. "It means having enough blood to produce an offspring, observing *namaz*, fasting, pilgrimage to Mecca, and alms-giving."

Shabnam's reiteration of the pillars of Islam was balanced by Miriam's comments. Circumcision, she said, is the recognition of the co-presence of male and female in everyone. Every human is composed of two elements, blood inherited from the father, and milk from the mother. In holding up the circumcised boy to her breast, the mother gives to her child the gift of milk, one that balances the blood of the father. Blood, she says, is red because it implies fire, under which everything is either incorporated or ravaged. It stands alone. She compared the singularity of blood to the first letter of the Arabic alphabet, *alif*. Both imply a movement of people toward the sky.

For Miriam, however, blood emerges from the earth and is nurturing. The prime example of nurturing is the milk of the mother. This milk balances and often counters the excessive strength and anger given in blood. By a balance she means that a person who has an excess of blood is disposed toward anger. If milk is preponderant, the person is inclined toward corpulence (*mutapa*) and sadness or hardship (*dukh*). In her opinion, women are born with blood and milk, whereas men are given the latter. This gift enables them to enter into the world of women. Hence, circumcision is for those who will become men. It is the necessary prelude to marriage, for in its absence the product of the union between man and woman is either sterile or consumed by violent passions. The gift of milk is the last gift of the mother to her child. From the point of view of the child, the ceremony, carried out in blood and pain, is rivaled by the nostalgia the mother feels while contemplating her relationship with her mature son: "With circumcision, he becomes his father's son."

The Barber

As a ritual specialist, the barber transgresses various boundaries, most importantly those that codify sexuality. For the duration of the present ceremony, she maintained a constant monologue on the state of sexuality among the Ansaris. Her monologue stopped as soon as the wailing child was handed over to her. She examined his penis and commented on its power to impregnate all of womankind. She mentioned that the boy was the penis, and without it he was nothing. Then holding the prepuce she snipped off the outer end in one smooth motion. The child had lapsed into whimpers. During the operation, not a drop of blood was allowed to fall to the ground. Subsequently, Sadiq Ali's father's brother whispered the *azan* (announcement to prayer) and the child's name in his (the novice's) right ear. Immediately after, the men offered prayers facing the western wall. The prepuce, recovered from the barber after she had placed a financial value on it, was buried under the nuptial bed in the quilt room.

In my conversation with the barber, she said that *khatna* ensured the sympathy between male and female. She designated this sympathy by the term *hamdami* (literally, "being of one breath"), for only this sharing of breath makes possible the male vision (*shuhud*) of the female and the female vision of the male. The conjunction between male and female has two aspects. In the male it is the *shauq* (desire or passion) for the female, and in the female it is the realization of this desire. *Shauq*, the barber adds, does not refer to two heterogeneous beings, but one person, either male or female, encountering him/herself as the other, at once a biunity, something that people tend to forget. In this interdependence each obtains recognition from the other.

Biunity, in the sense elaborated above, is a given, but one that must be uncovered by circumcision. The operation, the barber says, recognizes the biunity between male and female. The operating instrument, a small and sharp blade, called *naharni,* is also used to remove the hair of the bride a few days before marriage. The barber says that the *naharni* is used not coincidentally to remove excess bodily material from both bride and novice because both will experience a second birth. The *naharni,* then, is the instrument of *hamdami.* A sure sign of this being-of-one-breath is seen in the operation. If the act is swift and smooth, the circumcised will be potent. If, however, the prepuce cannot be removed in one flowing motion, he will find it difficult to marry and raise children.

In the above account, as distinct from that of the mother, the barber is situated outside the act. Her account is based on a framed portion of a prior world that she undertakes to represent accurately. For the mother, there is nothing to retrieve, except the act by which her child becomes alien to her. Simultaneously, she enlivens the system of signs given in the act of circumcision. The barber, on the other hand, is engaged in the theme of portraiture. Her portrait is organized around the removal of the foreskin, an act of violence by which the body is precipitated into an alterity. This alterity plots the progression of the boy's career in the domestic group: the laboring body, the impregnating body, the authorizing body, and so on. Also, with mutilation the biographical time of the body is encoded so that to enter into the life of the domestic group is to enter the community of Islam. Through violence, the body becomes a metonym of the social space of the domestic group and is simultaneously constituted as an imaginary space for the reception of Islam. The ritual wound, in this sense, has a double meaning embedded in it: religious legitimacy and a sexualized body.

The Novice

The double significance of the ritual wound may be seen in the relationship between the physical body and the signs impressed on it. This relationship may be understood through three terms: *ghusl, istibra,* and *kalimah* (the "word," one through which the novice is impregnated with Islam). Together these three terms constitute a state of being pure *(tuhr)* and show how masculinity is conceived. In mapping the three terms onto the physical body the latter acquires visible social organs and an authorized code of conduct.

Ghusl

As the major purifying ritual of the body, the main object of *ghusl* is to eliminate dirt. The prime source of dirt is the human body, a dirt that is dangerous since it impinges on the tidy insularity of the body. Dirt is composed of secretion. The second fear is of decay, a rotting in the depths of the body, which must be brought to the surface to be removed. The paring of nails, the first haircut, the oil massage, and the vigorous bath that follows are to be understood in this light.

Istibra

One of the many meanings circumcision lends itself to is the removal of impurity associated with urine. The removal of the prepuce prevents the residue of urine and sperm from accumulating inside the body. The circumcised male rids himself of the last drop of urine by an elaborate technical procedure. One must urinate with the buttocks resting on the ankles. After urination the penis, taken by the left hand, is rubbed several times against a stone. *Istibra* is continued until nothing remains in the urinary tract. *Istibra* is especially recommended for the recently married male.[14]

Thus, circumcision is an initiation into legitimate sexual desire, but one fraught with negative consequences. All the areas of the body producing secretion are imbued with a negative attitude. Bouhdiba says that circumcision is "a vaccination against the dangers of sexuality" (1985: 185). Circumcision and the deflowering of the virgin, then, occur within a frame where festivities, blood, pain, and exhibitionism accompany the traumata wittingly inflicted by the group to maintain its cohesion.

Kalimah

The connection with the configuration of belief and sexuality, as it is inscribed on the body, becomes clearer when we consider the utterances of *kalimah*. Through *ghusl* and *istibra,* the body acquires a socially recognized materiality. This recognition is incomplete if the body does not acquire sound. The murmuring of the *azan* in the boy's right ear is succeeded by saying his formal name. The murmur points in two directions: in the first he is initiated into the enunciation of the *azan;* in the second his name is linked to the verbal intonation present in the liturgy.

The union between the *azan* and the human form is one where the latter ingests God. For Sadiq Ali, the use of the formal name during the ceremony recognizes the omniscient suzerainty of Allah. I asked him, "Why do you call him Shujat and not, for example, by your name?" "My name, Sadiq, shows how this being [pointing to himself] manifests (*zahir*) the lord (*rabb*) in its own peculiar way. It would be sacrilege (*haram*) for me to call him by my name, for otherwise he [his son] will be unable to manifest the lord in his own way."

The above argument has two aspects. First, each name manifests the lord insofar as He has named everything in the universe. Second, since each human being carries a name designated by Allah, he is a particularized aspect of that manifestation. The sympathy between the two is dialogic: each name is an example of the conjunction between the spiritual and the corporeal. What is evident in Sadiq Ali's insight is that the acquisition of sound by the body occurs through the convocation with another voice.

The problem, however, remains: Why is the formal name uttered during the ritual? The gestural and verbal inscription on the body are two series regulated by the body. Through the first the body is marked so that it enters into the productive and reproductive life of the domestic group. The evidence is the wound as an eternal truth. The second series shows that through enunciation the body enters into the community of Islam. The evidence is the *azan* written on the body. The *azan* facilitates the transition from one series to another since communication between the verbal and the gestural is possible only after the *azan* is uttered. The name in this scheme guarantees the conjunction, albeit a particularized one, between the corporeal and spiritual.

The body of the novice thus described is understood through two sets of polarities: the gestural and graphic, and the corporeal and spiritual. The former shows how certain events are marked on the boy's body, while the latter shows how the body is related to its internal and external environment. Further, the first set refers to a series of events and the second set to a series of attributes. The two divide the body into a surface and a depth, and in the process show how the physical body is linked to the regime of signs impressed on it.

The Surface and the Depth

In terms of his body the novice is situated relative to the three realms of a depth, a celestial height, and a surface. The depth, in the sense of emissions that are polluting and dangerous, must forever be controlled. In the height he finds the word of God. He must always ascend or descend to the surface and thus claim the new status thrust on him. The body cannot be located in the celestial domain, because then it would, in the words of Miriam, have the characteristics of an ungrounded *alif.*

The surface is a kind of frontier available in a series of signs laying down an acceptable and accepted mode of behavior. These signs, embossed on the body through word and gesture, enter into a surface organization which assures the resonance of the series of events and of the attributes. The surface of signs does not, however, imply a unity of direction or community of organs. In terms of a series of events, it is primarily the sexuality of the male that is constituted at the surface of the body. The barber's comment that the boy is the penis, and without it he is nothing is an apt illustration. What is more important, the penis must be made visible and in this way forced into a hygienic sexuality. All the events of the ritual are, in this sense, coordinated in the genital zone. Here, the phallus does not so much play the role of an organ as of an image that shows the healthy male, thereby pointing to its synecdochic character.

Yet it is recognized that a body will emit fluid elements (urine, feces, phlegm, semen) and hard substances (nails, teeth). Elements and substances either emanate from the depth or detach from the surface. Sounds, smells, tastes, and temperatures refer to emissions from the depth, whereas visual determinations refer to the surface. The relation between the depth and the surface is one where emissions, arising from the depth, pass through the surface, and as they detach from the body are replaced by a formally concealed stratum.

If these signs emerge from the physical body and are simultaneously enacted on its surface, it is also evident that they are marks of the presence of the other. Emissions and substances, emerging from the physical body, must be socially censored. This censoring is the work of the other. The other is neither an object of gaze nor a subject. It is an a priori structure of the possible, designating the genealogical positions and conjugal relationships potentially available to the boy undergoing circumcision. Thus, the other is a distillation of time by which the rhythms of the body are broken into units.

There is a second way in which the other is conceived. Through the recitation of the *azan* and the whispering of the name, a theophanic other is created. The source of this home is an external environment, since it emerges from a celestial height. Creation has two sides. First, its seat of residence (the depth of the body) manifests divinity, by which it becomes transparent. Second, the recitation of the *azan* is embedded in corporeality and, because of this, linked to a particularized apprehension of divinity. Each recitation of the prayer in the ritual, in the sense noted above, is a recurrence of creation. The breath of prayer in the right ear of the circumcised introduces the guide who stands before the faithful. The other is the aid. The second part of the recitation, whispering the name in the right ear, is based on the attitude of the body prescribed during ritual prayer: erect stance (*qiyam*), inclination (*ruku*) and prostration (*sujud*). The name of man and the prayer of God are thus co-present. Umar mentions that each living being manifests one or all the three postures given in prayer. The upright stance of the faithful corresponding to Miriam's *alif* or the celestial height; the movement of animals corresponding to the surface of bodies; the descending movement of plants corresponding to the depth of the body. *Khatna*, he says, recognizes the three dimensions of prayer, since it has the three postures of the body built into it: erect stance of mother and child as they are draped over by the green cloth; the descending movement of the child's blood after his prepuce is removed; the burial of the prepuce under the nuptial bed. Each of these three postures is informed by the *azan*. Circumcision refers to the body in these three dimensions.

What is the body composed of after the ritual has been enacted? With its depth, it is constitutive of emissions that are to be purified and controlled. With a celestial height, the body is suffused with the word of God. And with a regime of signs playing on its surface, the body recognizes the presence of the other. This surface, in the words of the barber, is the communion of the body with its other, evidenced through vision (*shuhud*).

THE EVERYDAY DISCOURSE ON CIRCUMCISION

In the everyday discourse on circumcision the body becomes invisible. Instead, *musalmani* shows the simulated generation of differences between the circumcised and uncircumcised. Such differences cement a sense of community and posit pain as defining one's station in life. The ritual wound indicates forbearance, and as a referent it becomes an ornamental inscription on the sign.[15]

Everyday Speech and the Disappearance of the Body

We move now from the realm of the ritual to that of the everyday.[16] The speech on and about *musalmani* ranges for the act of weaving to casual social intercourse around a tea-stall. We are in an exclusively male space. The speech of women that punctuated the ritual is absent here. Further, the body of the circumcised male is also absented in two ways. The ritual wound is imbued with an incorporeal value, while the body is seen as the appendage of the community. *Musalmani,* when it refers to the genital zone, situates the latter within a speech domain where the emphasis is not so much on the physical condition of the body as on its incorporeal valuation. The incorporeality of the body emerges from the following conversation immediately after the *patwari* mentioned previously had made his comments and left us. The *patwari* asked his questions in a gathering of several people, among whom I knew four others: Azeer, Kalim, Itrat, and Rafiq. After the *patwari* left us, I asked Azeer the meaning of the term *musalmani.*

A: With *musalmani* we become Muslim.

DM: But what is the meaning of *musalmani?*

To the amusement of the others, Kalim visually mimed the operation from the perspective of the barber and then asked mockingly,

K: Do you want to become Muslim?

Ignoring the rhetorical question, I asked,

DM: What were you before *musalmani?*

K: The property of my mother.

Itrat and Rafiq nodded assent. Azeer, turning to me, asked,

A: Do you know what masculinity is?

I did not reply. Then Itrat, gently pushing me and in an ironic tone, opined,

I: What does he know? In the city everyone is adept at masturbation. With *musalmani* the body acquires strength, and we do not have any desire to masturbate. *Musalmani* and belief are twins.

DM: How does the body acquire strength?

I: Strength? I've already told you. We don't masturbate.

DM: So? If you don't masturbate you become strong? I'm asking what is the connection between strength and non-masturbation?

R: The meaning is clear. It is a miracle of nature that whenever a Muslim thinks of *musalmani,* his heart overflows with spiritual (*ruh*) words. With them the body acquires strength.

An obvious aspect of the conversation is how body and speech are related. First, we find a correspondence between seeing and speaking. Kalim, in miming the operation of *khatna*, presents his body to the gaze of the other, a gaze where the body making a gesture prompts an understanding contrary to what it indicates. The gesture evokes the sexual organ and ironically reflects on the preceding question: "But what is the meaning of the term *musalmani?*" Here the gaze divides the meaning of circumcision. While an explanation of *musalmani* is the operation of speech, pantomime is that of the body. This speech, in Rafiq's view, has a spiritual essence, since in his mode of reasoning it is animated with *ruh*.

However, we do not know whether the body is mimicry and speech is spiritual, for in the conversation one does not know if pantomime reasons or reason mimics. There is a complex relation between gaze and speech, for the latter takes on the mode of the former, while the body is effaced under a series of verbal signs. If sight is ironic, so too is speech. Just as Kalim's gestures are interpreted contrary to their indication, so also his question to me ("Do you want to become Muslim?") and Itrat's observations on city folk are ironic reflections.

Such speech mirrors the body in a particular way (Itrat's observations of the body as strength, belief, the retention of semen; Azeer's opinion of masculinity; and Rafiq's view of the body as spiritual). This speech substitutes verbal signs for the physical sign on the body: *musalmani* takes over and selectively arranges those meanings of *khatna* that evoke the tradition of Islam. In the process, this speech eclipses the range of meanings available in *khatna* and emphasizes the spiritual over the corporeal. When asked about the meaning of spirituality in *musalmani*, Rafiq says that it is a mark of remembrance, of having heard the Qur'an and voluntarily recited it. The moment *khatna* is made a mark of remembrance by reciting the Qur'an, it exceeds the body. This excess is the area of *musalmani*.

The inscription of the liturgy on the circumcised keeps the person's body within the limits set by the norms of various hygienic practices, legitimate conjugal relationships, and so on. Rafiq's account tells a more fundamental truth. It makes the body describe the order of *musalmani* since *khatna* is the precondition of *musalmani*. *Khatna* produces the practitioners of the norm of *musalmani*. To the extent that this norm, inscribed on bodies and recounted by them, is repeated in every act of *khatna*, we find the emergence of a discourse revolving around a tradition.

This tradition was particularized within weaving by Muhammad Umar after he had consented to teach me how to operate the loom. The craft of weaving, Umar says, demands the perfectly still body of the weaver, to be interrupted by regular and abrupt movements. Such movements are possible only if all the motions of weaving originate from the center of the body, the loins. For this reason, the loins must be particularly resilient. This resilience is given through the act of *khatna,* an act by which one learns the value of pain. The full understanding of pain, Umar says, comes from a knowledge of the lives of the prophets of Islam, all of whom endured Herculean hardship (the Prophet, Ali, Ayub Ansari, and Sis Ali). To be knowledgeable of their lives is to bear witness. The strength to bear pain makes the weaver "strong of speech" and a "wise weaver."

Umar isolates the gesture (the movement of hands and feet) to organize the discursive space of *musalmani.* Space is mapped so that occupants become available for observation and information: whether they are adequate Muslims and weavers. The gesture becomes visible when it shows the inadequacy of the functioning of the working body. A good gesture does not refer to the body but to the positive discourse of *musalmani,* which talks of pain, wisdom, and speech. Thus, a nondiscursive gesture is articulated in the language of *musalmani.* This gesture is a metonymic figure of *musalmani,* but also a figure by which the collective body of its practitioners is made to speak the truth of *musalmani.*

The Community

In the preceding conversations all those I talked to were united in their opinion on the connotation of *musalmani.* Each speaker maintained that *musalmani* represented a fundamental difference between Hindus and Muslims.

The dialogue given in the beginning of this section (among Rafiq, Kalim, Itrat, Azeer, and me) finally considered the difference between the circumcised and the uncircumcised. This occurred after Rafiq had left us.

> K: What is the connection between *musalmani* and *ruh? Musalmani* and pain are twins.
>
> I: You speak like a nonbeliever! There is some depth in Rafiq's statement.
>
> K (sarcastically): Then let me also understand?
>
> I: Rafiq said that with *musalmani* the body learns to recognize pain. The distinctiveness of this recognition is that with it our belief increases.
>
> A: Through belief we are separate from Hindus.
>
> I: Yes, but the meaning of the twinning [between *musalmani* and belief] is that their [Hindus'] pain does not "make" spirituality. The Hindu cannot tolerate his pain. True, he can have himself cut in hospital, but where is spirituality in that operation?

Later, Rafiq made the same point. When I asked him whether *musalmani* distinguished Hindus from Muslims, he said, "The other word for *musalmani* is belief that is distinctive to Muslims. This is how we are different from Hindus, because for us to be Muslim is to be pure and to have recited the Qur'an. The Hindus lack this purity because they are afraid of shedding their blood." In each of the conversations *musalmani* is suffixed by a metonymic and metaphoric progression of meanings. First, *musalmani* is linked to the recognition of pain, which in turn is associated with spirituality and subsequently becomes part of the belief of the group. Finally, this series of meanings empowers the body of the Musalman, distinguished from the Hindu: the pain of the latter is not spiritually elevating. In the second conversation Rafiq connects *musalmani* to the removal of bodily impurity, links the pure body to the recitation of the Qur'an, and concludes that this progression is the belief of the Musalman. The Hindu, in contrast, lacks bodily purity because he fears shedding his blood. *Musalmani* and the body are metonyms here. However, the full meaning of the term is achieved only when *musalmani* is linked to general metaphors by which the community is defined.

Common to the conversations is the ability of each speaker to talk on behalf of the community: the speakers use the plural in talking of *musalmani*. The community is framed in two ways in the conversations. First, such speech replaces the signs on the body by attaching to *musalmani* meanings that are external to those found in the ritual. *Musalmani* is an index of such externality and a way of separation from Hindus. Second, in the estimation of the speakers, the community is represented by the arrogation of a positive meaning. This is seen in the linking of *musalmani* to concepts such as belief, strength, and removal of bodily impurity. Here, *musalmani* exists in the form of a double meaning: the utterances related to *musalmani* signify like any other, but also intervene as an element of metasignification by which *musalmani* acquires a theme. As a symbol, *musalmani* harbors a double meaning: the obvious meaning both covers and uncovers a figurative one. It is a single signifier with multiple signifieds. Unlike a symbol, however, *musalmani* institutes a relation between itself and various metaphors. Through this relationship, the body is described (and eventually annexed). In other words, *musalmani* establishes a duplicative relation between itself and other terms, such as *iman, ruh, dard,* and so on. This is tantamount to saying that the relationship between *musalmani* and, for example, *iman* (faith) depends upon the decoder's ability to make the substitutions necessary to pass from one register to another. Yet, the understanding of *musalmani* is not solipsistic, since the task of establishing equivalence is already encoded in *musalmani*.

The speakers mention pain as the experiential core of the term. All of them reflect on *musalmani* but in such a way that pain is not linked to the physical impairment of the body. The experience of such pain is spatial not because it is restricted to any one body, but because the body of the community, taken as one whole, is a body formed in pain. Pain, in this sense, is incorporated into the definition of the community, neither disrupting the intentionality of its members, nor alienating them from the group.

From the account of the conversations, it is possible to make a further inference: the community becomes a presence when the characteristics used to describe it are those by which the body is so delineated. The speakers believe *musalmani* justifies the pain one feels during the ritual. There is one important way in which this presence is affected. When I asked each speaker whether he remembered his ceremony, I was categorically told that no one remembers his own ceremony, but that every male at some point in his life is expected to be present at someone else's. In this sense, participation in the *ummah* (brotherhood) arises only after the ritual has been presented to the witnesses.

The speakers base their sense of community on the claim to membership in the community of Islam. In so doing, they establish links to that tradition. Their interpretation conceals the work of the ritual not connected with pain and belief. An interpretation that reflects on the union of milk and blood and the combination of male and female, on the one side, and the issue of *hamdami,* on the other, is ignored. It is almost as if that view of the ritual is valorized which, in invoking tradition, constitutes the body as a zone of those hygienic practices that commemorate the community. The speakers establish the validity of their case by invoking Islam in one way or another. In this invocation, the material properties of the sign are replaced by a discourse which talks of belief and pain. The replacement of the embodied sign by the discourse of *musalmani* is evident in the establishment of a collective memory. In describing the common thread that binds one circumcised body to another, the speakers attach a retrospective ordering to the ritual. This ordering transforms individual bodies into a communal body.

The credibility of the discourse of *musalmani* operates through the instrument of the ritual wound, since the latter allows for the linking of *musalmani* with pain and prayer. Here, the wound is an instrument because it allows living beings to become signs which must recur from one body to another. By situating the wound within its fold, the discourse of *musalmani* incorporates the ritual of *khatna,* not as a repetition of the ritual in its filigreed detail, but as a community reminding itself of its identity as represented and told by conjoining *musalmani* with pain and belief. In effect, *musalmani* commemorates the past as a kind of collective autobiography—a master narrative, more than a story told. It is a cult enacted in its telling.

KATUA AND THE BESTIAL BODY

Following Scarry's argument, we might say that the body as a created object occupies two dimensions: the corporeal and the imagined. The body is corporeal to the extent that it "has all the sturdiness and vibrancy of presence of the natural world" (Scarry 1985: 280). The body is also imagination, because in the moment of its making it is embossed with a future. Much of this essay has followed Scarry's argument in the second half of her book.

However, rather than argue for a referential relation between pain and making, I have suggested that the link between pain and wounding institutes the imagination of *musalmani*. With the ritual we find an imagination that is projected on the physical surface of the body. Here, the act of wounding is willed and legitimated, since it restores the body to the community. In this legitimation the self-referentiality of the physical body (found, for example, in its emissions) is socially censored. Simultaneously, the wound constitutes the metaphysical body, but here the act of wounding is produced in accord with an already ordained world (found in the conjunction between the name and the *azan*). In incorporating the wound, everyday conversations do not recreate the ritual body. In fact, they deny it its complete referentiality (the union of male and female). In linking *musalmani* with pain and prayer, the speakers constitute the future and past as unlimited. For the speakers, the community must exist for all time, and every wound must recreate that existence. Each speaker, it is true, bears the wound within his body, but the power of the wound and its linking with pain is such that the body is invited into it. In this sense, the wound exists before the speaker. He is born to embody it. Thus, both the ritual and the conversations show how the whole body exchanges its organic will for a social and spiritual one.

In the relation between the ritual and the everyday, the presence and/or absence of the body is significant. Here we find that individual bodies are immersed in the Ansari social structure, and the overall meaning arising from such immersion both guarantees and is guaranteed by the tissue of values out of which everyday life is fashioned. During occasions of collective violence, the relationship between circumcision and society, as it exists, is incapable of sustaining the meanings found in *khatna* and *musalmani*. Instead, *katua* now designates the Muslim male.

It is not as if *katua* is used only in instances of sectarian conflict. In everyday conversations in Barabanki, this term was often employed by non-Muslims to designate Muslims. I will reproduce one such conversation with a cigarette and tea-stall owner with whom I had become friendly.[17] During Diwali (an important Hindu festival) he invited me to his house for what he called a pure vegetarian meal. After we had eaten in relative silence, he began his questioning: "How do you stay with Muslims? Does foul smell have no effect on you?" I provided an extended explanation regarding the nature of my work, the relation of weaving with domestic rituals, what I had found. Interrupting me, he continued: "Think for yourself. The vessel they use to clean up after defecating is the same that they drink water from. Go to their house and see for yourself. In the night they are either busy producing children, or sleeping with hens in their beds. In truth, each house has eight to ten children." When I objected to this stereotyping he gently rebuked me:

Hey boy! The wool has been pulled over your eyes. Forgive me, but you are a naive kid of the city. This *katua* is a bastard. On the surface he shows sympathy, but behind your back a knife. Ask me. There are too many of them in this country, and one day they will capture the parliament. In my opinion, with the *katua* you cannot live as either friend or foe. Why? With the right treatment he will behave like a bull, or, otherwise, a mad dog.

This conversation, as much a part of everyday life as those concerning *musalmani*, is not, in one respect, radically different from the Muslim speakers' understanding of circumcision. As with *musalmani*, the specificity of *katua* is situated within an ensemble of representations which stereotype the other (Hindus in the case of Muslim speakers and Muslims in that of the tea-stall owner). The Muslim is dirty—so much so that he makes no distinction between his mouth and anus. At night, when he is not copulating, he sleeps with hens. Further, given their fertility, the Muslims will become the majority community in India and begin to exercise political power. But we also find a second, parallel theme, one that constitutes the *katua* as animal-like. In this respect, this conversation is different from the conversations regarding *musalmani*. The *katua*'s animal character is classified as either dangerous (mad dog), or productive (the harnessed bull). The contrived animality of the Muslim allows for him to be framed in behavioral terms as not to be trusted, as someone given to ruse and stratagem. Read together with the Muslim's uncontrolled fertility, the speaker's knowledge denotes a function of fear.

In conditions of collective violence between Hindus and Muslims, the term *katua* does not occur within a system of representations. Instead, it is now affirmed in a set of procedures, a way of doing things specific to sectarian conflict. If with *khatna* and *musalmani* the Ansari community declares its allegiance to the Islamic community, we must also recognize that the wound, as used in the sense of *katua*, stigmatizes. Consider the following conversation.

While doing fieldwork in Bombay (1994, 1995) with the intent of gauging the effect of the violence of 1992–93, one of our informants, a Muslim from Aligarh in North India, said,

It was during the time of the Bhiwandi riots[18] when they [police] made us naked, took us in their trucks, and shoved their *lathis* (thick wooden sticks with iron at one end) up our arse. That's how they identified us. Whoever they caught was asked to strip. If they found the fellow was a *katua*, they would give him the *lathi*. [Laughing] Rameshlal Panwalla [a Hindu] was caught this way. The police asked him to strip. He is a *katua*, just like me. In spite of his protests, they gave it to him. When his *bhatija* (brother's son) intervened, they asked him to strip, too. He is also a *katua*. Now he walks like a pregnant goat.

The inscription of an identity built upon pain, so carefully marked out with regard to both *khatna* and *musalmani*, is now in terms of *katua* transformed into torture. Unlike the ritual and everyday, where "pain is not action but passion" (Asad 1997: 126), with the term *katua,* physical pain is degrading and dehumanizing. The wound—evidence of the group's relationship to itself—enters into a definite alliance with the torturer, one that is based on a contract with the other. That is to say, the wound outlines an alterity that imposes an identity on the community and its speech through acts of transgression.[19] Consider the account of another Muslim:

> You see, the roads were under constant threat. Groups of boys from outside would wait on the roads.[20] If they found anyone, they would strip him to discover his identity. We would spare all those who were *katua.* They [Hindus] call us *katua,* people who are not male (spits on the ground). Some of ours were knifed; others more fortunate were made to stand in a sewer and shout, "*Jai Siya Ram*" ("Hail Lord Ram and his wife Sita"—used as a form of greeting mainly among low-caste Hindus in this region). If they didn't, they were beaten.

A little later, this man said, "When they came in to attack, we could hear them shouting, 'Where are the *katua?*' (*Katua kahan hai?*), 'Catch the *katua*' (*Katua pakro*), 'See, there's another *katua,* cut it off' (*Dekho, wahan katua hai, kat do uski*).[21]

Manifested as voice,[22] the speech on and about *katua* is directed toward a violation of the body. It is not enough to say that such speech is deprived of reason or foreign to the knowledge possessed by the practitioners of circumcision. Such speech forms a secret pact between the Hindu and Muslim and not a silence of meaning in the plenitude of sound. But more than that, *katua* exploits the savageries of the other. As with *khatna,* the other signified by *katua* is an a priori. As a structure of the possible, it points to the structure of a frightening possible world. From the point of view of the attacker, it matters little whether *katua* as practice has been executed: past, present, and future are not distributed according to an empirical criterion. As practice, *katua* indicates the unfinished work of eliminating Muslims, of finding a common descendent in the man without name, without family, without self or "I." As for Muslim speakers, *katua* signifies that the riot and castration possess a secret coherence that excludes the Muslim. The speaker turns against his body, making it a signifying unit, independent of speech.

Here, in the accounts of Muslim speakers, the body is the other of speech: what is effaced is the speech of the body. Found in a muted way in the discourse of *musalmani,* it emerges in the discourse of *katua.* There are two signs attesting to the elimination of the speech of the body. First, *katua* signifies a loss to the extent that circumcision is a memory, a deformation. This deformation takes the place of the spiritual empowerment of the body, seen in *khatna.* The privation, occasioned by *katua,* is traced to the center of the body, allowing the attacker to treat the attacked as less than human. But *katua* is also an engraving of "being Muslim" upon the body. Meaning is produced by that which is taken away: it is a gesture that does not deceive, since it is a move toward castration. Between this loss and inscription, the existent difference between Hindus and Muslims is silenced. In this dispensation, *khatna* and *musalmani,* engraved on the body, are mute expressions, cannibalized by the power of the discourse of *katua,* one that assimilates a time of making in order to speak in its place.

NOTES

1. A preliminary version of this essay was presented, first in the Department of Sociology, Delhi University, and later in a conference in Delhi entitled "Violence, Political Agency and the Self" (March 1995). I am grateful to the audience for their criticisms and comments. The essay was extensively revised following the comments of Veena Das, Arthur Kleinman, and Mamphela Ramphele. My gratitude extends to the three of them.

2. Fieldwork, in this instance, was conducted in two villages, Mawai and Wajidpur, of the district of Barabanki, UP (1985–86) among a community of weavers popularly known as Julaha. The weavers call themselves Ansari. For a discussion of the term *Julaha,* see Crooke (1974) and Pandey (1990). I have discussed elsewhere the conception of weaving and its relationship to the Ansari social structure (Mehta 1997). See also Ansari (1960). As far as the circumcision ritual is concerned I cannot generalize for all Muslim communities in India. We could expect a considerable variation in the content of the ritual across castes. For one, the ritual specialist is different: among high castes, it is the male barber. Second, upper-caste Muslims in UP would not use the term *khatna,* but *sunna* or *sunnat.*

3. My aim is to analyze how masculinity is constituted rather than to see how circumcision is a ritual of entry. For circumcision as a ritual, see Bourdieu (1977), Lewis (1964), Mehta (1977: 181–98), and Trimingham (1964).

4. The Ansaris, like most other Muslim groups in India, do not practice female circumcision.

5. In this latter instance I draw on fieldwork in a slum in Bombay. Conducted with a colleague in 1994 and 1995, the fieldwork analyzed how the violence of 1992–93 was experienced. Such violence followed the destruction of the Babari Masjid in Ayodhya on 6 December 1992. Large parts of India witnessed what were euphemistically termed "communal riots." The city of Bombay saw savage fighting between Muslims and Hindus. Many of our informants were Muslim. In the aftermath of these conflicts, especially between those who had never met before, circumcision was the only way in which Muslim males could be identified.

6. I use the term *biunity* deliberately, for my concern is to show how the male body, in its unity, is composed of male and female elements. Co-presence of conjunction would always imply two bodies.

7. The male head of the dwelling, in consultation with the elders of his agnatic line, decides the date of his child's circumcision. Circumcision is usually done in the months of Id, the beginning of the new year, or in Chahullam, the most important Ansari festival.

8. In 1985 the controversy in Ayodhya had only just begun. It revolved around the Babari mosque, constructed in 1528 during the reign of the Mughal emperor Babur. It was alleged by various Hindu groups that the mosque had been built after razing a Hindu temple and that it was situated on the birthplace of the Hindu god Ram. In 1985 it was rumored in the field that the gates of the Babari mosque had been thrown open to the Hindu worshippers of Ram. It was widely believed that this move had been orchestrated by the central government in Delhi. Some of my friends in the field argued (in hindsight, presciently) that this would change forever the landscape of Hindu-Muslim relations. In December 1992 the mosque was demolished by various Hindu organizations. Less than twenty-four hours after its destruction, large parts of India went through paroxysms of Hindu-Muslim violence.

9. Srivastava and Punjabi Khatri are upper-caste Hindu groups in North India.

10. Pasi refers to untouchables, specifically those who tend to pigs.

11. The Khan Saheb are upper-caste Muslim groups in North India.

12. The house is the center around which both weaving and the circumcision ritual are enacted. Broadly, the house is divided into a male *(mardana)* and female *(zanana)* section. The male part consists of an uncovered courtyard and the work shed, while the female part consists of the room of the nuptial night, a covered courtyard, and the kitchen. The quilt room *(dula'i kamra),* located in the *zanana,* is the place where quilts are made and where a part of the weaving process is executed. For the purposes of the ritual, the quilt room offers a contrast to the courtyard of the *zanana:* it is the most interior of female spaces, while the inner courtyard is the most public.

13. None of the Ansari men I talked to remembered his ceremony, but was eloquent in describing someone else's. In this sense, descriptions concerning circumcision never refer to the speaker. They show how a collective memory is, through the ritual, inscribed on the body of its believers.

14. For Bouhdiba (1985), circumcision and deflowering occur within the same frame: both are marked by a cruel wound, a somewhat forced, narcissistic experience of oneself (187). Bouhdiba is able to establish a correspondence between deflowering and circumcision by excising religious legitimacy from the ritual. For him, circumcision is part of the sexual regime of the body. This essay argues that the ritual produces a correct male sexuality, but it also allows individuals to enter into the community of Islam.

15. This is not to suggest an irreconcilable difference between *khatna* and *musalmani.* An authority links the two and allows for an interchange between them. This authority, drawn from individual and collective memory, makes possible a reversal and a transition into a community. This community is delineated by recalling the ritual as it has been effected on someone else. Furthermore, this recall is founded not so much on an orthodoxy (of texts, ritual practices, and formal exegesis) as on the capacity of *musalmani* to enter into a duplicative relationship with other terms, such as *iman* (belief), *azan,* and so on.

16. I take the concept of the everyday from Heller (1984). Rather than argue for a separation between the everyday and the ritual, I will show how the former selectively incorporates the ritual.

17. This conversation reveals him in poor light. In spite of his opinion of Muslims, I found him helpful and generous.

18. Bhiwandi is a textile center near Bombay. Early in 1984 it witnessed extensive

warfare between Hindus and Muslims, part of which seeped into Bombay. The area where we did our fieldwork also saw sporadic trouble. Our informant mentioned this with the purpose of establishing a genealogy of communal trouble in his neighborhood. We have discussed this genealogy in a recent paper (see Mehta and Chatterji 1995).

19. The transgression indicated by *katua* presupposes the existing order. This transgression denudes the corporeal and spiritual body. In fact, it makes sense only if it assumes that the Muslim male possesses an individual body. But more than that, this transgression is thought to be inherent in the male Muslim's body. As transgression, *katua* represents an attempt, from the point of view of the attacker, to recover the possible. This possible is always seen as the future. Thus, every act of destroying the body of the Muslim male is each time represented as though it had never been carried out, as if all that is meant by *katua* is perpetually unfinished. Like *khatna* and *musalmani*, the symbolic image of *katua* draws together the present and the future, but always as unequal parts.

20. The phrase used here was *tapori chokras*. *Tapori* refers to thin iron rods that groups of young men carry as weapons. This is a favorite weapon of intimidation in the area of Bombay where we did our fieldwork.

21. A few hours after the Babari mosque was demolished, a cycle procession in Dharavi (the place of this fieldwork), organized by the Shiv Sena, rallied to slogans such as "*Hat men lungi, muh men pan, bhago landya Pakistan*" ("With loin cloth in hand and betel leaf in the mouth, runs the circumcised to Pakistan"). In Bombay *landya* is the colloquial term for the circumcised Muslim. Literally, it refers to the tail of the bull that has been cut (see *Srikrishna 1998: 69*).

22. This voice is not anchored in individual speech, but provides the background or the preconditions of "talk" about violence. Voice, as I understand it, always depends on something else to fill it out—in this case language—but it lacks the conditions of language, specifically an internal structure. It is, in this case, situated between language and noise.

REFERENCES

Ansari, G. 1960. *Muslim Caste in Uttar Pradesh.* Lucknow: Lucknow University Press.

Asad, T. 1997. "On Torture, or Cruel, Inhuman, and Degrading Treatment," in *Human Rights: Culture and Context,* ed. R. A. Wilson. London: Pluto Press.

Bouhdiba, A. 1985. *Sexuality in Islam.* Trans. A. Sheridan. London: Routledge and Kegan Paul.

Bourdieu, P. 1977. *Outline of a Theory of Practice.* Trans. R. Nice. Cambridge: Cambridge University Press.

Crooke, W. 1974. *The Tribes and Castes of North Western India.* Vol. 3. Delhi: Cosmo, 69–72.

Heller, A. 1984. *Everyday Life.* Trans. G. Campbell. London: Routledge and Kegan Paul.

Lewis, I. M. 1966. *Islam in Tropical Africa.* Oxford: Oxford University Press.

Mehta, D. 1977. *Work, Ritual, Biography: A Muslim Community in North India.* Delhi: Oxford University Press.

Mehta, D., and R. Chatterji. 1995. "A Case Study of a Communal Riot in Dharavi, Bombay." *Religion and Society* 4: 5–60.

Pandey, G. 1990. *The Construction of Communalism in Colonial North India.* Delhi: Oxford University Press.

Scarry, E. 1985. *The Body in Pain: The Making and Unmaking of the World.* New York: Oxford University Press.

Srikrishna, Hon. Justice B. N. 1998. *Report of the Srikrishna Commission Appointed for Inquiry into the Riots at Mumbai during December 1992 and January 1993.* Vols. 1 and 2. Mumbai: Bharat Press.

Trimingham, J. 1964. *Islam in East Africa.* Oxford: Clarendon.

Teach Me How to Be a Man

An Exploration of the Definition of Masculinity

Mamphela Ramphele

[B]eneath all the enfolded layers, there's the secret treasure: the story of identity and belonging, the myth of home, which places everyone in relation to mothers, fathers, to offspring, to here and to elsewhere, to time past and present—and in so doing lays the path to the future where we may or may not be saved.

M. WARNER,
Manhood: An Action Plan for Changing Men's Lives

Identity formation in almost all cultures is modeled on ideals of what it means to be a man or woman. Such ideals are often captured in myths that are told and retold with such authority that they leave little room for alternative formulations—things are what they are, and have always been like this, and would always be this way. Children in New Crossroads, a township in Cape Town, are enveloped in repeated stories of the ideal men and women they ought to become. Forms of storytelling are varied: Gentle cuddles, coaxing whispers, myths told around crowded rooms, firm drawing of boundaries, harsh words for nonconformists, or even physically imposed pain all find a place in the storytelling.

New Crossroads is a township established in 1982 for African people under pressure from their growing demands on the apartheid state to acknowledge their right of access to urban resources. A demographic survey we conducted in 1991 indicated that there was a total population of approximately 10,500, of whom 36 percent were fifteen years or younger, and only 3.5 percent were above sixty years of age. Thirty-two percent of households[1] were female-headed, with the average size of female-headed households standing at 5.59 and those headed by males at 6.16. Educational levels were relatively low, with 20 percent functional literacy, and only 18 percent of adults with matriculation certificates (high school graduation) or higher levels of education. Income levels, notoriously inaccurate in this setting, were reported to average US$330 per month per household; 79 percent of income was derived from wage earnings, 9 percent from pensions and other social security, and the balance from informal trading activity.[2] Violence, both structural and physical, in the public and private spheres is part of the everyday reality of the lives of children and adults in South Africa, shaping their definition of identities of the self and others in important ways. The meaning of childhood/adulthood; femininity/masculinity; the rich/poor; the powerful/powerless is forged in the crucible of violent confrontation—both in the structural and physical sense. According to a research report by the Medical Research Council of South Africa, in 1994 the homicide rate in the Cape Town area was 68 per 100,000, and transport-related deaths were 43 per 100,000 (*Business Day,* 29 November 1995). There were thus 1,789 homicides in this area, where 52 percent of the murder victims were black males. The legacy of apartheid, with its use of brute force to subjugate large sections of the population and confine them to overcrowded and under-resourced areas, is likely to remain important in the lives of many South Africans.

Violence against children is a serious problem in South Africa. Reported cases represent only the tip of the iceberg. In 1994 almost 23,000 cases were reported to the Child Protection Unit—up 36 percent from 1993. During 1993–94 officially reported child rape cases increased by 63 percent from 4,736 to 7,559 (*Argus,* 26–27 August 1995). An estimated 85 percent of the survivors of child rape know their attackers well—family members, friends, neighbors and baby-sitters. The National Council for Child and Family Welfare says it deals with 2,000 cases of child abuse every month nationwide, of which 50 percent involve sexual abuse.

Child abuse, particularly sexual abuse, undermines the very foundations of family and community life. The myths of adults as protectors and children as innocents are difficult to sustain under such conditions, but continue to be told and retold in part as an attempt to conceal the ugly reality of the disintegration of a caring ethos in many communities. Our research in New Crossroads suggests that this national tragedy has insinuated itself into the fabric of this community as well. All of the sixteen youths ranging from fourteen to twenty years of age whom we have included in a longitudinal study claim to know of at least one case of a man who has made his own child pregnant, of neighbors who regularly abuse unsuspecting little girls, and many other tragic stories which point to the dysfunctionality of social relations in this township. The cycle of abuse has also thrown up more myths to justify what is seen as abnormal. Child abuse is treated by some community leaders in New Crossroads township as a private family matter which should not be reported to the Child Protection Unit of the South African Police. When confronted with their actions, some of the men who abuse their own children simply assert that, like any producer of goods, a man is entitled to sample his own produce. Yet as international studies have indicated, there are likely to be many child abusers who abhor what they do and loathe themselves but are incapable of stopping the abuse (e.g., see Russell 1986).

In this paper I explore identity formation amongst young people in New Crossroads whom I have been observing in different contexts over the last four years. I am particularly interested in the development of their sense of identity as gendered individuals, as well as their sense of belonging within the collectives of family, community, and the wider South African society. I will present case studies of Bulelani and Bulelwa as windows into the complex web of issues with which young people must grapple in their struggle for a sense of self with a sufficient feeling of belonging to enable them to function adequately.

CASE 1: BULELANI

Bulelani is the firstborn in a family of two sons born to a single parent whose fiancé died before Bulelani's birth. He is an unusually tall young man, nineteen years of age, who speaks with a lot of passion and has interesting insights into the world around him. He has an attractive curiosity about how the world has come to be what it is, which came to the fore during the weekend field trips we did together. He often displayed gentleness and caring towards the smaller and younger members of the walking party, but got easily hurt if teased.

He speaks lovingly of his mother, who is a strong woman who has managed to raise both Bulelani and his younger brother under extraordinarily difficult conditions. She had to leave school as a teen mother, managed to study privately, educated herself, and completed high-school-level exams. She works as a salesperson and augments her income with part-time acting in serial dramas broadcast over the radio. She got Bulelani into a previously white school in 1991 through sheer determination. She entrusted him to the school principal, to whom she confessed her poverty and inability to pay for any of the school requirements because she was between jobs. She paid her debts as soon as she became more financially secure.

The loss of his father weighs heavily on Bulelani. He still maintains contact with his father's family in the Transkei, paying them occasional visits during school vacations. The loss of fathers does complicate the lives of children anywhere in the world, but it is a particular handicap in a community where fathers are the key to the entry into the world of men. It is the father who names one, introduces one to ancestors in the ritual of *imbeleko*, which ideally takes place in infancy, during which a goat is slaughtered, traditional beer brewed, and food and drink offered to both the living and the dead as one body of the clan to witness the entry of a new member into the corporate whole. Bulelani has had to rely on his mother's brothers to stand in for his absent father on ceremonial occasions such as these. The twin pressures of urbanization, with its dispersal of extended family members across a wide geographical radius, and the limited material resources at the disposal of most households in poor communities limit the capacity of uncles to play a meaningful role as substitute fathers.

Bulelani's mother has brought her sons up single-handedly and expects both boys to share domestic chores. Bulelani spends Saturday mornings cleaning the house and doing his own laundry. He can cook simple meals. He is a hard worker who has set his sights on a career in science. He studies regularly every day, including Saturday afternoons.

Bulelani grew up in Old Crossroads (a squatter settlement in Cape Town, born out of the structural violence of apartheid state policies which denied Africans the right of access to urban resources as a logical consequence of denying them their birthright as South African citizens). Power relations in both the private and public spheres in this settlement were in significant ways carved through violent conflict; survival of the fittest was the organizing principle.

The battle of the "fathers" versus "the comrades"[3] of the mid-1980s did not leave Bulelani untouched. Young males, some barely in their teens, were forced to do battle against the "fathers," who were regarded as conservative people who controlled the squatter camp with the support of the South African police. The "fathers" distinguished themselves in battle by wearing white head-dresses—hence the Afrikaans name *witdoek* (see Cole 1986 for a fuller description of this community conflict).

Fellow residents maimed and killed one another in the struggle for territorial control over the boundaries of what constituted "the struggle." Warlords violently carved out territories over which they could exercise absolute control and extract "taxes" for their own pockets. The South African police sided with the most conservative amongst them to drive deep wedges into the community, which had up to then successfully resisted some of the impositions of the apartheid government's anti-urbanization strategy against Africans in the Western Cape. The battle lines were not just drawn between the politically correct positions, but also around ideas of what constituted a "man." "Comrade" became the catch phrase, the password into "manhood"—the social leveler between "men" and "boys." The fracture in community relations occasioned by internal conflicts blurred the otherwise sharp distinctions drawn between "men" and "boys." Boys were suddenly thrust into the role of warriors. With the blurring of divisions between "men" and "boys" came role reversals and ambiguities. Young "comrades" presiding over "people's courts" between 1985 and 1988 publicly flogged errant male heads of households who were reported by their wives or children to have been neglectful or abusive. When asked how they felt about their sons flogging their own "fathers," a woman in nearby Nyanga township who was one of the complainants whom I questioned about this in 1988 had this to say: "What is worse—letting children handle corpses and preside over funerals or getting them to settle family disputes? There are no longer taboos against anything—if you let children near death, then you can't stop them from anything else." Bulelani's reflections on this period follow:

> It is difficult to grow up as a black child because you see things you should not see, and you hear things you should not hear. Language is also part of violence. Adults often use rude language which hurts us. I remember seeing dead bodies with their insides lying next to them. You know what a policeman looks like (a reference to the predominately white police force). A white child cannot grow up under such conditions.

Bulelani's mother, along with many other residents of the squatter area, moved to New Crossroads in 1982, battle-weary and impatient with the never-ending demands of warlords who extracted heavy levies from all households to finance their reigns of terror. The battle for access to urban resources had become a battle to enrich the few warlords and their loyal followers. What had begun as a struggle for justice had become the vehicle of further injustice.

"Comrades" who had become used to the power they wielded in the battles for control in Old Crossroads had to find a new form of expression in New Crossroads. The violent settlement of disputes had become embedded in the conduct of peer relations. Gang activity attained new heights. Young people involved in these criminal activities were referred to as "comtsotsis"[4] to indicate their tenuous relationship with "comrades" in the struggle.

Bulelani was forced to become a member of a gang. His explanation follows:

> The reason why I became a member is that one day I came home from the dentist via Nyanga (a neighboring township) taxi rank. I was called by a group of five boys, *amadoda*. They asked me where I stayed. I said New Crossroads. I did not know that there was something happening. I could see from their faces that they were people with no respect for anybody—*Zintswelo Mbeko*. One started to kick me. Another said I was the person they were looking for. When I asked what was happening, they said, "You are still asking?" I had to defend myself against a knife. I managed to run towards some houses.
>
> I was very angry and in great pain because I had just been to the dentist. I did not ask or think twice. I just took off my clothes, and I put on some funny ones and went out into the street. I hate to carry a knife, but I am very good at throwing a brick. I had to be on the side of the Badboys because they are from New Crossroads. Because of what happened to me, I decided to help them, and I hated Nyanga East groups from that day onwards. I have seen innocent people stabbed, but I did not stab anyone—I don't carry a knife on me; the only thing I use is the brick.

During the period from 1987 to 1988 the Civic Association and the residents of New Crossroads took the initiative to try to stop gang activity in their neighborhoods. The parents of children involved in gang activity were warned not to let those children back into their homes; otherwise they would be evicted from the township. Parents were ordered to give neither food nor accommodation to their gangster children as part of the campaign. Mothers had to hold back the nurturance of their errant male children as part of the process of redefining the disturbed lines of authority— violent behavior had to be met with further violence. The rallying cry was "Kwavukwa—umtshayelo nenkwenkwe" ("Wake up—a broom and a boy"). Adult men were literally being called on to clear boys off the streets with broomsticks or any object which came into their hands. A rule was established for boys to be off the streets by nine o'clock every evening. Bulelani's reflections on this follow: "The Comrades also joined the fray—they hunted down the Badboys and beat them. There was war between the Comrades and the Badboys for a long time. The residents of New Crossroads told themselves that they were going to fight—no boys were going to be allowed to rule New Crossroads. And the adults ultimately won." The clearing of the streets by adults was an important symbolic statement about their unwillingness to let chaos reign—they had to take back the neighborhood so that community relations, which were fractured by the gang activity, could be restored to more stable networks between the various parties.

Bulelani has handled a difficult living environment with great ingenuity and a sense of humor. He told us how he managed to convince his peers that his move to a "white school" in 1991 was not in any way a reflection of his weakening commitment to the struggle. There was general agreement amongst his peers that most teachers in the township schools were not equal to the task of guiding them through school. He suggested to them that by going to a better school, he would become a resource for them because he would be available to them as a tutor over weekends. He laughed as he told the story. How could a single young man become a tutor for all his peers? But he reminded us all of the risks attached to being labeled a sell-out at that time—the threat of a necklace murder was ever present. One had to be creative in order to survive.

Bulelani's school career has gone through ups and downs. Among its many milestones is the physical fight with a fellow student—a white boy from a poor working-class background whom Bulelani accused of hurling racist insults at him. The school principal diffused the tension by getting both boys into his car and driving around the Cape Peninsula, threatening not to stop the car until they had sorted out their problem. The school principal pointed out to both of them the similarities of their family circumstances and the need for one to control one's emotions even when provoked. Both boys were relieved when he stopped for lunch at a fast-food restaurant and gave both of them a treat. They may not have become the best of friends after that episode, but they have developed an empathy for each other and are on good terms.

Bulelani is often frustrated by the slow progress he makes in mastering science and mathematics—a legacy of poor foundations laid by apartheid education.[5] He also worries about his body image, which he describes in uncomplimentary terms. He sees himself as too tall and resents the scar he has over his forehead—a result of a car accident in childhood. He is given to banging his head against the wall when he is frustrated.

He wrote the following poem in 1994 as part of a school assignment:

My Love

Me . . .
I smile with Love,
I see with Love,
I dance with Love,
I wish with Love,
No wonder why I'm in Love.

Yes I walk with Love,
Socialise with Love,
Confused with Love,
And wonder when I'm falling in Love.

To me flowers mean Love,
The sea, the morning and night,
They all mean Love.

I speak about Love,
Talk with Love,
And give with Love,
But when am I going to receive Love?

We will leave Bulelani's interpretation of what "love" is till later. Let us first get to know another young person from the same township background.

CASE 2: BULELWA

Bulelwa is a cheerful eighteen-year-old to whom one feels immediately attracted. She is tall with a well-proportioned body and radiates self-confidence. She is the eldest of four girls—products of a broken marriage. The girls have been brought up largely by their maternal grandparents, who became their source of moral and material support. Bulelwa speaks with obvious warmth of both her grandparents, who have always been there for her since early childhood, when the children shuttled between their own home and that of the grandparents in the same street.

Her parents were in her view happily married until her father suffered a car accident about eight years ago which left him disabled and wheelchair-bound, for which he received reasonable financial compensation. They continued to enjoy a happy family life, unburdened by material want. From all accounts, the mother squandered the money and neglected their father, who then left her five years or so ago to go and live with his sister in another township, ending a long unhappy period. Bulelwa and her family have suffered financial hardship since the break-up of their parents' marriage, and have had to rely on grandparental support.

Their mother is given to wild mood swings which leave the children bewildered. Bulelwa is generous in her judgment of her mother. She acknowledges her weaknesses but does not ignore the good aspects of her mothering role. For example, their mother allows them to bring friends home and to entertain them without the harassment which Bulelwa has witnessed in other families with respect to male friends in particular. She also describes her sisters as being as good as friends to her—there is little sibling competition and rivalry in their relationships.

Bulelwa has also lived through the political and criminal violence described above which Bulelani has had to endure. Being a girl was a protective factor against most of the street violence: she did not have to join the "Comrades" to fight "the struggle," nor the "Comtsotsis" who followed in their wake, nor the gangs which violently carved out territories for themselves. Being part of the domestic space gives girls some protection, although it exposes them to the risk of sexual violence within the home. She was acutely aware of the dangers of the streets during the period described above, and is grateful for having come through the period unharmed.

Bulelwa suffered terribly after the loss of her grandmother three years ago. She expressed great sadness—her anchor was gone, and she felt that the problems she had with her mother would become unbearable. She drew closer to her grandfather, with whom she stays since the death of the grandmother in part to help look after him, but also to seek his loving support.

Bulelwa was one of six young people whom we encouraged to move out of township schools in 1994 to the same school to which Bulelani had moved. We sought to offer these youngsters better educational opportunities, given the appallingly inadequate township school system. Her school performance left much to be desired during the first year at the school. Teachers reported that she was often absent from school or left early in the company of young men driving cars. She predictably failed her Standard Eight exams at the end of that year. She has subsequently improved after repeating a year. She was made a school prefect in the third year of study in recognition of her leadership talents. She completed her final high school year in 1996.

Bulelwa shows all the signs of resilience in the face of adversity. She still has serious problems of inadequate emotional and material support from her mother, as well having to carry the burden of supporting her younger siblings, who suffer the pain of their mother's mood swings and abusive behavior.

Bulelwa is the only one of the sixteen young people included in our longitudinal study who has shown consistency in her participation in the programs set out: weekend trials, school vacation activities, and the aftercare programs at the New Crossroads Youth Center, which was built by our research project two years ago as an attempt to create quality space for the youth in that area. She works part-time at the center as part of a "child-to-child" program in which older children help younger ones. She is a good leader of the Environmental Cluster,[6] where she shows the benefit of four years of exposure to the Wilderness Leadership School's weekend trails.[7]

She is also popular with younger children who come to the Youth Center in the afternoons for storytelling and being read to. She is an animated reader who enthuses the young ones with a love for books. The little money she earns is important for her own upkeep as well as for sharing with younger siblings. He mother is known to demand whatever little she gets per month, which never exceeds US$100. It is a difficult situation, but she seems to be able to handle it in spite of the pain she suffers. She gets no support from her father, who has deserted her.

Bulelwa has set her sights on a professional career—"I see you as my role model," she has said to me on more than one occasion. She is determined to get a good pass in her final Matriculation examinations and go to university to study social science. When asked to indicate her career choice more precisely, she confesses that she knows too little about her options to be more certain. Her loving grandfather is her constant support.

GENERAL DISCUSSION

Both Bulelani and Bulelwa are products of complex family settings. Both have had to deal with the loss of the father as a source of support—Bulelani through death, Bulelwa through desertion after a broken marriage. Bulelani's mother is the stronger of the two mothers, but Bulelwa has had the benefit of her grandmother as a positive role model and continues to enjoy a supportive relationship with her grandfather, who has remained consistently loving after her grandmother's death. We have to look at personal factors and the social environment to identify important factors which shape the identities of these young people as gendered personae.

The Journey into Manhood

Bulelani's journey into manhood has to be negotiated along a poorly marked path across a terrain which gives conflicting cues to one so young and vulnerable. The definition of manhood starts at birth. His name is part of the process of defining who he is and his place in the body corporate, his role as a gendered body, and what dreams he is entitled to embody. Names given to male babies mark them out as historical actors. For example, *Bulelani* (give thanks), *Mkhululi* (the freedom fighter), *Vuyo* (joy), *Xola* (the peaceful one) all place historical agency in the hands of the boys. In contrast, female babies are marked as the recipients or objects of other people's actions: *Bulelwa* (the one for whom we give thanks), *Khululwa* (the one who has been liberated), *Vuyelwa* (the one for whom we rejoice), *Xoliswa* (the one who is endowed with peace). But names also convey the dreams of one's parents. Such dreams reflect hope, fear, grief, and many ambivalent feelings about one's offspring. These become indelible marks as one carries one's name around. Names such as *Kwanele* (it is enough), *Ntlungu* (pain), or *Nyembezi* (tears) are often given to children to capture the state of mind of the parents at the time of birth. I have given the two young people the two pseudonyms used here to reflect this naming practice.

Customary practice within this community stamps its seal on children in other important ways as infants, toddlers, pre-school pupils, school pupils, and later as adolescents—in the manner of dress, the tone of voice in addressing children with that ever-so-slight inflection of indulgence which is directed at favored ones, the hidden sharpness of the shaming custom which shapes one into conformity. Boys and girls are constantly reminded of their gendered bodies in injunctions such as, "Boys don't do that" or "Girls can't sit like that." Gender identity is defined through visible physical and sexualized signs of potency, with little emphasis on the virtues of communication skills, independent thought, and inner strengths.

The gender division of labor is blurred by the demands of survival, which require the cooperation of as many members of the household as possible to contribute to its smooth operation. Both boys and girls are required to make their contribution to household chores. As the boys reach middle and late adolescence, they feign incompetence and are subtly encouraged and allowed by others to get away with it. This reflects the ambivalence with which this society deals with the gender division of labor within both the household and the wider sphere. Boys are encouraged to conceive of themselves as merely helping out with domestic chores; it is not really their responsibility to nurture, and the closer they get to becoming "men," the more they need to distance themselves from household nurturing roles. "*Ozakunyaba kwedini xa osoloku uthe nca kunina*" ("You will be emasculated by hanging around your mother's skirts").

Boys in the New Crossroads community occupy that liminal space which is that of "an individual in the process of formation." Their individuality is in important ways not fully recognized. Signifiers of the liminal status of boys include, first, the lack of respect shown to boys by most members of the community. Scant attention is given to their needs for nurture—they are usually fed last, and the worst cuts of meat in line with the common adage that "*inkwenkwe yiinga*" ("a boy is like a dog"). Second, and in a contradictory sense, they are given the freedom, or indeed the license to act irresponsibly. This licensing may be partly to prove that they are boys—they have to misbehave for fear of being regarded as effeminate (a *morphie* in the local lingo), but it may also be related to the low level of expectation of good behavior which leaves boys with little to strive for in setting behavioral goals for themselves—"boys will always be boys" is a strongly held myth. Such misbehavior includes street fights, having multiple relationships with girls their age, and general scruffiness in appearance.

The encouragement of boys to operate as "individuals in formation" is a variety of the traditional practice which was common in most peasant communities where boys were treated as "apprentices" of older men in the community from whom they learned the art of being men. The boys learned by listening to, observing, and working alongside mature men. Excesses in the boisterous behavior of boys were promptly curbed by older men, who took corporate responsibility for all the boys—boys with absent biological fathers were taken care of within the network of men in the village.[8] Urbanization and poverty have weakened the web of networks which provided boys with a supportive environment in which to test the limits of permissible behavior.

In my view the absence of "apprentice masters" makes boys vulnerable to developing overly dependent relationships with peers who become an important source of support and protection against abuse by bully boys. The slide into gang activity is not surprising under such circumstances. Studies in the United States indicate that adolescents tend to fall back on peer support and advice in the absence of supportive parental relations even though they tend to prefer the latter (Dornbusch 1988: 74; Nightingale 1995).

Bulelani has shown resilience in the face of pressure from the world of gangs, which he entered for a brief period as a survival strategy. But he also showed ingenuity when presented with a tough choice between following his mother's advice to go to a "white school" and get better educational opportunities, and taking the risk of being branded a sell-out by his peers. He managed the risky situation with great skill.

Bulelani has also had to pass the final test—initiation into manhood. The circumcision ritual brings the definition of manhood as distinct from boyhood into sharp relief. Xhosa people in this setting hold the view that as long as a male is not circumcised, he remains a boy.[9] Boys can only escape their liminal status as a category of humanity awaiting initiation through the ritual of circumcision. Bulelani and his peers are quite emphatic about their identification with this cultural practice and its requirements:

> *Ukoluka lisiko elidala line nkqayi.* (Circumcision is a custom which is so old that it has become bald.) Our forefathers were circumcised, our fathers were circumcised, and we too will be circumcised, and our children and their children. We cannot throw that away. It is very, very important because you change from being a boy into being a man. Things which you did as a boy have to be left behind, and you do things which a man must do.

The importance of male initiation is recognized universally across many cultures and over the ages.[10] Michener in *The Fires of Spring* says that it is "the journey that men make to find themselves. If they fail in this, it doesn't matter what else they find" (quoted in Biddulph 1995: 192). What emerges as key to the success of finding "oneself as a man" is the management of the process of initiation by mature men who make themselves available as guides to the younger men on this journey. The following elements emerge from all accounts as important indicators of successful male initiation:

A clean break with the parents, especially the mother

Entry into the wilderness or forest, where communion with nature is encouraged

The communal nature of the ritual—one is initiated with one's peers and not alone

The preparation of the body of the boy through bathing, dance, and physical challenges such as contact sport (in Mandela's case, the boys had stick fights)

The wound which older men inflict on younger men as a seal of belonging and sharing the mysteries of manhood

The after care which molds the boy's body into a man's body

The emergence from the wilderness to take up one's place in society amid joyous celebrations which affirm one

Much has been lost due to the urbanization process as well as the breakdown in social relations as a result of apartheid's war on the poor and the loss of anchors which held communities together. The quality of male initiation has suffered immensely in poor urban communities such as New Crossroads. First, few mature men are willing or can afford to give of their time freely to pass on the secrets of successful manhood to the initiates. Some young men undergoing initiation end up suffering neglect and loneliness, which wound the spirit and expose them to the risk of developing serious infections. There is a danger under such conditions of initiation becoming no more than a sadistic practice.

Second, commercialization of the ritual makes it unaffordable for very poor people. They cannot raise the fees of the *Igcibi*, the practitioner who oversees the surgical removal of the foreskin,[11] nor the money to buy expensive clothes for the *Ikrwala* (the newly initiated who is no longer to wear the clothes associated with boyhood). Neither can they afford the elaborate feast which is expected by neighbors and relatives, who rarely make substantial enough contributions, as was customary.

Tensions arise between the expectations created in the minds of young men by this age-old ritual definition of manhood as distinct from boyhood and womanhood, and the social reality into which the newly emergent men are thrust. First, racism and inequity undermine the status which is presumed to come from the demonstrated ability to endure pain. Apartheid defined black men out of the community of patriarchs who constitute the powerful head of the body corporate. Black men, particularly African men, were categorized as belonging to a status below that of white women and children. The use of the term *boys* to refer to black men captures the symbolic position they were meant to occupy in the power hierarchy of racist South Africa—they were not men, and could never become men. The end of apartheid has not necessarily changed the reality of many poor men. Their only escape from complete powerlessness is the control they exercise over African women and children. It is not surprising that some of them become abusive of their own children and of the women in their lives. Many young black men are denied the rewards to which the status of manhood entitles them in a male-dominated society.

Second, apartheid undermined the role of black men as protectors. Few of the young men emerging from initiation ceremonies would have experienced the protective father figure who provided for the family. The father is either physically absent or emotionally, economically, and/or politically absent because of migrant labor or family structure. The inability of African men to protect their families became quite obvious during the apartheid era when women and children who dared come and live in cities were harassed by police, who raided their places of residence, arresting and deporting those defined as illegally resident in urban areas. In times of community conflict many men were unable to defend their homes against the onslaught of attackers. This failure often thrust women and children into the front line of the struggle, as was the case with the Old Crossroads community conflict, and it cast boys into a warrior role. New Crossroads women are regarded by all and sundry as powerful agents—*owakey* (the wide awake ones)—who have kept their families and the community going through difficult times. They head a third of New Crossroads households, and, where convenient, they play a strong supportive role to male leadership, which they help to install at strategic moments both in the private and public spheres.

Third, a man defined as a provider is often frustrated by lack of educational and job opportunities for the majority of poor Africans. Whereas women are prepared to do menial jobs, many men find taking up such jobs an intolerable further assault on their manhood. With 60 percent unemployment in some areas where poor Africans live, many households depend increasingly on women as providers. The provided-for "man" suffers further humiliation and may become violent.

The role reversal between strong women and weak men is a constant theme in New Crossroads. The weak position African men find themselves in is complicated by the humiliation of having to rely on the very female bodies they were initiated into despising and spurning as nurturers and providers. The deafening silence around this issue is interrupted only by outbursts of violence as men desperately attempt to reassert their dominance in both the private and public spheres in the only language they understand. Chatwin refers to the same phenomenon amongst Australians as that of strong women and "drained" men (1987: 112). The men's bodies are drained of all energy because their dreams are frustrated by a social environment which gives them mixed messages about their entitlements in society.

There is increasing refusal amongst former oppressed people to be part of the conspiracy of silence which protects men who have been brutalized by white racism who turn on their women and children (Morrison 1992). Black men in the African-American situation from the time of slavery often accused black women who complained against abuse or lack of support of working against the interest of the "group" (282–83), thus silencing women. Morrison and her colleagues argue that in daring to speak out, Anita Hill was projected as a witch by significant numbers of black political leaders and other members of the black community. But, like the witches of old, Morrison and her colleagues argue that the silenced voices would come back to haunt the African-American community as well as the wider American society which refused to listen to them. They note that closing ranks against a hostile, white, racist system is often done at the expense of black women and ignores class, age, and other differentials of power relations in society (394–95).

Fourth, the decision-making role is also not easily realizable for most men in New Crossroads. Until recently, most African men could not decide on even the most elementary of matters affecting their lives and those of their families in Apartheid South Africa. Poverty is an added constraint to decision making and is likely to remain so for the foreseeable future. One cannot enforce one's will on others unless one has the material means to do so, nor can one be taken seriously if there are no incentives to compliance with one's wishes.

Fifth, most women with whom Bulelani and his contemporaries are likely to get into contact as prospective partners and recipients of their protection and provision of material resources are not likely to resemble their own mothers. Bulelani's mother and her contemporaries have on the whole managed to tread a fine line between affirming the manhood of their menfolk and supporting themselves and their children. The myth of the man as supporter, protector, provider, and decision maker was carefully nurtured in an attempt to protect the community from a moral/ethical breakdown.

But what does being like a man mean to Bulelani, given his life experiences thus far? Does it mean being like "the father" of Old Crossroads? Or does it mean being like the tough men of New Crossroads who regard boys as *izinja* (dogs) awaiting evolution into fuller humanity? Or is he to become like the *"comtsotsis"* who are claiming their place in the new South Africa which seems to have turned its back on them without much acknowledgment of their warrior role in "the struggle"? How is he to understand manhood and its responsibilities as a husband, parent, and citizen? Who are his models of the man he wants to become?

Bulelani is at a tecknikon to train as an engineer. The poem he wrote in

1994 as part of a school assignment, quoted above, gives one a hint of his emotional turmoil. The interpretation of what "love" is, and its centrality to the affirmation of the self by others, are issues regarding which there is much silence. Violence, particularly sexual violence, directed at women and children tends to be the dominant form of communication to assert the right to claim the entitlements the male body has been promised.

Concluding Comments

The definition of "manhood" which runs through all stages of Bulelani's life presupposes a single notion of what it means to be a man. The common elements of manhood as traditionally framed include courage and leadership; a man is a fighter, warrior, protector, hero, provider, and initiator. These elements are reinforced at every stage of development by various strategies. Those willing and able to excel in demonstrating their "manhood," be it in the battles of "the struggle," "gang warfare," initiation ceremonies, or successful courtship and capture of the "trophy" called "woman," are celebrated. The "weak" are perceived as mere "women."

There are important dissonances between the traditional definition of "manhood" and the reality men find themselves in, which impinge themselves to a greater or lesser degree on men in South Africa, especially poor black men. African men are particularly vulnerable to these dissonances, as indicated above. The affirmation which one expects from being human and part of a whole is not often forthcoming in the lives of many African men.

The taste of "manhood" which "the struggle" provided, through the warrior role that teenage boys played, has left many of them in a confused state in the new South Africa. The violent confrontational skills that helped to render the country ungovernable through a strategy of calculated disrespect for authority figures are an embarrassment to the new government, which either looks the other way or threatens to clamp down on "unruly" behavior. Yesteryear's strengths have become today's weaknesses—the basis of one's rejection and marginalization. Confusion reigns in the minds of young former "comrades" who find their former friends unwilling or unable to acknowledge them as such. Whom are they to turn to?

The blows of the sculptor's chisel which define the outlines of the "manhood" leave many scars which cannot be smoothed over by the unrealizable dreams of future rewards as part of male dominion. Keen's comments in this regard are worth taking note of:

> The wounds that men endure, and the psychic scar tissue that results from living with the expectation of being a battlefield sacrifice, [are] every bit as horrible as the suffering women bear from the fear and the reality of rape. Rise a hundred miles above this planet and look at history from an Olympian perspective and you must conclude that when human beings organize their political lives around a war system, men bear as much pain as women. Our bodies

are violated, we are regularly slaughtered and mutilated, and if we survive battle, we bear the burden of blood-guilt. When we accept the war system, men
and women alike tacitly agree to sanction the violation of the flesh—the rape
of women by men who have been conditioned to be "warriors," and the gang
rape of men by the brutality of war. Until women are willing to weep for and
accept equal responsibility for the systematic violence done to the male body
and spirit by the war system, it is not likely that men will lose enough of their
guilt and regain enough of their sensitivity to weep and accept responsibility
for women who are raped and made to suffer the indignity of economic
inequality. (Keen 1991: 47)

The question of the appropriateness of male initiation rituals such as the
one applicable in New Crossroads has to be faced squarely in the light of the
dissonances it creates in a complex society such as South Africa. Is it fair to
young black males that their bodies continue to be marked for male dominance that they have little opportunity to attain other than through sheer
physical force? Is it not time to modify initiation rituals into processes
which prepare young males to negotiate more equitable gender relations?

The challenge would be to find the "apprentice masters" who would be
prepared to accompany young men as they undertake the journey into manhood. Feminism and the woman's movement of the late sixties have been
important in enabling women to explore the possibilities of redefining
womanhood. The redefinition of womanhood has left men in a difficult
position. They cannot be men in the mythical way in which they have
tended to project themselves without coming into conflict with the new realities around them. A man's movement has begun to make itself felt in
response to the need for redefinition of manhood.[12]

South African men share a common culture, be they African, Afrikaner,
Jewish, or English: patriarchy has been part of their social reality. Is it not
time for a humanizing man's movement in which young and old men can
start redefining who they are and thus teach young boys how to be real
men?

NOTES

1. The definition of "household" is a matter of some dispute amongst social scientists. The term is used here to refer to co-residential units whose occupants share
domestic resources and pool their incomes to meet the needs of all dependants.
Tenants who reside in shacks in some of the backyards of residential plots in this
township who pay rent to the registered owners or tenants are included.

2. Informal trading activity consists mainly of selling of fresh produce and meat,
but undisclosed activities such as the sale of marijuana and other addictive substances contribute substantial earnings to some families.

3. The expression "fathers" reflects the local custom of referring to any older

man as *utata* (father) as a sign of respect. "Comrades" became a popular name for those involved in the popular struggle for liberation in the 1980s and defined lines between "them" and "us."

4. *Tsotsis* is a colloquial term used by South Africans to refer to street-wise males who may or may not be thugs. The transformation of political activists into criminals is captured by the term *comtsotsi*.

5. Bulelani failed to get a Matriculation exemption in his 1995 final high school examinations, which ended his hopes of entry into university to pursue a science degree.

6. The New Crossroads Youth Center runs a number of programs clustered under interest categories: Environment, Life Skills, Academic Support, Music and Art, etc.

7. The Wilderness Leadership School is a national environmental activist NGO which focuses on leadership development through exposure to life in the outdoors under the guidance of a trained environmentalist. It draws on Jung's ideas of the environment as a spiritual healing medium for both individuals and social relationships.

8. For a detailed explanation of this corporate bringing up of young men by mature ones, see, for example, Mandela's description of his own childhood in his autobiography, *A Long Walk to Freedom* (1994: 1–40); see also Pinnock (1984), and Biddulph (1995: 110–38).

9. Mandela's account of his personal experience of this ritual in his autobiography (1994: 24–29) confirms the centrality of circumcision in the definition of manhood amongst the Xhosa. The cry of "Ndiyindoda" marks the initiate's point of entry into manhood at the moment of feeling the searing pain inflicted by the Igcibi (the surgeon who removes the foreskin). One's worthiness to enter manhood is measured by the extent to which one endures physical pain as an indicator of strength of character.

10. See La Fontaine (1985) for a good overview of the ritual; see also Robert Bly (1991) for an interesting interpretation of the ritual and its continuing symbolic significance in the struggle of men all over the world to define manhood in the face of the alienating challenges of modernity.

11. There are reports that in some cases parents have to pay up to R500 each to have their sons circumcised.

12. There have been several waves of this tentative man's movement arising from the angry backlash against feminism. Several men are writing and talking about their own journeys in an attempt to help others (see for example Bly 1991; Keen 1991; Biddulph 1994).

REFERENCES

Biddulph, S. 1995. *Manhood: An Action Plan for Changing Men's Lives.* Sydney: Finch Publishing.

Bly, R. *Iron John.* 1991. Dorset: Element Books.

Chatwin, B. 1987. *Songlines.* London: Picador.

Cole, J. 1986. *Repression and Reform: Community Conflict in Crossroads.* Johannesburg: Ravan Press.

Dornbusch, S., and Strober, M., eds. 1988. *Feminism, Children, and the New Families.* New York: Guildford Press.

Keen, S. 1991. *Fire in the Belly: On Being a Man.* New York: Bantam Books.

La Fontaine, J. S. 1985. *Initiation: Ritual Drama and Secret Knowledge across the World.* Middlesex, England: Penguin.

Mandela, N. 1994. *A Long Walk to Freedom: The Autobiography of Nelson Mandela.* Randburg, South Africa: Macdonald Purnell.

Morrison, T. 1993. *Race-ing Justice, En-gendering Power: Essays on Anita Hill, Clarence Thomas, and the Construction of Social Reality.* London: Chatto and Windus.

Nightingale, C. J. 1995. *On the Edge.* New York: Basic Books (paperback).

Pinnock, D. 1984. District Six Social Networks.

Russell, D. 1982. *Rape in Marriage.* New York: Collier Books, Macmillan.

———. *1984. Sexual Exploitation: Rape, Child Sexual Abuse, and Workplace Harassment.* London: Sage.

———. 1986. *The Secret Trauma: Incest in the Lives of Girls and Women.* New York: Basic Books.

Warner, M. 1994. *Managing Monsters: Six Myths of Our Time.* London: Vintage.

On Not Becoming a "Terrorist"

Problems of Memory, Agency, and Community in the Sri Lankan Conflict

Jonathan Spencer

This chapter focuses on the story of one person caught up in the political violence in Sri Lanka—a close friend from my anthropological fieldwork in a Sinhala village in the early 1980s, a young man whom I shall call Piyasena. His story, which involves both political commitment and political repression, can serve to illuminate and make immediate the general sociopolitical preconditions for political violence in Sri Lanka, and I have accordingly told it in a section entitled "Making 'Terrorists.'" My friend, though, did not become a "terrorist," however defined, and it is this act of apparently intentional passivity, or refusal to take on the role which local history had prepared for him, which stands at the nub of my argument. By shifting attention away from the blinding glare of violence itself, I hope to force some new reflection on the ways in which we attempt to explain the relationship between violence, agency, and community. Most analyses of collective violence pitch their explanations in terms of collective agents—"the mob," "the Tamils," "the Sinhalas," "radical youth." Piyasena, who at the time of the events I am concerned with was self-consciously a member of several of these categories (specifically, a radical Sinhala youth), reminds us that we need to understand the agency behind both violence and nonviolence: What are the circumstances which allow a space for the nonparticipant? This is part of my other theme, pursued in the final part of the chapter: the entanglements of agency and necessity, both individual and collective, in the ways in which violence is talked about and remembered.

In particular I explore the ways in which violence acts as a privileged marker in drawing the boundaries of community, such that an act which is both necessary and just to those inside the boundary may strike the outsider as arbitrary and unjust. Moreover, violence may, as it were, force the issue. The chronology of political violence often appears irreversible: past violence, in the form of memories of the dead, constrains the possible options for action in the future. Piyasena plays a smaller part in this section of my argument, which concentrates more on the different modalities of violence and memory in different parts of Sri Lanka, particularly the Tamil-dominated North and East and the Sinhala South, although it is his refusal to recognize the moral coherence of the claims of *any* of the parties involved in the political violence of the later 1980s which serves as my point of departure. Because he could not accept the moral force of the arguments involved, he found himself on the side of those who could only see the arbitrary and the unjust, those for whom violence could not, and must not, be allowed to "make sense."

Those are the arguments about violence and agency which I explore in this chapter. As for the construction of the self, I have decided to treat the problem of the self as necessarily also a problem of community. In Sri Lanka the problem of community is usually seen in terms of the continuing struggle between the dominant nationalism of the Sinhala majority and the secessionist nationalism of the Tamil minority, and that struggle provides the overall frame for my argument. For most of the years since I first lived and worked in Sri Lanka in the early 1980s, this struggle has taken the form of a civil war between the government and the forces of the secessionist group known as the Liberation Tigers of Tamil Eelam, the LTTE, or Tigers, for short. The end of my original fieldwork in 1983 coincided with one of the worst outbreaks of collective violence since Independence—a wave of attacks on Tamils and their property in selected towns and cities in the Sinhala-dominated south, and this paper starts with my reaction to that outbreak of violence in 1983, and particularly the way in which popular interpretations of the causes of the violence, especially as manifest in rumor, created the illusion of a single collective agent—the Sinhala people—who could be held to be collectively responsible for what happened. I returned to Sri Lanka in 1984 at a time of growing opposition to the government in the South. After that, I did not go back again until 1991; in the intervening years both North and South of the country were ravaged by major political violence. This chapter is also a record of my own relationship to the problems it discusses.

1983: RUMOR AND THE LIMITS OF COMMUNITY

In July 1983, after an attack by Tamil separatists on an army patrol in the North, a week of violence in the South resulted in whole residential areas of Tamil housing being destroyed, Tamil businesses looted, and up to three thousand people killed. There are two points that I want to make about these events here.[1] One is that they were predominantly orchestrated by a few government politicians, and most of the damage was done by organized groups of young men attached to the ruling party. This is not, of course, the whole story, but it is a very important part of the story.

The second concerns my position and the place of rumor. During the week of violence there was little credible news released by the government, but the country was swept by rumors. These involved the sighting of members of the separatist fighters, the LTTE, in various unlikely disguises, on their way to attack symbolically important Sinhala targets in the South. In the world of rumor, the violence was construed as defensive, a necessary response to the threat of the Tamil militants. Indeed this argument was given official endorsement in the broadcast speeches of government politicians at the time (Nissan 1984). Moreover, as I later discovered, while the sighting of the "terrorists" and the inventive reconstruction of the Tigers were new phenomena, many of the same rumors had been recorded in earlier outbreaks of collective violence—in 1958, for example, or even in the anti-Muslim violence of 1915 (Spencer 1990a: 618–9; cf. Kannangara 1984: 155–8; Rogers 1987: 190–1).

Within the violence itself, rumor played a more active role. Attempts at self-defense, attempts to escape even, were interpreted by attackers as evidence that particular Tamils were "really" Tigers. When this happened, they were killed—sometimes by the crowd, sometimes by the security forces—in particular stylized ways.[2] Far from being random, senseless, or wild, the killings of July 1983 can be seen as informed by a moral framework, intended as acts of just punishment for the collective errors of the Tamil people, a view implicitly endorsed by the government of the time in its early reactions to the violence.

The personal impact of the rumors was particularly disturbing. After nearly two years fieldwork, I suddenly felt that I could not communicate with the people I thought I had come to know well. The official Sinhala media, particularly the radio news on which the village depended, barely mentioned the suffering of the Tamil victims of violence, to the extent that one neighbor assumed the "refugees" mentioned in one bulletin were *Sinhala* victims of Tamil violence. I instead listened compulsively to the BBC World Service and Voice of America, hearing detail after detail of atrocities in the cities. Even as my neighbors seized on every new rumor which seemed to make sense of what we all suspected might be happening elsewhere, I simply could not believe these stories. The result was an almost suffocating sense of cultural and moral isolation.

One way to analyze this situation was in terms of what Bourdieu might call a double "misrecognition" (*méconnaissance*).[3] The first misrecognition was that created in the intersubjective space of rumor, which had the effect of making fleeing, terrified civilians appear to their attackers as aggressive terrorists. This same misrecognition then extended outwards to include most members of the Sinhala population (as far as I could tell), for whom the rumors supplied a morally acceptable explanation for the violence (at least temporarily). Then, stripped of their more outlandish details, they were re-presented by government leaders in their appeals to the nation. In the then-president's own words, the violence was caused by the harmful actions (*hinsaka väda*) of the minority community. By this he meant agitation for separatism and acts of violence against the State; the attacks on Tamils, in this interpretation, were the expression of an inevitable and explicable response by the Sinhala community as a whole.[4]

One other point about this moment of misrecognition. The world of rumor was not, as far as I can tell, produced by the powers-that-be, and it certainly was not controlled by them. Nevertheless, it would take a mighty, and misguided, hermeneutic effort for me to rework the rumors of July 1983 into the reassuring language of "revolt and resistance" favored by some recent writers on rumor.[5] In Sri Lanka in that week in July 1983, the world of rumor served to restore a sense of moral order in terms of a set of propositions about the Sinhala people and their place in the world, *shared by powerful and powerless alike* (within the Sinhala population), even as it created the possibility of more acts of violence that would appear to undermine or compromise that sense of order. It also occurred in the extraordinary time of the riots themselves—a time of curfew and almost complete censorship of news. In this classically liminal moment, historical time collapsed, as events and stories from the past were used to justify and explain actions in the present. Similarly, everyday social distinctions collapsed, as Tamil neighbors and colleagues, people with their own names, and personalities, and networks of social relationships, became instantiations of the generic figure of the Tamil or, more specifically, of the threatening figure of the Tamil terrorist.

What of the second misrecognition? This was mine. The acceptance or nonacceptance of the rumors seemed to mark a clear boundary between Sinhala and non-Sinhala; it was only later that I met and talked to Sinhala people who shared my understanding of what had happened in the violence. The misrecognition involved a failure to recognize how temporary or ephemeral the appearance of the Sinhala people as a unified interpretive community actually was.[6] What was lost in my own first reaction was the *variety* of responses to the violence I encountered. These ranged from the blood-curdling exultation expressed by a few men in the village, who clearly regretted the lost opportunity to "get" a few Tamils themselves, to the embarrassed attempts to change the subject of other people who, despite it all, found the whole episode deeply troubling. From not recognizing this variation, it was but a short step to identifying the agent of violence as some collective entity called "the Sinhalas" (or "Sinhala culture") instead of asking *which* Sinhalas participated under what historical circumstances.[7]

MAKING "TERRORISTS"

There is of course a particular political history behind the Sri Lankan violence of the 1980s. Violence has been a part of political life in Sri Lanka at
least since the beginning of mass electoral politics in 1931. In Sinhala areas,
elections and party politicking have been accompanied by a steadily growing level of violence since the populist victory of S. W. R. D. Bandaranaike in
1956. (The 1994 elections were the first to reverse this trend.) After
Independence in 1948, power changed hands between two Sinhala-dominated parties—the left-of-center SLFP (Sri Lanka Freedom Party) and the
right-of-center UNP (United National Party)—in 1956, 1960 (very briefly),
1965, 1970, and 1977. From 1977 to 1994 the country was ruled by the
UNP in a regime whose "liberal" economic policies attracted continued,
huge support from international donors, even as its own actions generated
ever more violent internal protests (Moore 1990).

Tension between the minority Tamils and the majority Sinhalas manifested itself in the form of anti-Tamil "riots," in 1956 and 1958, and again
in 1977, 1981, and most traumatically of all in July 1983. Since then there
has been no major outbreak of anti-Tamil violence in the Sinhala-dominated South of the country, but the conflict has coalesced around the government's war against the separatist LTTE, who have controlled much of
the North and East of the country since the mid-1980s.[8] Between January
and April of 1995, the new government agreed to a ceasefire with the LTTE
and attempted to start negotiations for a political settlement. In April 1995
the LTTE unilaterally broke off negotiations and resumed its attacks on the
state security forces; in December of that year government troops took the
LTTE's stronghold of Jaffna. The government has published radical proposals for a political solution to the conflict, although at the time of writing
it seems unclear that they can carry the support of either the Sinhala or
Tamil population for these measures, and the war drags on.

Between 1987 and 1990 Indian troops were stationed in Sri Lanka in
order to police a peace agreement foisted on all the actors by the Indian
government of Rajiv Gandhi. The Indian troops were soon involved in their
own war with the LTTE in the North and East, while the rest of the country
was convulsed by a wave of terror as young members of a group called the
JVP (Janata Vimukti Peramuna, or People's Liberation Front) attacked the
government not only for betraying the nation by allowing the Indian presence, but also for its own unjust political and economic policies. The JVP
had been involved in an earlier uprising in 1971 which was almost mil-
lenarian in its hopeless, brief moment (Alexander 1981; Obeyesekere
1974); it had enjoyed a brief phase of constitutional legitimacy in the late
1970s before going underground after being falsely accused by the government of fomenting the 1983 anti-Tamil violence.

The 1987–90 violence, with which I am most concerned in what follows, was almost entirely contained within the majority Sinhala population. The JVP targeted agents of the State, particularly those closely identified with the ruling UNP, as well as its own enemies on the left. The government responded with a wave of terror, directed at young males in particular, which reached its climax with the capture and murder of the JVP leadership in late 1989. As far as we can tell, the government won the day by concentrated terror—killing so many young people, whether JVP activists or not, that the opposition ran out of resources and leadership. Although a precise figure will never be possible, one independent source estimates a death toll of around forty thousand for the second JVP rising (Moore 1993: 593, n2). Since 1990, violence and disappearances have abated in the South. In 1993 and 1994 almost all the leading personalities of the UNP government of the late 1980s were killed in a series of assassinations (probably the work of the LTTE). Finally, in 1994 the UNP was defeated in elections, and a new government installed, above all on its promise to settle the Tamil issue by peaceful means.

There are strong parallels between the two major eruptions of anti-State violence, that spearheaded by the LTTE in the North and East, which continues, and that led by the JVP in the South, which was terminated by ruthless state terror at the end of the 1980s. Both movements can be legitimately viewed as the products of state repression of earlier nonviolent protest. This chapter describes the local effect of such repression in a Sinhala area in the 1980s, but the LTTE also emerged after twenty years of state repression, sometimes violent, of peaceful Tamil protest (cf. Wilson 1988). Both combine elements of Marxist rhetoric with appeals to the nation, the Tamil nation of Eelam in one case, the Sinhala Buddhist nation of Sri Lanka in the other. Both have been associated not merely with the use of violence as a political weapon, but with forms of violence which have been aestheticized to the point that expressive violence has become a political goal in itself (as much as the intrumental means to some identifiable political end).

While at the end of my argument I will draw some sharp contrasts between the JVP and the LTTE, it is fair to say that these movements have very similar social roots. Both movements have emerged from situations which could be described as characterized by "uneven modernity." This unevenness is most starkly manifested in the mismatch between high levels of education and low levels of employment for the educated, but it is also apparent in the generational divide between the educated young and their less-educated mothers and fathers. Many commentators have fallen back on the frustrations of underemployed rural youth as the explanation for Sri Lanka's political problems.[9] There are, however, aspects of both the JVP and the LTTE which render narrowly instrumental interpretations problematic.

What renders the instrumental interpretation problematic is the place of violence in both movements. The LTTE has developed a highly elaborated cult of martyrdom—expressed in speeches, memorials, books, songs, and videos—around the figures of its dead cadres. In the words of the LTTE leader Prabhakaran, "Our history of liberation has been written in the blood of these *Maha Veerar* (great heroes). Their passing away are not losses without meaning. Their deaths have become the power that move forward our history—[they are] the life-breath of our struggle. They are the artisans of freedom; . . . they will be worshipped in the temple of our hearts throughout the ages" (quoted in Bose 1994: 120). While the JVP also remembered its dead comrades, as much emphasis seems to have been placed on the victims of violence. Those killed were sometimes mutilated, their bodies often accompanied by posters denouncing their crimes. Victims' families were ordered not to conduct public funerals, or not to carry the corpse to the funeral at normal shoulder height. Needless to say, the forces of the state responded with at least equivalent brutality.

The JVP's official communiqués dwelt mostly on the violence of the government, combining calls to patriotism with rage at the president and his supporters:

> The power hungry traitor [President] J. R. Jayawardene, who during the last eleven years put the nation and the people into distress, harmed and repressed the masses, betrayed our fatherland to foreign imperialists, brought their invasion armies to this country, got them to commit murders, destituted hundreds of thousands of people, sacrificed innocent families to Tamil Eelamists, is now bold enough to transform our fatherland to a pool of blood by getting people shot and dead in order to suppress the wave of protests rising from all the directions of the country. [I]t may be only those who work for the sinister objectives of beastly Jayawardene and long to lick the bones thrown by him that would remain silent. (JVP communiqué, 12 October 1988, quoted in Gunaratna 1990: 290)

The rhetoric and symbolism of the LTTE is heavily focused on the figure of the dead "liberation hero," as in these words from Prabakharan:

> The death of a liberation hero is not a normal event of death. This death is an event of history (*carittira nikalvu*), a lofty ideal, a miraculous event which bestows life. The truth is that a liberation fighter (*vitulai viran*) does not die . . . Indeed, what is called "flame of his aim" which has shone for his life, will not be extinguished. This aim is like a fire, like a force in history (*varalarru caktiyaka*), and it takes hold of others. The national soul of the people (*inattin teciya anmavai*) has been touched and awakened. (Prabakharan, quoted in Schalke 1997: 79)

The martyrs of the LTTE's struggles are remembered on their own death anniversary and in the annual rituals of Great Heroes Day (Schalke 1997). The landscape of the Jaffna peninsula, at least in the years of LTTE control, was everywhere marked with memorials—in the names of lanes, in pictures and posters, even in a children's playground with toy weapons—to the martyrs.

I shall return to the moral world of the JVP and the LTTE in the closing section of this chapter. Before that I want to provide a more immediate account of the sort of environment from which the JVP emerged. Between April 1982 and October 1983 I lived in a village on the eastern border of Sabaragamuva Province in southern Sri Lanka. The village was not especially prosperous. Most of the residents were relatively recent settlers, migrants who had taken advantage of the unoccupied land in the area in order to pursue a life of wage labor, small-time searching for precious gems, occasional cash-cropping, and anything else that came along. The village elite, such as it was, was mostly composed of more established residents whose families owned the village's few paddy fields and shops. The most remarkable events of my fieldwork had occurred during the election campaigns of 1982, when the village had split into rival SLFP and UNP factions, the air fizzing with antagonism and real or imagined injustice. In the first campaign President Jayawardene was reelected, not least because his principal opponent had been stripped of her civil rights and barred from standing against him. In the second campaign, the life of the existing parliament had been extended for a full term by a referendum in which the ruling party had openly used intimidation and impersonation to gain a victory.

I left Sri Lanka in late 1983 and returned for a few months in the summer of 1984. Two days after I arrived in the village I walked into the house where I was staying to find it being searched by a police patrol who had arrested my host, Piyasena, a young man in his early twenties who had become my closest friend on my earlier visit.

Piyasena was born in the late 1950s, the fifth son of a poor but respectable sharecropper, unschooled but literate, and his illiterate wife. Piyasena's older brothers became farmers like their father, but the family quietly prospered through the 1960s: one brother received an allocation of new land on a nearby irrigation scheme, another got a steady job with the government Archaeology Department, another moved into petty trade and acquired a shop and tea-room in the center of the village. What was left over from this modest prosperity was invested in the education of the younger members of the family. Piyasena studied as a part-time student for an external degree from the University of Colombo. His younger brother had gone one better and was studying full-time for an arts degree at another unversity near the capital, and his youngest brother and sister were busy trying to acquire the exam grades to go on to university themselves.[10]

Piyasena and his siblings did more than devote themselves to their own education. They were extremely active at the local Buddhist temple, helping to organize new forms of collective village worship which, among other things, brought the village together as a homogeneous community of

Sinhala Buddhists (Spencer 1990b: 52–70). And they were strongly identified with the opposition SLFP and thus often at odds with the local bosses of the ruling UNP. In the 1982 presidential election, the main SLFP rally in the village was held at one of the brothers' houses, where it was drunkenly interrupted by the belligerent figure of the village's UNP boss. When his side had clearly won, the same man lead a carnivalesque victory procession around the village. Outside Piyasena's house they stopped to taunt him with chants lampooning the beard he had recently grown.

Piyasena was also a reader and a thinker: concerned to understand himself and his place in a world which he recognized as not merely changing but in need of change. His intelligence and capacity for self-conscious reflection made him an excellent companion for a lonely anthropologist, glad to talk to anyone who recognized his own problems of living half in and half out of this particular social world. His beard, a mark *par excellence* of the young intellectual, was one of many signs of his position as a rural modernist. I have already mentioned Piyasena's involvement at the temple. He was a committed Buddhist of pronounced rationalist leanings, eschewing the gods and demons of his parents' cosmology. I have no record of his views on the 1983 violence, which suggests that he was one of those who were lost for words at the time. But I do find a note of a conversation some time later when he was lamenting what had happened to some of his erstwhile classmates from the secondary school in the nearest town, apparently intelligent and educated young men (crucial compliments in his vocabulary), who had inexplicably acquired a taste for various kinds of unsavory activity ("bad work"; *narak väda*). The examples he quoted were drinking, shooting wild animals, and burning Tamil houses.[11]

The circumstances of Piyasena's arrest in 1984 were these.[12] I had returned to Sri Lanka at a moment of student unrest. A week earlier, students who were celebrating the end of their examinations made the mistake of celebrating too playfully too close to a new police post that had been set up, to general dismay, on the campus of the University of Peradeniya. The police opened fire; a student died. Protest quickly spread to other campuses; there was police firing, and another student died. Student and opposition leaders called a national strike of all students and school children. The government responded by denouncing the protest as the work of "terrorists" and threatening to file charges against the parents of any children who stayed away from school on the appointed day.

In the village on the morning after I arrived, mysterious graffiti had appeared, painted on walls and on the road, attacking the government and calling the president and his ministers a bunch of "murderers." The village party boss immediately filed a complaint with the police, identifying Piyasena as the ringleader. He was arrested under the Prevention of Terrorism Act, his rooms were searched, and he was taken to the nearest

town for questioning. After a pause to recover my equilibrium, I quickly followed, in the company of various friends and relatives intent on using our
combined influence to get him out of detention. After twenty-four hours,
including an especially surreal interview between the ethnographer and a
senior policeman, and the intercession of a number of sympathetic local
worthies, we eventually succeeded. Piyasena, thoroughly shaken, came
home thirty-six hours after his arrest and proceeded to keep his head down
for the rest of my stay. Under the pressure of government threats, the student protest gradually fizzled out. As far as I know, no one was ever charged
in connection with the police killings. When I returned seven years later,
Piyasena reminded me of my last words to him when I left the village in
1984: "Be careful."

This incident perfectly illustrates the role of the state in creating the
problem of "terrorism" in the 1980s. There was, for example, nothing especially new in villagers filing complaints to the police against each other. A
pattern of village *appropriation* of the state's legal apparatus for the continuation of village disputes by other means can be traced back at least as far as
the mid-nineteenth century (Spencer 1990b: 208–31; cf. Rogers 1987;
Samaraweera 1978; Wickremeratne 1970). Party politics, which had split
the village since the mid-1950s, represented a continuation of an old pattern involving the use of the courts, the police, and petitions to local admin-
istrators. What was at stake varied—in the past it was often small amounts of
land, but these were themselves tokens in a tournament of social value
aimed at establishing a claim to social position or even, in certain cases, the
right itself to be considered a member of the same moral community
(Selvadurai 1976). And, in talking about the divisive effects of party politics
on the local community, people habitually used an idiom of displaced
agency: it wasn't necessarily their own fault if two neighbors quarreled; it
was "politics" (*desapalanaya*) which caused them to fall out.[13]

Nevertheless, if politics seemed to be a continuation of an older pattern,
it also introduced irreversible changes. Political power involved some control over the increasingly important material resources—jobs, loans, sometimes even land—distributed by the state. In the late 1970s and early 1980s,
huge aid inputs (from international bodies eager to establish a positive
example of unfettered capitalism in the region) greatly increased the state's
capacity for *largesse* (Moore 1990). Those politically connected prospered,
while the everyday injustices of village argument became reinforced and
inflamed by a growing sense of distributive injustice.

The state itself was not a stable element in local politics either. Obviously
the gradual increase in the repression of peaceful protest, from the 1950s
on, played a big part in directing people toward less peaceful mediums of
protest. Similarly, the use of violence and intimidation by members of the
ruling party educated a generation of young people into the notion that vio-

lence was the only effective means of political communication. And finally, measures like the Prevention of Terrorism Act (modeled on the British legislation of the same name) introduced new possibilities and constraints into the system. One of the senior policeman explained to me on the day Piyasena was arrested, "Normally we would have released him by now, but because of the nature of the charge, we can't do that on our own authority."

Piyasena's arrest has to be viewed first of all in this context. In this village, as in many other Sinhala villages at this time, party politics had insinuated itself into the capillaries of everyday sociality, providing a medium for the working out of all sorts of animosities. Arguments based on caste or family, minor economic rivalries, all could be worked through in the idiom of local party political rivalry. But politics was not a neutral idiom. With the growth in state *largesse* in the boom years of the late 1970s, political alignment made more and more difference to someone's life-chances, or lack of life-chances, while repeated tinkering with the rules of political engagement at the national level increased the sense of political injustice at the village level.

The history of the 1984 protest is especially illuminating. The protest started on the university campuses, which had become the main source of public criticism of the government outside the secessionist North and East. However provocative their protests might have been, the brutality of the official response gave the students the moral high ground. Some of these students would have been members of the JVP, a real force in campus politics despite its proscription by the government the previous year, but the protests drew in many more young people, like those I knew in the village, who were as suspicious of the JVP as they were of the government. These young people were often the best educated, so far as I could tell, and networks of classmates and former classmates ("batch-mates" in the local idiom) from urban secondary schools served to carry plans of the protest from city to town and town to village. These, I suspect, were the networks through which the JVP consolidated its support a few years later. The government's heavy-handed crushing of the protest before it could spread—by labeling all protestors as "terrorists" and treating them as such—must also have played a part in turning young, educated people away from peaceful protest and toward more violent methods.

The issue of local justice and morality was central to the JVP's project. When the cycle of killings and counterkillings took off in the second half of 1987, one troubling aspect of the reports that reached human rights organizations outside Sri Lanka was the general sense that the state's violence was indiscriminate and immoral, while the JVP's violence, while perhaps excessive, was discriminating and, in its way, moral. As Mick Moore, who was conducting research in Colombo at the height of the JVP rising, puts it, "There developed a general presumption that, if someone were killed by the JVP, then s/he had done something which deserved punishment"

(Moore 1993: 628). Partly this was a matter of bringing to justice "bad" people—wife-beaters, thieves, and so on. But also it was a matter of bringing to justice the "right" people—the people the JVP wanted to punish *and no one else*. To a great extent, the violence of the JVP flowed along those capillaries of local political sociality I have already described. There was some symmetry in this, as other people used the apparatus of official denunciation to destroy local enemies with no special connection to the JVP, but in general the security forces tended to employ ever more indiscriminate tactics: they targeted anyone who was an opposition member, anyone who might have attended a protest ordered by the JVP, any young man in an area where the JVP had just struck. The very existence of these clandestine killers seemed to demonstrate the collapse of the government's old regime of precise information, while the apparent precision of the JVP's actions appeared to demonstrate both their power and their claims to moral superiority.[14]

When, in the middle of 1989, the JVP decided to up the stakes by announcing that it would kill the *families* of police and soldiers who continued to serve the state, two things happened. The security forces responded with a final ferocious wave of violence that broke the power of the organization, but they also seem to have finally broken the JVP's moral hold over the populace too.

ON NOT BECOMING A "TERRORIST"

The late 1980s in Sri Lanka were no time for anthropologists to be carrying out fieldwork. I returned apprehensively for my first visit in seven years in the summer of 1991 and was amazed to discover that the village in which I had lived had miraculously escaped the worst violence. Many people on both sides had been killed in the area around the village, and everyone had friends and relations who had either died or disappeared. Nevertheless, the village itself had survived, as had those friends, the young men most hostile to the government, for whom I had feared most in the intervening years. In particular, Piyasena, who had been detained as a "terrorist" seven years earlier, while as angry as ever with the government's excesses, had kept his distance from the JVP and their activities. His words on recent events (paraphrased here) provided the stimulus for this whole chapter: the two years of troubles had been like hell (*apaya vage*), he said, not like anything we recognized or expected in our own country; the JVP turned our customs upside down and attacked our culture, but the government was just as bad with so many killings. I think we may be able to see these comments as in some way parallel to my own earlier sense of interpretive exclusion at the time of the 1983 violence: Piyasena was also acknowledging the impossibility of maintaining a sense of moral community with either side during the terror of the late 1980s, despite the fact that his own history and social position might have been expected to make him a prime candidate to join the militants of the JVP.

Compare, for example, Piyasena's story with the conclusions of the Presidential Commission which reported on the causes of youth discontent in 1990:

> The ever widening disparity in opportunities for advancement between rural and urban youth captured with telling effect in the popular youth slogan, "Kolambata kiri apata kekiri" [Colombo gets the milk, we just get cucumber]; a pervasive sense of injustice "Asadharanaya" arising principally from political patronage in employment which culminates in a demoralising denial of merit; the use of the English language by the urban elite as a sword of oppression "kaduva" to deny social mobility to rural youth; and the emergence of corruption and bureaucratic apathy as major phenomena debilitating the foundations of society; have provided the ideal prescription for youth discontent which has spilt over into violence embroiling a significant section of the youth of our country. (Report 1990: viii)[15]

These were all topics on which Piyasena and his friends could argue eloquently and with real conviction and experience. To the commission's list of causes we have to add two others: the systematic closing down of alternative modes of protest in the late 1970s and early 1980s (which the commission did discuss, albeit in terms of a crisis of faith in democratic and legal institutions); and the moral force of Sinhala Buddhist nationalism, which lay at the heart of the JVP's language of "traitors" and "patriots" (cf. Moore 1993: 616–7).

Certainly Piyasena and his friends considered *themselves* the likeliest recruits to the JVP. "If anyone had started anything here, it would have been us," as his brother told me, while it was generally agreed in the village that it would have required only one action for the cycle of violence to have taken off there. The same brother was in fact asked to carry a message for the JVP, as it turned out by a plainclothes policeman acting as a *provocateur.* He refused. The younger siblings buried all their books, as any sign of education was a potential source of suspicion. In 1991 Piyasena told me that they had literally "lost" many of their friends, who had disappeared, and were either dead or still in detention—no one knew. The government, another brother chipped in, had been quite cunning (*kapati*), because those who had disappeared were the cleverest and best educated young people in the area, and thus posed the greatest long-term threat to the powers-that-be.

There is one dimension of the JVP's project which I have left undiscussed—its employment of the appeal of Sinhala Buddhist nationalism. There is no doubt that this was the factor which, at the moment of the Indian intervention in 1987, transformed the JVP into a movement of mass protest, and there is equally no doubt that Piyasena was deeply attached to his sense of his own Sinhala identity. Why, then, did he still not join these radical defenders of the nation? I can only speculate, but I think we might begin to answer this by looking at the interaction of violence and community, which in turn leads on to the question of past and present, history and memory, what has to be remembered and what must be forgotten.

Writing about violence in the Punjab, Das and Bajwa (1993) analyze two different models of the link between violence and community. In one, exemplified in the act of martyrdom, violence creates a community of common substance based upon an idiom of sacrifice. In the second, exemplified by village feuds or vendettas, violence creates a community based upon the agonistic exchange of killings in the cycle of vengeance. The world of "normal" politics in village Sri Lanka with its exchange of insults, accusations, and occasional violence, is an obvious example of the second mode, violence as agonistic exchange within the community. The world of the LTTE, with its highly developed cult of martyrdom, is an equally obvious example of the first—violence as sacrifice on behalf of the community—even if its own supporters sometimes feel uneasy with the oxymoronic model of the martyr who kills.

I suspect that the vision of the JVP was also closer to this case, an imagined community of sacrifice and martyrdom in which, paradoxically, responsibility for the violence was displaced onto those killed—those "bad" people who could be said to have deserved their punishment. To the extent that the same interpretive move was made in talk about the 1983 riots—in which the harmful actions of the Tamils *necessitated* the reluctant but just violence of their attackers—there is a parallel between the different moments of violence I have discussed so far. But the deployment of this model of violence and community in a situation predicated upon the reciprocal exchange of harmful actions had particularly devastating consequences,[16] just as the state's repressive rewriting of the rules of local political exchange had devastating consequences.

Both the LTTE and the JVP, it can be argued, trapped themselves within a present of permanent, necessary violence. Both, at different times, have confronted the possibility of real political power as the government offered major concessions. Both responded by escalating the violence, almost as if peace would deprive the movement of its *raison d'être*. In a recent article on the imagery of blood in the making of nations, John Kelly takes issue with Benedict Anderson's claim that the willingness to die for the nation is the central problem posed for us by nationalism. It's not so much death that counts, as what nationalism *says* about death: "Martyrdom stories signal an effort to force a social alignment, to force a decision about a social truth." And "it is always very difficult to argue against death stories" (Kelly 1995: 489; cf. Anderson 1991: 7). While we may feel uneasy about Kelly's apparent dismissal of the mystery of the martyr's own agency, his formulation does help us to make better sense of movements like the LTTE and the JVP. Viewed in this light, they can be seen as pursuing the politics of certainty, in which death is the mysterious but unambiguous point of reference upon which to build a moral world and a sense of community.

But the two movements seem to have differed in the extent to which they were able to externalize the source of the mystery. Although the LTTE has been a source of terror within the Tamil population, it has nevertheless directed most of its energy, most of its violence, and expended most of its martyrs in the struggle against forces which are fairly clearly "external": the Sinhala-dominated government and security forces or the Indian troops sent by Rajiv Gandhi. Until very recently it has had, moreover, the power to impose its own selective memory on the landscape of Jaffna—the martyrs are commemorated, and the traitors erased. The LTTE also speaks to a vast audience of diaspora Tamils, who bring their own politics of loss and guilt to the situation. The JVP in contrast worked within a situation where political divisions had permeated the capillary relations of everyday interaction: your political opponents would be neighbors usually, kin often, former friends sometimes. Death in these circumstances would always be a dangerous foundation on which to build a new vision of community, because one person's just death would always be someone else's unjust death.

This contrast seems to me to be now manifest in the different problems which memory poses in the North and South of Sri Lanka. Obviously the LTTE, with its constant reminder of the facts of martyrdom, is not about to deny or forget the recent history of violence and death. But even those Tamils who might prefer to distance themselves from the LTTE and its mission, in the ravaged villages of the East coast or in the refugee camps, are hardly likely to deny their own suffering, not least as this is often the one point of collective reference which can still bring people together.

In the South it is all rather different. For me as an outsider who never witnessed what happened, any return to familiar landscapes is eerie. Here, on the university campus, is the pond around which the security forces carefully arranged the heads of young men they had abducted and killed. In these villages, by these roads, piles of bodies would appear, disfigured or partially burned on heaps of tires. But there is little (so far) in the landscape to mark these events, and people seem to proceed with their lives as if nothing had happened. In 1995 the talk in Colombo was of rehabilitation as the key to any settlement, but rehabilitation was almost always taken to be a matter of bricks, mortar, and tarmac, a problem for the North and the East where the infrastructural wreckage of war was everywhere. There seemed to be some reluctance to acknowledge that there was even a need for rehabilitation in the South, where villages and towns were still standing, whatever the damage done to individuals and families in the years of violence. There people face the everyday fact of "living with torturers," to borrow a phrase from Sasanka Perera (1995).

There have been some official attempts to come to terms with the traumas of the JVP rising and its suppression. The Presidential Commission on Youth, which I have quoted, was one early response by the government. In 1991, under pressure from donor countries and human rights NGOs, the government set up a Presidential Commission of Enquiry into the Involuntary Removal of Persons—but with a mandate to investigate only cases that occurred after its establishment (i.e., more than a year after the repression of the JVP rising). The new government in 1994 created new commissions to enquire into disappearances in the late 1980s, but these have sat in closed session, with witnesses protected from publicity, and until their reports are made public, they cannot offer even the flawed catharsis found, for example, in Argentinian attempts to come to terms with recent political violence in the 1980s (Perelli 1994).

At this point we might recall Renan's dictum that "forgetting . . . is a crucial factor in the creation of a nation," especially that paradoxical feat of knowing exactly what must be forgotten: "Every French citizen has to have forgotten the massacre of Saint Bartholomew" (1990: 11). Nowhere has this been better documented than in recent historical ethnography from the Balkans (e.g., Collard 1989; Denich 1994). In his comments on an early version of this chapter, the Sri Lankan anthropologist Sasanka Perera suggested that there may be no secular solution to the problem of dealing with the divided past. In his own work, he has started to analyze people's use of possession, oracles (*anjana*, or "light-reading") and sorcery (*vas kavi*) in dealing with the grief and loss of political violence (Perera 1995: 46–55). Elsewhere in this volume, Patricia Lawrence describes the work of religious and ritual idioms in a world of torture, sudden death, and disappearance among Tamils on the East coast of Sri Lanka. There are other possible routes to symbolic resolution. Sri Lanka's Buddhists have a standard act of remembrance for the dead in which alms are given to Buddhist monks and the merit thus generated is not just transferred to the departed person, but also diffused more generally (cf. Keyes 1983). These alms-givings take place at regular, but increasing, intervals—one week, three months, a year—and then usually fade away. They are called *mataka dane*, literally "memorial gifts," and represent a way of coming to terms with death neither through its counterfactual denial, as in the aftermath of the JVP violence, nor through its oppressive remembrance, as in the cult of martyrdom which is both symptom and cause of the LTTE's entrapment within an eternal present of violence. No one, though, has yet found a way to employ such an idiom as an act of public and collective remembrance for loss on this scale.

Which leaves me with Piyasena, who opted to stay aloof from the exchange of deaths. How self-conscious an action was this? Certainly he is a very self-conscious man, dedicated in a hundred different ways to a project of scrupulous self-fashioning. When the violence subsided, he took a decision and legally changed his name, from his old name which was rooted in the specificities of caste, family, and village, to a new one which, roughly translated, meant "warrior of the Sinhala people." The word used for "Sinhala" was a very specific one, employed in the twentieth century to denote an originary Lankan people and culture, rooted before the coming of Buddhism and the distinction between Sinhala and Tamil. In that gesture, with its ironies and contradictions, we have some sense of an impossible but necessary yearning for a vision of community not based on violence.

In a recent article on political violence in India, Veena Das has lucidly summarized a theoretical argument she develops from the work of Feldman. Agency, and specifically political agency, is "not given but achieved"; it is a product rather than an author of social practice: "The very act of violence invests the body with agency—not only the body of the perpetrator of the violence but also that of the victim and the survivor" (Das 1996: 173). On this basis she reconstructs the local power relations in Delhi which could be seen, in retrospect, to create the possibilities for acts of violence: acts of violence which would, in turn, create yet further political and social possibilities, while closing off possible alternatives. So, in this paper, I have started with the general political preconditions which made what the state called "terrorism" seem the only political and moral possibility to so many young men and women of Piyasena's generation. But I have also tried to show how the use of violence had very different moral consequences in the Tamil North and the Sinhala South. These consequences can be seen, on the one hand, in the necessity for public remembrance—the LTTE's cult of the martyrs—and, on the other, in the sheer impossibility of public remembrance. But those consequences include many other actions, including, I would suggest, Piyasena's considered refusal to act.

There is, I think, an important lesson to be learned here, a lesson which connects back to my moment of radical isolation amid the rumors of July 1983. As social scientists, of whatever theoretical persuasion, we are trained to offer illumination, to provide explanations where before there was confusion, or to empathize and patiently reconstruct the coherence of someone else's moral world. To some extent this chapter has been an exercise of that sort, as I have tried to make some sense of the world of the young militants of the JVP and the LTTE. Yet I started with my own moment of incomprehension, and I have structured my exposition around Piyasena's incomprehension of both sides in the violence. What Piyasena's example can teach us is that incomprehension is not necessarily a failure: it may represent an intentional refusal to comprehend. This refusal to comprehend the moral force of the argument for violence can in turn provide the space for an intentional refusal to act. The question then would be not what was it about this person, this family, or even this village, but what was it about the agonistic exchange of violence in the South which left a space for Piyasena to insist on his capacity for incomprehension? Similar questions arise for those Tamils in the North who have also managed to maintain a distance from the imperatives of martyrdom. Rather than arguing too hastily across the moments of misrecognition or incomprehension in our encounters with violence, we may instead choose to reflect on them and learn from what they can teach us.

NOTES

For criticisms, comments, and suggestions, I am grateful to the participants at the Delhi workshop, as well as those in Bielefeld, Edinburgh, and at the fifth Sri Lanka Conference at the University of New Hampshire, all of whom patiently listened to highly preliminary versions of this paper. In addition, Sasanka Perera, Ajith Serasundera, and Veena Das provided acute comments on the written text while Elizabeth Nissan helped with characteristically wise advice on the history of human rights initiatives in Sri Lanka.

1. This section summarizes and develops the argument of two earlier papers on collective violence, where readers will find a fuller account of the place of rumor and the political context of the 1983 violence (Spencer 1990a, 1992)

2. For accounts of the violence from the Tamil perspective, see Kanapathipillai (1990) and the chilling conclusion to Selvadurai's novel *Funny Boy* (1994).

3. My point in invoking this unwieldy term is twofold: to draw attention to the structural or nonarbitrary nature of these moments of opacity and failed understanding; and to locate the reflexive element in my argument within Bourdieu's project for a reflexive sociology, rather than in the more confessional mode of much "reflexive" Anglo-American anthropology (cf. Bourdieu and Wacquant 1992).

4. The government response started with this recitation of the "just" grievances of the Sinhala people. Later speeches by ministers introduced a second theme—much of the violence was engineered by anti-State forces working in league with the separatists. See Nissan (1984).

5. See, for example, Bhabha (1995) and Spivak (1988), both of whom are commenting on Guha (1983); see also the discussion in Feldman's contribution to this volume.

6. This creation of community out of the shared need to explain or justify an act of collective violence is brilliantly explored in Amitav Ghosh's novel *The Shadow Lines* (1988). Some readers may have felt some of its powerful compulsion in their reactions to others' reactions to events like the Gulf War or the Falklands War.

7. Writing from the perspective of Tamil survivors of the violence, Kanapathipillai sounds a similar warning: "Violence homogenizes people and renders them indistinct: Kemala [a Tamil survivor] found that, regardless of her political ideology, she was identified as a Tamil" (1990: 341). This is a major problem with Kapferer's analysis of the same events, concerned as it is with "the transformation of a normally peaceful people ["the Sinhalese"] into violent and murderously rampaging mobs" (1988: 101).

8. This is broadly true of the whole post-1983 period, although in June 1995 the murder of a prominent Buddhist monk, presumably by the LTTE, was followed by the burning of Tamil shops in the southern city of Galle.

9. A great deal of evidence for this argument is collected in the *Report of the Presidential Commission on Youth* (Report 1990); Moore (1993) stresses the combination of general socioeconomic preconditions and particular political causes, especially the UNP regime's abuses of local power, in the background to the JVP uprising.

10. To some extent this educational investment paid off. By 1991 all four of the youngest children, including Piyasena, had jobs as schoolteachers in the area.

11. The burning occurred in August 1981 when UNP leaders in the area organized attacks on local Tamils in what was to be a dry run for the 1983 violence elsewhere on the island.

12. After Piyasena's arrest I deliberately destroyed what notes I had taken about the incident; the version here is necessarily a product of memory and reproduces the view from the village. Colleagues more directly involved in the events in Colombo and Kandy have different memories of what actually happened nationally.

13. This version has often been uncritically adopted by anthropologists who also speak of politics "dividing" hitherto peaceful communities (e.g., Robinson 1975).

14. One of the special features of the political structure of the early 1980s was the role played by local information in patronage transactions. What local party bosses offered up to their MPs and superiors was not a guarantee of votes—because the rural electorate was neither homogeneous nor compliant—but a guarantee of information (Gunasekera 1994: 188–9). Nobody could buy off or suppress all protests and grievances, but a successful local political boss had to be able to warn the powers-that-be exactly where and from whom trouble might be expected. The swiftness and specificity of the reaction to these events in 1984 is a good example: the party boss knew exactly who he felt was responsible and acted accordingly.

15. The commission which drew up this report included among its members the leading academic and human rights worker Radhika Coomaraswamy as well as Professor G. L. Peiris, who was to emerge as a leading figure in the successful opposition to the UNP in the 1994 elections. The report itself was remarkably independent and direct in its attribution of responsibility to the excesses of the incumbent government.

16. As indeed, it had in both the Sikh and Tamil cases, where much of the violence has been deployed against traitors within the community.

REFERENCES

Alexander, P. 1981. "Shared Fantasies and Elite Politics: The Sri Lankan 'Insurrection' of 1971." *Mankind* 12, no. 2: 113–32.

Anderson, B. 1991. *Imagined Communities.* London: Verso.

Bhabha, H. 1995. "In a Spirit of Calm Violence." In *After Colonialism: Imperial Histories and Postcolonial Displacements,* ed. G. Prakash. Princeton: Princeton University Press.

Bose, S. 1994. *States, Nations, Sovereignty: Sri Lanka, India and the Tamil Eelam Movement.* New Delhi: Sage.

Bourdieu, P., and L. Wacquant. 1992. *An Invitation to Reflexive Sociology.* Oxford: Polity.

Chandraprema, C. 1991. *Sri Lanka: The Years of Terror. The JVP Insurrection of 1987–89.* Colombo: Lake House.

Collard, A. 1989. "Investigating 'Social Memory' in a Greek Context." In *History and Ethnicity* (ASA Monograph 27), ed. E. Tonkin, M. McDonald, and M. Chapman. London: Routledge.

Das, V. 1996 "The Spatialization of Violence: Case Study of a 'Communal Riot.'" In *Unraveling the Nation: Sectarian Conflict and India's Secular Identity,* ed. K. Basu and S. Subrahmanyam. New Delhi: Penguin.

Das, V., and R. S. Bajwa. 1993. "Community and Violence in Contemporary Punjab." In *Violences et Non-Violences en Inde,* Purusartha, no. 16, ed. D. Vidal, G. Tarabout, and E. Meyer, 245–59.

Denich, B. 1994. "Dismembering Yugoslavia: Nationalist Ideologies and the Symbolic Revival of Genocide." *American Ethnologist* 21, no. 2: 367–90.

Ghosh, A. 1988. *The Shadow Lines.* London: Bloomsbury.

Guha, R. 1983. *Elementary Aspects of Peasant Insurgency in Colonial India.* Delhi: Oxford University Press.

Gunaratna, R. 1990. *Sri Lanka: A Lost Revolution? The Inside Story of the JVP.* Kandy: Institute of Fundamental Studies.

Gunasekera, T. 1994. *Hierarchy and Egalitarianism: Caste, Class, and Power in Sinhalese Peasant Society.* London: Athlone Press.

Kannangara, A. 1984. "The Riots of 1915 in Sri Lanka: A Study of the Roots of Communal Violence." *Past and Present* 102: 130–65.

Kannapathipillai, V. 1990. "July 1983: The Survivor's Experience." In *Mirrors of Violence: Communities, Riots, and Survivors in South Asia,* ed. V. Das. Delhi: Oxford University Press.

Kapferer, B. 1988. *Legends of People, Myths of State.* Washington: Smithsonian.

Kelly, J. 1995. "Diaspora and World War: Blood and Nation in Fiji and Hawaii." *Public Culture* 7, no. 3: 475–97.

Keyes, C. 1983 . "Merit-Transference in the Kammic Theory of Popular Theravada Buddhism." In *Karma: An Anthropological Enquiry,* ed. C. Keyes and E. V. Daniel. Berkeley: University of California Press.

Moore, M. 1990. "Economic Liberalization versus Political Pluralism in Sri Lanka?" *Modern Asian Studies* 24, no. 2: 341–83.

———. 1993. "Thoroughly Modern Revolutionaries: The JVP in Sri Lanka." *Modern Asian Studies* 27, no. 3: 593–642.

Nissan, E. 1984. "Some Thoughts on Sinhalese Justifications for the Violence." In *Sri Lanka in Change and Crisis,* ed. J. Manor. London: Croom Helm.

Obeyesekere, G. 1974. "Some Comments on the Social Backgrounds of the April 1971 Insurgency in Sri Lanka (Ceylon)." *Journal of Asian Studies* 33: 367–82.

Perelli, C. 1994. "*Memoria de Sangre:* Fear, Hope, and Disenchantment in Argentina." In *Remapping Memory: The Politics of TimeSpace,* ed J. Boyarin. Minneapolis: University of Minnesota Press.

Perera, S. 1995. *Living with Torturers and Other Essays of Intervention: Sri Lankan Society, Culture, and Politics in Perspective.* Colombo: International Center for Ethnic Studies.

Renan, E. 1990 [1882]. "What Is a Nation?" In *Nation and Narration,* ed. H. Bhabha. London: Routledge.

Report. 1990. *Report of the Presidential Commission on Youth.* Colombo (mimeo).

Robinson, M. 1975. *Political Structure in a Changing Sinhalese Village.* Cambridge: Cambridge University Press.

Rogers, J. 1987. *Crime, Justice and Society in Colonial Sri Lanka.* London: Curzon.

Samaraweera, V. 1978. "Litigation, Sir Henry Maine's Writings, and the Village Communities Ordinance of 1871." In *S. Paranavitana Commemoration Volume,* ed. L. Prematilleke et al. Leiden: E. J. Brill.

Schalke, P. 1997. "Resistance and Martyrdom in the Process of State Formation of Tamililam." In *Martyrdom and Political Resistance: Essays from Asia and Europe,* ed. J. Pettigrew. Amsterdam: VU Press.

Selvadurai, A. 1976. "Land, Personhood, and Sorcery in a Sinhalese Village." *Journal of African and Asian Studies* 11, nos. 1–2: 82–96.

Selvadurai, S. 1994. *Funny Boy.* London: Cape.

Spencer, J. 1990a. "Collective Violence and Everyday Practice in Sri Lanka." *Modern Asian Studies* 24, no.3: 603–23.

———. 1990b. *A Sinhala Village in a Time of Trouble: Politics and Change in Rural Sri Lanka.* Delhi: Oxford University Press.

———. 1992. "Problems in the Analysis of Communal Violence." *Contributions to Indian Sociology* n.s. 26, no. 2: 261–79.

Spivak, G. S. 1988. "Subaltern Studies: Deconstructing Historiography." In *In Other Worlds: Essays in Cultural Politics.* New York: Routledge.

Wickremeratne, L. 1970. "The Rulers and the Ruled: A Study of the Functions of Petitions in Colonial Government." *Modern Ceylon Studies* 1: 213–32.

Wilson, A. 1988. *The Break-up of Sri Lanka: The Sinhalese-Tamil Conflict.* Honolulu: University of Hawaii Press.

The Ground of All Making

State Violence, the Family, and Political Activists

Pamela Reynolds

[T]he unmaking of civilisation inevitably requires a return to and mutilation of the domestic, the ground of all making.
ELAINE SCARRY, THE BODY IN PAIN

INTRODUCTION

Prior to the democratic elections of 1994, the South African state committed systematic violence against the institution of the family among Africans.
A consequence for many people is a dramatic disjuncture between the
ideals and the experiences of family life. High mobility and state interference have made it difficult for adults to establish families in accord with
norms that approximate ideals. This, in turn, has profound implications for
the formation of identity. Here I examine individual experiences of family
life within the context of political upheaval, state oppression, and economic manipulation.[1] The experiences reported on are those of political
activists who participated in the revolt among youth against the apartheid
regime. What emerges from a close examination of the first twenty years of
their lives is the extent of disruption of their family ties and their security as
a consequence of apartheid policies.[2]

A gulf seems to exist between conventions about kin ties and actual experiences of kin relations. If, after Strathern (1992b: 6), we see kinship as a
modeling of ideas about intimate relations and human nature, then the
character of kin ties that are maintained during periods of high stress and
rapid change may inform us about these ideas. Strathern observes that
"when the places of things change in relation to one another, everything is
novel" (1992b: 7). Change in South Africa has forced apart categories that
convention held together.

There are two strong sets of models in South Africa that affect relations
among kin. One set derives from values placed on kinship that link kin ties

to the order of things both supernatural and natural. The other set derives from ideas that inform and direct state policies to do with employment, social security, health provision, housing, education, tax, inheritance, and so on, which in turn shape the nature of families.[3]

Children can fall into the cracks between convention and new permutations as the difference between social and biological parenting is renegotiated. There are profound implications for a child in the public recognition of kinship links. These include rights of access to parental care, rights to ritual attention, and rights to incorporation within communities bounded by acknowledged kin links.

To illustrate this I shall sketch the invidious position in which a Xhosa woman in Cape Town is caught. She gave birth to a son out of wedlock. The infant was not recognized by his father and not ritually welcomed into the father's set of kin. After some years, the woman married, and her husband did not want her to bring the child to live with them. The child was sent to live with the woman's mother in a rural area far from Cape Town. Recently the woman's mother sent her a message to say that the boy, now sixteen years old, has become unmanageable. He is playing truant from school and mixing with dubious company. The woman's husband refused to allow her to bring him to their home, and he said that she may not even visit him. He suspected that she would go to her son and kept watch at the main bus terminus. The woman is a nurse with a good position in a clinic. One day she left for work but went not to the clinic but to another bus terminus some distance from her home and caught the bus to the Transkei where her mother and son were living. She consulted with her kin at home, who advised her not to risk her marriage for the boy's sake, and a joint decision was made to send the child to live with kin in another city. The woman returned to her husband in Cape Town.

Because the boy was not part of his mother's husband's kin group, he was denied access to his mother. What is more, the woman's rights to care for her child were seen to be in conflict with her role as a wife. Given that the illegitimacy rates are growing and divorce is increasing (see Burman and Preston-Whyte 1992), many children fall into the vacuum between convention and actuality in terms of adults' recognition of their rights to care and of their value as members of kin groups. It may be that conventions are changing and that the value placed upon children and the rights accorded them will alter. However, ideals about kinship are still reinforced by state policies and practices among kin. The nature of kinship is flexible, modifiable, but the forces of convention are strong. Communities may fail to be cognizant of the extent to which ideas or norms are out of kilter with experience. Without cognizance of disjuncture, the cost to individuals is unlikely to be weighed. A child is positioned in relation to others. Moral obligation is limited to the circle of effective social ties (Strathern 1992a:

81). There is almost an undoing of obligations towards certain children—a decomposition of nurturance.

Strathern holds that "practices associated with conception or conjugal relations turn out to be underpinnings of the social order providing symbols of relationships that do not just make sense *in* the context of people's arrangements but make sense *of* them in their representation of fundamental values" (1992b: 6; emphasis in the original).

What sense are young people making of the values as represented in the practical arrangements in which they find themselves among kin during the years of their childhood? The young people whose experiences are reported here resisted domination by forces both outside and within families in actively engaging in political activity against the state. They contributed to shifts in meaning by taking action. "Shifting the grounds of meaning, reading against the grain, is often something done through practice, that is, through the day-to-day activities that take place within symbolically structured space" (Moore 1994: 83).

THE PARTICIPANTS IN THE STUDY

Beginning the Project

In April 1991, at the University of Cape Town, I began to explore what social means of support some students who had been political activists had drawn upon in surviving the consequences of political involvement in South Africa. Initially, I worked closely with ten students. They were not a randomly selected sample. Between them they have spent about forty years in prison and fourteen in exile, ranging from fifteen months in prison (Nomoya) to ten and a half years (Siyavuyo). Each has been beaten, interrogated, tortured, and kept for months in solitary confinement, except Enoch, who was in exile but not in prison. One of them spent almost three years in solitary confinement. They do not dwell on their awful experiences but, when asked, recount them in a matter-of-fact way. One of the ten was tortured so severely and so frequently that he attempted suicide. Another was left alone for so long that she yearned for the interrogators to come just to have contact with someone. A third was treated so badly that it took him three years to regain equilibrium while he was on Robben Island. Many of the details that follow are drawn from their accounts of their lives.

Given the time (just after the amnesty granted political activists following President De Klerk's speech on 2 February 1990) and the vulnerability of the students, their selection and the methods used in the study had to be done with care and close consultation with those who participated in the project. We explored the nature of their political activities in relation to their experiences of childhood, the character of their families, and their networks of support amongst peers and, later, comrades in political organizations. In doing so, we examined notions of childhood, the family, and parenting. This was done through interviews and group sessions, all of which were unstructured, taped, and transcribed, and through some basic questionnaires.

I interviewed each of the students individually on a number of occasions, and we met in small groups (three or four of us) and larger groups. At the end of the first year, three of them worked with me for two months interviewing students from other educational institutions and their relatives. During 1992, another two members of the original group and three students who were not participants in the project interviewed students, kin, colleagues, and some older political activists. The result was a spiraling outwards of connections among political activists, including young people at other educational centers and some older political activists. I used the method with the intention of achieving a multivocality. My view is but one among others, although my role as writer gives my voice a dominance.

By the end of 1993, the study had involved 62 people, of whom 40 were, at the time, students in tertiary educational institutions, and 22 were their kin, or mentors, or colleagues in political organizations. The analysis focuses on the 40 students. Of the 40 students, 26 are at university, 7 are at technikons, and 7 are at colleges. When we began the project, most of them had recently been released from prison, and some had just returned from exile. Some of them talked hesitantly and showed signs of the stress involved in adjustment after years of incarceration. Most grew increasingly articulate and confident during the next three years. They are members of a variety of political organizations and come from different areas in South Africa. Of the whole sample of 62 people, 43 are male, and their ages range from 20 to 60 with the majority between 20 and 40. The average age is 31.5 years. The students are linked by a network of friendship and political commitment. Their willingness to participate in the project emerges from their acknowledgment that the effects of a system of oppression on their lives and on the lives of their kin should be examined and documented.

The material upon which this analysis depends is the construction of the past by students. It is upon reflection, often in groups of peers, that the students give shape to and test out what they have lived in practice. Checks on the veracity of their histories lie in the group sessions, the fact that many of the interviews were conducted with another member of the group present, and the testimony of kin. I obtained information on and transcripts from their court trials but have not drawn on them here, as I have used pseudonyms.

I have drawn, too, on the reconstruction of the political activities of young people as represented in a burgeoning literature on the years between 1960 and the present. The focus of the project, however, is on the young peoples' construction of their experiences. It is their reflection on the forces that shaped their political commitment that interests me: this paper touches on only one angle of the study. Descriptions of their past soon exposed the flaws in the definitions proffered by social scientists of basic categories such as "the family," childhood, and parenting. For this reason reconsideration of these concepts is important here.

Questions about the Family

It soon became clear to me while working with the students that in order to describe their relationships as children with kin and other caretakers, I had to rethink descriptions of the family from the child's point of view. We know something about the ideals various societies hold about families and the nature of childhood, but there is little systematic documentation of children's experiences either in the past or present. In part this is because much of the experience of childhood is intangible and because of the paucity of our techniques for documenting children's lives. What we do know is that there must be close ties between adults and children (and between children and children) to secure the conditions necessary for the experience of satisfactory childhood. Ties between adults and children are determined, in part, by the ideal description of family relations that societies variously propagate. These ideals need to be realigned in accord with detailed descriptions of children's lives.

Over time, transformations occur in the ways that childhood is experienced, and at any one moment in history it is unlikely that policies affecting children are made in relation to accurate accounts of their experiences. Varieties of childhood patterns coexist even within one nation-state, yet decisions to do with tax, housing, education, child welfare, and other matters that shape children's lives are often made in the light of concepts to do with the nature of families and of marriage, the pattern of children's growth, needs, and expectations that, at best, reflect the situation of only some children. I suggest that there can be no transformation without description. That is to say, attempts to direct changes are unlikely to be successful unless they are founded on accurate descriptions of children's experiences in the context of other forces of change. Too often we obscure children's lives by molding our observations and designing our policies in accord with ideologies (particularly theological or political) or the experiences of people within certain strata of societies. Few of the world's children, now or in the past, live in ways that approximate the supposed norms as described by adults.[4]

Questions about Childhood

We need to recognize the extraordinary complexity of childhood as a category. Childhood is a social institution (having rule-bound or patterned natures of behavior). It is marked by stages that are often ritually highlighted. It is not biologically fixed in its details and shape. It is variable across time, across classes, and across cultures. It follows that the idea of a child cannot be fixed. Outside forces change the idea of the child: forces that include political, economic, and ideological factors.

Societies (however defined) seem to establish child-rearing patterns that differentially make sense of the way children fit with adult worlds; that set conventions to do with ways of caring for children, ideas about nourishment, rules to do with the division of labor, etc.; and that aim to offer security and adequate environments for growth. Children, however, are seldom, if ever, treated equally, and societies variously use and abuse children. Children are particularly vulnerable when a group's ideas of what a child ought to be no longer fit many children's experiences. When the integrity or sense of whole that binds adults and children breaks down, then children are exposed to the likelihood of greater harm or neglect than usual. Colonial domination, famine, civil turmoil, and war are the most obvious forces of destruction. The integrity of patterns of child-rearing are also challenged from within.

We form ideas about childhood in relation to our histories: we see children through the eyes of the past. Our ways of seeing are defined, in part, in childhood: we learn some of our affinities and our prejudices as children, and it is difficult to describe others' childhoods. As children we learn to interpret our experiences in relation to the stories we are told; to our own positions in the social structure and in the hierarchies of age and gender; to the interpretations that others (especially adults) place upon our actions; to our access (or lack of access) to resources and the uses of them; to the opportunities available to us; and so on. That is to say, we see childhood, and so interpret others' experiences as children, differently depending on our own experiences.

All societies distinguish between adults and children, but they differ in their ways of defining childhood; in their criteria for evaluating the behavior of children in different age groups; in the places assigned children in sociocultural groups; and in the ways in which the transition into adulthood is negotiated. Norms and conventions about childhood may be drawn from the dominant discourses of particular classes as presented in the media and academic formulations, so that "universals" of childhood are given an idealized, ethnocentric, and mythical tone. The wide variations in childhood experiences are not on record. The source of our knowledge about childhood is deeply embedded in the myths and sociopolitical structures of particular societies. Consider the effect on children's lives of the myth of race or the myth of intelligence tests. All of the above points suggest that in order to begin to describe the experiences of children in South Africa, we must return to the reality of practices rather than depend upon the analysis of custom (or norms).

In her important book, *Faces in the Revolution: The Psychological Effects of Violence on Township Youth in South Africa* (1992), Gill Straker worries about the negative image of black youth created by campaigns in the 1980s that were aimed at halting the devastation caused by apartheid, protecting black youth from further attacks by the state, and urging the state to put an end to violence. They were portrayed as the "Khmer Rouge generation," or "Lord of the Flies" boys; as a broken, brutal mass, though there was little hard data to justify this depiction. On the home front this image lent itself to "use and abuse by various hostile forces" (2). The state promoted an image of youth as conspirators and revolutionaries or as victims of manipulation by outside forces—with the intention of justifying its use of repressive measures. However, Straker points out, the youth involved took on none of these images, but projected themselves as freedom fighters and heroes. Her writing is based on her work as a psychologist with sixty Leandra activists ranging in age from twelve to twenty-two years who were forced to flee their homes at the time of conflict in their community and who sought sanctuary in a church center; Straker believes that the leaders or initiators of political activity by youth against the state were "highly functioning, intelligent, and socially sophisticated individuals" (21). All the youth in the Leandra group could be considered to be at risk for psychological disturbance within the purview of the traditional literature.

A follow-up study of the sixty suggested that about 50 percent manifested signs of psychological disturbance. Straker comments:

> This incidence figure at first sight seems very high, as it means that one in every two persons in the Leandra group at the time of follow up was not coping in these terms (those set by the various criteria applied). However, . . . one out of every two persons was coping against tremendous odds. Given the extraordinarily high levels of trauma this group sustained in the context of their backgrounds, which already encompassed multiple hardships, it could be argued that this figure is a testimony to the resilience of the human spirit. (1992: 35)

Straker stresses recent criticisms of the literature which traces adult psychopathology to trauma in childhood:

> Far greater emphasis is now being placed on factors which may mediate the impact of stressors on the individual. It is increasingly recognized that adverse circumstances are not experienced as equally stressful by all individuals, in all circumstances, all of the time. The actual experience of stress is dependent on the individual's assessment of the seriousness of a particular situation, as well as his or her assessment of resources available to facilitate coping with it. There is an increasing focus therefore on factors which encourage resilience (33–34).

The Question of Resilience

A triad of factors has been shown by numerous researchers to be associated with resilience.[5] The triad includes constitutional factors, the presence of supportive family networks, and an external support system (Straker 1992:

36). Straker's study unequivocally shows that the factor that best promotes survival is the opportunity for secure bonding and attachment. Survival is most easily undermined by poverty (72). She adds, "We know what facilitates the psychological development of youth and protects them most effectively from breakdown—the establishment of strong, enduring emotional bonds with consistent caretakers" (142).

I have referred in some detail to Straker's work for two reasons. First, it is one of the very few detailed studies of the young who were caught up in political conflict in South Africa. Second, I hope to contribute to the description of the factors associated with survival (they include the factors mentioned below). The effects of traumatic events must be considered in the light of the context in which they occur.

Factors Promoting Resilience

There are as I see it, five layers in the support system upon which the students drew in surviving the turmoil of the fifteen years after the killings of 1976. The first layer comprises the ingredients of each one's individuality. I shall not attempt to explain the forces that shape identities at this level. The second layer is the family. What interests me here, and is the concern of this paper, is the need to explore the range from the minimum provision of love and care that can be enough (given the interplay of other factors like individual character and communal or institutional succor) to the best available. Another concern in relation to the family is the need to acknowledge the cost and effort on the part of adults who provide nurturance to children—and not only to their own biological offspring. A third concern is the need to recognize the active part that children play in negotiating and establishing relationships with adults, that is to say, to recognize both parties of the dyadic pairs within families as having and pursuing active strategies in the process of developing and sustaining those relationships.

The third layer is that made up of the peer group and, for the children of 1976, peers were central in the formation of political consciousness and in political activities. The students moved from the peer group, especially in schools and community involvement, into political comradeship and, finally, into prisoner solidarity—the fourth and fifth layers of support. The layers are not, of course, discrete. What I want to suggest is that within communities, and between communities, it is possible to establish varieties of institutions that offer individuals opportunities to achieve adequate attention and nourishment as they grow.

It is widely said in South Africa that those who have grown up since 1976 are "the lost generation"—lost in terms of having been denied an adequate education and not having developed structures of discipline and respect that lead to responsible citizenship. The phrase insults youth and is used to screen a paucity of commitment by those with access to resources to use those resources in the interests of youth. It is dangerous in that it fosters a myth that excuses those in power from assuming responsibilities and absolves us from assessing the scale of young people's needs.

Youth in South Africa mobilized their energies using a range of tactics in relation to planned and sustained strategies that, drawn together, formed a large-scale movement. To discuss their problems as those of poverty, or unemployment, or anomie is foolhardy. They have, for fifteen years and more, created structures of support that warrant close attention. Even within families, they have negotiated and shaped relationships in accord with the sociopolitical demands of the times.

Students Talk about Their Families

However imperfectly, families acted as support systems for the students as they became embroiled in politics. We can learn from the students' interaction with their kin because their political engagement involved them in processes often stretching over years, during which time family members had to negotiate the consequences and reach decisions about censure and/or support. If we understand something of the process, we may be better able to contribute to the analysis of the forms families have taken during the tumultuous period leading up to the beginning of a new political dispensation in 1994.

The students talk about their kin in terms of respect. None blames them for having failed at all, even when care was denied, compulsion used, or important decisions made without consultation. Indeed, each talks with tenderness and admiration of those who nurtured them. It is only from interviews with their family members that one gathers some sense of the neglect and isolation that some of them suffered. The students are adults. They have each acquired a consciousness in relation to revolutionary struggle and, in doing so, have formulated a sense of individual responsibility which seems not to countenance the assignation of blame onto others.

However, some of the students came into conflict with their kin, or caused conflict among them. Malusi, for example, lived for some years with his older brother, who taught in the school he attended. He and fellow scholars organized a school boycott, which meant that he missed an exam set by his brother and, in consequence, he was beaten by his brother. Malusi's second oldest brother was also a political activist but later became a policeman, the result of which was that Malusi felt in danger even within his own family.

Another example of conflict within families comes from Thabo. He was expelled from residence at the University of Transkei for political activities, and his mother insisted that he then live with conservative kin who watched his movements closely and reported to friends in the security police.

A number of themes run through their discussion of parents and caregivers. One is their respect and gratitude for care given and attention paid despite what were often extremely difficult situations. One of their mothers admitted to having been dismissed from the cleaner's job that she had held for fifteen years at Groote Schuur Hospital because she stole food for her children. Her son did not tell me that, but he recalls having to walk home four kilometers from school in order to eat lunch and then back for afternoon classes because his mother could afford to give him only five cents for lunch, and that was too little. He remembers, too, having to wait until after the night shift for his dinner, as his mother would return with leftovers from the hospital kitchen.

When we met as a group, the students and I would select a topic on which to focus our attention. Topics included fathers, mothers, siblings, pain, betrayal, and friendship. At our first meeting, we talked about fathers. Zolile spoke first. Eight points in his talk are worth attention as themes taken up by most of the students in subsequent interviews:

> Young activists adopted protective attitudes towards their parents and treated them as if they did not know what was happening.
> Parents were drawn into political involvement despite the youths' attempts to protect them.
> They felt a sense of failure in not living up to parents' expectations, for example, that educated youth would begin to support the family once qualified.
> They experienced a growing sense of isolation, of becoming a stranger in the family, as insecurity and threats accumulated and their own behavior became more unpredictable.
> Mothers kept closer contact, demanded more information, followed events more closely as their children were drawn into political activity than did fathers.
> Fathers expected sons to assume responsibility for the consequences of their political action.
> Young activists valued the solidarity from family and community expressed in response to danger or trouble.
> They felt pain at witnessing the intense humiliation inflicted by police on their parents.

Zolile, for example, described the humiliation of his parents by the police and its effect on him. The first time he was arrested was in July 1976. The police did not inform the family of his arrest; it was reported to the family by schoolchildren. They did not know where he was being held. Zolile says that it fell to his mother "to go up and down to the lawyers, to the organizations, to the South African Council of Churches, and others to try to find [me]." She would tell Zolile's father, "He is said to be in such and such a place." But his father took no action.

While in prison before being brought to trial, Zolile was allowed no visitors. "It was only after several appearances [in court] that my father began to appear in court—to meet me." He was aware that his family was exposed to "a very, very intense humiliation from the police":

> Your mother visits you, brings you clothing or food, [she is] shouted down by the police, insulted, . . . is the one who is mostly bearing [the] brunt. She will keep on visiting you, and that's what is painful when you are . . . in detention, that element. Because sometimes you'll see, you are in court, you are behind bars, they see you when you are coming in with the van, you are taken into the cells, you are waiting there to go up to the court-room. They will be calling you down there, wanting just to get your voice and talk to you. You'll see the police dragging them, kicking them, you just see them kicking your mother, the police, and . . . [they] are very young, of your age, you know, policemen. That humiliation affects you. It's worse when you are in prisons [outside the main cities] in the '76 period, after the beginning of the whole thing. The prison authorities, the Boers, they were so rude, that if you are talking to your mother [during a visit], they just cut off everything, they push her outside, tell her to go out of the prison, and even insult her. So that affects you.

Malusi was arrested and held for three months in solitary confinement in an isolated prison. His family did not know where he was. He was severely tortured on a regular basis, and then he was moved to a prison in a small city and was able to smuggle out a message to his mother, "so she came round and brought me clothes, but they didn't allow her to see me. But when she came, she spoke, so I realized that this was her voice, so she came around to the back of the police station. I shouted. She shouted. I told her that, 'No, I'm okay and thanks for the clothes.'"

He was later sentenced on four counts to over twenty-one years imprisonment, with some sentences running concurrently, making an effective twelve-year sentence. He spent five years on Robben Island.

The students say that it was the bravery, especially of mothers, in tracking down their children, in going from prison to prison, from officer to officer, withstanding rudeness and physical abuse, in smuggling messages, in taking advantage of opportunities to write, to send food and clothing, that helped them withstand the horror of prison and the pressures to give up or give in (see White 1994). Lizo laughs in telling the story of his father's first visit to him in jail. They had not seen each other since Lizo had gone into exile three years ago. Lizo had been caught while training people in the countryside. A member of his group had informed the Security Police about their activities and their hiding place. Lizo had spent seven months in solitary confinement before he was visited by anyone from his family. His father set rules for his mother before he would allow her to visit their son. Lizo said, "My sisters came first and then my brothers. In fact my mother had to (agree to) some conditions before she could come to meet me. My father gave her some conditions because she used to cry. . . . And then she came after some time and she behaved. She never cried, although it was quite an emotional moment."

They were not allowed to touch each other. I asked Lizo if he cried, and he said, laughing, "No. No matter how you feel, you seldom cry especially in the presence of our people, because we always try to strengthen them. When they find you crying, they go back with very bad memories of you."

He said his fellow detainees refused to be defended in court because they considered that the legal system was illegitimate. The prosecutor called for death sentences, and the advocate defending the local people accused along with them was so angered that he spoke up in court on their behalf. The judge gave sentences of between twelve and eight years. Lizo was given ten.

The testimony of the students confirms that the family is vital in giving members love, trust, care, a sense of security, and a basic set of values. The students celebrate that which they received from their kin, despite having stood against the immediate interests of family members in pursuing political strategies—the consequences of which they knew to be potentially immeasurably harmful to themselves and to their families. In so doing, they reversed their roles as sons and daughters, assuming parenting roles, attempting to protect, and soothe, and comfort as if they were fathers and mothers. Their cognizance of their responsibility for pain caused was fully realized. Once the students were in deep trouble with the state, parents resumed roles of caring, but still the students attempted to shield them from full knowledge of the horror and terror that they were experiencing.

The representatives of the state, that is the police and the security police, went to great lengths to destabilize families and undermine their sense of trust and unity. Four examples will suffice.

Thabo was taken into police custody in 1986, and the police carefully covered all traces, keeping his whereabouts a secret. They placed an announcement on the radio station calling for kin to come and identify the body of a young man badly smashed in a car accident in the Ciskei, over one thousand kilometers away. Details of his clothing, possessions, and vehicle were given that matched Thabo's. His mother was preparing to leave for the Ciskei to identify what she supposed was the body of her son, when an anonymous caller at midnight told her where Thabo was being held. She alerted lawyers, who were able to secure police confirmation that he was in detention. The caller had been a prison staffer whom Thabo had persuaded to contact his mother; he is convinced that the call saved his life.

Zolile believes that police harassment caused his mother's death in 1983. Although he was serving an eight-year sentence on Robben Island, the police raided his mother's home during the night, claiming that Zolile had escaped and that they were searching for him. Zolile's mother had a heart attack and died soon afterwards. It was only upon his release from prison

three years later that he learned of her death. Prison authorities had withheld the telegram and letter that his brother had sent bearing the news.

The third example concerns a woman of sixty-four in Zululand who was
arrested for harboring "terrorists," one of whom was Lizo. The police
tricked her daughters into giving evidence against her. She was kept in a cell
alone for eleven months until after the trial. She was not treated for her
high blood pressure and was ill. Lizo explained,

> See, one thing about the system, it's very bad. For instance, they like destroy-
> ing family, you see. For instance, they took some of her daughters and made
> (them into) state witnesses against her, you see. And it was all cunning,
> because I'm sure they told them that, no, they would only be giving evidence
> against us, you see. But when they called them in the witness box, they found
> them asking many questions, less about us and more about their mother, want-
> ing to incriminate the mother and the whole thing and so on. But they didn't
> have any case against her finally, and that was why she was finally acquitted.

Lizo said that they had talked with the woman about the state's motive—"to
manipulate and break up the family"—and she forgave her daughters. She
was, he says, a very strong woman.

The final example is drawn from Sipho's story. During a night in early
1986 the security police broke into his home, beat him for two hours, and
beat his wife, who was five months pregnant. They threw her into a puddle
on the ground outside, and one officer stood with his foot on her neck while
the others dealt with Sipho. The police ruined their furniture. Then, Sipho
says,

> I was bundled into a van and given some clothes by the police. They just
> grabbed whatever they wanted to from my room, and when I got into the van
> I was just in underpants and a T-shirt, and I was wet with blood and water, and
> they gave me my wife's maternity dress. . . . [B]efore we had even reached the
> police station, the headquarters in town, it was already wet with blood because
> I was bleeding, so they took it away, so I had to battle until today I never got it.
> [O]n the second day in detention they came to my cell and refused to take me
> to CT to the doctor, but anyway they spoke in Afrikaans and made me aware
> of the fact that they have detained my wife, and the first thing that strikes you
> when you are in detention is to think about how your family is being treated
> by the police after you've been detained. Are they also arrested? If not, what
> is the situation at home, and who's going to maintain the family? Who's going
> to pay the accounts? Who's going to make groceries and all that? And that
> emotional attachment that exists within the family, is it still going to continue
> with the same spirit as before you were arrested? And if you were the core per-
> son in the family, are they going to manage without you? Then come the secu-
> rity police trying to convince you to work for them if you want to get out of this
> hell: "You just give us information and become state witness, and you are out
> one, two." It's as easy as that to them. What keeps you strong and determined

to withstand whatever befalls you is the determination, commitment, and confidence in what you struggle for. You are able to withstand or to defy the police or refuse to accede to what they persuade you to do, that is, to be a traitor against your comrades if you know what exactly you are fighting for.

Four days later he was told that his wife had lost the baby. It was three months before he was allowed to receive a letter from her: she had been permitted after a month to send food parcels but no messages, and Sipho was allowed no visitors. Her first letter requested names for the baby that was soon to be born; only then did Sipho realize that the police had lied to him.

I give these examples to emphasize the importance of family solidarity. It warranted gratuitous intervention by the police as they sought to break those held in prison.

PARING DOWN THE FAMILY

Malinowski's early definition of the family is centered on the child as object (Malinowski 1913). He said that the family is universal because it fulfills a universal human need for the nurturance and care of children. He defined the family as consisting of (1) a bounded social unit which was distinguishable from other similar units; (2) a physical location (home) where the functions associated with child-rearing were performed; (3) a specific set of emotional bonds (love) between family members (in Moore 1988: 23).

In this definition the family, the home, and the domestic arena are conflated and separated from the public sphere of work, business, and politics. Henrietta Moore (1988: 23) argues that the definition is compelling because it accords well with Western ideas about the form and function of the family. Malinowski's definition of the family has been challenged by later anthropologists, but I refer to it here because I found it useful as a tool of analysis, as described later in the paper. Analysis of family patterns has shown that there is a wide range in the composition of domestic groups and in the assignment of particular tasks of child-rearing across societies.

Moore calls our attention to the fact that not only mothers care for children, that domestic units are not necessarily built around biological mothers and their children, and that the concept of "mother" in any society is not necessarily constructed through maternal love, daily child care, or physical proximity (1988: 26). She emphasizes the point that "culture constructs the possibilities of human experience, including those of giving birth and motherhood" (28). Not every culture confines the processes of life-giving to women or the "domestic" domain alone: they can be social concerns of society as a whole. Physiology presents possibilities; it does not determine cultural elaboration (30).

State policy in South Africa as it affects the family has been formulated in relation to the definition of the family as nuclear. It describes the nature of only a segment of families in the country (which is not to say that it is not the ideal to which many more aspire). Many families aspire to different ideal family patterns, and many have been unable to establish and maintain consistent family forms in accordance with any ideal because of the terrible destruction that the apartheid system has wrought. That is not to say that families have not existed, nor even that families have not been created in accordance with accepted norms and conventions. Rather, it is to say that families in South Africa may resemble those described by Stacey (1990: 17) in postindustrial societies, where household arrangements are characterized as being diverse, fluid, and unresolved.

Whatever their character, we must acknowledge that families are groups engaged in social reproduction, as are other groups, including the typical groupings of modern industrial societies that are designated by the name "classes" (Bourdieu 1990: 75). Bourdieu believes that the most fundamental questions raised by all societies include, "those of the specific logic of strategies which groups, especially families, use to produce and reproduce themselves, that is, to create and perpetuate their unity and thus their existence as groups, which is almost always, and in all societies, the condition of the perpetuation of their position in the social space" (74).

"Belonging to a group is something you build up, negotiate and bargain over, and play for," says Bourdieu (1990: 75); for him, families participate in sets of strategies within society: "I am thinking for instance of strategies of fertility, of educative strategies as strategies of cultural investment or of economic strategies such as investing or saving money, etc.—through which the family aims to reproduce itself biologically and, above all, *socially*: aims, that is, to reproduce the properties that enable it to maintain its position, its rank in the social world under consideration" (68–9).

Matrimonial strategies (the first step in establishing new families) are written into the system of strategies of social reproduction. Matrimonial exchanges are the occasion for complex strategies. Marriages are complex operations that demonstrate the social uses of kinship. They can mobilize members of two groups as they negotiate the distribution of economic and symbolic capital. Mobilization of this sort can be traced particularly clearly among prestigious groups, but Bourdieu claims, too, that even within the laissez-faire policy of free market societies, marriage is part of the reproduction of groups. This is done in various ways, including spontaneous affinity produced from similar social conditions and conditioning, and through the effect of closure linked to the existence of socially and culturally homogeneous groups.

Family groups have to be kept going at the cost of a permanent effort of maintenance. When families' participation in social reproduction is blocked, as has happened to many families in South Africa, then the effort of maintenance is no longer made as a joint enterprise. Instead, some persons (most often women) attempt to shoulder burdens of reproduction (biological and social) that are not meant to be carried by individuals isolated from the momentum of strategic forces of reproduction in society.

There is a "patchwork quilt" of social forms in South Africa and, even in the process of responding to the forces of change, people hold onto a belief in the sanctity of certain kinds of relationships. These are variously preserved despite the power of outside forces, including strong pressures to institute a particular family form, as expressed, for example, in state regulation of the family institution.

Bozzoli (1983: 159) sees the creation of particular family forms as the outcome of class and domestic struggles, as well as of economic manipulation. She points out the need to provide analytical space for a notion of struggle to be applied to family forms in South Africa (1983: 168). We need, she says, to examine the discourse about the struggles between men and women within the family and the struggles between the family as a social unit and the wider system within which it is located. Conflicts and contradictory forces located in the "domestic sphere" are relevant to explanations of social change (1983: 144), for the outcome of these "domestic struggles" may in fact condition and shape the very form taken by capitalism in that society. It is not only that "domestic struggles" are the key to unraveling the evolving subordination of women; they also provide a crucial dimension to our understanding of a variety of other factors, ranging from the composition of the labor force to the form of the state (1983: 146–7).

Bozzoli claims that "in most cases it may be assumed that the household as an entity will adopt a defensive self-protective attitude towards external forces; but that different protagonists in the internal domestic struggle will adopt different individual attitudes" (1983: 147). She suggests that by identifying internal and external dimensions of that struggle, one has a key heuristic device to unravel the differential responses to men and women. A household can be an arena of defense against the intrusion of outside forces as well as an institution that serves those forces. Different household types possess relative strengths and weaknesses, as well as various strengths among the protagonists in particular household struggles, that influence the emergence of class hierarchies, and the places and experiences of men and women respectively (160–1).

Motherhood, Fatherhood, and Childhood as Cultural Constructions

In recent writing, fatherhood as a concept has come under close scrutiny. It is more clearly a social status than is motherhood and has widely varying rights and duties, privileges and obligations. The cross-cultural variability in the concept of fatherhood is less easily obscured by generalized notions of what is "natural" or universal than in the case of motherhood.

The concepts of motherhood and fatherhood are not merely given in natural processes but are cultural constructions elaborated differently across societies. In the same way, childhood is a variable construction. It varies historically and culturally. We cannot describe its hues without examining our notions of motherhood, fatherhood, and the family. What we in southern Africa need, of course, is a description of each of these categories that gives an account of the prevailing forces of the century: how these forces have pared down what once were elaborate family connections to the bare minimum. It is thus not possible to analyze the nature of the family without simultaneously analyzing or at least understanding the role of the state. The state, nowadays, determines where and how families constitute themselves. It does so through its legislation.

Few studies grant children an active role in determining their life paths. A central concept in the work of the sociologist Anthony Giddens is that every person is a "competent human agent." This, he says, is because "human actors routinely and chronically constitute and reconstitute their qualities as agents in recurrent processes of social interaction" (Giddens 1989: 283). And so do children.

In working with children in southern Africa I have been impressed by three facets of children's experience within families: the intricacy and effectiveness of children's strategies; the power of particular adults to sustain children's growth, that is, the importance for children of core members within sets of relationships; and the net of possibilities that societies articulate in terms of kinship for the provision of sustaining relationships. Each of the facets has, of course, a negative side which can predominate at any given time. For example, the impotence of children in the face of force, authority, and abuse; the vulnerability of central figures to poverty, oppression, ill-health, and despair; and the foreclosure of options based on class, gender, race, and so on.

Children utilize kinship links as a resource and nurture relationships that hold them fast. It is not often that a child actually chooses with whom to live, although some communities enshrine the child's right to choose with whom to live, as do the Tonga of the Zambezi Valley (Reynolds 1991a). But frequently a child negotiates close ties with a particular adult: the sustenance of the relationship is thus a two-way process.[6] Children actively participate in the struggles of individuals and households to maximize their resources and opportunities under the circumstances in which they find themselves.

Sean Jones (1990) documents the effects of the migrancy system on the family from the children's point of view. He traces the number of times a sample of children living in Lwandle hostel in the Cape have moved and notes the switches among their caretakers. He shatters the impression given by a general reading of the literature on the nature of households in rural South Africa that children lead relatively staid and sedentary existences in rural areas, albeit with only their mothers, kin, or substitute figures. Jones comments, "Our vision is thus one of absent and mobile parents, usually only fathers, and children who remain secure within the nurturing net proffered by the agnatic household or some other form of extended family grouping" (1990: 123). Jones points out two reasons for our failure to document the actual experiences of children. One is the nature of research projects that focus on people's lives at a particular time, and fail to account for mobility across time. The second is that most studies concentrate on households as basic units of analysis.

Jones (1990) traces fluctuating relations between parents and children and the lack of security in relationships built up between children and those from whom they sought succor and support. He shows that even for those children "who enjoyed relative degrees of *residential* stability over time, the quality of the relationship which they formed with significant others around them, and the relationships themselves, were clearly far from constant" (133). Sporadic separation from parents and the pain of leaving one important person to live with another play havoc with children's emotions. Parents are forced by circumstance to choose among their children, keeping some with them while parting with others. Jones finds that "it is not unusual for one or a number of siblings in a family to experience little separation from parents whilst others in the same family are isolated for long periods of time" (142).

In order to describe childhood experiences, it is necessary to trace the particulars in relation to the fluidity, fragmentation, and mobility that have characterized so many communities in the country. A redefinition of the family may be required. Perhaps the family can be defined as a cluster of relationships that is distinguished by connections across time that operate in accord with kin ties that have proved supple in their accommodation and flexible in their role allocation.

The Support Structures of Students in the Study Group

In working closely with the activists, I used Malinowski's definition of the family because I found that the three functions he defines are useful in analyzing the patterns of children's experiences within the families. Using the definition as a tool of analysis, I separated each function and examined the first twenty years of each student's life in relation to a bounded social unit, a physical location, and a specific set of emotional bonds, charted on separate diagrams. Each of the three functions he attributes to the family can have its own history. The analysis revealed that the young had to be adaptable in order to cope with series of changes in their bonding, in their places of residence, and in the nature of the social units within which they were placed.

I was able to trace the particulars in relation to the fluidity, fragmentation, and mobility as experienced by individuals. The analysis allowed for an account across space and time, and it gave a perspective on family life and the household unit from the child's point of view. Having schematized the experiences of the political activists with whom I worked most closely, I then took a sample of twenty-four from the study to explore the explanatory value of the model. The twenty-four were chosen because I only wanted data on about a third of the group for the purpose and because there were careful checks on the accuracy of the data collected from the recall of the childhood experiences of these respondents.

Table 1 gives data on the childhood experiences of twenty-four of the respondents.[7] The data is drawn from their responses to questionnaires, kinship diagrams, figures that trace their family histories (as described above), and interviews. The data are based on the interviewees' own recall. The various methods of recording allowed for checks to be made. The table suggests that most of the respondents did not experience the security of stable families over extended periods of time during the first twenty years of their lives. Given the nature of the oppressive state under which they lived, this is not, perhaps, surprising. However, there is little written material that documents the complexity of the changes that people have experienced.

Section A of the table gives details of the families in which the informants grew up. A quarter of their fathers had no formal education; 62 percent had less than a Standard Six schooling (that is, a full primary education); and 21 percent had passed Standard Eight or above. Fifty percent of their fathers were laborers, four were teachers, and one a priest with a university education. Forty-two percent of their mothers had no education; 8 percent had less than a Standard Six schooling; and 29 percent had passed Standard Eight or above. In terms of years of formal education, the women had enjoyed more than had the men. Forty-two percent of the respondents' mothers were domestic workers, and 8 percent were factory workers, while 17 percent were described as being housewives. Three were employed as teachers, one as a secretary, and another as an office worker. A range is apparent in both the education and work of mothers and of fathers.

The three middle sections of the table on Bond, Place, and Unit carry the burden of the narrative. From what they recall, respondents tell about experiences in the first twenty years of life in relation to the following: the number of bonds with a caretaking adult (usually a mother, father, grandparent or parent's sibling) that were broken because of death, illness, moves, migrancy, or marital disruption; the number of changes in places of residence experienced by the respondent as a child; and the changes in the size of the social unit (people living in the household) that the respondent experienced. These are often, but not necessarily, a consequence of the child's moving from one household to another. The changes in size of domestic unit are often dramatic: for example, the sixth respondent on the chart moved from a social unit composed of seven people to one of thirteen and then to one of only two.

The three sets of data often overlap, but they do not tell the same tale.

TABLE 1   Life Experiences with Families over the First Twenty Years: Data from Models of Emotional Bonds, Place, and Social Units

													Respondent												
	1	2	3	4	5	6	7	8	9	10	11	12	13	14	15	16	17	18	19	20	21	22	23	24
A. Family details																								
Parent's marital status	M	S[a]	M[b]	M	M	M	SEP	M	M	M	SEP	SEP	M	M	M	M	S[c]	M	WR[d]	M	WR[e]	M	M	M
Father's occupation	FAC	BUS	CHA	T	T	LAB	PRI	MEC	RAI	LAB	—	LAB	RAI	FAC	T	T	—	OFF	FAC	RAI	LAB	LAB	FAR	BUI
Father's education	4	0	0	8 (PTD)	8 (PTD)	0	10 (COL.)	6	0	0	2	0	0	0	8 (TT)	8 (TT)	—	6	0	0	0	2	0	3
Mother's occupation	DOM	FAC	DOM	DRE	T (PTD)	DOM	PRT	SEC	FAC	HOU	DOM	OFF	HOU	DOM	HOU	T	DOM	HOU	DOM	DOM	—	DOM	FD	FAR
Mother's education	5	6	8	8	8	0	7	7 (GCE, SEC)	0	6	2	8	0	0	8	8	0	6	0	0	0	3	0	0
Number of children of same father and mother	7	1	5	7	6	5	4	1	3	7	3	2	7	5[f]	8	6	4	3	4	4	1	2	8	5[g]
B. Bond:																								
Number of bonds broken with caretaking adults	0	2	3	3	4	4	5	2	1	1	1	1	1	2	2	1	5	8	4	2	8	7	6	4
C. Place:																								
Number of changes in places of residence	3	0	5	0	4	3	6	2	4	0	2	0	0	1	2	1	4	4	4	1	5	2	6	4
D. Unit:																								
Changes in size of social unit over 20 years[h]																								
First	8	3	10	9	6	7	7	3	4	10	3	4	9	6	10	7	5	3	4	6	7	9	10	7
Second	—	—	6	—	7	13	6	8	5	—	4	3	—	4	2	8	9	7	3	7	8	3	3	8
Third	—	—	4	—	7	2	7	—	—	—	—	—	—	1	1	—	3	2	4	—	3	5	3	5
Fourth	—	—	3	—	8	4	4	—	—	—	—	—	—	—	—	—	1	3	2	—	1[i]	—	3	1
Fifth	—	—	—	—	—	—	—	—	—	—	—	—	—	—	—	—	—	6	6	—	3	—	—	—

TABLE 1 Life Experiences with Families over the First Twenty Years
(continued)

	1	2	3	4	5	6	7	8	9	10	11	12	13	14	15	16	17	18	19	20	21	22	23	24
D. Unit: (continued)																								
Years spent in nuclear family	20	20	0	0	12	5	14	3	0	0	0	0	0	0	12	8	0	2	.5	20	0	9	9	16
Years spent living with father	20	20	8	20	12	5	14	3	0	0	10	0	0	3	16	8	0	8	.5	20	0	10	9	16
Years spent living with mother	20	20	20	20	12	12	15	3	17	20	20	20	20	5	12	20	7	2	15.5	20	2	18	9	16
Years spent with kin of father and mother	0	34	0	40	14	8	8	17	6	40	0	0	0	10	0	0	12	30	15	3	25	22	6	0
E. Current situation:																								
Marital status	S	M	S	S	S	S	S	M	S	M	S	S	S	M	M	S	S	S	S	S	M	S	WR	S
Own children	0	1	3^j	0	0	2	0	0	6	3	2	1	0	5	0	1^k	0	0	2	1	3	0	3	1
Composition of current household^l	5	2	3	6	8	4	7	2	11	5	4	9	10	1^m	2	1	1	1	6	1^m	5	1^m	4	1
	F/H	M/H	F/H	M/H	M/H	M/H	M/H	M/H	M/H	F/H	F/H	F/H	M/H	M/H	M/H	M/H	M/H	M/H	F/H	M/H	M/H	F/H	F/H	M/H
Number of generations in the household	3	1	2	2	3	2	2	1	3	2	3	3	3	3	1	1	1	1	3	1	2	1	2	1

NOTE: Superscript letters are as follows: a, parents never married, and the respondent never lived with either of them; b, father had five wives; c, father never lived with the respondent nor contributed to his maintenance; d, the respondent's father died before the respondent was one year old; e, father was a migrant, and his son seldom saw him; mother died when the student was very young; f, father had nine children; g, father had twenty-three children; h, reflects the changes in the number of people in a household during the first twenty years of the respondent's life; the data do not reflect how many of the members of the household changed, but the changes usually represent different casts of characters each time as a child is sent from one household to another; i, as an adolescent, this person spent a year living in a migrants' hostel in order to be close enough to a school to walk to and fro; he had no kin in the hostel; j, the respondent had three children while he was in exile; k, this respondent gave birth to a child in 1993, but the child died a few weeks later; l, gives the number of residents in the current household (1992) and whether or not the household is headed by a female or a male; and m, these respondents cannot return home as they feel under threat in their home areas: one from the State Security forces, one from residents who hold political allegiance different from his, and one from a variety of forces that are targeting political leaders.

ABBREVIATIONS: M, married; S, single; SEP, separated; WR, widower; DOM, domestic worker; FAC, factory worker; BUS, businessman; CHA, chauffeur; T, teacher; LAB, laborer; PRI, priest; MEC, mechanic; SEC, secretary/secretarial courses; RAI, railway worker; HOU, housewife; DRE, dressmaker; OFF, office worker; FAR, farm laborer; FD, farm domestic; BUI, builder; GCE, General Certificate of Education; PTD, Primary Teacher's Diploma (or equivalent); PRT, preschool tacher; TT, teacher training college; COL, college; F/H, female-headed household; and M/H, male-headed household.

For example, the fourth child on the table experienced three breaks with caretaking adults, yet she never changed her residence. Only dramatic changes are likely to have been remembered. I shall draw out some of the data to demonstrate the extent to which children had to deal with the flux in their relationships and change in their home bases.

> *Bonds:* Only one child (4 percent of the sample) had no break with a caretaking adult, while 23 (96 percent) had one or more breaks. Ten people (42 percent) had four or more bonds broken in the first twenty years (a broken bond means either a final break, caused, for example, by a death or a divorce, or a break lasting many months or years, as when a mother or a father migrates to a city in order to work).
>
> *Place:* Five (21 percent) of the respondents did not change their places of residence, while twelve (50 percent) moved three or more times.
>
> *Unit:* Five (21 percent) lived in more or less the same social unit for twenty years, while nineteen (79 percent) had from one to five changes in the size of their units. Nine (38 percent) of them had four or five changes.

The last four rows under section D detail the years that respondents spent living as part of nuclear families; years spent living with their fathers; with their mothers; and with kin—fathers' and mothers' parents and/or siblings. These figures add to the description above of children having to cope with changes in their bonding with kin. Ten children (42 percent) never lived in nuclear families (with father, mother, and siblings), and only two (8 percent) lived in nuclear families for all of their first twenty years. Eighteen (75 percent) of the informants lived for ten years or less in nuclear families. If all the years spent in nuclear families are added up, then we see that only one-third were spent thus. If policy decisions are taken on the assumption that children usually spend most of their growing years in nuclear families, then the decisions are in danger of attending to the needs of less than a third at any one moment. It is, of course, not necessary for children's stability that they live in nuclear families, but closer examination of time spent in extended or compound families shows that these barely exist as stable units over time. For example, only three of the subjects spent more than half their time as children with a set of grandparents: respondent number two never lived with her parents but spent seventeen years with her mother's father and mother; respondent number four spent twenty years with his father, mother, father's father, and father's mother—the only child who lived in a fully-constituted extended family for a long period; and respondent number ten lived for twenty years with her mother, her mother's mother, and her mother's father.

The row on years spent living with father shows that eight children (33 percent) never spent a long period of time with their fathers and that only three (13 percent) spent all of their childhood years with their fathers. Fifteen (63 percent) spent less than half of their years living with father, and 38 percent more than half. The row on time spent with mothers tells a different story. Nine respondents (38 percent) spent all twenty years with mother, and only one never lived with her. Seven (29 percent) spent less than half of their years living with mother, and seventeen (71 percent) spent more than half—a mirror image of time spent with father.

The final row under Section D shows how many years the informants lived with their grandparents and/or the brothers and sisters of their parents. The figures are a composite. I shall make four observations about the details that go into this composite.

1. Of the total number of years spent with grandparents, 64 percent of the years were spent with grandmothers and 36 percent with grandfathers.
2. Of the total number of years spent with parents' kin, 67 percent of the years were spent with mothers' kin and 33 percent with fathers' kin.
3. Sixty-eight percent of the years were spent with female kin of the fathers and mothers, and 32 percent with their male kin.
4. Few of the informants spent long periods with their parents' kin, yet eighteen (75 percent) lived with kin other than parents for part of their childhood.

The picture that emerges is of women caring for children—mothers and mothers' kin. Twenty-five percent of the informants' first twenty years were spent with grandmothers and 15 percent with other female kin of parents: that is, 40 percent of their years were spent with parents' female kin (not necessarily without the presence of their parents). So children need kin of older generations to support them, and parents need their parents and kin of their own generation to help bring up their children. While this may seem obvious enough, it is the fragmentation of care, the fact that caretakers seldom look after children for the bulk of those children's years in a situation of security and interdependence that is not so obvious unless the details of children's experiences are documented (see Kotze and van der Waal 1995 on insecurity and mobility among children in two areas of the north of South Africa).

The last section of the table, E, is on the current situation of the informants. It shows that seventeen (71 percent) are single, six (25 percent) are married, and one (4 percent) is a widow. Yet thirteen (54 percent) have children. Six do not see themselves as members of households, eight belong to male-headed households, and ten to female-headed households. Despite the fact that their average age is 31.5 years, there is no clear pattern of marital stability. Three informants live with their spouses only, and another three live with their spouses and their children only; six live alone; and twelve live with a variety of kin. Nine (38 percent) live only with others of the same generation; seven (29 percent) live with kin of two generations; and eight (33 percent) with kin of three generations. This section suggests that the flux and complexity which characterized their childhood years may be continuing in their adult years. Whether or not this is a consequence of their involvement in political activity, years of imprisonment, and delayed tertiary education can be determined only later.

Concluding Discussion of Data in the Table

Let us draw from the table the worst scenario and the best scenario.

The best scenario: Among the respondents,

4 percent had no breaks with their primary caretakers,
21 percent experienced no change of residence,
21 percent lived in the same social unit for their first twenty years,
8 percent lived in nuclear families,
13 percent lived with their fathers for most of their childhood years,
38 percent lived for over half of their childhood with their fathers,
38 percent lived all their years with their mothers,
71 percent spent over ten years living with their mothers, and
25 percent spent over ten years with any one of their parents' kin (that
     is, as a consistent caretaker).

The worst scenario: Among the respondents,

96 percent experienced one or more breaks with caretaking adults,
42 percent had four or more breaks in their bonds,
50 percent changed residence three or more times,
79 percent had one to five changes in their social units,
42 percent never lived in nuclear families,
75 percent lived in nuclear families for less than half of the time,
33 percent never lived with their fathers,
63 percent lived for less than half of their time with their fathers,
4 percent never lived with their mothers,
29 percent lived for less than half of their childhood with their mothers,
     and
75 percent lived with parents' kin for some of their childhood years, but
     all of these for less than half of those years.

The best scenario is not very good; it includes many indications of instability and absence of consistent care. The worst scenario shows children on the move between caretakers, between residences, and among sets of household members. I do not intend that this description of people's own recall of their first twenty years should be an exercise in bewailing the breakup of the family. *Indeed, it seems to me that many adults make superhuman efforts to stay married, work for their children, establish homes for their children, keep contact with their children, and ensure care of their children despite powerful destructive forces that militate against the establishment and maintenance of families.* The South African state consistently and severely undermined the ability of people to form and nourish families over time. Ensuring the best interests of children depends upon the existence of infrastructure and services that enable people to attend to those interests.

ANALYSIS OF SURVEY RESULTS

I began to model the experiences in families of political activists with whom I worked closely. Then I applied the model to data from a sample of twenty-four. Finally questions were asked of data collected from 8,800 households across South Africa during the first South African Project for Statistics on living Standards and Development, conducted under the auspices of the International Bank for Reconstruction and Development (IBRD) and the South African Labour and Development Research Unit (SALDRU) from August to December 1993.[8] Pieter Le Roux (1994) computed data from the survey in accord with questions concerning parental presence in households, and the difference between racial groups, gender, rural and urban areas, etc. We asked what proportion of young people in each of these different circumstances were in the care of both parents, what proportion had only one parent present, and what proportion were in a household where neither parent was there. The composition of the households was analyzed; for example, an analysis was made of the proportion of households that consist of nuclear families or of families in which there are only mothers and no fathers.

Two sets of figures were extrapolated: one was on membership of households and the other on actual presence in households. The first was termed *de jure* membership and the second *de facto.* People were included, in the survey, as members of households if (1) they lived under the same "roof" or within the same compound/homestead/stand at least fifteen days of the preceding year and (2) shared food from a common source when they were together and (3) contributed to or shared in a common resource pool. Thus, the parent who is a migrant worker and is home only fifteen days a year should be included as a member of the household. On the household roster the question was asked whether each member of the household had been in the household for fifteen days of the preceding month. If not, a person was excluded from the rest of the survey, and not considered to be a *de facto* member of the household. Many people considered to be members of the household were actually absentee fathers, husbands, brothers, and, at times, mothers, wives, and daughters. Many were away from the households as migrant workers.

Just over half of all children in the sample were recorded as having both parents as members of the household (*de jure*). Of Indians and whites,[9] 87 percent were reported as having both parents in the households, while only 48 percent of African members up to the age of eighteen years were reported as having both parents in the households. When parents who had not been home for more than two weeks in the month prior to the survey were excluded, the figures changed dramatically: both parents were *de facto* at home in the case of only one-third (34.36 percent) of African children. Migrancy affects only a very small proportion of white and Indian children, and in the case of those classified as colored, the effect is much smaller than in the African case (children with both parents present drop from 68.82 percent to 58.66 percent).

The above data confirms the findings based on the sample of twenty-four, namely, that only one-third of their first twenty years were spent living with both parents. It was only in framing pertinent questions and then extrapolating details from the survey data that the actual presence of mothers and fathers in children's lives was given. The national census does not show if a child is living with his/her mother and/or father. It seems likely that, as a result of this analysis, the next census will.

It is worth emphasizing points having to do with methodology here. A model of a child's experiences within a family was initially formulated on the basis of close examination of ten students' experiences. Confirmation of the descriptive powers of the model was sought in applying it to a sample of twenty-four. Finally, survey data based on over eight thousand questionnaires was extrapolated and the results confirmed the initial description.

CHILDREN AND SYSTEMS OF SOCIAL ACCOUNTING

There is a dearth of statistical data about children. Even in Europe, children are not visible in systems of social accounting. Jensen and Saporiti (1992: 9) suggest that children must become the objects of special focus, the unit of observation. Children are typically represented by adults, most often by parents. "Changing the statistical unit from 'family,' 'household,' 'mother,' 'father,' etc. into *child*, also changes the ideas of the phenomena discussed." The two authors are concerned to link children to a generational perspective, as much data on children concerns only children, so that it is difficult to compare other ages on living conditions. They observe that "the lack of comparable data of the whole generational span supports a public ideology of children as a private responsibility. Such a privatisation of children's living conditions may conceal systematic biases when compared to other population groups; and at the same time, it represents a barrier against public discussion" (Jensen and Saporiti 1992: 10). Without taking children as the unit of observation, it is difficult to visualize their contributions to society and to families. Jensen and Saporiti illustrate the difference that taking children as the focus of statistical analysis makes to measures of household composition, migration figures, labor, and family size. They argue against the common perception of children as receivers of adults' services, money, and time. The declining childhood population, a biased distribution of resources between generations, and the invisibility of children's contribution may all illustrate that children occupy a marginal position in industrialized societies (1992: 66). The situation in a country like South Africa is unlikely to be better, although the childhood population is not declining dramatically, as it has recently done in Europe. It is clear from what has been said so far that the nature of families, of households, and of resource distribution is not, for some sectors of the population, accurately described and that children remain, to a large extent, invisible.

CONCLUSION

The effects of state violence against the family in South Africa have been to disrupt ties between adults and children and between children and children. The extent of the disruption for some people has been documented here. The demands placed on the young to negotiate loss and separation are enormous. Veena Das (1992: 390) points to the writings of Bowlby (1980) and Lipton (1967), who suggest that death, loss, and separation are psychically interchangeable.

In order to describe the experiences of the young in families, we need alternative models for the analysis of the family. Moore (1994: 87) examines alternative models for the analysis of the household based on contracts, bargaining, and negotiation. In these situations, questions of power and ideology become prominent. The new focus is a response to the recognition that the outcome of bargaining and negotiation is determined not only by economic factors but also by socially and historically specific views about the rights, responsibilities, and needs of particular individuals. Bargaining power, she argues, is significantly affected by membership in certain demographic groups. I have suggested in this paper that children do have bargaining power in families, and that some manage to secure adult attention and care despite disruptions in relationships, changes in the composition of household units, and high mobility among family members. The young with whom I worked were conscious of the effects that their political activities had on their families, and they carry with them both a deep sense of the value of their kins' support, especially their mothers', and feelings of guilt at having exposed them to the awful intrusion of the state's security forces. Membership in families is not assured for some children, and their ability to negotiate is therefore curtailed. Given that the state offers services and designs infrastructure around the notion of secure nuclear families, the lack of membership undercuts many children's access to social and political security. Given the absence of statistical data on children's experiences and the lack of adequate description of families from their points of view, any attempts to improve the situation of the young will be hampered.

Finally, I agree with the philosopher Martha Nussbaum, who supposes "that the capacities of children, rather than the institution of the family itself, are what society is committed to supporting" (Nussbaum 1992: 48).

NOTES

1. I acknowledge with thanks funds received in support of this project from the University Research Committee of the University of Cape Town and the Family and Marriage Co-operative Programme of the Human Sciences Research Council of South Africa. I thank Lesley Fordred for editing the manuscript. One section of the paper appeared in *Children and Families in Distress: Working Papers*. Pretoria: HSRC, 1993.

I am deeply grateful to the students (and to the scholars and older people) who worked with me on the project. The lives of some of them are, at the time of writing, under threat, and so I cannot acknowledge them by name. The names in the text are pseudonyms.

2. In this paper I take the essence of the family to be kinship relations; thus I sometimes overlap the use of the terms.

3. Here is an example drawn from the definitions of the family used in determining policies to do with housing. Implicit in the approaches to mass housing provision in South Africa is a "model" based on a house on its own, however humble, on its own plot, in a "properly planned" township (Spiegel, Watson, and Wilkinson 1994: 6). Housing needs have been conceptualized in terms of a series of unexamined assumptions about the population. Need is defined as the number of units required to provide for a population of hypothetical "average" or "standard" households. The de Loor Task Group, formed in 1990, shaped the new framework for a national housing policy. Underlying the basic vision is the concept of "essentially nuclear families occupying their own, fully serviced, four-roomed houses in stable, permanently settled communities." According to this vision, housing consists of

> a formal house providing separate living quarters for parents and children and separate living quarters for children of different sexes once this becomes necessary. The concept must be further expanded to provide [for] private ablution facilities and facilities for the preparation of food. The structure itself must also provide adequate protection against the elements, protect the privacy of the inhabitants, provide for security of tenure, and allow for integration into a system of housing which in fact relates to the evolution and development of viable communities. . . . In these shelters, the family/household must at least have access to potable water, sanitary facilities, energy, and refuse disposal. (quoted in Spiegel, Watson, and Wilkinson 1994: 7)

The nature of the family or the household is not addressed explicitly in the report. "Intentionally or otherwise, however, the Task Group appears to have equated the 'normal' household with the nuclear family, and this enables it to translate projected population growth unproblematically into the anticipated demand for new housing, simply by dividing the population growth figure by a hypothetical or statistically derived 'average' family size—six in the case of the african [*sic*] population" (7).

4. I use the word *child* to refer to anyone under the age of eighteen, following the United Nations' definition, and the word *youth* to refer to anyone in that period between childhood and adult age. I have not attempted to define the line between a child and a youth because the actions of political activists blur the differences.

5. The term *resilience* is widely used in reference to young people who cope with trauma. I dislike the term, as it suggests a passivity—a boxer's punching bag—and would prefer a term that suggests agency, such as *determination* or *courage*.

6. I have written about these kinds of bonds among the Tonga (Reynolds 1991a) and the Zezuru (Reynolds 1986).

7. Twenty-one of the 24 respondents are students—15 at universities and 6 at colleges, including technical colleges. Their average age in 1992 was 31.5 years. Their ages ranged from 20 to 40, with 76 percent aged between 25 and 35 years. The other 3 respondents are women in their fifties: like the students, they are political activists, and they are also close relatives of young activists. Two-thirds of the sample are men.

8. The first report is entitled "South Africans Rich and Poor: Baseline Household Statistics," published by IBRD and SALDRU, 1994.

9. The classifications as used by the former government are still employed in the collection of statistical data.

REFERENCES

Bourdieu, P. 1990. *In Other Words: Essays Towards a Reflexive Sociology.* Tr. M. Adamson. Cambridge: Polity Press.

Bowlby, J. 1980. *Loss, Sadness and Depression.* Vol. 3. *Attachment and Loss.* New York: Basic Books.

Bozzoli, B. 1983. "Marxism, Feminism, and South African Studies." *Journal of Southern African Studies* 9, no. 2: 139–71.

Burman, S., and E. Preston-Whyte. 1992. *Questionable Issue: Illegitimacy in South Africa.* Cape Town: Oxford University Press.

Das, V., ed. *Mirrors of Violence: Communities, Riots, and Survivors in South Asia.* Oxford: Oxford University Press.

Giddens, A. 1989. "A Reply to My Critics." In *Social Theory of Modern Societies: Anthony Giddens and His Critics,* eds. D. Held and J. B. Thompson. Cambridge: Cambridge University Press.

Jensen, A-M., and A. Saporiti. 1992. *Do Children Count? Childhood as a Social Phenomenon: A Statistical Compendium.* European Centre for Social Welfare Policy and Research. Vienna: European Centre.

Jones, S. W. 1990. "Assaulting Childhood: An Ethnographic Study of Children Resident in a Western Cape Migrant Hostel Complex." Master of Arts Thesis, Department of Anthropology, University of Cape Town.

Kotze, J. C., and C. S. van der Waal. 1995. *Violent Social Relationships and Family Life in Two Transvaal Lowveld Settlements.* Pretoria: Human Sciences Research Council.

Le Roux, P. 1994. "Parental Care and Family Structure: Some Interesting Findings from the SA Living Standards Survey." Unpublished paper delivered at the *Living Standards and Survey Workshop,* 8 December, SALDRU, University of Cape Town.

Lipton, R. J. 1967. *Death in Life: Survivors of Hiroshima.* New York: Random House.

Malinowski, B. 1913. *The Family among the Australian Aborigines.* London: London University Press.

Moore, H. L. 1988. *Feminism and Anthropology.* Cambridge: Polity Press.

———. 1994. *A Passion for Difference. Essays in Anthropology and Gender.* Cambridge: Polity Press.

Nussbaum, M. 1992. "Justice for Women!" *New York Review,* 8 October, 43–48.

Reynolds, P. 1984. *Men without Children.* Second Carnegie Inquiry into Poverty and Development in Southern Africa. Cape Town: University of Cape Town.

———. 1986. "Concepts of Childhood Drawn from the Ideas and Practice of Traditional Healers in Musami." *Zambezia* 13, no. 1: 1–10.

———. 1991a. *Dance Civet Cat: Child Labour in the Zambezi Valley.* London: ZED Press.

———. 1991b. "Children of Tribulation: The Need for Healing and the Means to Heal War Trauma." *Africa* 60, no. 1: 1–38.

———. 1991c. "Youth and Trauma in South Africa: Social Means of Support." Paper delivered at the International African Institute Conference on Healing the Social Wounds of War, Windhoek, Namibia.

Scarry, E. 1987. *The Body in Pain: The Making and Unmaking of the World.* Oxford: Oxford University Press.

Spiegel, A. D., V. Watson, and P. Wilkinson. 1994. "Domestic Fluidity and Movement Patterns among Cape Town's African Population: Some Implications for Housing Policy." Paper delivered at the Africa Seminar, Centre for African Studies, UCT.

Stacey, J. 1990. *Brave New Families: Stories of Domestic Upheaval in Late-Twentieth-Century America.* New York: Basic Books.

Straker, G. 1992. *Faces in the Revolution: The Psychological Effects of Violence on Township Youth in South Africa.* Athens: Ohio University Press, and Cape Town: David Philip.

Strathern, M. 1992a. "Parts and Wholes: Refiguring Relationships in a Post-Plural World." In *Conceptualising Society,* ed. Adam Kuper. London and New York: Routledge.

Strathern, M. 1992b. "Unanticipated Contexts: The Representation of Kinship in the Context of the New Reproductive Technologies." *BASAPP Newsletter,* no. 11 (spring): 5–7.

White, H. 1994. *In the Shadow of the Island: Women's Experiences of Their Kinsmen's Political Imprisonment 1987–1991.* Pretoria: Human Sciences Research Council.

Violence, Suffering, Amman

The Work of Oracles
in Sri Lanka's Eastern War Zone

Patricia Lawrence

THE EXPERIENCE OF VIOLENT CONFLICT IN EASTERN SRI LANKA

Days in eastern Sri Lanka's coastal plain begin at first light with the distinct sound of reed rakes rhythmically combing the sandy surface of each household's compound, effacing footprints and entrances to ant tunnels, and erasing marks of the confluence of activity from the day before. Now, during the long "problem times" (*piraccanai nṭkal*), the staccato of hovering chopper blades competes with women's steady raking and the early morning creaking of well-sweeps in this matrilocal region of South Asia. A day is as likely to begin with the sound of shelling, approaching army vehicles, or the resounding explosion of a land mine followed by the crackle of gunfire. Militant and security forces operations have left many houses in ruins throughout Paduvankarai, a fertile, paddy-cultivating area on the western side of the lagoon. Paduvankarai, as its name implies, is the land over which the sun sets—the "sunset shore." For all the families, times are indescribably hard there in this fifteenth year of civil war. Sri Lankan Air Force operations and long-range shelling are intrusions they must contend with, for their villages and hamlets are close to the jungle. Still, women in Paduvankarai adhere to the Tamil adage: *Pularvu mun alaku eṭu,* "Before the dawning, take the rake." Day-to-day life must go on even as the chaos and destruction of war continue.

Villages inside the military boundaries that cordon off Sri Lanka's eastern region from the rest of the island state have become sites of repeated retaliation killings. Ordinary Tamil families caught in the prolonged struggle between the Liberation Tigers of Tamil Eelam (LTTE), fighting for the establishment of a separate state, and government security forces drawn from the Sinhalese majority population, must face violence and death as a

171

part of their everyday existence. No single militarized group has been able to maintain stable control of any particular part of the eastern war zone, so families cannot simply work out a modus vivendi with the forces of oppression. Instead, noncombatants find themselves in the impossible position of facing conflicting, life-threatening demands from the various arms of the Sri Lankan security forces, paramilitary forces, and LTTE in their day-to-day lives.[1]

During the advance of the Sri Lankan army into the eastern region of the island in 1990, the entire civilian population of the village of Vellaveli was displaced. On the afternoon when the ground and air attack on Vellaveli began, the people panicked and ran, scattering through the rice fields and fleeing down the road toward the Periya Porativu Kali temple without carrying anything, running for their lives. At first, most of the displaced people stayed as refugees in the Periya Porativu Kali temple, surrounded by the security forces, although some who sought safety inside the temple were extrajudicially executed by the security forces during the first weeks of displacement.

After the demoralizing transformation of Vellaveli, only fourteen homes were left standing, while the rubble of the rest of Vellaveli's shelled homes was used for construction of a thick wall of medieval appearance around the area controlled and occupied by the security forces. The large Vellaveli school was burned, and what remained was converted into barracks. All of Vellaveli's public offices were destroyed. The rice fields around the Mariyamman temple were mined. Vellaveli became a government security force's camp.

It is widely surmised that Vellaveli was targeted in 1990 because it was considered a "Tiger village." Vellaveli was the natal village of an LTTE leader named Reagan, who, with other members of an LTTE strike unit, summarily executed twenty-nine Sinhalese Buddhist priests and two civilians in an attack on a bus near Aranthalawa, Ampara District, on 2 June 1987. The "Aranthalawa massacre," as it came to be known, was an event of violence that made clear the LTTE's capacity for ruthless action. It is less widely known outside the eastern war zone that after the Aranthalawa killings, a Special Task Force unit of the Sri Lankan security forces retaliated by ordering Reagan's family members to stand before them in their Vellaveli homes, and after reading their names from a list on a piece of paper, shot them to death and dismembered their bodies.[2] Two years later, as the intense violence of Eelam War II began, Tamil bodies were burned at junctions and in paddy fields in the eastern region—then as the government's configuration of army, police, and Special Task Force camps was put into place in the east, Tamil bodies were burned on tires inside several detention camps as well. After the ground and air attack on Vellaveli in 1990, the village's residents dispersed into at least seven locations in Paduvankarai and to the outskirts of Batticaloa town.

Vellaveli's recent history is but one case which demonstrates that, in the villages of Sri Lanka's eastern war zone, one violent event leads to the next in the perpetuation of loss of life and the destruction of social habitat. The list of villages which have been marked as sites of retaliation killings in the island's eastern region is long. The victims need not be active participants in the fighting, yet serve as targets for retaliatory violence because they belong to a particular place and are perceived as embodying a particular identity. National identity cards are required for passage through the plethora of security forces' checkpoints in Sri Lanka. The provision of the name of the individual's village on national identity cards may be sufficient to provoke arbitrary arrest and abusive treatment under the Prevention of Terrorism Act and Emergency Rule.[3] After tens of thousands of deaths and "disappearances," ordinary Tamil people perceive their lives as inextricably subjected to relations of power over which they have no control.

PALUGAMAM: WHAT A VILLAGE HAS BECOME

About three miles northeast of Vellaveli, the village of Palugamam waits out the war, clustered around its temple for the goddess Tiropataiyamman. Slightly more than one-third of Palugamam's population remained after the mass exodus from the area in 1990. By 1994, an estimated 150 people of the village had been killed or "disappeared" in the fighting. Recounting the assassination of the head of the village council along with the names of other residents of Palugamam, several elders admitted that they had lost access to any political voice that could help them gain control over their future. "Now," they assured me, "politics means killing."

The clay or plastered walls of almost every house in Palugamam had scars from shooting and shelling, and as I entered more and more houses in the beginning of my fieldwork, pointing out this evidence seemed part of the ritual of being received. I interpreted this as a collective message from the people who were still living in Palugamam—a message which described what a house has become. When I initially asked the mother of the first matrilocal household cluster where I lived if I could stay with them, she took me into the kitchen and showed me the space underneath the waist-high concrete hearth. "We stay here when there is shooting." Family members had spent whole nights crouched together under the hearth. In the center of the village, houses have large chunks of plaster gouged from the walls of the entry room where guests are received. The Sri Lankan army drove armored cars through the center of Palugamam, firing into homes on both sides of the narrow sandy lanes. Few people were in their homes during the attack, as it is the practice of people in Palugamam to take refuge in their temples.

Bullet scars on houses in Palugamam have many sources; the damage is not all attributable to the Sri Lankan army's invasion in 1990. In the late

1980s the Indian army, remembered for the inscription of violence upon women's bodies, established its presence. Palugamam was selected as a site for a military camp because the stands of mangroves along the edge of the lagoon are so thick that bullets can't reach cadres hiding inside them. Internecine battles between different armed Tamil organizations then filled the narrow, sandy lanes of the village as one group of Tamil cadres replaced another. Camps of several arms of the Sri Lankan military apparatus have been constructed and dismantled and reestablished in a long succession of violent events carried out by militarized forces. With each intrusive effort to control the village, a renewed experience of extortion, arrests, and interrogation practices beset the people. In 1994 the army was replaced by the Special Task Force (a division of the police). At this writing, Palugamam is once again defined by the government as an "uncleared area," or an area under the control of the LTTE, destined to become again a site for state "clearing operations" (Thangarajah 1995: 214).

THE STRANGENESS OF THE ORDINARY
IN A WORLD ALTERED BY VIOLENCE

Survivors' narratives disclose the manner in which they are forced into vulnerable positions and experiences of loss of trust in the immediate world. Deaths in the paddy fields and deaths of paddy farmers in the prisons and military camps were everyday occurrences in the first years of the 1990s.[4] Those arrested in the fields were often taken away blindfolded. One day, seven of those killed were women who were bathing by a well. I asked "Why did they shoot them?" The answer: "The people here are frightened. When the people hear a gunshot they start running. The army sees that, and thinking they are 'Tigers,' they shoot at them." Since the late 1980s there has been very little income-producing work in the village. To be involved in lumber or firewood implied involvement with the LTTE because the Tigers control the inland forest zones.

Kumaravelu, a member of Palugamam's *Attiyānār kuti* (a high-ranking Velalar matriclan), eighty-four years old some days and seventy-four others, was a paddy farmer who held a prestigious position in the village Tiropataiyamman temple. He was also a local healer who had committed many healing verses to memory. I asked him for his views on the war in 1992, a time when there were successive deaths in the village and the immediately surrounding hamlets. In a loud voice he offered, "We are paddy farmers, and we can't farm the paddy. Sometimes, when we are just sitting around talking, we say the best thing would be if one big bomb would come and kill all of us at once." His statement was not a death wish but a comment on collectively experienced grief within the close kinship nexus of Palugamam. During some growing seasons, the LTTE ordered village farmers to cultivate their fields, an endeavor which had become life-threatening. In the first half of this decade, many rice fields were burned by the security forces before harvest throughout the coastal plain. Kumaravelu's complaint came at a time when the security forces had implemented plans designed to prevent rice cultivation, as well as transportation and sale of the harvest, so that the crop could not benefit the LTTE.

During harvest seasons in eastern Sri Lanka it is quite common to see farmers who were still trying to grow paddy pouring out sacks of rice onto the ground at one military checkpoint after another. In this manner, the security forces ascertain that LTTE weaponry is not being transported with the harvested rice. As the now meager harvest is sold, the LTTE impose clandestine harvest taxes, while the state security forces step up arrests and interrogations. The harvest seasons are now times of trepidation in the fertile, once productive, coastal plain.

THE CHANGED NATURE OF EVERYDAY RELATIONS

In order to speak of the violation endured, there is the basic necessity for a safe space and a safe witness. In 1991 when there was no Sri Lankan government military presence in Palugamam, and the village was solely under LTTE control, I was interrupted by several women on a narrow, sandy pathway winding through the village's houses and asked to come to a certain house. At the house, I was greeted warmly and invited to have tea by a man in his late fifties. We sat under a tree in the compound garden—a relatively safe space—and after some time I became the witness. Initially, he wanted to tell me about the deaths of a number of village residents. When government security forces were occupying the village, they had insisted on the use of his well for washing. He had noted their respectfulness toward his family. He said he had given them food cooked in his house. The security forces soldiers had gone out of their way to say good-bye and in particular to tell him not to worry. Minutes after their kind departing words, which he had taken to heart, he noticed that a small building nearby was burning. Eight people from Palugamam who were tied up inside died as the building burned. The fact that the soldiers were burning these villagers to their deaths in the same moment that he accepted their kind departing words in good faith still overwhelmed him. There was a long speechless pause, as we sat under the tree where he had first confronted this truth one year earlier. His one painfully unfinished sentence, suspended in ineffable emotion, was, "Why (has) God made me see these things?"

He continued. He moved his wife and children out of the village because he felt it was unsafe for them to remain there. The LTTE buried landmines in the pathways of security forces' patrols around Palugamam. Whenever the security forces discovered a mine, the soldiers would wait until the next villager came along and would then order the local resident to dig the mine up at gunpoint. Twice, as he was leaving the village to visit his wife and children, he was forced to dig out mines with his bare hands while soldiers stood by with guns aimed at him. Boastfully, he explained that he was intelligent enough to disconnect the detonator wires, or he would not be telling me the story. I asked him if the LTTE, watching from a distance, would have blown him up as he bent over the mines, and he answered with affirmative certainty that they would. He went on to elaborate the LTTE's new method: "Now they set three landmines in a row, one in the middle, and one on either side of the pathway, so the security forces and TELO-PLOTE boys (paramilitaries) who stand at a distance will also get caught."

A set of three landmines had exploded near the Mavetkuda Pillaiyar temple two days prior to the telling of this story, and four local people, one TELO boy who was an army informant, and two security forces soldiers were killed. Stories that circulated house by house in the village stated that the villagers were not killed by the mine, but were dragged from nearby houses, shot, and dismembered by the security forces to make it appear that the mine explosion had killed them. He accepted this version of events as truthful, and added that he heard gunshots after the sound of the mine explosion. Not once in his commentary that day did I hear a hint of criticism or resentment at the price villagers were paying for the LTTE's violent politics, which seemed to operate under the assumption that all Tamils should be willing to give their lives in the struggle for Tamil Eelam. The uncanniness of the ordinary—the kind words uttered by the security forces while they had just burned alive his fellow villagers, and the absence of voiced resentment after digging up landmines exemplifies the manner in which people must live out their day-to-day lives.

ALTERED KINSHIP AND NEIGHBORHOOD RELATIONS

Most of the families and individuals I came to know in the interior of the eastern war zone lacked the resources to leave during the major exodus from the region in the late 1980s and early 1990s. Some of the families I lived with had managed to send one or more children abroad to safety, but the lifeworld of these families was rooted to a kinship nexus and to paddy lands on the eastern coastal plain. In unrelenting ways, noncombatant Tamil families' day-to-day existence has been pulled apart by the simultaneous military occupation of the eastern region and the controlling commands of the LTTE which doubly pressed upon them.

With a generation of men lost in the fighting, there were many unmarried women and widowed women in the village of Palugamam. The priest of a Pillaiyar temple had five unmarried daughters. All three of his sons, who had been assisting him in temple rituals, were executed by the security forces in 1990. Dowry houses stood unfinished due not only to the absence of traditional matrilocal marriage alliances, but also to the economic paralysis of the war and possible imposition of LTTE taxes which are demanded from families engaged in the construction of houses.[5]

The mother of a household where I tried to pay visits of respect somewhat regularly once described changes in the people after the security forces had reestablished a camp on Palugamam's village perimeter. The lines between who is friend and who is enemy have become impossible to draw. She had lived long enough to remember the period before the war with deep nostalgia. She lamented, "Now there is no value for life here. [*Ippō, iṅkkē oru perumatiyum illai.*] Now the people have a stone heart. [*Ippō ūr makkaḷūkkellām kal neñcam.*] When there is crying and shouting next door in the night, people in this village can't go over and ask, 'Why are you crying?' because we don't know if the LTTE or the army is there." One aspect of her experience that is most difficult for her to bear is her inability to go next door and help calm the family.

In Palugamam, there are clearly defined matriclans and matrilocal household clusters (McGilvray 1982a, 1989). Thus the "crying and shouting next door in the night" is usually within a close circle of female kin. In this case, the house next door belongs to her sister. She has lost her ability to act as an influential woman in the village as well as within a close circle of kinship relationships. Under the Prevention of Terrorism Act, continuing Emergency Rule, and Sinhala-Tamil conflict over control of her village, she is now embedded in a set of relationships over which she has little control and which have altered the present and the future in irrevocable ways.

Like other mothers who could gather enough resources, she has sent her children out of the country. Mothers can be heard to say, "This is no longer a place for young people." In the village's traditional matrilocal social organization women were rooted to place, but this is changing as a result of the war. The loss of these female networks is felt not only by women living between the government forces, paramilitary forces, and the LTTE, but—even more acutely—by women living in camps for the displaced, or in cities of the Sri Lankan Tamil diaspora like Toronto, where increasing numbers of suicides of Tamil women are being reported.[6]

The mother of another Palugamam family I had known for five years began a conversation about her family's latest problems with the question, "What justice?" Her husband has been severely disoriented since 1990, when he watched several of their family members being killed and when their home was burned. Repairs on their house have been sufficient to continue to live in it. They have three daughters whom they feel should be married by now and two sons. The mother also suffers from chronic illness. In 1996 the LTTE visited her and asked, as they had previously, for money to support their goal. Other options they presented to her were to provide information to them about the security forces, or to give one of her children to the LTTE for combat training. It is no longer uncommon for young unmarried women to join the LTTE as fighters (Trawick 1999). Upon my return to the United States, I received a telephone call from her brother, who now lives in Toronto, Canada, and I explained her family's plight in the course of our conversation. He was unaware of the severity of his sister's predicament, and lamented that during rare telephone conversations with relatives still living in the east the practice of self-censorship and the conscious attempt to avoid discussion of politically sensitive issues prohibit the exchange of the most crucial information. The fear of tapped telephone lines is similar to the fear of exposing information in letter-writing, as it is a practice of the security forces to open mail entering and leaving the region—a practice imposing strict military scrutiny of mail received or sent out from the interior villages. Thus, within the village or neighborhood, and in communications between family members who remain inside the war zone and their members living abroad, everyday sensibility of kinship relations must be suppressed.

In eastern Sri Lanka, there is a pervasive sense of living out life without the possibility of extrication from unrelenting political violation pressing upon the daily lifeworld. Middle-aged people in families I lived with generally expected the violence to continue for the rest of their lifetime. They often remarked that they held the hope that their youngest children would not live in conditions of war.

"SILENCING" AND THE CHANGING PLACE OF THE TEMPLE

In this region of protracted war, people live with many kinds of silences: protective silences, some silences that may be understood as empowering—and the muteness of intimidation, trauma, erasure, and loss. "Silencing" and denial are common coping practices widely reported in contexts of violence where there have been large numbers of "disappearances" and extrajudicial executions (Das 1996b; Kordon et al. 1988; Menon and Bhasin 1996; Suarez-Orozco 1992; Taussig 1992). Ordinary families caught in the violent conflict silently tolerate the impunity of the security forces and the demands of the LTTE—they have learned how to know what not to know. One ultimate consequence of this silencing is the erasure of history.

Systematic use of trauma to impose political silencing and intimidate witnesses (Kleinman 1996: 175; Somasundaram 1998) often takes extreme forms in the practices of the LTTE and the Sri Lankan security forces. When I worked in medical clinics in camps for the displaced, I met a mother of five children whose husband was arrested by a government countersubversive unit in 1991 and incarcerated under the Prevention of Terrorism Act for more than three years without being charged for any criminal offense.

When she was first allowed to visit him in the Batticaloa prison, she found that he was unable to hear her voice. Two years later, her husband was unable to eat after his tongue was repeatedly cut during interrogation in a Colombo prison. Following one of the monthly visits to the prison in this period she told me, "My husband was unable to speak. But he cried. I also cried." Although this Tamil father was eventually released, and accomplished the journey from the last prison in which he was detained in the south back to the east coast where he was reunited with his family, by the time of their reunion he had lost the faculty of speech.

These are historical moments when dissent is impossible, but inside the eastern war zone there is one distinct exception to the oppressive silencing: the emotional outpourings at local Amman temples. In Batticaloa District there is a particular cultural response to violation which reverses social withdrawal: ritual practices at local Amman (goddess) temples which overcome political silencing. Amman "oracles" or trance mediums (*teyvam āṭumākkaḷ, kaṭṭāṭikaḷ*) embody, interpret, and acknowledge the injury of war. The work of oracles came into increasing prominence during the 1980s and early 1990s rather than collapsing along with the health care infrastructure and the judiciary system during the prolonged conflict. The resurgence of oracular revelation stems from experiences of ordinary families and intractable dilemmas created by suffering. In the aftermath of occupation by the Sri Lankan security forces and many thousands of "disappearances," people could not take their problems to government authorities. Tamil people who remained behind during the exodus from the region have increasingly availed themselves of a different form of agency found within local Amman cult practices.

The revitalization of territorial Hindu goddess cults in eastern Sri Lanka is closely tied to the belief that the local Amman (a divine epithet meaning "Mother") can ensure the well-being of devotees and their families and protect the boundaries of household compounds, neighborhoods, and villages from negative influences, including the intrusiveness of army, Special Task Force, countersubversive units, and other militarized groups. An increase in oracular revelation, a central part of local Amman cults, can be observed throughout the region, particularly during annual propitiatory rituals at local temples.

The lived experience of war is articulated in the process of "telling oracles" (*vākku solluṟatu*) in many ways. The shattering of close circles of kinship and the unresolved grief of "disappearances" are experiences shared with oracles in their everyday work. As the embodiment of the agency of local goddesses, oracles facilitate a process of testimony that overcomes political silencing and acknowledges broken kinship connections, abductions and arrests, extortion practices, socioeconomic paralysis, and torture. In the local context, Amman oracles facilitate resolution of some moral dilemmas that arise from political fragmentation and the need to respond to each other.[7] An active and embodied critique of the effacement of local violence from public record is also apparent in the work of some Batticaloa oracles (Comaroff 1985).

AMMAN CULTS AND THE INJURY OF WAR: THE WORK OF ORACLES

There are many "teyvam dancers" (*teyvam āṭumākkaḷ,* or "oracles") in the village of Palugamam. One afternoon when I was interviewing a group of women and men who "dance" in states of oracular possession by the goddess, and when I asked about their relationships with the village goddess Tiropataiyamman in the present context of terror, they replied,

> Every day gunshots and other sounds are heard. For a long time we're having all these problems. Still it's continuing. Problems are still going on. Who knows whether we would always be like this? Somehow our life goes on with anxiety. When a gunshot is heard over there, here we worry in our hearts, and then again when there is a gunshot here we are worrying—in this way we're always living with anxiety. This is our life work. When we go to her (*Tirōpatai-yamman*), we tell her the suffering that is going on. "Why, Mother, have you closed your eyes to these? Are you not going to open a way out for us?"

The Amman oracles are ordinary people surviving in an extraordinary historical circumstance of violence, who experience additional trauma of bearing witness to and affirming the terror of annihilation. They are as vulnerable to the injury of war as other noncombatants who seek their assistance. They are men and women of both high and low castes who are part of a social body of sufferers. In many instances a close member of the oracle's same kin group, often one deceased, had also experienced oracular possession. The agency of the oracle centers upon dissolution of a previous sense of self and identification of the body-self with the Amman.

In eastern Sri Lanka it is understood that "every Amman is very powerful" (*ovvoru ammanum mikavum vallamai uṭaiyavarkaḷ*). *Sakti,* often translated as the "active female energy of the Hindu cosmos," may be used as a synonym for *Amman* in Batticaloa District. Summoning of *sakti* is central to some local forms of healing ritual in this region. Oracles receive empowerment of *sakti* (*saktivalimai*) through profound identification with a particular local goddess. The moment of commingling of the oracle's body and the presence of the Amman is referred to in Tamil as "assuming form" (*uruvarutal*). Oracles describe *sakti* possession as a painful sacrifice of the body. They report feelings of unbearable heat and pain, and describe their trembling (*saṇṇatam*) as resembling the "shivering when one suffers from fever." During *sakti* possession, the person is sacralized and accorded respect as a living presence of the Amman. The speech and body language of oracles is not considered their own. They understand the Amman's "coming upon them" as an experience in which the self is being acted upon and affected by her will, and they are therefore not held responsible for their words and actions.

Oracles say they cannot remember what transpires during possession experiences. They explain that when the hot energy of *sakti,* traveling upward through their trembling bodies, reaches the level of the throat, they lose the ability to speak in their individual human voices. Then they may burn camphor on their tongues. After that, "only the deity speaks" (*teyvamtānēccollura*).

One of the most dramatic scenes I witnessed in an Amman temple was entirely lost to the memory of the oracle who performed it. At the Kallady Kali temple in 1992, several thousand local people had gathered to witness firewalking on the seventh evening of the annual propitiation. It was dark, and the crowds were kept clear of the wide sacred area around the firepit by constant patrolling of the temple *vaṇṇakkar* (trustees). The firepit was prepared for hundreds of devotees to walk over the fire in a few minutes. The oracle who would lead the firewalk was wearing a red sari with white plumes of *kamukampū* at his waist. At this heightened moment of ritual, three tall Army officers from the nearby camp strode boldly into the cleared circular space surrounding the long, hot bed of coals as if to position themselves there for the event. There were rumors that arrests were imminent. Suddenly, the oracle rushed from the shrine, tore furiously across the space, and, growling angrily at them in the unbearable rage of Kali, chased them out. And the officers did move quickly out.

Local temple events are the only social gatherings in many places inside the eastern war zone, and at these events I witnessed a tremendous range of behavior on the part of individual oracles. In Batticaloa, oracular revelation is sometimes presented as a genre with its own conventions, such as speaking in verse or in the ritual vocabulary of oracular possession. Eclectic and experimental practices also arise during the emotional intensity of ritual, particularly during *vākku solluṟatu* (telling oracles) or at times when ritual intermingles with the immediacy of political violence.[8]

AN ORACLE FOR KALI

My fieldwork involved extensive amounts of time with women and men who are well-known oracles and priests at Amman temples, both in the context of temple ritual and in their homes. One evening a local Amman temple priest took me to the home of an oracle for Kali. The oracle whom we visited that night, Saktirani, has a very close relationship with the local aspect of Kali known as Pattirakaliyamman at Punnacholai. The priest, who was a childhood friend of Saktirani's, thought it was important that I meet with her. As I would learn, Saktirani is an unsilenceable local woman who would

even speak about sexual victimization of women during the war without hesitation. I would hear her state several times that she is certain that in her
next life she will take rebirth as a man. In this life, she is feared, respected,
and criticized. We traveled to Saktirani's house by bike at dusk through
sandy lanes close to the sea to avoid army checkpoints on the main road.
She was bathing at the well when we arrived. We sat quietly and waited.

Saktirani surprised me by overcoming the usual cultural hesitancy to
speak about sexual victimization, and told me that some of the women who
had been raped during the recent Kokkadiccolai massacre had come to her
for assistance. She spoke openly and without hesitation, and it was in a matter-of-fact manner that she commented on the women coming to her first.
I asked, then, if she knew what happened in the temple for Kannakiyamman
(a local goddess representing "wifely loyalty" and "chastity") at Mahiladitivu.
Her response was that the women had been assaulted and raped in the temple. At that time in my field research I had gained some understanding of
the protective capacity people attributed to their local goddesses, and I
wanted to understand how she interpreted this experience of violation in a
temple for Kannakiyamman. Saktirani's interpretation of this event of sexual victimization led through a sequence of events of natural and human
disaster, a temple dispute, and finally the destructive capacity of an offended
local goddess.

Saktirani began her explanation by referring to the terrible cyclone
which devastated the east coast in 1978, a storm so fierce it was frequently
used as a historical mark in local stories. During the storm, 28,000 acres of
coconut palms and many homes were destroyed, and descriptions I had
heard of the storm seethed with emotion. While listening to emotional outpourings during stories of their survival of this terrible storm, I often
thought that these were healing narratives. Locked in the ineffable emotion
of the present suffering, there was nothing politically incorrect in speaking
about the violence of a natural storm. People emphasized hiding in the
safest corners of their houses, much as they do under aerial attack. They
described the fierceness of the wind which whipped palm trees in circles
until their splintered trunks were severed from the earth. In her description
of crawling over broken trees on her hands and knees with her children
toward the temple in the middle of the night in the terrible wind, one
elderly mother suddenly became confused and could not remember if the
experience she was describing was during the cyclone or during a military
attack. At least one other aspect of the cyclone narratives which I thought
was healing was the fact that they had survived it and it had passed.

According to Saktirani, the temple for Kannakiyamman at Mahiladitivu
was severely damaged in the cyclone of 1978. She began to rub her fore-
arms with a slight expression of discomfort and showed us the sensation on
the surface of her skin, which is referred to in Tamil as *mēl silittal* or *mēl*

sūsutal. While she excused herself to bring drinks from the kitchen, the priest quietly explained that *mēl silittal* is an indication of the Amman's presence. As she carried the drinks to us on the tray, she began to tremble uncontrollably, and we had to catch the tray to save it from falling. She explained that the *saṇṇatam* (uncontrollable trembling caused by the goddess' presence) would not leave her since the day before, when someone seeking information about "disappeared people" (*kāṇāmalpōṇṇākkaḷ)* had brought her a list of forty names of missing people in Jaffna. Saktirani, as I would later witness many times, is especially well known for telling the fate of the "disappeared."

For Saktirani, the massacre at the Mahiladitivu Kannakiyamman temple is but one of many violent events she has confronted day-to-day during more than a decade of close interaction with those injured by the war. Her religious interpretation of events during the massacre is consistent with her work as an Amman oracle, in which she assists disoriented people with problems of "disappearances," sexual violation, torture, and atrocity on a daily basis. In the late 1960s, confronted by personal dilemmas and pain, Saktirani sought safety and a way of lessening the agony of loss by absorbing herself in religious practices of Amman cults. As I came to know her, I heard her reiterate almost daily that the Amman protects the people (*mākkalaikkāpparrinar*). However, in the cosmology of local oracles, both the destruction and the preservation of life are attributed to the ambiguous nature of the Amman. In the case of this massacre, the Amman was said to have withheld her protection because she was not properly attended through religious ritual. When people bring problems to Saktirani, she often urges them to participate in household and temple rituals which propitiate the Amman.

At annual propitiation ceremonies for local goddesses, which sometimes last as long as fourteen days and nights, there can be no question that some collective agency resides in the gathering of devotees, who usually live within the *ur,* or the locale, that each goddess is thought to protect and control. At Batticaloa's Amman temples, "telling oracles" (*vākku solluratu)* is part of every *puja,* or ritual of worship. Large numbers of people wait to take their turn before Amman oracles at local temples. However, telling oracles is not limited to the temple *puja,* and may spontaneously become integrated with household rituals, such as a house-compound protection ritual (*valavu kāval paṇṇutal)* or a ritual of foretelling the future with a margosa wood bow (*villukkuri).*

Saktirani tells *vākku* (oracles, truth) at the Pattirakaliyamman (Bhadrakali) temple, and every day at her house. There is not much between her home and the sea other than dunes and slender eucalyptus trees with aromatic leaves. Slightly to the north, there is an old Nagatambiran shrine under a large *arasū* tree where a well-attended *poṅkal* ceremony is held once a year. To the south, on the edge of the dunes, there is a cemetery. Temples for the goddesses Pecciyamman, Kaliyamman, and Mariyamman are situated within a short walking distance. From outside, her home is deceptively ordinary in appearance, with the exception of clusters of people talking by her gate. Beyond the gate, one can immediately see the confluence of people filling doorways, spilling out of the main room, and occupying hand-woven mats spread out in the sandy side veranda.

Saktirani's home is a place of protection and healing for disoriented and traumatized people. There are also regular visitors and neighbors who spend time there frequently. White-haired Marimuttu, over one hundred, often came slowly but steadily from her house nearby. If she had a problem to share with Saktirani, it was usually concerning an issue of respect (*korava kuṟaivu*), which this stately lady felt she deserved from everyone in her circle of kinship. Saktirani often praised her, "She is steady!" She has six children living and seventy grandchildren, so she has everything." Taking the tray to chew betel, Marimuttu would respond to Saktirani's praise of her by lifting the iron areca nut cutter in her gnarled hand while sending off a brusque order in Saktirani's direction: "You do your work!"

Sometimes people who have come a long distance spend the night at Saktirani's when there is trouble on the roads and the journey through military checkpoints on the return to their villages is considered too dangerous. Extremely ill or severely disoriented people sometimes are cared for in the shrine room. Usually by late afternoon most of the people have gone back to their respective homes. Then Saktirani takes her single daily meal. Before that, she only drinks "cooling" lime juice. Cordon and search operations frequently sweep the area where she lives.

People gather at her house beginning at about 6:30 in the morning from towns, villages, and hamlets all over the eastern coastal plain. People of any caste, any ethnicity, or any role in the conflict may come. The majority are Tamil people with desperate problems. During lulls in the violence, people from Muslim enclaves also often seek her advice. After the death of Saktirani's husband in 1994, the press of people seeking guidance at her gate each morning moved Saktirani to discontinue her observation of seclusion and speak to their problems. When she begins her work, she comes directly from the shrine and sits down in the sand at the end of her veranda before a small table, facing the sea. She refers to the sea as "the place of all the goddesses (*pattinikal*)."

First she requests that those present not smoke cigarettes and that menstruating women not sit in the veranda. For those who have gathered for the first time, she sings an introduction, listing the types of issues she will address. It is a list in which consequences of arbitrary arrest, arbitrary execution, and displacement intermingle with everyday concerns of the sort Saktirani addressed before the intensification of the war—indicative of the way life must and does go on amidst destruction and loss of life in the immediate world.

> Theft, article missing, arson, arrest, anonymous letters, letters that have not been received from abroad. Thoughts. Goat, cattle, poultry, living beings. Wife-husband, love, conspiracy, all these. Disaster. Say "Disaster" and place the betel. *Ketuti* (a local euphemism for "lost" or "disappeared"). Spade, axe, bicycle, motorcycle, theft. Property and sickness. You can ask about income and illness. Jewelry lost. Disappearance of son (*makaṇakkāṇalla*). I am able to tell immediately. You have to offer betel leaves. Hindus offer betel and flowers. Christians could ask with flowers and rosary. Muslims shouldn't place flowers on their betel leaves.

Through her engagement in *vākku solluṟatu* for more than twenty years, she has become an exceptional, unconventional woman. She is a woman widely believed to embody the dangerous divine, to have such a close relationship with Kali that she is part of her, so she is both feared and respected. She is also criticized, particularly by older men who are well-versed in Amman cult practices. Their criticism is directed at her bricolage of ritual practice, and my sense is that they are jealous of her popularity. Some accused her of incomplete knowledge or unorthodox ritual practices. Others expressed absolute certainty that communication with Kali was part of her everyday experience, often embellishing this belief with a story of her prediction about the future or the fate of a "disappeared" person which had indeed proven to be true. Sometimes when an arrest by the army had occurred, Saktirani told the family members to bring a new garment to her Kali shrine to be blessed. After she rubbed sacred ash into the garment while uttering mantrams, she ordered the family members to deliver the article of clothing (usually a sarong) to guards at the detention camp or detention center; promising that the detained individual would be released if the article of clothing was received and worn. I learned of a case in which the arrested person was transferred to another prison and not released, an outcome which tarnished Saktirani's credibility in that particular family. I discovered skepticism about her ability to predict the fate of the "disappeared" in a hamlet where six youths remained lost without a trace of further information. There were other cases of incorrect revelations about the "disappeared," but on the whole her reputation was impressive.

Saktirani told me with unshakable confidence that she had the ability to cure cases of madness (*paittiyam*). I observed cases in which Saktirani was considered the only person able to care for them. These cases, treated at her home, included people from both Tamil and Muslim families. Some were said to be possessed by *pey* (evil spirits or ghosts). Once in a rare while she treated cases of *paittiyam* experienced by Sinhalese boys in the army who had violently turned upon others, including their superior officers. Not knowing what to do with them, army personnel sometimes brought these severely disoriented soldiers to Saktirani. Women who had experienced rape by soldiers were also cared for by her. One case of "madness" was a silent, withdrawn young woman covered with cigarette burns from interrogation practices at a temporary army camp set up for paddy harvest in the interior. Saktirani settled her in the shrine and took care of her there. One of the first steps of her treatment was to administer *naciyam* (an herbal inhaler with a cotton wick and a funnel fashioned from palm leaf strips).

Saktirani embodied the extremes of the goddess Kaliyamman. When she expressed anger, other people witnessing this told me it was the presence of Kaliyamman in Saktirani. Those who embody the agency of Kali often describe an overwhelming feeling of *āvēcam* (fury, wrath, or uncontrollable emotion). She overturned gender boundaries in her mimicking of male and female voices. Saktirani was not constrained by the often cited "four qualities" of Tamil femaleness: timidity, shyness, delicacy, and modesty (*accam, nāṇam, maṭam, payirppu*). She was indifferent to expected deference behavior. She chewed betel with gypsies (*kuravar*) who were passing through and enjoyed joking intimately with them; when influential men came for help, she often scolded them for neglecting the goddess. She blatantly disregarded gendered presentation of her body, and often appeared to have emptied her consciousness of her femaleness. This was particularly true when cases related to torture were brought before her. Saktirani dressed simply and wore none of the usual jewelry of a Tamil wife when her husband was alive in the early 1990s.

She regularly warned young males of arrests, torture, and bullets. She soothed mothers whose children had recently "disappeared." She scolded mothers for not disciplining children, and she scolded children for not respecting their mothers: "You should listen to your mother. When you get caught (arrested) your friends won't come to help you. At the moment when you're in difficulty only your mother will come. Listen to your mother." To mothers of teenagers she would sometimes sing, "Is it enough to give birth to a child? Discipline is needed don't you know?" Saktirani tenderly gave a blind fisherman advice on how to improve his relationship with his wife, compassionately asking him not to be "suspicious" of her activities while he was away. She also frequently gave instructions on the treatment of illnesses.

There were periods when it was clear that she enjoyed what she was doing. Whatever problems people brought with them through her gate, Saktirani was expert at responding in unexpected ways. She often encouraged youth to succeed in their studies; "computer course," "bioscience," and "technical" were a few but frequently used English phrases when she predicted future studies abroad. Saktirani had a style of imaginative wit, yet she remained sensitively in touch with the anguish of families trying to cope with unresolved grief and survivors' guilt. In many cases parents who had sent their sons out of the country to "a safe place" felt grief at the loss of their children. One such case of "lost connections" (*toṭarpu illai*) reveals Saktirani's inventive methods of establishing a sense of connectedness:

> Parents from a small Tamil village near Eravur paid a visit to Saktirani about their son, who had traveled to Sweden through an illegal travel agency for two lakhs—approximately $4,000 U.S. This is the minimum fee; the "better" illegal travel agencies ask $10,000 U.S. The son was languishing in a Swedish immigration prison. He hadn't written for a long time, and the parents were deeply concerned. During the interaction, Saktirani lay flat in the sand, and then cocked one leg over the other, jiggling the raised foot in a thoughtful rhythm, with one arm bent behind her neck. (Theatrical gesturing such as assuming a European body position is but one example of her transgressive creativity.) Saktirani complained, in the son's voice, about the food in the prison and about not having a job. As she portrayed him, the son seemed to be feeling miserable. Then Saktirani sat up and told the parents to write a letter that would calm him. There are dozens of letters placed on the shrine, where mantrams will be uttered over them before they are mailed to family members who have joined the vast Tamil diaspora. She ordered them to bring *muntiriyamparuppu* (cashews) to be blessed on the shrine before sending them to him by post. When he eats these cashews, according to Saktirani, he will be compelled to write.

In her manner of responding to people's desperate problems or voicing people's fate, Saktirani had respect for truth, and this was perceived as her expression of concern and caring. When people returned to her who had previously lost family members, there were sometimes cases in which she had correctly predicted the deaths. She would often give predictions about other family members. Sometimes she would warn mothers fiercely, "Watch your children carefully—more bullets will come to your family." She scrutinized young wives whose husbands had been shot by the LTTE, or the STF, or some other group, commenting, "You have grown thin." (Thinness is viewed as unbecoming.) Saktirani might tell women, "Your life is spoiled." While talking with women about husbands, it was not uncommon for her to state, "He will face death." She might warn, "Someone in your family will take poison."

With blunt and caring honesty, the agency of the oracle and the agency of the Tamil mother were blurred in Saktirani's work. She would tell young boys they were going to be arrested. A twenty-year-old youth was told, "You will be arrested. I don't know if you will end up in the Forestry Camp, or Boosa, or dead" (places of detention reputed to use torture). Saktirani was lying down in the sand and repeatedly sucking in her breath very deeply as she foretold his future. She often scolded boys for not being careful with their national identity cards and predicted that they would lose them. She chastised them for cycling and visiting friends in the evening. "Stop your cycling! At the same time be careful with your identity card. Stay at home, or you will have a problem." She scolded them for not concentrating on their studies and predicted that if they were conscientious students, they would then have a chance to go abroad.

This is not to say that she did not express compassion and empathy. She often told those who were frightened that there was no need to be afraid. She would give encouragement: "Don't put your head down for anything." Her deep identification with the pain of others could embarrass the gathering on any given day. This was, in part, because the issues she addressed and exposed were the issues that had to be kept hidden. The range of emotion she traversed in an hour or a day was indicative of the desperate conditions of life in Batticaloa District.

The fierceness of her *vākku* (truth, oracles) could be extremely harsh. As a young mother from the Punnacholai Vannar (Washerman) settlement, whose husband had disappeared, once commented, "People say that she tells the truth even when it is bad." One afternoon I described the following interaction with Saktirani to another oracle, a man known to speak as the *talateyvam* (temple deity) of a nearby Amman temple with whom I had many long conversations. I asked for his reaction. He simply said, "Sometimes Kali will speak out like that." The case represents the brute social habitat that Saktirani was sometimes compelled to reflect during oracular revelation— and the harshness of her response may be understood as a form of redemptive realization:

> As on many mornings, we could hear the Sri Lankan Air Force bombing Paduvankarai and the Thanthamalai jungle, and there was irritable disagreement among the gathering about whether we were hearing thunder or bombing, even though we could feel the vibrations of the impact through the straw mats on the sand. (Similarly, through what I interpreted as a protective form of denial, people sometimes saw black smoke on the horizon as cloud formations.)
>
> An agricultural laborer from paddy fields in the interior was brought in front of Saktirani shaking uncontrollably. He was accompanied by his wife. He had just been released from his third arrest. His home is Ayttiyamalai. He has four children, and he is not an LTTE freedom fighter. He has lost the sight of one eye, and there are deep wounds in the tops of his feet where he says his army interrogators ground and gouged wounds with their boots.
>
> Saktirani did not express horror at torture, and looked steadily at him. There was no alteration in his uncontrollable tremors. Still looking hard at him, Saktirani stated, "This will happen to you again." She told them to go and bring three *ilaner* (young, green coconuts) to the shrine. Someone went off with the wife of the torture victim to get the coconuts. When they returned, Saktirani placed the three *ilaner* in front of the statue of Kali and called *sakti* into them. He drank one of the green coconuts in the shrine room, and she explained that this would heal the wounds.

One especially notable comment made during the collective discussion of his experience among the gathered people on the veranda was, "For his problem he needs money" (to bribe the army to release him because he must cross through many military checkpoints). Saktirani then added her own perception, "The people who are involved (in perpetrating violence) run away with stolen money and leave the innocent to suffer here."

It is difficult to know how to assess the immediate interpersonal experience in cases like this one. The laborer seemed to benefit simply from close contact and connection with Saktirani, whom he believed had Kali in her. Saktirani's religious imagination incorporates and reflects the world of violence in which both she and those who seek her help live.

Her physical frailty was certainly related to the difficulty of her work. She is known, before everything else, for her ability to feel the pain of others. Sometimes, for days on end she would complain that she could no longer bear feeling others' suffering in her own body. There were many moments when she did not differentiate herself from others' suffering. As cases given below further indicate, Saktirani understands pain as an inevitable part of experience, and directs her work toward acknowledgment of suffering, "seeing" the condition of pain, feeling it in her own body, and guiding people through its experience. Particularly in cases of "disappearances," interactions with Saktirani may take a form of redemptive remembering.[9]

ON BECOMING AN ORACLE

Although Saktirani was born on 14 December 1948, into the respectable Velalar caste and Maluvaracan matriclan, the deity with whom she has a close relationship today is situated in a low-caste Washerman settlement of about one hundred and fifty families. She was educated through Advanced Level, and people commented she was quite attractive in her youth. Her father, who sometimes experienced *sakti* possession, died before Saktirani was married. As Saktirani's family could not provide her with a dowry house or matrilineal property upon marriage, she endured a succession of shifting residences early in her marriage. This was stressful for her in a social setting where women are distinctively rooted to place through matrilocal residence and matrilineal inheritance of property upon marriage (McGilvray 1989: 192–235). She longed to have a permanent house. When she was unable to conceive a child, she adopted a daughter and almost immediately found that she was pregnant. Saktirani has six children, two of whom are adopted.

One of Saktirani's children was adopted before his birth. As she explains it, in 1985 a thin woman came to request that her future be foretold. The young woman placed the betel leaves, areca nut, and flowers in front of Saktirani and confided that she was pregnant, and she did not want to keep the child in her womb. Saktirani told her to bring the infant to her when it was born. The birth was very premature, and no one in Saktirani's household expected the infant to live. Today he is the youngest of Saktirani's sons. The mother is listed today as one of the thousands of cases of "disappearances" that have occurred in the eastern region.

Saktirani is one of the individuals who leads the annual firewalking while also keeping the vow of *vāyalaku* (mouth arrow), in which her cheeks are pierced with a single, long, silver needle with a three-pronged *sūlam* (trident) on one end. The *sūlam* is described as an instrument of the Amman's protection. In June 1996, the fifth year of our friendship, Saktirani shared part of her motivation by stating this wish immediately before enacting her *vāyalaku* and firewalking vows: "To solve the problems in this country. To solve the ethnic problem. No danger should fall on the children, the relatives, on the neighborhood. For this I walk the fire. *Arōharā! Ammakku Arōharā! Parasaktikku Arōharā!*"

She presented a statue of Kali which was placed in the temple's third hall, the place that corresponds with the center of the human body, where *teyvam* dancers merge with the hot, active, female energy of *sakti* during temple ritual. Saktirani described the gifted statue of Pattirakaliyamman, one which clearly presents the inverse of passivity, in the following way: "Intense. Wrathful. (Saktirani put out her tongue, pointing it down, with eyes full of fury.) Arms brandishing the conch, *cakkaram,* anklet—every aspect will appear. (Saktirani stretched out her arms as she spoke.) After the death of one of her daughters, Saktirani dreamt of Kali as a child holding a *sūlam.* The child-Kali gave Saktirani an inscribed *ola* leaf as she stated, "Now you are able to tell oracles." The next morning she started telling *vākku* to everyone who visited the funeral house. She says, "I don't know how, but I told *vākku* to everyone. After that, I continued telling oracles at the Punnacholai Pattirakaliyamman temple. I became very close to her." When she "dances" in a state of possession at the temple, she "has in her" the divine beings Kaliyamman, Mariyamman, Murukan, and Veerapattiran. Her closest relationship is with Kali, or Pattirakaliyamman, with whom she talks every day. Saktirani believes that Kali took her daughter's life in order to give her the ability to tell oracles. She once stated, "My child died; then I got the power to foretell. Only after the human sacrifice (*narapali*) I received the power (*vālayām*)."

Saktirani believes her own death will be instantaneous, and that in her next life she will not be reborn in Sri Lanka. She expresses certainty that her husband will be reborn as a female, and, as I mentioned, that she will be reborn as a male. Saktirani has confronted the death of her parents and the sudden death of her daughter, the deaths of a brother and son-in-law who were shot by the security forces, and most recently the death of her husband. Furthermore her familiarity with death and bereavement has continued to grow through her work, in which she regularly helps those undergoing agonizing experiences of "disappeared" family members. Just as her own bereavement brought her into this work, unresolved grief brings many others to her.

INTERPERSONAL EXPERIENCE OF *VĀKKU SOLLURATU* (TELLING ORACLES)

Like others who "dance with the divine being" and who offer their bodies and tongues to the Ammans, to the male guardian deities of the Ammans, and to the god Murukan, Saktirani states, "I forget myself completely telling oracles." In her profound identification with divine beings, most consistently with Pattirakaliyamman, her previous self is lost. For several decades Pattirakaliyamman, who "speaks out," has been "with her" and a part of her identity.

The following cases reveal the pain involved for the oracle engaged in oracular possession and for the survivors inside the war zone. They bring us closer to the interpersonal world and social experience of sufferers engaged in *vākku solluratu* (telling oracles) in everyday experience. During the course of a day, while attending to requests from as many as ninety people, some of whom have often traveled a long distance to see Saktirani, she moves in and out of her individual identity as Saktirani and the identity of Kali. Her identification with Kali enables her to help those who are traumatized by terror. It is understood that Kali has empowered her with *vālāyam* (a word used in local dialect for the miraculous power of Kali), which, in the eyes of the daily gathering at her home, imbues Saktirani with immense moral power.

The following interaction between Saktirani and a mother from a hamlet next to the village of Palugamam in Paduvankarai concerns a "disappearance."

> An elderly mother with white hair, a faded blue cotton sari, and a striking air of grace rose from the crowd and took the place in front of the oracle for *vettila vaiccu kēkkiratu* (putting betel and asking). Her natal home is beyond Kovilporativu, where people say the helicopters are strafing. This mother has lost eight members of her family, including her husband. Her surviving daughter and grandchildren have moved in with her. The army is occupying her home now—a common practice in the area—so they have moved to an abandoned house. The most recently "disappeared" family member is a son who went to sell paddy and never returned. She has come to ask if he is alive. Saktirani confirms his death by singing the lines from an old popular film (*Pālum Palamum*) while looking into the mother's eyes:
>
> pōnāl pōkaṭṭum pōtā
> inta pūmiuil nilaiyāy vālntavar yāratā
> *"Let things gone be gone;*
> *Who in this world is living eternally?"*

Saktirani advises the mother, "Now you are with your daughter and three grandchildren. It's your responsibility to take care of them now. Live for them." She placed the offering of betel leaves, areca nut, flower, and a ten-rupee note back into the mother's hands. Her practice is to return the *vette-laipākku* offering when the person asked about is dead. She may return as many as ten offerings a day.

Others who have gathered, bringing their own problems, then ask the elderly mother questions about where she has come from, and about how she is managing, showing their concern. They also talk with her about rice rations which she is eligible to obtain.

Before they depart, the mother is reminded by the oracle that earlier, before the problems, they worshipped Kali and Veerapatiran annually in the house compound. In a commanding voice, Saktirani tells her this must be done where she is now living. (Her instruction to resume a performance of religious devotion is a common closure in interactions with families of the "disappeared.")

In the case of this mother, as in many cases, those gathered on the veranda mats shared in her agony, and her desperate question about the last missing member of her family incited questions from others on the mats about current threats from the security forces in her area, and LTTE activity there, so that in the general discussion which ensued, others' accounts of fear, abuse, and loss were integrated. The veranda narratives often included outbursts of rage that were understood and accepted in the Kali-permeated space Saktirani had created.

INJURY BEYOND LANGUAGE

A large part of the Saktirani's work today is acknowledgment of unspeakable injury—trauma that is beyond language—forms of injury that are further covered in a second veil of their political unspeakability. In the interior of the region named the "Eastern Theater of Operations" by military strategists, those who are compelled by the local Ammans to engage in "telling oracles" are entrusted with the task of bearing witness. The following interpersonal experience on the veranda concerning a "disappearance" illustrates this point:

A father whose son was one of 158 persons arrested by the security forces at the Vantharumulai refugee camp on 5 September 1990 positions himself before Saktirani. In this instance of mass arrests and "disappearances," the entire refugee camp witnessed the arrests, and those who shouldered the responsibility of organization in the camp compiled a detailed list of the individuals who were arrested. Not even one of the individuals has been found. This father has come to Saktirani after receiving an official letter from the Ministry of Defense informing him that a thorough check of their detention records has been completed, according to which his son had neither been arrested nor imprisoned. He holds the letter of the so-called final report on his son in his hand, which in effect denies his son's existence as a still-living prisoner, or as dead.

He has come to ask the fate of his son, who has now been missing for almost three years. In response, Saktirani uses both body and voice as an instrument for reenacting the son's experience of torture, experiencing his pain, calling out incoherently for approximately fifteen minutes, sometimes voicing the word *erivu* (burning), then vomiting. She returns his *vettilaipākku* offering and lapses into an unconscious state lying on the sand. She then stands half bent as though being beaten, and vomits again. She holds her head, arms, neck, back, and legs—saying that she feels pain all over. Saktirani complains that it is too difficult for her. She crawls to the shrine room. We hear her retching. By the time she eventually returns, those gathered expect her pronouncement of the death of his son. She does not attribute his son's death to the army. She reveals that he was incarcerated in Boosa (a large prison where thousands of Tamil people were incarcerated in 1987 and following years) and survived to be released. She tells the father that his son is living in the south near Galle, and he has changed his identity by becoming a Muslim. The father is crying. He asks helplessly, "Now how am I going to find him there?"

Voicing the incoherent sounds of the tortured, representing injury on behalf of those silenced, Saktirani transforms absence into presence, giving pain a place in the world. It seems that she is not attempting to make sense of unacceptable social suffering but is trying to find a voice to express unresolved grief in an altered world where the rule is to "keep quiet" (*maunamāka irukkavum,* or *amaityāka irukkavum*) about broken connections in the closest circle of human relationships.

The way Saktirani defied social norms of covering the body while rolling and moaning on the sand in a semi-conscious state, and the way she retched and vomited so often, was a sort of counterpoint to the manner in which people moved—it seemed as though people made an immense effort to hold pain stiffly inside to shield the truth from exposure. Freedom of movement is absent in Batticaloa only partly as a result of military checkpoints which are configured so closely that the next point of military scrutiny can often been seen from the point at which one is being searched by checkpoint soldiers. Gendered boundaries and management of appearances place even stricter constraints on sexually mature women in the context of war. Saktirani's seemingly unlimited and inventive ways of embodying the inverse of what had become the norm was perceived by others as the embodiment of Kali.

A FATHER'S *SAKTIYINMAI* (LIFELESSNESS)

The story of Pattini's father exemplifies the efficacy of Saktirani's work in strengthening interpersonal relationships. I met Pattini at a Kali temple on the first night of the annual propitiation. Not many had come for the first night, but we all slept on the sand around the temple because it was not safe to walk home in the middle of the night. Pattini slept near me. She was twelve years old, the youngest in her family. The next day *vākku solluṟatu* (telling oracles) was held for the people during the *puja*. Pattini's mother brought a bottle of oil for temple lamps as an offering, and anxiously asked a female oracle if she had done something wrong, thinking that the goddess was punishing her because her daughters were suffering from *ammāḷ*. (The term for disease which causes pox is referred to as *ammāḷ*, which was, in this case, chicken pox.) Marked by unbearable heat and itching, *ammāḷ* is thought to be caused by a temporary inner presence of the goddess (McGilvray 1982b; Egnor 1982). One by one, each of Pattini's sisters had been overcome by *ammāḷ*. Employing a familial trope of benevolence and authority, the oracle addressed Pattini's mother as *kuñcan* (little one), and replied to her concern: "Don't worry, she (*Kāḷi*) is just playing with you. She likes you, and that is why she is at your place. She won't let go of her hold on you; she will not take her hand away."

As Pattini insisted upon it, I went home with her and her mother for a tumbler of tea after her interaction with the oracle at the temple. One of Pattini's sisters was lying in the main room of the house on a white sheet sprinkled with "cooling" margosa leaves. A cut lime was nearby. As *ammāḷ* is thought to be caused by the burning heat of the Amman's temporary residence in the body, the treatment is to "cool" the person. Then I noticed Pattini's mother talking to her husband, who was lying on a cot in the shade. He was not well, and I only learned that whatever was wrong, it was not that he was experiencing *ammāḷ*. After several more visits, I understood that he spent most of his time on the cot and did not usually rise to greet guests. Pattini and her sisters told me, "The army beat him." He was not the first father of a household I had encountered who would not rise up from a cot in a corner or on a side veranda to interact with guests. I knew the female members of one household in which the father had become so withdrawn he would not speak even to his wife and children.

The following month, I saw Pattini's mother and father at another Amman temple. They were sitting in a special area reserved for those with health problems under a tree sacred to that Amman. Once again, I went to their home for tea. This time I learned that the father was first arrested in a "round-up" at Karadiyanaru in the interior by the Special Task Forces in 1984. Like others, he was beaten. They used a timber to beat him after they had tied his hands behind his back with a nylon rope and hoisted him up so that his feet no longer touched the floor. After that arrest he suffered from pain in his chest and the back of his head. Then, in 1987, he was arrested at an Indian army (IPKF) checkpoint coming home from his paddy fields in Ayttiyamalai. In 1990 he was arrested again, this time by the Sri Lankan army, as he tried to travel between his home and the family's paddy fields in the interior. He was beaten a third time and, after a few days, released. He gave up the idea of farming the fields. Now he complained of body pain in the head, back, and chest, and he said he was unable to do any physical work. Yet they had five daughters to marry, and in this matrilocal region, responsibility falls upon the parents and brothers to build dowry houses for each daughter's marriage. There was only the foundation for the first dowry house under construction, and none of the daughters were married. They had no sons, so there were no brothers to share in this responsibility.

Pattini's mother said her husband's health was growing worse. He experienced loss of appetite and complained of chest pain, and his "withdrawn behavior" was worrisome. I asked if they had visited Saktirani, because I had seen them talking with Saktirani's brother-in-law, who is an Amman temple priest. She said she wanted to take him there but had not yet gone, so we arranged to meet at Saktirani's house.

When Pattini's mother and father sat down in front of Saktirani on her veranda, Saktirani lay down in the sand, and abruptly called to one of her daughters inside the house, asking for a sheet. The sheet was draped on her, and she rocked back and forth, stretched out in the sand. Through an edge of the sheet in her clenched teeth, she was saying, "*noy*" (pain). Then she covered herself up completely, like a corpse, and lay still. After about four minutes of this stillness and absolute silence on the veranda, she uttered, "Should assault. Should assault." Then she began rolling in pain again and moaning, unconscious of the exposure of her body; by this time the sheet covered very little of her, and she held her arms and her legs as though they were filled with pain. "Kali will do the judging. Don't be afraid. You are in the house; nervous and mental disorder comes." The father then complained of his "uselessness." Saktirani announced almost absent-mindedly to the empty space above the people gathered on the mats that thinking too much causes madness (*yōcicci yōcicci paittiyam vāra*). She talked quietly with both of them then, and the rest of us could not hear. She ordered Pattini's parents to bring a bottle of water from their well the next day, which was to be placed on the shrine where it would be blessed and imbued with *sakti*. After that they were to sprinkle some of the water around the rooms of their house and pour the remainder back into their well. She ordered them to make a vow to please Pattirakaliyamman.

Pattini's father seemed to be more active in family life after visiting Saktirani. He sat with me and took tea when I next visited. I suggested that we visit a doctor at the hospital who had recently returned from a period of exile in London. They knew of that doctor, and we kept an appointment that same week. The nurses produced a medical file on his case, which was more than could be expected given the constraints and interruptions in the hospital's functioning during recent years, a period in which all rural health facilities had collapsed. The hospital not only faced an extreme shortage of medical staff, but also struggled with essential equipment in disrepair and shortages of drugs, oxygen cylinders, and water. During the visit he mentioned his pain and his inability to work, and his wife mentioned the general state of *saktiyinmai* (lifelessness) her husband had been experiencing. After prescribing antidepressants, the doctor explained to me that the main problem he could foresee was that this patient would stop taking the tablets, or would not be conscientious in taking the medication as prescribed. He allowed that there was not much more he could do for these types of cases.

Whether it could be attributed to Saktirani's ritual work of calling *sakti* into their well water and strong local belief in Amman ritual which suffuses this collective form of agency with possibility, or the London-trained Tamil doctor's antidepressants, Pattini's father began to work again. He was given a job as a watchman that included some light gardening work around the building he guarded near the sea. Some would deem him fortunate in a district where so many paddy-farmers are unable to attend their fields or to find alternative employment amidst the economic paralysis of protracted war. In comparison with many who have experienced months or years of imprisonment under the continuing Emergency Rule, he would also be considered fortunate in that he was detained for relatively brief periods and lived to be released.

EMBODIMENT OF OTHER'S PAIN

Like many people living in the war zone, the young man whose story follows came to Saktirani for help, and was both hesitant and fearful because the oracle might expose secrets that were unspeakable: his participation in events of violence that had to be kept hidden; experiences of his own victimization; experiences that he did not wish to reveal before a public gathering. Saktirani not only exposed his experiences of torture, she performed and inscribed a shared perception of his pain on the skin of her body and his, and on the memory of the gathered collectivity:

A young Tamil man in his early twenties sat in front of Saktirani and said, "*Ninaittakariyam*" ("Thoughts"). He had the appearance of a healthy young man with a promising life ahead, but as he positioned himself before the oracle, his fearfulness was evident to the rest of us. He then stated that he wanted to know about the possibility of "going out," (leaving the war area to live in the diaspora). Suddenly, Saktirani collapsed into the sand, and for about six minutes moaned and writhed in pain. She also covered her genital area with her hands. She took a pen and drew on the skin of her arms and legs, encircling large areas, and asked him if this was where the pain was most intense when he was detained. He struggled with his response. Saktirani asked when he was arrested. He mumbled an answer, and she immediately told him where he was incarcerated. He agreed that this was correct. He also complained of feeling stomach pain (*vayiṟṟuvali*). Saktirani then took the pen and wrote or drew something on his abdomen, and uttered inaudible words into his abdomen. They discussed his education, and she predicted a "computer course" in his future. She ended this interaction by stating that she would prepare a copper *yantiram* (a geometric design on copper foil that represents the goddess) which would bring him success abroad.

Elaine Scarry (1985) points out that the body and voice are the most elemental categories we have, which we use in moments of creativity. Torture, as both E. Valentine Daniel (1994) and Elaine Scarry have so well described, destroys the capacity of speech. The language-destroying pain of torture disintegrates the content of one's world and self. Torture has been the dominant weapon employed in the protracted ethnic conflict in the eastern region. Saktirani's ability to bring into knowledge the most inaccessible otherness of the tortured body, or the experiences of the "disappeared," gives shared acknowledgment of pain a place of entry into the everyday. As an oracle, she creates an opening for inner trauma to make its way into collective experience and memory. Through the oracle's body and voice, the event of pain is brought from depth to surface not as a symptom, but as her felt experience—an experience shared. Saktirani is, to borrow a phrase from Arthur Kleinman, an "active agent in a moral and political process," as she is a creative participant in the remaking of the local world by morally reinforcing what is at stake for survivors (Kleinman 1996: 189).

Torture and "disappearance" are but two forms of the many desperate problems brought before Saktirani and other Amman oracles. Wives whose husbands have just been arrested come to ask in which of the many places of detention they are being held and to participate in rituals for their release. Families whose members have been abducted for ransom seek reassurance and advice from oracles. Mothers come deeply distressed about missing daughters and sons, for large numbers of young people are now responding to recruitment drives of the LTTE freedom fighters—and "disappearances" of Tamil people continue to occur under the new Peoples' Alliance government. Oracular revelation may answer questions about safety during movement when arbitrary arrests at road checkpoints increase. In Batticaloa, Tamil people who have lost their national identity cards, or who have been ordered by soldiers to tear up their identity cards, chew them, and spit the pieces onto the side of the road, may bring their difficulty to an oracle. Parents consult Saktirani to ask whether they should send their children abroad, knowing they may not see them again in this lifetime. An innovator of culture, Saktirani is inventing ways to address "lost connections" of the family, including the dispersion of close relations to Tamil communities from Sri Lanka which have formed in Canada, England, Australia, France, Switzerland, Germany, Denmark, the Netherlands, Singapore, the United

States, and smaller communities in more than fifty other countries. In 1994, people distressed about "lost connections" (*toṭarpu illai*) began bringing letters written to displaced relatives in the diaspora to Saktirani, asking her if she would bless them on the shrine for Kali before they mailed them abroad. In a simple ritual which soothes the pain of separation, Saktirani chants mantrams over many letters on her shrine now, and puts sacred ash (*vibuti*) inside each painstakingly written letter. During the interpersonal experiences on her veranda, she frequently speaks with the voices of family members who are now living somewhere in the vast Tamil diaspora.[10]

CONCLUDING OBSERVATIONS

This paper has taken seriously the work of local oracles in eastern Sri Lanka, who now embody and interpret the injury of war. It has become their work to address agonizing doubts about lost connections, memory which cannot be erased, and wounds which cannot heal.[11] Tamil families caught in the war zone say they have no control over the activity of the government, Muslim and Sinhalese paramilitary groups working with the security forces, armed Tamil militant groups which have allied themselves with the government forces, or the LTTE, and attempt to distance themselves from connection with political activity. Many Tamil people alienated from the government also carry within them unvoiceable resentment of the ruthless politics of the LTTE. They experience deeply ambiguous feelings because the LTTE represents the need for self-government by the Tamil minority and an end to the impunity of the government security forces under long years of Emergency Rule. Although the LTTE control large areas in the eastern region, in 1996 it was clear that they were not in a position to respond to hardships suffered by the local Tamil people—with lack of medical care and public transportation high on the list. The LTTE is careful to avoid dividing Catholic, Protestant, and Hindu sectors of the Tamil minority living in the north, up-country, and in the east. They articulate their thirst for a separate state of Tamil Eelam in political and linguistic, but not religious terms. Many of the people still living in eastern Sri Lanka reject all sides of the protracted political conflict, and have turned their attention to the practices of Amman cults.

 With the collapse of the health care infrastructure and the judiciary, and the loss of many thousands of lives in the last two decades, the temple and the work of the oracle have been left to expand—providing a place of safety where social interaction can still take place. The oracle and the Amman temple bring some sense of safety to an everyday world altered by the state's configuration of military checkpoints, bunkers, camps, prisons, and other places of detention. The following passage by Arthur and Joan Kleinman resonates with this response to violence:

Studies of dissociation show that when individuals and small groups are under great pressure of traumatizing occurrence or other deeply disturbing events, there is a focusing of attention and narrowing of the field of awareness away from what is menacing toward absorption in a safer place. That place may be one's imaginings, an alternative self, or concentration on a highly focused part of the social field. Perception, imagination, and memory are absorbed into that particular focus. (Kleinman and Kleinman 1994: 717)

Ordinary Tamil families caught in the eastern war zone concentrate on the Amman, who is believed to be imbued with power to return children who have "disappeared," to protect homes vulnerable to the intrusiveness of military oppression, to compel children who have fled into the diaspora to maintain connections through writing letters, to provide information about how to respond to extortion, and to put pressure on military officers to release incarcerated family members undergoing interrogation in detention camps. Oracles now "see" and experience what is happening in places of incarceration under the Emergency Rule and the Prevention of Terrorism Act, in immigration prisons in the diaspora, and in places within and without the war zone that are difficult or impossible for the immobilized population to reach. In the oracle's work we find a counterpoint to the muteness of political silencing and the restriction placed on freedom of movement.

The agency of the oracle is not individually constructed, as it is surrounded by strong collective belief and inextricably intertwined with experiences and sources of trauma. Is the oracle truly transformative? Agentive moments located in the work of oracles are not resolving the trauma of the sociopolitical condition; however, people must still live in the chaos that prevails in the middle of the violence, and the acts of oracles engage this violence. They do so by addressing the pain and loss of trust in the everyday world of this region marked by chronic political trauma.

The collages through which Saktirani begs, borrows, and steals what she can from narrative and cultural practices create a place in which to speak of abductions, arrests by the state, and conscription by militant organizations. She provides moments which interrupt silencing so that moral dilemmas that arise from political fragmentation may be resolved. She creates new practices for maintaining connections with family members in the diaspora. Her motherly chastisements are directed at strengthening kinship relations in shattered families. She helps people overcome trauma and loss, and in this work she does not differentiate herself from the suffering of others.

Saktirani's religious imagination incorporates and reflects the world of chaos in which both she and those who seek her help live. Criticism is directed at her bricolage of ritual practices—theatrical gestures, lyrics of popular film songs, motherly chastisements, words of empathy, traditional and invented rituals. Herein lie the gestures or words which may give to others a sense of future and create new dispositions to an altered world.

To speak of unspeakable violation, people need a safe witness (Felman and Laub 1992), and through her presencing of the local goddess, Saktirani provides this witness. Veena Das (1994) and Lindsay French (1994) ask whether making sense of suffering is necessarily the concern of people whose lives rest on power relations over which they perceive they have no control. Veena Das has suggested that "making meaning of suffering" is a discourse of the powerful. In the cosmology of oracles, who are compelled to act as embodied agents of the local Amman, and who serve as witnesses to the painful histories of shattered families, suffering is considered an inevitable part of human experience.

Possession by the Amman is described by the oracles themselves as a painful sacrifice of the body. Oracles become part of a moral and political process by entering a form of expressiveness which necessitates dissolution of a previous sense of self. During possession, Saktirani is known, before anything else, for her ability to feel the pain of others. Identification with the painful experience of others is a form of engagement which poses one of the most extreme tasks of human capability. With *vālāyam*, or empowerment, of Kali, Saktirani witnesses the painful fate of the "disappeared"—she relives suffering under torture, brings the experience of others who are lost into the depth of her body, and allows family members a shared memory they can incorporate into the process of grieving. In a local world of extreme hardship, she directs her work toward acknowledgment of suffering by bringing the pain of others into her body-self (Das 1996a: 80–85).

Against years of infliction of systematic trauma, silenced families come to Saktirani with fear they must elsewhere conceal, confusion and criticism they cannot elsewhere express, and anxiety which must be hidden at a plethora of military checkpoints between their homes and hers. Erasure from official history of arbitrary executions and the use of systematic violence continues to be part of the work of the military, but it is the work of oracles to speak. In this place, as everywhere throughout the war zone where the ambiguous and dangerous divine resides, words and acts are powerful. Amman oracles are creative participants in the remaking of the local world in a community of suffering—where the irredeemable effect of atrocity and loss must be endured. Inside the Amman temple gate, through oracles' embodiment and witnessing of the injury of war, unshielded truth is expressed, pain is acknowledged, and relationship with death is restored into its process.

NOTES

This paper is based on research made possible by the SSRC-MacArthur Foundation Program on Peace and Security in a Changing World. I have deemed it necessary in several places to alter personal names, place names, and time sequences in order to protect people whose lived experiences are part of continuing suffering inside the eastern region under the Prevention of Terrorism Act and Emergency Rule. I have drawn from my fieldwork in the years 1991–94, and a return to the region in 1996. An earlier version of this paper was presented at a conference on violence organized by the Social Science Research Council in New York and the International Center for Ethnic Studies in Colombo, held in Colombo, Sri Lanka, 28–31 March 1996.

1. While the historical and political origins of violent Sinhala-Tamil conflict in Sri Lanka have received wide attention in the anthropological literature (cf. Tambiah 1986; Spencer 1990; Nissan and Stirrat 1990; Jeganathan 1993), extended scholarly analysis has concentrated less on the consequences and actual experiences of violence.

2. Local versions of the story of these revenge killings conclude with descriptions of Reagan's younger brother, who survived, carrying his mother's corpse from the house in a dismembered state. On 12 September 1996, the LTTE again raked a bus with gunfire near Arantalawa. Loss of noncombatant lives has been immense in the eastern war zone.

3. The Prevention of Terrorism Act (PTA), which defines "terrorism" very broadly, provides no safeguards on conditions of detention and permits renewable administrative orders for detention without judicial review which can be retroactively applied. Under Emergency Rule and the PTA, people are reported to have been incarcerated for more than five years without having a court order or even a charge filed against them (INFORM 1995). As Elizabeth Nissan points out,

> Despite maintaining a democratic parliamentary system since independence, Sri Lanka has in practice been ruled under a declared state of emergency for well over 26 of the past 42 years, with emergency law operative in all or part of the country; . . . the PTA and emergency powers have contributed to the ability of the security forces and the government to commit serious violations of human rights with impunity. They dispense with the normal safeguards against arbitrary detention, disappearance and torture that are found in the ordinary law, and thus facilitate abuse. (1996: 33)

Imposition of strict limits on the extent of emergency powers requires revision of the constitution and judicial review of existing legislation.

4. There have been many extrajudicial executions of Tamil civilians in the eastern region during the course of the protracted political violence. I have documented elsewhere the collective summary executions of 184 civilians from Saturukondan, Pannichaiyadi, Pillaiyaradi, and Kokuvil on 9 September 1990, an event in which 68 of the victims killed in the army camp were twelve years old or younger (Lawrence 1995; 1999).

5. The LTTE has imposed taxes on almost all forms of local economic activity in the east for years, and the organization is well known for its international fund-raising practices.

6. In 1994–95, concerned women of Toronto's Sri Lankan Tamil community began organizing women's groups to help Tamil women adjust in the diaspora. One women's center offered assistance in legal, immigration, and marriage counseling, and operated a hot line for emergencies such as sexual assault. However, young Tamil women who cannot speak English are isolated and do not know how to get

help once they are severed from kinship networks. In some cases of suicide, Tamil women have jumped from windows in Toronto's high-rise apartment buildings where they were locked in.

7. I am indebted to Darshan Ambalavanar for a conversation on this point.

8. An example of this is the attack on Palugamam during the annual propitiation of the village goddess Tiropataiyamman. One of the oracles began speaking as the goddess and giving commands to the crush of frightened and confused people who sought refuge inside the temple, as victims of the gunfire fell on the temple grounds during the fighting outside.

9. E. Valentine Daniel thoughtfully suggested the notion of "redemptive remembering" as one aspect of Saktirani's work as an oracle.

10. The creativity of those who are profoundly engaged in work with ritual, collective, and personal symbols in Sri Lanka is explored in the pre-war writings of Gananath Obeyesekere (1978, 1981) as well as his writing in *The Work of Culture* (1990).

11. In *Holocaust Testimonies: The Ruins of Memory* (1991) Lawrence Langer points out that trauma may transform durational time, so that the sense of long-term future is lost, and death becomes unforgettable.

REFERENCES

Comaroff, Jean. 1985. *Body of Power, Spirit of Resistance: The Culture and History of a South African People.* Chicago: University of Chicago Press.

Daniel, Valentine E. 1994. "The Individual in Terror." In *Embodiment and Experience: The Existential Ground of Culture and Self,* ed. Thomas J. Csordas. Cambridge Studies in Medical Anthropology. Cambridge: Cambridge University Press.

Das, Veena. 1994. "Moral Orientations to Suffering: Legitimation, Power, and Healing." In *Health and Social Change in International Perspective,* eds. Lincoln C. Chen, Arthur Kleinman, and Norma Ware. Boston: Harvard University Press.

———. 1996a. "Language and Body: Transactions in the Construction of Pain." *Daedalus* 125, no. 1: 67–92.

———. 1996b. "Sexual Violence, Discursive Formations, and the State." Paper presented at the conference entitled "Violence Against Women: Victims and Ideologies," 28–31 March. Sri Lanka Foundation, Colombo, Sri Lanka.

Egnor, Margaret Trawick. 1982. "The Changed Mother, or What the Smallpox Goddess Did When There Was Smallpox." *Contributions to Asian Studies* 18: 24–45.

Felman, Shoshana, and Dori Laub, M.D. 1992. *Testimony: Crises of Witnessing in Literature, Psychoanalysis, and History.* New York and London: Routledge.

French, Lindsay. 1994. "The Political Economy of Injury and Compassion: Amputees on the Thai-Cambodia Border." In *Embodiment and Experience,* ed. Thomas J. Csordas. Cambridge: Cambridge University Press.

INFORM. 1995. *Sri Lanka Information Monitor: Situation Report.* 5 Jayaratna Avenue, Colombo 5: Sri Lanka, 5 February.

Jeganathan, Pradeep. 1993. "All the Lords Men? Perpetrator Constructions of Collective Ethnic Violence in an Urban Sri Lankan Community." Paper presented at a workshop entitled "Violence, Suffering and Healing in South Asia,"

27–28 August. Department of Sociology, Delhi School of Economics, Delhi, India.

Kleinman, Arthur, and Joan Kleinman. 1994. "How Bodies Remember: Social Memory and Bodily Experience of Criticism, Resistance, and Delegitimation Following China's Cultural Revolution." *New Literary History* 25: 707–23.

Kleinman, Arthur. 1996. *Writing at the Margin.* Berkeley, Los Angeles, and London: University of California Press.

Kordon, Diana R., L. I. Edelman et al. 1988. *Psychological Effects of Political Repression. Efectos Psicológicos de la Represión Política.* Buenos Aires, Argentina: Sudamericana/ Planeta.

Lambek, Michael. 1993. *Knowledge and Practice in Mayotte: Local Discourses of Islam, Sorcery, and Spirit Possession.* Toronto: University of Toronto Press.

Langer, Lawrence. 1991. *Holocaust Testimonies: The Ruins of Memory.* New Haven and London: Yale University Press.

Lawrence, Patricia. 1995. "Work of Oracles: Overcoming Political Silencing in Mattakkalappu." Paper presented at the fifth Sri Lanka Conference, University of New Hampshire, 10–13 August.

———. 1999. "The Changing Amman: Notes on the Injury of War in Eastern Sri Lanka." In *Conflict and Community in Contemporary Sri Lanka,* ed. Siri Gamage and I. B. Watson. New Delhi and London: Sage.

McGilvray, Dennis. 1982a. "Mukkuvar Vannimai: Tamil Caste and Matriclan Ideology in Batticaloa, Sri Lanka." In *Caste Ideology and Interaction.* Cambridge Papers in Social Anthropology, no. 9, ed. Dennis B. McGilvray, 34–97. Cambridge: Cambridge University Press.

———. 1982b. "Sexual Power and Fertility in Sri Lanka: Batticaloa Tamils and Moors." In *Ethnography of Fertility and Birth,* ed. Carol P. MacCormack, 25–73. London: Academic Press.

———. 1989. "Households in Akkaraipattu: Dowry and Domestic Organization among the Matrilineal Tamils and Moors of Sri Lanka." In *Society from the Inside Out,* ed. John N. Gray and David Mearns. New Delhi and London: Sage.

Menon, Ritu, and Kamla Bhasin. 1996. " 'They Wanted to Die': Women, Kinsmen, and Partition." Paper presented at the conference entitled "Violence against Women: Victims and Ideologies," 28–31 March, Sri Lanka Foundation, Colombo, Sri Lanka.

Nissan, Elizabeth. 1996. *Sri Lanka: A Bitter Harvest.* London: Minority Rights Group International Report.

Nissan, Elizabeth, and R. L. Stirrat. 1990. "The Generation of Communal Identities." In *Sri Lanka: History and the Roots of Conflict,* ed. Jonathan Spencer. London and New York: Routledge.

Obeyesekere, Gananath. 1978. "The Fire-Walkers of Kataragama: The Rise of Bhakti Religiosity in Buddhist Sri Lanka." *Journal of Asian Studies* 37, no. 3: 475–76.

———. 1981. *Medusa's Hair: An Essay on Personal Symbols and Religious Experience.* Chicago and London: University of Chicago Press.

———. 1990. *The Work of Culture.* Chicago and London: University of Chicago Press.

Scarry, Elaine. 1985. *The Body in Pain: The Making and Unmaking of the World.* New York and Oxford: Oxford University Press.

Somasundaram, Daya. 1998. *Scarred Minds: The Psychological Impact of War on Sri Lankan Tamils.* Thousand Oaks, CA: Sage.

Spencer, Jonathan, ed. 1990. "Introduction: The Power of the Past." In *Sri Lanka: History and the Roots of Conflict.* London and New York: Routledge.

Suarez-Orozco, Marcelo. 1992. "A Grammar of Terror: Psychocultural Responses to State Terrorism in Dirty War and Post-Dirty War Argentina." In *The Paths to Domination, Resistance, and Terror,* ed. Carolyn Nordstrom and JoAnn Martin. Berkeley, Los Angeles, Oxford: University of California Press.

Tambiah, Stanley Jeyaraja. 1986. *Sri Lanka: Ethnic Fratricide and the Dismantling of Democracy.* Chicago: University of Chicago Press.

Taussig, Michael T. 1992. *The Nervous System.* New York and London: Routledge.

——. 1993. *Mimesis and Alterity.* New York and London: Routledge.

Thangarajah, Yuvi. 1995. "Narratives of Victim as Ethnic Identity among the Veddas of the East Coast." In *Unmaking the Nation: The Politics of Identity and History in Modern Sri Lanka,* ed. Pradeep Jeganathan and Qadri Ismail. Colombo: Social Scientists' Association.

Trawick, Margaret. "Reasons for Violence: A Preliminary Ethnographic Account of the LTTE." In *Conflict and Community in Contemporary Sri Lanka,* ed. Siri Gamage and I. B. Watson. New Delhi and London: Sage.

The Act of Witnessing

Violence, Poisonous Knowledge, and Subjectivity

Veena Das

My concern in this paper is to see the meaning of witnessing in relation to violence and the formation of the subject. An important signature of the catastrophic violence of the Partition of India in 1947, and more recently of the ethnic wars in the former Yugoslavia, was the magnitude of violence against women (see Das 1995a, 1997; Menon and Bhasin 1998; and Butalia 1998). The violations inscribed on the female body (both literally and figuratively) and the discursive formations around these violations made visible the imagination of the nation as a *masculine* nation. What did this do to the subjectivity of women?

As many recent contributions to the theory of the subject have argued, the experience of becoming a subject is linked in important ways to the experience of subjugation (Butler 1997; Mohanty 1993). Thus we need to ask not only how women were made the victims of ethnic or communal violence through specific gendered acts of violation such as rape but also how they may have taken these noxious signs of violation and reoccupied them through the work of domestication, ritualization, and re-narration. In some of my earlier papers on these themes I have analyzed the discursive formations through which a particular type of subjectivity was attributed in discourses of power to women-as-victims of rape and abduction (Das 1995a). Yet women's own formation of their subject positions, though mired in these constructions, were not completely determined by them. I have argued that women spoke of their experiences by anchoring their discourses to the genres of mourning and lamentation that already assigned a place to them in the cultural work of mourning (Das 1986, 1990,1997; see also Briggs 1993; Seremetakis 1991), but they spoke of violence and pain *within* these genres as well as *outside* them. Through complex transactions between body and language, they were able both *to voice* and *to show* the hurt

205

done to them and also to provide witness to the harm done to the whole social fabric—the injury was to the very idea of different groups being able to inhabit the world together.

In this paper I hope to explore the meaning of being a witness to violence—to speak for the death of relationships. In the literary imagination of the West, the figure of Antigone as witness provides a kind of foundational myth that explores the conditions under which conscience may find a voice in the feminine. Hegel (1920), as is well known, saw a conflict of structures in this story. In his reading, Creon is opposed to Antigone as one principle of law is opposed to another—call it the opposition between the law of the state and the law of the family.

> The public law of the state and the instinctive family-love and duty toward a brother are here set in conflict. Antigone, the woman, is pathetically possessed by the interest of family: Creon, the man, by the welfare of the community. Polyneices, in war with his own father-city, had fallen before the gates of Thebes, and Creon, the lord thereof, had by means of a public proclamation threatened everyone with death who should give this enemy of the city the right of burial. Antigone, however, refused to accept this demand, which merely concerned the public weal, and, constrained by her pious devotion for her brother, carried out as sister, the sacred duty of interment. (210)

As long as we are, with Hegel, looking at the dialogue as constituting the arena of the play, it is difficult to find other meanings in this tragedy except in the conflict of these two discourses. In contrast, Jacques Lacan (1997) invites us to shift our gaze to the *tragic setting* of Antigone. What is the nature of the zone that Antigone occupies in this setting? Lacan specifies it variously as the *limit*, as a happening between two deaths, as the point at which death is engaged with life. The scene of Antigone's death is staged in this particular zone, from which alone a certain kind of truth may be spoken.

Lacan rejects Hegel's interpretation that Creon is opposed to Antigone as one principle of law is opposed to another. Instead he is more sympathetic to Goethe's view that in striking Polyneices, Creon had gone beyond the limit. The issue, Lacan feels, was not that of one law versus another but whether the law of Creon could subsume everything, including the funerary rites to the dead. For Lacan it was never a question of one right versus another, but of a wrong against something else that is not easily named. Lacan insists that Antigone's passion is not for the sacred rights of the dead—it is not that she speaks for the rights of the family against the claims of law. Instead he draws attention to the famous passage in Antigone's speech which has caused much discussion among its commentators. This is the speech Antigone makes after every move has been made—her capture, her defiance, her condemnation, her lamentation. Antigone is facing the tomb in which she is to be buried alive when she makes this speech, paraphrased thus by Lacan: "Understand this. I would not have defied the law of the city for a husband or a child to whom a tomb has been denied because after all if I had lost a husband I could have taken another and even if I had lost a child I could have made another child with another husband. But it concerned my brother, born of the same father and the same mother" (1997: 255).

It appears that there are two points here—the first that Antigone has moved toward the limit at which the self separates into that which can be destroyed and that which must endure. Antigone is making that speech when she can imagine herself as already dead—and yet she endures this awesome play of pain to affirm not her own desires but the non-substitutability of her brother. Lacan, taking the voice of Antigone, says, "My brother may be a criminal, she is saying, but from my point of view my brother is my brother, the register of someone who has been named must be preserved" (1997: 255).

To Lacan, it appears that it is Antigone speaking from this zone between two deaths, who can voice the truth of the uniqueness of being. The truth whose name she speaks goes beyond the laws of the state, and one may say that in affirming the uniqueness of her criminal brother, her passion evokes the crime underlying the law of the city. This is an important formulation on the emergence of voice—it emphasizes the emergence of voice in the moment of transgression. What distinguishes Lacan's formulation though, from the hundreds of papers appearing every year on desire, pleasure, transgression, and location of agency, is that the affirmation of uniqueness of being against the scripting of law is not located in submission to immediacy of desire. Instead the zone between two deaths is identified as the zone from which the unspeakable truth about the criminal nature of the law might be spoken. Why is it Antigone who must affirm the uniqueness of the person whom the law of the state has condemned as a criminal and whom it wishes to consign to an eternal forgetfulness?

For Lacan, the unbearable truth that Antigone speaks is too terrible to behold. For, in questioning the legitimacy of a rule that would completely efface the uniqueness of a being even in death, she shows the criminality of the social order itself. This truth, says Lacan, needs the envelope of beauty to hide it and yet make it available to the gaze. While there is a sense in which one can find the suspicion of vision, which many authors have noted in Lacan (e.g., Jay 1993; McCannell 1986), the relation between voice and vision is a complicated one in the articulation of this unbearable knowledge.

The theme of the woman who finds voice when she is occupying the zone between two deaths is an important one in the Indian imaginary: it builds on but also separates itself from the gendered division of speech and silence in mourning laments. But the truth articulated from this zone is rarely enveloped in beauty or splendor, as even the well-known female figures of

Indian mythology, such as the goddess Kali or Sitala, would testify. Instead of looking at this contrast at the level of the imaginary as articulated in mythology and literature, however, I want to take the argument in a different direction. How does one bear witness to the criminality of the societal rule, which consigns the uniqueness of being to eternal forgetfulness, not through an act of dramatic transgression but through a descent into everyday life? Thus, how does one not simply articulate loss through a dramatic gesture of defiance but learn to inhabit the world, or inhabit it *again*, in a gesture of mourning? It is in this context that one may identify the eye not as the organ that sees but the organ that weeps. The formation of the subject as a gendered subject is then molded through complex transactions between the violence as the originary moment and the violence as it seeps into the ongoing relationships and becomes a kind of atmosphere that cannot be expelled to an "outside." I want to evoke at this point Wittgenstein's (1953; para. 103) sense of there being no outside and the image of turning back that he offers, though the context in which he spoke was obviously a different one. "The ideal as we think of it, is unshakable. You can never get outside it; you must always turn back. There is no outside; outside you cannot breathe."

This image of turning back evokes not so much the idea of a return as a turning back to inhabit the same space now marked as a space of destruction in which you must live again. Hence the sense of the everyday in Wittgenstein as the sense of something recovered. How you make such a space of destruction your own not through an ascent into transcendence but through a descent into the everyday is what I shall describe through the life of one woman, here called Asha. If the figure of Antigone provided one way in which we could think of voice as a spectacular, defiant creation of the subject through the act of speech, the figure of Asha shows the creation of the gendered subject through engagement with knowledge that is equally poisonous but is addressed through the everyday work of repair.

THE ETHNOGRAPHIC CONTEXT

This paper is based on my fieldwork among urban Punjabi families, some of whom had been displaced after the Partition of India. In the years 1973 and 1974 I was engaged in the study of a network of urban Punjabi families with a view to understanding their kinship system (Das 1976). The core of this kinship network was located in Delhi and consisted of ten families who had fled from Lahore at the time of the Partition. Other families in this network were scattered in several cities, including Amritsar, Bombay, Calcutta, Ferozpur, Ludhiana, Jullundher, and Simla. In the initial stages of my fieldwork I started by collecting kinship terminology, making genealogies, recording gift transactions, and trying to trace the marriage alliances. I was very interested then in the politics of kinship and accordingly attended closely to disputations during weddings, funerals, and the narratives of relationships that were obsessively discussed and debated. The Partition had created significant differences of wealth and income within the kinship network—thus help from those who had survived the destruction better than others was an essential component of the strategy of survival. This help took the form of adoption or foster care for the children of one's siblings who had died or become destitute as well as a flow of material help in the form of gifts, temporary shelter, or loans of money. Relatives who were fleeing from Lahore or Gujranwala were given shelter by their more fortunate relatives who had homes in the Indian side of the border. Yet the other side of these kinship relations was the constant allusion to betrayal of trust, to infidelities and the failure to live up to the high moral ideals of kinship solidarity. The manner in which such disappointments in one's relationships were staged, the performance of accusations, and the delicate encoding of references to the past favors granted and relationships betrayed made up the aesthetic of kinship (see Das 1976, 1990, 1995b). It was not that there was any taboo on the mention of the Partition or that no reference was ever made to the homes that were left behind. Yet the personal violence endured or the betrayals of which I was to be made aware slowly seemed to be always on the edges of conversation. There was a delicate aesthetic of what could be proclaimed as a betrayal and what could only be molded into a silence. The memories of the Partition were then not in the nature of something gone underground, repressed, hidden away, that would have to be excavated. In one way these memories were very much on the surface. Yet there were fences created around them: the very language that bore these memories had a certain foreign tinge to it, as if the Punjabi or Hindi in which it was spoken was some kind of translation from some other unknown language. For the moment, I leave this idea here as a signpost for a possible way of conceptualizing what many have spoken of as an inner language and turn instead from questions of representations to the notion of "work" in the formation of the subject. One feature of my own work was that my understanding of the lives of women was arrived at through an attention to the concreteness of relations in which they were embedded. Though there were long conversations, these were in the contexts that sprang up in the course of daily living—thus there are no stories here that were offered in response to the question, What happened? Let me first describe the case of Asha, in whose case, as we shall see, the originary moment of the violence of the Partition got woven into the events of her life because she was already vulnerable as a widow in a kinship universe of Hindu upper-caste ethos. But to be vulnerable is not the same as to be a victim, and those who are inclined to assume that social norms or expectations of widowhood are automatically translated into oppression need to pay attention to the gap between a norm and its actualization.

WIDOWHOOD AND VULNERABILITY

Asha was fifty-three or fifty-four years old when I came to know her. Married into an affluent family of the trader caste, she had lived with her husband and his two elder married brothers in the ancestral home in Lahore. She had been widowed at the age of twenty in 1941. Her husband had typhoid and died within three weeks of his illness. He was the youngest brother in a fraternally joint family. In addition he had been very close to his two older married sisters, who had virtually brought him up since their mother had died in childbirth. She said that the grief of her husband's sisters had been as fierce as her own grief.

She recalled the earliest period of her bereavement as one in which she had received enormous affection and support from them. She continued to live with the family of her husband's elder brother. The fact that she was childless weighed very heavily upon her. She said that she had lost all interest in life. In order to reawaken her interest in life, her husband's younger sister gave her own son in "adoption" to her. The child was not taken away from his own mother, but it was presumed that as he grew into adulthood, he would take the responsibility of caring for her. Such arrangements were common within a kinship group even thirty years ago, for women often treated their children as "shared." (*Bache te ji sajhe honde hain;* lit. "Children belong to all.") It was, therefore, not unusual for various combinations of relationships to evolve over a single child. This was one way by which a community of women took care of a particular member who had become bereaved. In some ways they evolved cultural subtexts, which were anchored upon the dominant patriarchal texts of the society, yet created spaces for new and caring relationships. In this case, for example, it would have been out of the question to let the widow adopt a child outside the patrilineal kinship group—marking one child from within the kinship group as especially hers was intended to create a special relationship between them. In the women's understanding and construction of human nature, a woman, it was felt, experienced the lack of motherhood most acutely; hence, her husband's sisters tried to fill this emptiness in Asha's life. It may be argued that this very construction of female "need" constrains women to invest desire in maternity rather than, let us say, sexuality. Hence it constructs the female self in accordance with the dominant cultural paradigms. This is true, yet we shall see that the cultural representations do not become completely mapped upon the self. If the social context alters suddenly, a different definition of female "need" may be evoked by the woman herself, or by other social actors. Thus individual lives are defined by context, but they are also generative of new contexts. The turbulent period of the Partition, by opening up the relation between social norms and new forms of subjectivity, became such a time for Asha. It is not that older subject positions were simply left behind or abandoned; rather, there were new ways in which even signs of injury could be occupied. In that sense, the question of how one makes the world one's own had to be re-posed for her, and she moved between different ways in which she could find the means to recreate her relationships in the face of the poisonous knowledge that had seeped into them.

During the Partition Asha's conjugal family lost everything and had to escape from Lahore empty-handed. Her husband's elder sister died in the riots. It was never clear whether she had killed herself or whether she had been abducted. In all the narratives about Lahore that I heard in this family, there was a blanking of this period. For instance, I have seen photographs of the whole family in which, this woman—now dead—appears in various happy contexts. The occasions on which the photographs were shown usually evoked narratives of the event portrayed in the photograph, but no reference was ever made to her present absence. A question such as, "What happened to her?" was met with a cursory answer: "She died in that time."

As I have explained earlier, in the months just preceding and following the Partition, residential arrangements were very unstable. People moved from one place to other in search of jobs, houses, and ways to reformulate their existence. Asha's natal family lived in Amritsar, the nearest town near the border on the Indian side, so they became the first source of support for her conjugal family. At one time she recalled that forty relatives were being given shelter in their house. Slowly, within months, as other relatives in Simla, Delhi, and Ferozpur came forward to help, Asha's conjugal kin began to scatter in different places. Asha was left with her "adopted" son in her father's family. But while her parents were supportive, her brother and his wife did not want to take this extra burden upon themselves. This would never have been directly stated by them but would have been communicated through veiled speech and an aesthetic of gestures. As with any utterance that gets its meaning from the context (which is not to say that it cannot be itself generative of context), the fragments of her speech that I shall quote are bristling with unstated words, performative gestures, and a whole repertoire of culturally dense notions that surround the utterances. Thus, while I do not wish to suggest an objectified idea of meaning ("Here a word, there a meaning," as Wittgenstein put it), it appears to me that filling out this repertoire to which the fragments point allows us to construct meaning as a process in which the spoken utterances derive their meaning from the lifeworld rather than from the abstract notions of structural semantics.[1]

Asha philosophized on what she construed as her brother's reluctance to give her a home in the following way:

> A daughter's food is never heavy on her parents, but how long will one's parents live? When even two pieces of bread are experienced as heavy by one's own brother, then it is better to keep one's honor—make one's peace—and to live where one was destined to live.

Asha's formulation—an indicative utterance—also constitutes her reproach to life. I offer an exegesis by taking different phrases of this formulation and filling up the dense cultural encoding which may be said to provide the context for understanding her reproach.[2]

First Fragment

A daughter's food is never heavy on her parents, ...
  Beti di roti ma pyo te pari nahin hondi, ...

Asha is evoking the cultural idea here that even though the norms of kinship orient a daughter toward her affines, the natal kin have some residual obligations toward married daughters if they have met with misfortune. A woman can always lay claims on her father and mother for support in case of trouble—parents do not consider the obligation to provide the daughter with support as a burden because of their love for their daughter (but one should note that the emphasis is only on support for survival; if parents try to provide more to the daughters, it would create resentment among their sons, who think of themselves as the legitimate heirs). Hence what the daughter claims as food from the father's house is not experienced as *heavy* (i.e., burdensome) by them. Clearly there is a form of subjectivity here attributed to parents when Asha takes the voice of the daughter to claim entitlement: yet the most wounding idea in Punjabi life is that this entitlement can be rarely realized, making the daughter into a permanent exile.[3]

Second Fragment

  ... but how long will one's parents live?
  ... ma-pyo kine din rehenge?

When a married daughter makes a claim on her parents because she is facing misfortune in her husband's house, she tends to forget time's effacement of relationships. There will inevitably come a time when parents will not be there to offer her welcome—power will pass into the hands of her brother and his wife. Then the two pieces of bread she is laying claims on in her parental home will become *heavy* on her brother and his wife. A daughter must always keep the ephemeral nature of her claim on her parent's home in mind. The concept of time as a destroyer of relationships occurs as a constant refrain in Punjabi life and accounts for the fact that the actual moment in which one is living is imaged in relation to the eventual. Thus the subject is conceived as a plural subject, inhabiting the present moment but also speaking as if she were already occupying a different moment in the future. This has important implications for understanding the temporal depth in which the subject is constituted and the manner in which traumatic memory opens up time to construe the blindness of the present already from a projected point in the future.

Third Fragment

When even two pieces of bread are experienced as heavy by one's own brother, . . .
  Jad do rotiyan wi apne hi pra nun pari pein lagan, . . .

In Punjabi society, the relation between brothers is acknowledged as fraught with tensions stemming from their coparcenery status. There is a further tension between the principle of hierarchy, by which the elder brother is to be treated as a father, for he inherits the moral obligation to look after his younger siblings, and the principle of equality, by which all brothers have equal rights over the ancestral property and are to be treated as equals. In contrast the relation between the brother and sister is valorized as a sacred relationship in which the sister provides spiritual protection to the brother. In exchange she is the honored gift-receiver in her brother's house (Bennett 1983). A married sister who visits on ritual occasions, carries gifts for her brother's children as is appropriate, and receives gifts given freely and lovingly from the brother's house, is said to bring honor to both families. But a destitute married sister who has been compelled to leave her affinal home to make a place for herself in her brother's house comes to be an object of mistrust, especially by the brother's wife, who suspects that she may use her position as a beloved daughter to usurp a share of the brother's property. Many of the women's songs capture this sense of the married daughter being an exile—her desire to visit her father's home being seen by the brother as an excuse to demand a share in the father's property (see especially Trawick 1986). This is why *the two pieces of bread that the sister consumes come to be seen as heavy:* they point to a time when the anguish of the sister will not be *heard* any more in the natal home. The framing of the future in these terms makes it unbearable for Asha to imagine her transfiguration from a beloved daughter and sister to a burden on the family. It is important to note that Asha is not complaining of neglect that she has already experienced but imagining where her story might go within a possible societal emplotment of such stories.

Fourth Fragment

. . . then it is better to keep one's honor—
  . . . pher apni izzat bacchaye rakho—

Asha knows that in the altered circumstances, her affinal kin were hard-pressed to support her. Yet it is better to keep your honor, she says, by putting up with humiliations in the affinal home—that is considered a woman's lot. In contrast the parental home is imagined as a place where she is *entitled* to receive honor. Thus if she fails to anticipate the inevitable souring of relations and claims what is her right, she will lose her honor. Yet there is more than a hint of disappointment here that the individual story could not rise above the culturally given plot in which the temporality of the brother-sister relation is imaged.

> . . . *make one's peace*—
> *shanti banaye rakho*—

Making your peace does not have the sense of a passive submission here but of an active engagement—the constant doing of little things that will make the affinal family see you under a different aspect than that of a widow who is a burden. For example, while Asha must completely efface her sexuality, she must be always available for chores that others shrink from—rolling *papads* for hours, cleaning a young child's bottom, grinding or pounding spices. Similarly the expression of affect has to be managed carefully (see Trawick 1990). Asha's face, as befits a widow, must always portray the presence of grief—the parting of the hair being emptied of the auspicious red vermilion, she told me, was symbolic of all that is in the nature of a void in the cosmos. The performance of the gendered identity of widowhood has the force of a compulsory social ritual. Yet if grief is too flamboyantly displayed, it makes everyone uncomfortable, as if they were betraying a departed brother, or an uncle, by laughing or enjoying a special snack. There is a special aesthetic of the senses here. A widow, especially a young childless widow, understands her vulnerability for she must incorporate in her behavior the culturally held belief that she is inauspicious—all the outward criteria by which her inauspicious status is conveyed are present in her embodiment—yet her own relation to her body is not simply a mapping of this exterior on to an interiorized self. She reminds everyone in the family of a much-beloved brother whom they have lost to untimely death, yet whose memory must not be allowed to interfere with other tasks of getting ahead in life. Her face and her body must constantly enact this aesthetic. Again I do not mean to say that there are feelings, thoughts, and sensations that are "inner" and behavior that is "outer." But the whole deportment of the body as providing external criteria through which others may read the "inner" is an important cultural move embedded, in this case, in the grammar of widowhood in Indian society.

> . . . *and live where one was destined to live.*
> . . . *te jithe kismat lei gayi, othe hi rao*

Here there is the evocation of the cultural idea that a woman's destiny lies in the husband's house. This is reiterated for girls, whose socialization emphasizes their future in the husband's house. Older women often expressed the idea that a girl goes into her husband's house in the bridal palanquin *(doli)*—and should come out riding on the shoulders of four men as a corpse.

The exegesis of this single statement makes clear how much of Asha's voice was shaped by the cultural, patriarchal norms of widowhood, yet it must be remembered that before the Partition she did not have to consider these choices. It was not that the norms were different earlier, but that the composition of the family and especially the close relations she had with her husband's sister did not invest these norms with the force that they later acquired. Though a widow, Asha had felt loved and had been given the familial support that made her feel that she had a rightful place within her affinal family.

With the Partition came an enormous decline in the family's fortunes. Each unit of the previously joint family was facing new and what appeared to be insurmountable problems. Where would they live? Where would the children go to school? One of the children was ready for medical school. How was his father going to raise money for his education? Under the new kinds of tensions to which the families were now subjected, Asha found a subtle change in the way she was being treated. Whereas earlier the death of her husband was seen as a great misfortune for her, now blame came to be attached to her for his death. She was slowly being pushed into the position of a scapegoat. Sometimes her female affines, that is, her husband's brother's wife and her husband's sister, would suggest by innuendo that she had been unable to lure her husband from the edge of death back into life. As Asha described it, "They began to hint that he had been very disappointed in my looks. He was such a handsome man and I was such an ordinary woman. They said that perhaps he lost interest in life because he did not really like me. This made me so guilty and remorseful that I often thought of killing myself."[4] Asha moved between her natal family, her husband's brother's family, and her husband's sister's family for the next four years. Over several conversations, this is what she conveyed to me.

Everywhere I tried to make myself useful. I would work from morning to night. I was so fond of the children that I was prepared to put up with anything for their sake. But soon the taunts became worse. And what was unbearable was the fact that my *jija ji* (brother-in-law, HZH), who was now a widower, began to make sexual passes at me which were very difficult to resist. I was torn between loyalty to my dead husband, his sister whom I had loved very much, and the new kinds of needs that seemed to be aroused by the possibility of a new relationship. I began to see that I would always be the person who was available for experiments. He never suggested marriage, which would have created a scandal since I had lived in their house for so long.[5] Finally, I wrote to a very dear friend of my husband's who lived in Poona. He suggested that I come to visit his family. When I went to Poona, he persuaded me that I had long life stretching ahead of me and that if I did not wish to be constantly degraded, I should get remarried. There was a wealthy man in Poona. His wife had left him. He was much older than I was, but this friend arranged a marriage between us. I then wrote both to my natal family *(peke)* and to the members of my conjugal family *(saure)* that I had been remarried. There was a complete furor, and they swore never to see me again. They said I had disgraced them with my behavior. And, indeed, I had disgraced them. They had showered me with so much love 'til their own lives had become disrupted, and I had responded by sullying their white turbans *(pagdis.)*[6] They would not be able to show their faces in the community. But I was helpless.

Then followed a period of great tension for Asha. Although she was remarried and in the next four years had two children, she seemed unable to forget her connections with her earlier conjugal family. Her new husband also appeared disinclined to sever his own ties with his first wife, who visited them from her village often to reiterate the rights of her children to the property and affection of their father. In fact, one of her sons came to live with his father and seemed to consider himself as the proper heir to the father's property. My impression, after many informal talks with Asha in which this topic would come up, was that she regarded herself more as a concubine of her new husband than his wife. For instance, when I asked her how she felt as a young woman when her husband's previous wife visited their house, she looked a little surprised and said, "But she had the right to visit him."

This way of forming a new relationship but never quite giving up the older conjugal ties may be an expression of the strong religious commitment to the conjugal relationship that Obeyesekere (1984) argues is the core of Brahmanical values. What struck me, however, was that the first husband did not seem to preoccupy Asha in the same manner as did his surviving sister or the child who had been "given" to her. She did everything possible to reestablish the broken links with the family of her first husband, always referring to it as "that house"— *os ghar nal sambandh bana rahe* (may the relationship continue with that house). This was remarkable when one considers that these relationships could have been easily obliterated from her life, for they were the source of painful memories, and though she never spoke about it, it appears to me that it may not have been easy for her to explain her continued attachment to that family to anyone in the light of her much disapproved remarriage. During the first five years of her marriage to the second husband, she continued to write letters to the surviving sister of her husband. She heard from her that there was no possibility of rapprochement. Her first husband's elder sister, as I said, had died under circumstances that were never made clear. The sexual interest shown by the dead woman's husband toward Asha and her struggle over this relationship had perhaps made him defensive toward her. As a result he was virulent in his attacks on her morality. But the husband's younger sister continued to make attempts for rapprochement, and finally, after eight years of her new marriage, she was invited to come and visit the family from Poona.

I was curious as to why it had been so important for her to continue her relationships with her earlier conjugal family. Her answer was that she felt an extreme attachment to the husband's sister, who had given her young son to Asha. She also felt that by going away she had made the child feel that he was of no importance in her life, whereas the fact was that she felt she owed her very life to the child and his mother.

Then there was the temporal depth in which she saw her relationships. "When I married," she said, "my husband's sister was very young, and she became very attached to me. We had evolved all kinds of games as a sign of our special relationship; for example, we always exchanged our *duppattas* (veils). When we sat down to eat, we ate from the same plate. She would feed me one [mouthful] and then I would feed her one. Everyone in the family used to laugh, but we really had fun." She did not articulate her relation to her husband's young sister as an *individuated* relationship but tended to derive it from the relationship with her dead husband. Thus we could say that the relations between the women were conducted under the shadow of patriarchy, for they could acknowledge their love only through the mediation of a dead brother/husband.

"I don't know. I had such little time with my husband. It was almost as if a flower that was to blossom was picked off a branch. But I had so many desires that in some other time, some other place, they are bound to bear fruit. The only important thing is that I must keep my connections with that house alive."[7]

One is bound to ask, What was the meaning of the second marriage to her? That marriage had, after all borne fruit. There were two lovely daughters to whom she seemed very attached. In one rare moment of explicit formulation of her relationships, she said,

> I have been very happy, very lucky that I found someone so good to marry me. He has really looked after me. To the best of my own conscience I have provided him with every comfort. But I was drawn to this marriage because of this wretched body—it has needs, it has an existence over which I have no control.
>
> I don't mean just my needs. I could not help it when men looked at me with lust in their eyes. It was not I, it was this body which attracted them. If *jija ji* had not begun to make passes at me *(ched chad na karde),* I might have lived an ascetic life, appropriate to a widow, in my husband's house. But after what happened between us, how could I have faced my sister-in-law? How could I have faced my husband in my next life? With him it is a connection for eternity. With my present husband—it is like two sticks brought together in a stormy sea—the union of a moment and then oblivion. I want all accounts settled with him in this life—all *lena dena* (giving-receiving) must be completed. Then I can depart without sorrow. After all he has another wife, and in god's eyes it is she and not I who will stand with him. I am a sinner *(papin).*

It may seem from the above account that Asha had a deep attachment to her dead husband. Yet, in conversations with her it often appeared to me that her husband was a very shadowy character to her. She once remarked that when she saw old photographs of herself with her husband, she felt that she was looking at two strangers. It is also remarkable that memories of her husband's sisters appear to be far more concrete and vital in her narrative and that it was the first husband's sister who slowly overcame the objections of the men to allow Asha back into their lives.

I would suggest that for many women such as Asha, the violence of the Partition lay not only in what happened to them in the riots and the brutal violation of their bodies but also in what they had to witness—*viz.* the possibility of betrayal coded in their everyday relations (see Butalia 1998; Das 1990, 1991, 1995b). Think for a moment about what was taken to be the givenness of life in Asha's account and how that involved a form of concealment of which she was to be made aware only in the unfolding of events. Who could have predicted that a major political event would reveal the possibility of betrayal in much-loved relationships? I have described other cases of such betrayal in my earlier work—the point being that the horrendous violence of communal riots solidifies the membership of a group at one level, but it also has the potential to break the most intimate of relations at another level (Das 1990). The obverse of this is that people are moved to offer support beyond all normal expectations (e.g., neighbors from the other community are sheltered at the risk of one's own life)—hence, the heterogeneous experience one has of these events, in which one encounters not only hate and violation but also an experience of sympathy that can display heroic virtues, cutting short the lengthy chains of claims and responses of everyday life. However, how these passionate moments are carried forward into everyday life requires a different kind of story to be told, and my unease with many such accounts of passionate hatred or equally passionate heroic altruism is that we don't see how such moments are then carried into everyday life.

I have elsewhere described the case of Manjeet (Das 1991, 1996). Some of the memories of Partition for her were of a brother leaving a packet of poison with her while he went out every day, with the instructions that she should not hesitate to swallow the contents if Muslim mobs came to the house. Manjeet, then barely thirteen years old, had the vague sense that while he himself indulged in the deadly games of murder and rape, he expected her to die rather than court dishonor.[8] This had been an experience as frightening as the experience of waiting every day expecting to be attacked or the experience of being rescued by the army. In Asha's case it was when the protector of yesteryear became the aggressor that her life had to be reformulated. In all this, it was the solidarity forged between the women that helped her to not only escape a suffocating situation but also to connect the present with the past. Yet she was unable to acknowledge that it was the community of women that healed, framing this relationship itself within the dominant male-female relationships. Perhaps this suggests that even when a woman has broken the most important taboos, as Asha did, she may not feel that she has really transgressed against the idealized norms. Asha did not feel that she had become another person—only that she had entered into temporary arrangements while her true relationships remained suspended for a while.

I propose that Asha's way of telling her story also tells us something important about the hyphenated relationship between legislation and transgression. It is not that first there is a law and then a transgression—first an individual who has completely incorporated the norms and then one who transgresses. Rather, in breaking the taboo against a widow's remarrying and earning censure for it, Asha felt that she had broken the norms and yet not quite obliterated them in her life. This is evident in her statements that divide her against herself: "I am a sinner," and then, "But after what happened between us, how could I have faced my sister-in-law? How could I have faced my husband in my next life? With him it is a connection for eternity."

In Lacan's (1997) rendering of the passion of Antigone, she spoke from the experience of that limit in which she could see her life as already lived. In juxtaposing the far less dramatic mode of speech that Asha used with the dramatic speech of Antigone, I hope to have shown that women such as Asha occupied a different zone by descending into the everyday rather than ascending toward a higher plane. In both cases, however, we see a woman as witness not only in the sense that she is within the frame of events but that she is herself marked by these events. The zone of the everyday within which Asha spoke had to be recovered by reoccupying the very signs of injury that marked her so that a continuity could be shaped in that very space of devastation.

WITH THE EYES OF A CHILD

Until now, I have described the events of Asha's life primarily in her voice. I want to give one vignette of how her first visit (after she was remarried) had appeared to her "adopted son" (Suraj), who was then about eight years old. After news of her remarriage had come, Suraj, now an adolescent, said he remembered how bitterly everyone would talk about her—the narrative was always about how they had showered affection on her, but she had betrayed them. For instance, her (first) husband's brother would say that "we had clasped her to our heart thinking she was the only sign of our dead brother, but she wanted to take out a different meaning/purpose." (The phrase *matlab kadna* in Punjabi can refer to a manipulative use of others for self-serving purposes.) A common genre of family conversations among urban Punjabis is to address an absent person as if he/she is present. In this case she was made the subject of taunts; for example, "*Vah ni rani—tu badi laj rakhi sadi*" ("Kudos to you, oh queen—you truly preserved our honor").[9] Her adopted son said that only his own mother would mutter to herself sometimes in his presence, What is the life of a woman? Such speech in which no one is directly addressed, but one deliberately sets it up so that one is "overheard" is a common genre of women's speech in the Punjab.

Suraj had been very tense at the prospect of seeing her, his "other" mother. The family conversations had built a diffused image of her as a shameless woman who had betrayed the family and especially betrayed a special trust by abandoning him, her "special" son. When she came, she looked well, clearly had lots of new clothes and some jewelry. Her body was not a proclamation of her widowhood—he had himself wanted to avoid looking at her, as if she were too dazzling. But she did not display her newly found wealth—she settled into helping in the domestic chores as she used to. Suraj remembered one particular occasion, for he had become adamant that they should all go out to eat ice cream. The whole family had been gathered, and the elders were not particularly encouraging. But he said he wanted his will to prevail—he wanted to claim that he had special claims over her against everyone else. Conceding to his demands, she went in to change and came out wearing a colorful sari. A tonga was called to take them to the market and as they—Asha, Suraj, and a cousin—were going to embark, his uncle (the same man who had subjected her to sexual advances) said, "There is no need to show the stylized charms *(nakhre)* of a *sethani.*" The term literally means the wife of a *seth,* or a rich trader, but is used among Punjabis to refer to a woman who is lazy, does not perform household chores, and is only interested in dressing up and displaying her wealth. Asha's eyes filled with tears, and as they sat in the tonga she put her arm around Suraj and said, "See, for your sake I have to listen to such derision" *("Boliyan sun-ni paindiyan hain").*

REFLECTIONS

The writing of history and anthropology in recent years has been strongly influenced by the literary analyses of narratives. As Good (1994) has noted in the context of illness narratives, however, the narrator of the story is relating a story that is not yet finished. In the context of the Partition, historians have often collected oral narratives that are formulated to answer the question, What happened? In this paper I have chosen not to frame the question in these terms. In that sense my work has been animated by seeing how the violence of the Partition was folded into everyday relations. Another way to put this is to say that I am not asking how the events of the Partition were *present* to consciousness as *past* events but how they came to be incorporated into the temporal structure of relationships. Thus I hope to remain especially mindful of the projecting character of human existence.

In the case of Asha we saw that she defines relationships of kinship much more through ideas of care, and in her story the brutality of the Partition lay in what violence could do to alter the ways in which kin recognize or withhold recognition from each other. Thus the traumatic memory of the Partition cannot be understood in Asha's life as a direct possession of the past. It is constantly mediated by the manner in which the world is being presently inhabited. Even when it appears that some women were relatively lucky because they escaped direct bodily harm, the bodily memory of being-with-others makes that past encircle the present as atmosphere. This is what I mean by the importance of finding ways to speak about the experience of witnessing: that if one's way of being-with-others was brutally injured, then the past enters the present not necessarily as traumatic memory but as poisonous knowledge. This knowledge can only be engaged through a "knowing by suffering," as Martha Nussbaum (1986: 46) puts it.

> There is a kind of knowing that works by suffering because suffering is the appropriate acknowledgment of the way human life, in these cases, is. And in general: to grasp either a love or a tragedy by intellect is not sufficient for having real human knowledge of it. Agamemnon *knows* that Iphigenia is his child all through, if by this we mean that he has the correct beliefs, can answer many questions about her truly, and so on. But because in his emotions, his imagination, and his behavior he does not acknowledge the tie, we want to join the Chorus in saying that his state is less one of knowledge than one of *delusion*. He doesn't *really know* that she is his daughter. A piece of true understanding is missing.

In the case of Asha, she was also *known* in her role as the widow of a much-loved brother—her body was incorporated, not only ritually, but also in everyday interactions in the family, in the body of her dead husband. This was the only *acknowledged* aspect of her being. Yet there might have been other subtexts operating—the love between her husband's younger sister and herself, the recognition that she was a sexual being whose sexuality had been forcibly effaced by the death of her husband and the demands of family honor. It appears to me that these were the subtexts that came to be articulated as a result of the turbulence of the novelty that was born during the Partition. Once her sexual being was recognized in the new kind of gaze—someone in the position of a surrogate brother revealing himself to be a lover—she was propelled into making a choice.[10] Would she wish to carry on a clandestine relation and participate in the "bad faith" upon which Bourdieu (1990) recognizes the politics of kinship to be based? Or would she accept the public opprobrium to which she subjected the family honor for a new definition of herself which promised a certain integrity, although as an exile from the life projects she had earlier formulated for herself?

In the process of this decision the subject may have become radically fragmented, and the self may have become a fugitive, but I think what I have described is the formation of the subject, a complex agency made up of divided and fractured subject positions. This becomes evident not necessarily at the moment of violence—but in the years of patient work through which Asha and her first husband's sister repaired the torn shreds of relations. There was the poisonous knowledge that she was betrayed by her senior affinal kin as well as her brother, who could not undertake to sustain the long-term commitment to a destitute sister. *What was equally important for her* was the knowledge that she may have herself betrayed her dead husband and his dead sister by the imagination of infidelity, and made a young child, her "special" adopted son, feel abandoned. It was not any momentary heroic gesture but the patient work of living with this new knowledge— *really knowing* not just by intellect but through the passions—that made the two women's work, described simply as *ais ghar nal sambandh bana rahe* (let the relation between these two houses continue), an exemplary instance of agency seen as a product of different subject positions—transgressor, victim, and witness.

The relation between the formation of the subject and the experience of subjugation was captured by Foucault in his analysis of the discipline of the body by an imprisoning metaphor, "The soul is the prison of the body" (Foucault 1977: 30). In the context of the prison, he argued that the discipline of the prison is not just one that regulates the behavior of the prisoner but invades the interior and in fact produces it. Though reversing the relation of interiority and exteriority, of body and soul, does manage to produce a shock, he seems to me to be still placing himself within our established languages of inner and outer. In her important study of the psychic life of power, Butler (1997) suggests "that where Lacan restricts the notion of social power to the symbolic domain and delegates resistance to the imaginary, Foucault recasts the symbolic as relations of power and understands resistance as an effect of power" (98).

In coming to understand the complicated relationships between the folding of an originary political violence into the ongoing relations of kinship through the life of Asha, I have found the models of either power/resistance or metaphors of imprisonment to be too crude as tools to understand the delicate work of self-creation. Instead I have found that in exploring the temporal depth in which such originary moments of violence are lived through, everyday life reveals itself to be both a quest and an inquest, as Stanley Cavell (1988) once put it. Thus, instead of using metaphors of imprisonment to capture the relations between outward criteria and inner states, body and soul, one may think of these as lining each other, of having a relation in which they are next to each other but joined as legislation and transgression are joined.

It is this relation of "nextness" between norm-setting legislation and transgression that seems to have allowed Asha to have experienced herself as laying claims to the very culture and the relationships that had subjugated her. Clearly the terrible violence of the Partition signaled the death of her world as she had known it. It also provided a new way by which she could reinhabit the world. From some perspectives, her attachment to the past might be read through the imprisonment metaphor—something she is incapable of breaking out of. From another perspective, however, the temporal depth in which she constructs her subjectivity shows how one may occupy the very signs of injury and give them a meaning not only through acts of narration but through the work of repairing relationships and giving recognition to those whom the official norms had condemned. I see that as an appropriate metaphor for the act of witnessing, which is one way to understand the relation between violence and subjectivity.

NOTES

I am grateful to the participants of the seminar entitled "Violence, Political Agency, and Self" for the stimulating discussion. My gratitude to Arthur Kleinman for his enduring interest in the issues we have explored together over the years and to Pamela Reynolds for her critical comments. I have learned much from the writings of Stanley Cavell, and am especially indebted for his generous reading of this text.

1. I am obviously aware that the rules of structural semantics render the meaning of utterances as linguistic entities, but these are disembodied utterances. The introduction of the subject as the maker of this speech necessitates an introduction of context—not only linguistic context but also lifeworld as context. Yet I am hesitant to introduce the idea of intentionality here because of the givenness of language as *parole* requires a certain forgetfulness of the act of speech, as Gadamer (1985) suggests. The fact that Asha was never explicitly telling me the story of what happened in the Partition but narrating here and there, as the occasion arose, certain fragments of her world, makes this forgetfulness an important part of what was said.

2. I am reminded here of several performative genres in India, especially in dance, in which a small phrase can be augmented through facial and eye gestures for anything up to an hour.

3. The genre of women's songs especially those that take the voice of the younger sister articulate this hurt and are common in many regions of India. See Trawick (1986); Gold, Grodzing, and Raheja (1994).

4. I am translating the Punjabi word *gila* as a composite of guilt and remorse when it is a first-person reflexive statement (e.g., "*Mainu apne te aina gila hoya* ["I experienced guilt/remorse on myself"]). It is better rendered as a composite of *accusation* and remorse when the addressee is someone else, but this form of accusation is only appropriate among those who are closely related.

5. The implication is that there would be gossip that they had had a long-standing sexual relationship that was now being formalized.

6. The *pagdi (turban)* is the sign of honor—whiteness here refers to unsullied honor.

7. See Nicholas (1995) for a similar analogy of divorce being represented in Ben-

gali culture as a relation not fully realized rather than one which has torn two people apart.

8. I think what might have been a vague knowledge sensed as a child probably became certainty as she reflected and worked on this memory as an adult. I have described elsewhere how she encoded this knowledge in her story (Das 1996).

9. The English word *taunt* was incorporated in Punjabi especially as a form of doing (e.g., *bada taunt karde si;* "they did very much taunting").

10. I must emphasize that the moral stakes for Asha can only be understood if we can enter a lifeworld in which she felt that her eternity was in jeopardy. A passing comment by a reader who was puzzled as to how the presence of a "horny" brother-in-law could cause such a major dilemma for Asha makes me want to revisit the point about the temporal depth in which Asha saw her relationships. Especially important was her conviction that her relation with her second husband was a momentary alliance of interests, but that in some future life her relation to her first husband, to whom she had been married before the sacred fire as witness, would be resumed. It shows that the moral stakes in her lifeworld cannot be understood outside that frame. This is not to deny that this story is also about the way that patriarchy structures the "inner" in Hindu society.

REFERENCES

Bennett, Lynn. 1983. *Dangerous Wives and Sacred Sisters: Social and Symbolic Roles of High-Caste Women in Nepal.* London: Oxford University Press.

Bourdieu, Pierre. 1990. *The Logic of Practice.* Stanford: Stanford University Press.

Briggs, Charles S. 1993. "Personal Sentiments and Polyphonic Voices in Warao Women's Ritual Wailing: Music and Poetics in a Collective Discourse." *American Anthropologist* 95, no. 4: 929–57.

Butalia, Urvashi. 1998. *The Other Side of Silence.* London: Routledge.

Butler, Judith. 1997. *The Psychic Life of Power: Theories in Subjection.* Stanford: Stanford University Press.

Cavell, Stanley. 1988. *In Quest of the Ordinary: Lines of Skepticism and Romanticism.* Chicago: University of Chicago Press.

Das, Veena. 1976. "Masks and Faces: An Essay on Punjabi Kinship." *Contributions to Indian Sociology* (n.s.) no. 1: 1–30.

———. 1986. "The Work of Mourning: Death in a Punjabi Family." In *The Cultural Transition: Human Experience and Social Transformation in the Third World,* ed. Merry I. White and Susan Pollock. London: Routledge.

———. 1990. "Our Work to Cry: Your Work to Listen." In *Mirrors of Violence: Communities, Riots, and Survivors in South Asia,* ed. Veena Das. Delhi: Oxford University Press.

———. 1991. "Composition of the Personal Voice: Violence and Migration." *Studies in History* 7, no. 1: 65–77.

———. 1995a. *Critical Events: An Anthropological Perspective on Contemporary India.* Delhi: Oxford University Press.

———. 1995b. "Voice as Birth of Culture." *Ethnos* 3–4: 159–81.

———. 1996. "Violence and the Work of Time." Paper presented at the University of Edinburgh on the Conference on Boundaries. October 5–7.

————. 1997. "Language and Body: Transactions in the Construction of Pain." In *Social Suffering*, ed. Arthur Kleinman, Veena Das, and Margaret Lock. Berkeley: University of California Press.

Foucault, Michel. 1977. *Discipline and Punish: The Birth of the Prison*. New York: Pantheon.

Gadamer, Hans-Georg. 1985. "The Hermeneutics of Suspicion." In *Phenomenology and the Human Sciences*, ed. J. N. Mohanty, 73–85. Boston: Martinus Nijoff.

Gold, Ann Grodzing, and Gloria Goodwin Raheja. 1994. *Listen to the Heron's Words: Reimagining Gender and Kinship in North India*. Princeton: Princeton University Press.

Good, Byron. 1994. *Medicine, Rationality, and Experience: An Anthropological Perspective*. Cambridge: Cambridge University Press.

Hegel, Georg W. H. F. 1920. *The Philosophy of Fine Art*. Vol. 2. Tr. F. P. B. Osmaston. London: Bell & Sons.

Jay, Martin. 1993. *Downcast Eyes: The Denigration of Vision in Nineteenth-Century French Thought*. Berkeley: University of California Press.

Lacan, Jacques. 1997. "The Splendor of Antigone." In *The Ethics of Psychoanalysis: The Seminars of Jacques Lacan*, ed. Jacques-Allain Miller, 7: 243–57. London: N. W. Norton.

McCannel, J. F. 1986. *Criticism and Cultural Unconscious*. London: Nebre.

Menon, Ritu, and Kamla Bhasin. 1998. *Borders and Boundaries: Women in India's Partition*. New Brunswick, NJ: Rutgers University Press.

Mohanty, J. 1993. "The Status of the Subject in Foucault." In *Foucault and the Critique of Institutions*, ed. John Caputo and Mark Yount. Pennsylvania: State University Press.

Nicholas, Ralph W. 1995. "The Effectiveness of the Hindu Sacrament *(Samskara)*: Caste, Marriage, and Divorce in Bengali Culture." In *From the Margins of Hindu Marriage: Essays on Gender, Religion, and Culture*, ed. Lindsey Harlan and John Courtright. London: Oxford University Press.

Nussbaum, Martha C. 1986. *The Fragility of Goodness: Luck and Ethics in Greek Tragedy and Philosophy*. London: Cambridge University Press.

Obeyesekere, Gananath. 1984. *The Cult of the Goddess Pattini*. Chicago: University of Chicago Press.

Seremetakis, Nadia C. 1991. *The Last Word: Women, Death, and Divination in Inner Mani*. Chicago: University of Chicago Press.

Trawick, Margaret. 1986. "Internal Iconicity in Paraiyar 'Crying Songs.'" In *Another Harmony: New Essays on the Folklore of India*, ed. Stuart Blackburn and A. K. Ramanujan. Berkeley: University of California Press.

————. 1990. *Notes on Love in a Tamil Family*. Berkeley: University of California Press.

Wittgenstein, Ludwig. 1953. *Philosophical Investigations*. Ed. G. E. M. Anscombe and R. Rhees. London: Macmillan.

————. 1982. *Last Writings*. Vol. 1. London: Basil Blackwell.

The Violences of Everyday Life

The Multiple Forms
and Dynamics of Social Violence

Arthur Kleinman

[Y]ou take what comes, when it comes, you do not struggle against the
war, or against life, or against death, you pretend, and the only master
of this world is time.

SEBASTIAN JAPRISOT,
A Very Long Engagement

THE PROBLEM

Students of *political violence* have extended the concept from wars between
states and civil conflicts to include the oppressive practices of governments.
In a recent publication, my colleagues Veena Das, Margaret Lock, and I have
argued that *social suffering* is the result of "the devastating injuries that social
force inflicts on human experience" (Kleinman, Das, and Lock 1996).
Suffering, in this anthropological perspective, is the effect of the *social violence* that social orders—local, national, global—bring to bear on people.
Diseases and premature death are unjustly distributed; institutions protect
some while exposing others to the brutal vectors of economic and political
power; everyday life, principally for the poor but also for other classes, does
violence to the body and to moral experience; the immense cultural power
of the media in the world order enables appropriation of images of violence
as "infotainment" to feed global commercialism, while at the same time it
normalizes suffering and turns empathic viewing into voyeurism—a violence is done to the moral order. But social suffering is also seen in the
response to human problems by the institutions of social policy and programs that are in principle organized to ameliorate the problem.

In this paper, I examine four instances of social violence: the institutional
and political economic abuses that fostered the AIDS epidemic among
hemophilia patients; the local effects of Maoist totalitarian control over the
lives of ordinary Chinese people; the structural violence in middle-class and

inner-city American society; and the cultural violence of appropriated and naturalized images in the media. I seek to show that social violence has multiple forms and dynamics. I take the implication of this anthropological demonstration to be that current taxonomies of violence—public versus domestic, ordinary as against extreme political violence—are inadequate to understand either the uses of violence in the social world or the multiplicity of its effects in experiences of suffering, collective and individual. The ethnography of social violence also implicates the social dynamics of everyday practices as the appropriate site to understand how larger orders of social force come together with micro-contexts of local power to shape human problems in ways that are resistant to the standard approaches of policies and intervention programs.

The term *structural violence* has been used to designate people who experience violence (and violation) owing to extreme poverty. That violence includes the highest rates of disease and death, unemployment, homelessness, lack of education, powerlessness, a shared fate of misery, and the day-by-day violence of hunger, thirst, and bodily pain (Farmer 1992, 1996; Scheper-Hughes 1992). The World Health Organization (1995) estimates that 20 percent of the world's population lives in extreme poverty. Authors writing about this population, especially ethnographers, use the phrase "the violence of everyday life" to indicate the violence such structural deprivation does to people (Scheper-Hughes 1992; Bourdieu 1993).

The examples are myriad. The hidden injuries of class, the wounding of the self under racialism, the spoiling of identity due to stigmatizing social conditions, the variety of forms of normative violence toward women: all are salient. One of the most inclusive of ethnographic accounts of the *violence* of everyday life is offered by Das (1995) in her studies of the experience of communal violence in India. In that impressive work, Das shows that even in the setting of obvious political violence—say, the old Delhi streets where Hindus killed Sikhs after the assassination of Indira Ghandi or the case of the thousands killed and the hundred thousand women abducted during the Partition—there are differences not only in the dynamics of violence, but in its forms as well. Explosions of communal violence, mobilized for political purposes, are intensified or diminished by differences of gender and geography; they are built up out of structural violence, and, in extending from one unfolding event to another, deepen it. They leave in their wake deep existential fractures for the survivors.

Those breaks in physical bodies and social bodies are further intensified by violence done to female survivors by their own community, by their families, by the patriarchal ideology, and not least by their own inner conflicts between personal desire and transpersonal duty. Thus there is a cascade of violence and its effects along the social fault lines of society.

I prefer to discuss this subject with a slight change in the wording to the phrase "the *violences* of everyday life." But this is a difference, I believe, that makes a difference, because structural violence occurs in a variety of ways that affect people throughout the social order. I do not contest that social force grinds most brutally on the poor. Yet the violent consequences of social power also affect other social groups in ways that are often not so visible, perhaps because they are also not so direct and also, not surprisingly, less likely to be labeled "violence," as we shall see below.

Here I will advert to examples from my field notes and from other ethnographic experiences to deepen this appreciation of the multiplicity of the social forms and dynamics of violences of everyday life in order to look anew at why policies and programs aimed at relieving the suffering that results from such violences so regularly fail.

VIOLENCES OF EVERYDAY LIFE: BOURGEOIS VARIETIES

In an influential account of liberation theology, Rebecca Chopp (1986) observes that while liberation theologians make suffering the core of moral practice and teleology, not all suffering, for them, counts. "Against the bourgeois subject, liberation theology listens to a new subject who suffers: these are the subjects on the underside, on the margins, in death itself" (121). Liberation theology privileges the oppressed, especially those living under the degrading conditions of extreme poverty. Like liberation theologians, orthodox Marxists privilege the suffering of the poor, and like both liberation theologians and Marxist commentators, many anthropologists of suffering and violence (including the author of this paper) work under the presumption that the object of inquiry of societal violence is those who belong to the lowest social strata: those who cannot resist power and out of whose struggles power itself is created by oppressors. While there is overwhelming evidence, as I have already noted, that the poorest poor indeed live under the greatest social pressure and do regularly experience the most violence, have the weakest resources and the worst (health and social) outcomes, violence (and suffering more generally) affects members of all social strata.[1] The lion's share of ethnographic description has dealt with the violence of everyday life almost as if that form of violence were equivalent with the social experience in shantytowns and slums in poor countries or in the poorest inner-city ghettos of wealthy nations. But the *violences* of everyday life also include other kinds of violence in the social order; and it is one of these other kinds of violences in the social reality of everyday life that I will now describe, as I search for a plural subject.

Jane Huffberg stands as a bourgeois protagonist of a fairly common narrative of everyday violence in middle-class North America, albeit one that is not labeled as such. I am drawn to the analogy because of something Jane Huffberg, forty-two, daughter of a Holocaust survivor, guidance counselor in an African-American, inner-city school, and sufferer from chronic pain and exhaustion, said to me after concluding one of our many conversations during the course of a research project on the social experience of chronic illness. "You know, it's strange to say, but in a way, I think my problem is violence too, just like the violence these kids I work with have to go through. I'm not talking about street violence. You know, they are the victims of a violence our society does to them, and so really am I. Only a different kind really."

For seven years, since her divorce from a physically abusive man, Jane has visited doctors in the suburban North American town where she lives because of pains in various parts of her body, exhaustion, and weakness. She has been diagnosed as suffering from a variety of problems: fibromyalgia, chronic pain syndrome, chronic fatigue, immunodeficiency syndrome, depressive disorder, anxiety disorder. She has been treated with an equally wide spectrum of therapies: medicines, psychotherapy, physiotherapy, acupuncture, therapeutic massage, and relaxation, among others. Yet her complaints persist.

> Sometimes, you know, I think . . . I mean life is a violence. It does violence, kind of. You know, family, work, things you got to live with, yourself really. I'm not talking big stuff, but that too; I mean the whole damn thing. All the things! I've got teenage girls; you really, you know, you can't say to them. They couldn't get it, you know. . . . But that's how I feel it is, you know: violent.

The way Jane tells the story, whatever causes her complaints, they are made worse by bad days at school and pressure from her three teenage daughters, who are angry about the divorce, about Jane's boyfriend, and about the amount of time she devotes to her work. But once she gets going, Jane doesn't stop with these issues. She transfers fluidly from complaining about pain and exhaustion to complaining about her former husband, who was an alcoholic who beat her and threatened the children when he was drunk. She also rails against incompetent supervisors at work as well as at the unwillingness of her current boyfriend to commit himself to marriage. Occasionally she talks about her father, a Holocaust survivor, and her mother, a chronic complainer, as Jane describes her. The family lived in near poverty during her childhood. She feels bitter about that. The metaphoric range of her bodily complaints, then, extends deep within the social world.

Her home is a modest, two-story house on a pleasant, if overbuilt, suburban street. When I visited, I discovered that her daughters are almost constantly angry at her; it seemed largely because of the lack of attention they feel. They are hostile to her friend, Brian, and openly negative about their mother's work. In the face of such hostility, Jane hardly defends herself.

I learned that Jane works an extremely long and demanding week.

Driving to and from school takes close to two hours; school is an eight-hour day, but often Jane stays for another hour or two to work with problem students. Once a week there is an evening meeting with students' parents; more at certain times of the academic year. Several times over the past few years, in order to enhance her professional credentials, Jane has herself taken evening courses. On the weekend Jane shops for her family and for her parents, with whom she has a Sunday meal. Because of greatly different schedules, Jane eats most of her dinners alone, her daughters eat earlier, and Brian works until 9:00 P.M. On Saturday nights, Brian expects Jane to go out with him; sometimes Sunday nights too.

Jane describes herself as like her father: quiet, "a workhorse," persistent, a survivor. "I can cope with anything, you know," she observes sadly more than boastfully. "I don't show my anger. I let people get angry at me. But really, you know, I think I'm angry all the time. I'm angry at life, I think. Really, I am. It gets to you. It's too much, really—life is!"

While the hidden meanings of Jane Huffberg's bodily complaints could be analyzed with respect to the hidden psychodynamics of anger, I am more impressed by what her story has to say about the more overt sociodynamics of the everyday violences of middle-class life. There are many middle-class traumas—the "death of a salesman," "falling from grace," "success at any cost," "betrayal of ideals," are among other examples so well known they have become the main material for TV sitcoms and soap operas (see, for example, Newman 1989). Jane Huffberg's interpretation suggests another kind: the violence of oversubscribed time. She has no time to spare; she experiences the loss of time and the pressure of time with exhaustion and anger. The demands of external time usurping the priorities of inner time—this is the violence the social order holds for her. Life is also painful because of how one must cope, what and how much one must do, in order to succeed. Jane Huffberg experiences her life as the trauma done to her by the constraints of social life, which are fierce and have dangerous effects. This *apercu,* that the force of social pressures inflicts wounds, some of which are part of one's defensive resistance to force, describes a core thread in middle-class social experience in North America. That thread in popular culture is often described by the word "stress." As Jane herself puts it: we can cope with anything, adjust to even inhuman regimens. That too, she insists (and I concur), is a form of everyday violence. It is the violence of what "stress" does to us, even as we cope with it.

This sociosomatic way of putting things runs against several related global ideologies: psychologization (attributing social problems to mental states) and personal responsibility/self-help ("Don't blame us, we'll blame you"). Talking about the everyday violence of social reality when physical violence to the person is not the issue may seem a distraction. I choose to focus on it because the societal violence I am personifying through Jane Huffberg's story is widespread, can be devastating, too often goes unrecognized, and can be a major barrier to human flourishing. It offers, moreover, a cultural critique of the normal as well as of the normative social order.

VIOLENCE OF IMAGES

A second form of the violences of everyday life is the violence of images. In several recent publications Joan Kleinman and I (1996, 1997, 1999) have explored how the appropriation of images of violence by the media in turn performs social violence—moral, aesthetic, and experiential.

I take an example literally from today's newspaper. The topic will probably come to stand as one of the three great icons of political violence of the twentieth century's fin de siècle: Bosnia. In the *New York Times* of Tuesday, 18 July 1995, the International Rescue Committee (founded by Albert Einstein in 1933) has taken a full-page advertisement to appeal for funds (p. A9). The top half of the page contains two black-and-white photos placed parallel to each other. In the left panel there is an image labeled "Ethnic cleansing, 1943": armed soldiers are forcing families, apparently Jews, out of a dilapidated ghetto residence. The civilians are dressed in coats and hats. Their hands are raised in the air. In the foreground, a young boy of eight or ten in a coat, short pants, long socks, and woolen cap, his hands in the air, stands before the camera: his eyes are lowered. He appears so anguished you can almost smell his fear. To his left (our right), a woman, also with raised hands, looks back over the boy toward a soldier whose gun is pointed almost casually at their legs. Emerging from the building, out of the darkness into the light, is the shining helmet of a Nazi officer, who is behind another woman and man with raised hands; a cloth tied around the arm of the woman, the reader must presume, is a star of David.

The picture is an icon of Nazi savagery, probably the forced removal of Eastern European Jews from one of the large Jewish ghettos to the death camps. In the panel next to it is a picture captioned, "Ethnic cleansing, 1995." The picture is of a Bosnian woman, her face a grimace of fear and shock; she is clutching tightly her little girl, probably her daughter, who also seems frightened. Though their cheeks are pressed together, the overall effect of the artistry of the photojournalist (Anthony Suau of Liason International) is to evoke extreme tension, as caught in the tightness of the mother's hand gripping hard onto her child, the intense terror and shock expressed by her eyes, and the tightly controlled grimace around her mouth.

The words below the pictures give voice to the serious problem of Bosnian refugees after the fall of Srebrenica. The International Rescue Committee (IRC) makes clear that while Sarajevo may be next, and the UN may pull out its forces altogether, the IRC will stay as long as it is possible to offer assistance. At the lower side of the advertisement is a form that can be cut out and mailed in with a financial contribution.

The pictures, with great artistry, have captured the traumatic effects of political violence. The connection is made between the Bosnian civil war and the Holocaust. That connection cannot stand up on historical grounds, of course. (Nor, to be sure, can the analogy drawn by hemophilia-AIDS families that I discuss below.) For the Nazis, the "final solution" of the Jewish problem—the destruction of all of European Jewry—was a systematic policy, a war waged on a people to the death. The Jews were not uprooted to become refugees; they were uprooted to be killed; and that killing was bureaucratized by the machinery of the state as institutional extermination. But the pictures placed side by side enable the use of the analogy in spite of historical difference: the horror of Bosnia is the horror of the Holocaust. The appeal that follows in powerful prose about Bosnia simply allows the logical conclusion to be drawn about the comparison with the Holocaust. There was no help for the Jews in the 1940s, and they were exterminated; therefore, the reader must act now to assure that this fate does not await the Bosnian Muslims.

It is an enormously effective appeal. One can only hope that it was successful. I have no reason to doubt the sincerity of commitment of the IRC or the usefulness of their humanitarian assistance. And yet the pictures, so visually arresting, also tell us about the crucial mediatization of violence and trauma in the global moral economy of our times. As Joan Kleinman and I have shown (1996), the mediatization of violence and suffering creates a form of inauthentic social experience: witnessing at a distance, a kind of voyeurism in which nothing is acutely at stake for the observer. Perhaps the deep advertising principle behind the IRC advertisement is that by sending money to the sponsor we don't so much feel good about helping refugees as we feel a reduction in the guilt of not being there. They (the refugees) are present as a "hyperreality" in our world; but we are an unreality, a silence in theirs.

The moral implications of violence at a distance are even more disturbing when we consider the change in social experience that is occurring in society. The appeal of experiences of suffering to mobilize solidarity and social action are transformed via the media into a dismay of images. We are outside the field of responsibility; we need feel nothing, risk nothing, lose nothing. We can change the channel, or turn the TV off, or (in the instance cited) turn the page. When we don't, we are caught up in a confusing and morally dangerous process of commodification and consumption of trauma. We require ever more detail of hurt and suffering to authenticate the reality. Over time, as this experience of representations of human misery becomes normative, we alter the social experience of witnessing from a moral engagement to a (visual) consumer experience. We consume images for the trauma they represent, the pain they hold (and give?). The implications of that change are deeply compromising to the very idea of existential responses to human conditions, such as witnessing.

Images are an absence of presence (Shapiro 1988: xii). The artistry of the photojournalist personifies collective violence as the trauma felt by mother and child. What is left out is the politics, political economy, institutionalization, and moral economy of the Bosnian disaster. The image materializes complex problems in the simplifying picture of mother and daughter and the "natural" shock of the comparison piece. This is part of the process of essentializing trauma, providing it with a normative space and normal appropriations in the global order. Yet what fails to project into the photo is precisely the specifics of the social context that make this historical situation distinctive. It is the danger of normalizing images of violence that is the matter; for that process transmogrifies moral experience, appropriating it for new uses—commercial, political—and for purposes of cultural control.

FEAR AND HATRED:
THE TOTALITARIAN STATE'S LEGACY OF VIOLENCE

From 1949 until the present, China has been ruled by an oppressive dictatorship, the Chinese Communist Party (CCP). Although most attention from critics has focused upon the spectacular periodic public convulsions—Mao's vicious dispatching of a million landlords, the Anti-Rightist Campaign so devastating to China's intellectuals, the enormous policy catastrophe of the Great Leap Forward, which produced the world's most destructive famine, the near total turmoil of the Cultural Revolution, and Deng's Tiananmen Massacre—the toll the CCP has extracted from China's 1.2 billion people includes the equally infamous yet humdrum terror of the police state, especially the use of the threat of violence to silence potential critics and to prevent moral recrimination for the CCP's widespread and extreme failings. While police brutality and diffused oppression in work-units and block committees are now less widespread and extreme, though still present, during this phase of economic reforms, the legacy of the recent past haunts the present in widely diffused sentiments of fear and hatred together with political alienation.

From 1978 until the present I have conducted field research in China—field research that was also haunted by the traumas of recent history. To illustrate the routinization of political violence as a social violence of the everyday, I draw upon my field notes for an evocative instance.

It was gray, hot and humid. There were moments of darkness and sometimes light, but mostly things looked gray. The two of us walked slowly through the winding streets of our section of town. The year was 1980; the place a city in the interior of China. I was there to conduct research. He was a member of the hospital staff. We had gotten to know each other over the months of my visit. Ever the diplomat, I thought he had never taken my research project seriously enough to inquire into the details of the interviews with victims of the Cultural Revolution, or rather by not inquiring he protected himself from the consequences if I created any serious difficulty. After five months there had been no serious difficulty, save for my precarious health, and he had nothing further to fear, I thought. Nonetheless, I was surprised when he asked me to walk with him. After ten minutes and the usual clichéd pleasantries, he turned to me and said, "You ask all these patients about their experiences of the bad years, but you don't ask me. Well, I'm going to tell you, once."

Then he launched into a narrative of his bourgeois background, the chaos of the year of liberation which separated him from the rest of his family, who escaped abroad, and so on. When he came to talk of China in the 1950s and 1960s, he stopped speaking about his own life. As we turned a corner, he asked me to look at a large building. He said that during the past he would never have dared look at the building directly. Even now he felt troubled doing so. Each place we passed, he recounted a story about its recent history: Party office where campaigns had been launched, prison, police station, home for the disabled, including those whose bodies and health were broken by political movements, a work unit where something bad had happened.

I didn't get it, at first. Then slowly I began to understand that he was describing to me (through its social location) the core emotion of those decades, and by extension, I assumed, the present. He spoke in hushed tones, often looking around to assure we were not overheard. When I tried to ask questions or interpret what I thought I had heard, he changed the subject. I was seeing fear, pure fear, sedimented in his furtive movements and haggard, wary face.

I understand now that he was giving me a farewell gift. He was showing me what the moral universe of China in the hold of Maoism was like, what the effect of having to endure oppression meant. The ordinary ethos was fear—pervasive, unappeased, based in terrible realities, yet amplified from a relatively small number of events into an emotion close to terror that was present every day. And terror experienced, not far below the surface of the ordinary, on a daily basis created cowardice, betrayal, and abiding rage.

Suddenly, the quiet, hesitant tones hardened into something else. We passed a small gray building. "In there," he said, "we knew the cadres had their special store. They could buy things we couldn't. I hated that! Their special stores, their special schools, I hated that! They had privileges, and we didn't. But we were all supposed to be equal. It was a lie. I hated that!"

Hatred at masters whose hypocritical words extolled the egalitarianism and collectivism of Communism at the very same time that Party members had access to prestige, and power, and things unavailable to ordinary people. He was most upset by the special stores and schools. "They lied to us!" he exploded, shaking his head hard in bitter resentment.

In totalitarian states, complete control of the expression of criticism leads over time to what Chinese refer to as "eating bitterness." You are "deaf and dumb," you "can't speak out," you "eat the seeds of the bitter melon." The suppression of criticism and dissent leads to a deep reservoir of rancor, bitter resentment, and fantasies of revenge.

This same friend explained to me what it was like to live in work units side by side with those who had attacked you politically and physically. You had to get along. There was no time at work for recrimination; yet in your dreams you planned revenge.

This man, my friend of eighteen years, is generally mild-mannered and easy to get along with. He has an excellent way with senior colleagues, though he is somewhat stern and authoritarian to those who are younger. But periodically he would become explosively enraged. At such moments, it was not always immediately clear what had set him off. Thinking about a co-worker or superior who had oppressed him was one cause that he recognized.

Elsewhere Joan Kleinman and I (1994) have argued that the collective experience of fear and hatred among Chinese is part of a profound delegitimation crisis that has shaken not only engagement with the ideology of Communism but even the traditional moral orientations of Chinese culture. The violent consequences of this crisis have not yet been played out. The legacy of burning revenge and unappeased recrimination can be seen in other former Communist states after the breakdown of the totalitarian political order. People feel misled, cheated, betrayed; they deeply resent the social dynamic that brought into being a cluster of violence, terror, deception, capitulation, and secret histories of silent resistance—a cluster that still haunts China.

This too is part of the multiplicity of violences of everyday life. Possessing different histories, sustained by different social dynamics, we assume, nonetheless, that the outcome in trauma and suffering is the same. But why should that be? Why shouldn't the trauma and suffering be as different as a different form of violence or its sources are? And if trauma and violence are different, don't they require different responses? Isn't the implication of multiplicity that policies and intervention programs also must be different? The problem may be global, but the intervention needs to be oriented to a local world.

THE AIDS AND HEMOPHILIA TESTIMONIES

Hemophilia patients in North America in the early days of the AIDS epidemic claim that they were routinely exposed to infected blood products.[2] Thousands have died from AIDS in what patients and families call a "IIolocaust." They assert that conccrn to avoid corporate losses led the blood products industry as well as the government agency responsible for assuring their safety to disregard scientific evidence and led their physicians to bypass the requirement for informed consent. Patients and family members (including foreign ones given U.S. blood products) say that they were not told at the early stage of the epidemic that by using certain blood products to control their bleeding disorder they were at very high risk for HIV infection; nor, many hold, were they informed that safer products existed. Thousands of hemophilia patients not only were unknowingly infected, but infected their spouses, who in turn gave birth to children with AIDS (Keshavjee, Weiser, and Kleinman forthcoming).

A controversy swirls around this little-appreciated corner of the epidemic. Those with hemophilia who were infected by contaminated blood and their family members contend that the U.S. Government's Centers for Disease Control as well as individual health scientists had warned in the early 1980s that the blood supply was potentially unsafe, yet the industry responsible for blood products chose to disregard warnings and continued to provide products that were later recognized to contain HIV. They argue that the industry refused to clear the shelves of blood that was likely to be contaminated because of the economic cost. Doctors, in turn, routinely prescribed these products for their hemophiliac patients without fully appreciating the consequences and without recommending forms of blood products that were safer, condemning almost an entire age cohort of hemophiliacs to being infected by the virus that causes AIDS. Patients and families blame the relevant government agencies for massive negligence in overseeing the blood supply. This position is hotly disputed by the blood products industry, which claims that the scientific data were unclear, that they simply didn't know that they were fostering the epidemic among hemophiliacs by providing blood that had not been tested for the virus. In response the hemophilia-AIDS community acrimoniously contests that industry chose profits over safety and that government and doctors abetted them.

In the course of charge and countercharge, lawsuit and countersuit, the Department of Health and Human Services of the U.S. Government funded a study by the Institute of Medicine of the National Academy of Sciences that was charged to sort out what had actually occurred. The committee that organized the study held a hearing at which, among others, members of the hemophilia community spoke about their experience with HIV and about their efforts to determine what had happened to them. Two students and I were invited by the Committee to summarize the testimony offered by those who participated in the hearing.

Our analysis documented that those with HIV and hemophilia who testified held a common perspective on what had happened to them. AIDS-infected hemophilia patients and family members came to define themselves as innocent victims of a system of negligence; their sense of innocence betrayed is a collective experience of explicit identification with the Holocaust. They charge collusion among commercial and bureaucratic interests as the source of their suffering. Their narratives turn on anger, intense anger at the government agency responsible for the blood supply, the companies that produce the blood products they require, and the doctors who advised them. They are also angry with themselves for having accepted an overly dependent relationship with medicine and industry. And they are angry as well because of their sense that they have been "forsaken" without recourse to justice or retribution for preventable suffering that, in their collective story, results from valuing profits over human lives.[3]

The testimonies by persons with hemophilia and AIDS, their family members, and scientists and medical experts working with them are enormously powerful. They brought the Institute of Medicine's panel of experts frequently to tears. They are difficult to listen to because of the extreme suffering and the deepening repetition of a collective memory. That memory is told, not unlike experiences of those who have undergone ethnic violence, war, and atrocity, in order to commemorate but also to provoke social action. These survivors say that they will not forget or allow others to forget that their reliance on biomedicine, the blood industry, and the government was betrayed, and that something must be done to bring those responsible for the catastrophe to justice, to compensate those who are its victims, and to protect others in future.

Repeated in these analytic terms, the collective narrative sounds overly simple. Nothing could be further from the reality. The testimonies must be understood within a context of AIDS in America, in which those with hemophilia and AIDS feel that their story has not received (indeed cannot receive) the attention it deserves. To gain that attention (and also to express their own existential reality) they use the idea of "innocence"—a powerful metaphor in America—to separate their own group of AIDS sufferers from those whose AIDS is blamed, in the popular culture, on personal behavior (unsafe sex, IV drug abuse, etc.). By doing so, the hemophilia-AIDS community seeks to open a moral space separate from the stigmatized space of AIDS. From that moral space, these sufferers further seek to project a critical perspective on professional authority, the commodification of health and health care, and power and powerlessness in American society. Their experience of suffering is explicitly seen as an extreme and systematic social violence done to them by the American political economic order. The legal battle now underway can be understood as a struggle over moral, legal, and political representation of this catastrophe. In one view it is the result of the nature of risk: no one bears responsibility (see Gigerenzer et al. 1989: 37, 236, 270, 288); on the other, it is a routinized violence of everyday life experienced by those unprotected from abuses of the social dynamics of power.

CONCLUSION: SOCIAL THEORETICAL IMPLICATIONS OF THE VIOLENCES OF EVERYDAY LIFE

In a recent review of Nancy Scheper-Hughes's (1992) moving and important ethnography of structural violence in a disintegrated *favela* in a city in the Northeast of Brazil, I pointed out that anthropology lacks a social theory for framing comparisons of everyday violence in local worlds (Kleinman 1996). This is a subject that still calls out for theoretical elaboration. What then are the theoretical implications of the case I have been making in this paper? That case rests on an appreciation of the *violence of everyday life* as *multiple,* as *normative* (and normal), as the outcome of the interaction of changing cultural representations, social experience, and individual subjectivity.

Phenomenological accounts of everyday life experience show that social experience involves overarching requirements of relevance and exigency (Kleinman and Kleinman 1991). Wheresoever power orients practices—and that is everywhere—there is violence. That is to say, social power is responsible for (and responds to) relevance and exigency. Hierarchy and inequality, which are so fundamental to social structures, normalize violence. Violence is what lends to culture its authoritativeness. Violence creates (and reemerges from) fear, anger, and loss—what might be called the infrapolitical emotions. Violence, in this perspective, is the vector of cultural processes that work through the salient images, structures, and engagements of everyday life to shape local worlds. Violence, thus, is crucial to cultural processes of routinization, legitimation, essentialism, normalization, and simplification through which the social world orders the flow of experience within and between body-selves.

Such social (or cultural) violence is most clearly seen in the brutal deprivations and predations found in settings of extreme poverty (Bourdieu 1993; Farmer 1996; Bourgeois 1996). But as the phrase "the *violences* of everyday life" is meant to indicate, this is only one kind of social violence, albeit the most degrading and destructive of local worlds. The violence of images and the violence in middle-class life under the regime of disordering capitalism, the violence of social institutional practices, such as that experienced by the hemophilia community in the time of AIDS, and the violences that oppressive political structures do to local moral economies in the production of resentment and resistance—all are forms of social and cultural violence that shape (and are shaped by) social experience. Through violence in social experience, as mediated by cultural representations, social formations are not just replicated, but the ordinary lives of individuals are also shaped, and all-too-often twisted, bent, even broken.

Perhaps when compared to the extremes of political violence—the Holocaust, World Wars I and II, the uprooting of entire populations due to so-called low-intensity warfare—cultural and social violence may seem like another order altogether of violent events and their traumatic effects. And indeed such violence is distinctive. Yet, for this very reason, the study of the violences of everyday life is significant, because it offers an alternative view of human conditions that may give access to fundamental, if deeply disturbing, processes of social organization.

These processes interfuse the social body and the lived body (Turner 1992). They are sociosomatic interconnections between local moral worlds and people living in those worlds. Everyday violence occurs in collective experience *and* in the subjectivity of personal experience. Large-scale political and economic forces—war, economic restructuring, displacement—have the power to break through the constraints of local contexts, to overwhelm local power relations, to make whole classes of people victims. To some extent, local worlds (communities, networks, families) can modify these effects: here dampening them, there intensifying the outcomes. A political movement encouraging communal violence may be a national or regional phenomenon; but determining who to attack, whether to protect neighbors, when to turn on friends is a local process that emerges from contexts of relationships (Das 1995; Tambiah 1997). Out of this interplay of national/international and local forces, both the trauma and resilience of persons emerges as a narratized fate and an experienced agency. Massive political violence must work through local worlds in which social and cultural violence is already a routine part of day-to-day living. And in its aftermath, the response of a community, or a neighborhood, or a family to short-term horror is inseparable from that humdrum background of violence as usual.

Rather than view violence, then, simply as a set of discrete events, which quite obviously it also can be, the perspective I am advancing seeks to unearth those entrenched processes of ordering the social world and making (or realizing) culture that themselves are forms of violence: violence that is multiple, mundane, and perhaps all the more fundamental because it is the hidden or secret violence out of which images of people are shaped, experiences of groups are coerced, and agency itself is engendered. Because the cultural prefiguring and normative social workings of violence shape its consequences as forms of suffering and means of coping, such violence must also be at work in the institutions that authorize response and in the ordinary practices of engagement. Policies and programs participate in the very violence they seek to respond to and control. Bureaucratic indifference, for example, can deepen and intensify human misery by applying legal, medical, and other technical categories that further burden social and individual experience (see Das 1995; Herzfeld 1992).

The violences of everyday life are what create the "existential." In this view, the existential is not the result of a uniform human nature but rather emerges out of the inherent multiplicities, ironies, and instabilities of human conditions (shared and particular) in local moral worlds. It is this instructive process of the *naturalization* of social experience and individual agency that must become the object of inquiry of ethnographies of the violences of everyday life.

NOTES

1. Violence among the near poor, the working class, and the middle class includes street violence, domestic violence, and violence related to state terror, forced uprooting, and other traumatic consequences of civil conflict. But as I illustrate in the case of Jane Huffberg, there are also the social violences associated with

work and the brutalizing compression of space and time under the regime of disordering capitalism. These include the negative health effects of sociosomatic pressures and problems such as the psychosomatic effects of joblessness, underemployment, downsizing, inadequate retirement support, downward social mobility, and a host of other forms of social violence. The delegitimation of the moral order, which includes alienation at interpersonal and subjective levels, is yet another example of such social trauma.

2. The materials for this analysis come from testimony given by hemophilia patients and their family members, including those with AIDS, on a public panel organized by a Committee of the Institute of Medicine, National Academy of Sciences, on 12 September 1994 that was charged with the responsibility for studying the questions concerning the U.S. blood supply in the era of HIV. Estimates are that between 1981 and 1985 over half of the hemophilia patients in the United States were infected by HIV via contaminated blood products, with more than three thousand developing AIDS.

3. There are active lawsuits litigating this charge. Although the issue has been settled in Japan and a number of European countries with court victories on behalf of hemophilia patients with AIDS and their families that include financial awards and also jail sentences for officials held responsible for negligence, this has not happened in the United States. In America, it is still an open question as to whether the hemophilia community will prevail in its quest for justice and compensation.

REFERENCES

Bourdieu, P. 1993. *La Misere du Monde*. Pana: Editions du Seuil.

Bourgeois, P. 1996. *In Search of Respect*. Cambridge: Cambridge University Press.

Chopp, R. 1986. *The Praxis of Suffering*. Maryknoll, NY: Orbis.

Das, V. 1995. *Critical Events: An Anthropological Perspective on Contemporary India*. Delhi: Oxford University Press.

Farmer, P. 1992. *AIDS and Accusation: Haiti and the Geography of Blame*. New York: University of California Press.

Farmer, P. 1996. "On Suffering and Structural Violence: a View from Below." *Daedalus* 125, no. 1 (special issue entitled *Social Suffering*): 261–83.

Gigerenzer et al. 1989. *The Empire of Chance: How Probability Changed Science and Everyday Life*. New York: Cambridge University Press.

Herzfeld, M. 1992. *The Social Production of Indifference: Exploring the Symbolic Roots of Western Bureaucracy*. New York: Berg.

Japrisot, Sebastian. 1994. *A Very Long Engagement*. Trans. Linda Coverdale. New York: Plume/Penguin Books, 172–73.

Keshavjee, S.; S. Weiser; and A. Kleinman. Forthcoming. "AIDS and Hemophilia Testimonies: A Collective Experience of Illness and Suffering." Paper prepared for the Institute of Medicine, National Academy of Sciences' Committee on AIDS and the American Blood Supply.

Kleinman, A. 1996. *Writing at the Margin: Discourse between Anthropology and Medicine*. Berkeley: University of California Press.

Kleinman, A.; V. Das; and M. Lock, eds. 1996. "Introduction." *Daedalus* 125, no. 1 (special issue entitled *Social Suffering*): xi–xx.

Kleinman, A., and J. Kleinman. 1991. "Suffering and Its Professional Transformation: Toward an Ethnography of Interpersonal Experience." *Culture, Medicine, and Psychiatry* 15, no. 3: 275–301.

———. 1994. "Cultural Revolution. How Bodies Remember: Social Memory and Bodily Experience of Criticism, Resistance, and Delegitimation Following China's Cultural Revolution." *New Literary History* 25:707–723.

———. 1996. "The Appeal of Experience: The Dismay of Images: Cultural Appropriations of Suffering in our Times." *Daedalus* 125, no. 1 (special issue entitled *Social Suffering*): 1–23.

———. 1997. "Moral Transformation of Health and Suffering in Chinese Society." In *Morality and Health,* ed. P. Rozin and A. Brandt. New York: Routledge.

———. 1999. "The Moral, the Political, and the Medical: A Sociosomatic View of Suffering." In *Medicine and the History of the Body: Proceedings of the Taniguchi Foundation International Symposia on the Comparative History of Medicine,* ed. Y. Otsuka, S. Saskai, and S. Kuriyama. Tokyo: Ishiyaku EuroAmerica.

Newman, K. 1989. *Falling from Grace: The Experience of Downward Mobility in the American Middle Class.* New York: The Free Press.

Scheper-Hughes, N. 1992. *Death without Weeping: The Violence of Everyday Life in Brazil.* Berkeley: University of California Press.

Shapiro, M. 1988. *The Politics of Representation: Writing Practices in Biography, Photography, and Policy Analysis.* Madison, WI: University of Wisconsin Press.

Tambiah, S. 1997. "Friends, Neighbors, Enemies, Strangers: Aggressor and Victim in Civilian Ethnic Riots." *Social Science and Medicine* 45, no. 8: 1177–89.

Turner, B. S. 1992. *Regulating Bodies: Essays in Medical Sociology.* London: Routledge.

World Health Organization. 1995. *World Health Report.* Geneva: WHO.

Body and Space in a Time of Crisis

Sterilization and Resettlement
during the Emergency in Delhi

Emma Tarlo

On 26 June 1975 Indira Gandhi declared a state of internal emergency in India.[1] Her announcement was followed by nineteen months of tightly implemented state control, during which many of the policies that had been hovering in the background of Indian politics were suddenly implemented with rapid and brutal efficiency. In Delhi, the two policies with the most widespread impact were the Resettlement Scheme and the Family Planning Scheme: the former aimed at demolishing all "unauthorized" dwellings and shifting the inhabitants to the outskirts of the city; the latter at controlling the "exploding population" by promoting family planning. In both cases the people most directly affected by the schemes were those from the lowest socioeconomic strata who inhabited the largest proportion of "unauthorized" dwellings and were the easiest to target for family planning. They included rickshaw walas, sweepers, peons, laborers, craftspeople, street vendors, and their families. The fact that such citizens generally refer to the Emergency as *nasbandi ka vakt* (the sterilization time) and that some even think that the term *emergency* means "sterilization" gives an idea of the atmosphere of the times.

While the demolition drive intruded deep into the private space of the home, the sterilization drive went one step further, threatening the individual at the level of the body. And although the two policies initially functioned in isolation, it was not long before they began to operate in unison, trapping their victims at the vulnerable point of intersection. For those caught in the middle, the only way to lessen the impact was to divert the effects of one policy by participating in the other. This became a common survival strategy, but one which often involved the transfer of victimhood onto friends, neighbors, and total strangers in the effort to save oneself. This set rolling a process of co-victimization, whereby the obvious targets of the Emergency also became active agents in the search for yet more victims. How ordinary Delhi citizens were drawn to participate in the growing market that developed for bodies and space in the capital city is the main theme examined in this paper.

Despite the passing of two decades, it is not difficult to meet the people who once found themselves the primary physical targets of Emergency policies in Delhi. Many live in the various resettlement colonies[2] that line the outer edges of the city. It was here that the interlocking of housing policies with family planning policies was at its most explicit. This was true both in the early resettlement colonies established in the 1960s and in the sixteen new colonies established during the Emergency itself.[3] This study is based on the particular experiences of people living in an East Delhi trans-Jamuna colony officially known as "Seelampur Phase 3 and 4," but locally known as "Welcome."[4] Like other resettlement colonies, Welcome houses people from all over Delhi, and in this sense its population can be considered representative of a wide range of different Delhi experiences. Some inhabitants had been living and working in the factories, workshops, and streets of Old Delhi when their homes were demolished and they were "resettled" during the Emergency; others had been working in building sites and commercial centers in New Delhi, and still others were already located in the colony and its environs when the state of emergency was declared. Since the colony was initially established back in 1963, it provides interesting insight into the nature of the different problems faced by those already settled in the colony and those who joined it during the Emergency years. But before examining their experiences, I must outline the structure of the family planning policy, the housing policy, and the process by which the two became interlocked in Delhi.

FAMILY PLANNING DURING THE EMERGENCY

The structure of the Family Planning scheme which, by February 1976, had become part of Sanjay Gandhi's "four-point program"[5] is relatively well known (see, for example, Gwatkin 1979). In Delhi the force of the scheme lay in its centralized grip not only over government institutions: schools, colleges, hospitals, police stations, transport bodies, and all offices of the MCD (Municipal Corporation of Delhi) and DDA (Delhi Development Authority), but also over private industries, civic bodies, traders, shopkeepers, cinema halls, and, to some extent, even trade unions (Dayal and Bose 1977: 120–57). By April 1976, it had become clear that the main thrust of the program was not that people should plan their families but that they should cease to reproduce altogether once they already had two children. This was to be achieved through the quick and relatively easy operation of vasectomy and, to a lesser extent, tubectomy.[6] What rapidly emerged was a pyramid of pressure for sterilization, headed by Sanjay Gandhi (the Prime Minister's youngest son, whose political experience and credentials were questionable), flanked by members of the "Family Planning Motivation Committee"[7] and the heads of government offices, civic bodies, and major industries. Situated further down the pyramid were senior employees, followed by their juniors. At the bottom were low-income workers: peons, cleaners, coolies, gardeners, packers, delivery men, and transporters. The intention was to create a structure of motivation which was to function through an elaborate package of "incentives" and "disincentives." Heads of institutions were provided targets for sterilization and were instructed to recruit their victims from their staff. They were threatened with "severe consequences" if they failed to meet these targets and promised substantial increments and rewards if their efforts proved successful. And it was through this same structure of threats and rewards that the pressure worked its way down the human chain to the bottom of the pyramid where unskilled workers who had more than two children found their salaries withdrawn until they got themselves sterilized. While the pressure for sterilization worked from the top downwards, the accumulation of cases worked from the bottom up. If a lower-level official could boast that he had motivated twenty cases, then his superior might be able to accumulate as many as one hundred cases, and the head of a large institution as many as one thousand. Rewards, in the form of cash, promotions, and increments would then be duly distributed, providing people with a further incentive to motivate yet more cases in the hope of outdoing rival officers, institutions, or companies and reaping further benefits. These institutional pyramids, when slotted together, contributed to the achievements of the Union Territory of Delhi. Meanwhile individual states were left to raise their own targets and exceed them by almost whatever means they could, thereby creating an atmosphere of interstate competition. Delhi, as the capital, was to set a spectacular example.[8] According to official statistics, in the year 1975–76 it more than doubled its target of 11,200 sterilizations, and in 1976–77 it more than quadrupled its target of 29,000,[9] thereby achieving a record of 138,517 sterilizations—477 percent of the target (Ministry of Health and Family Planning 1975–1977).

There is no doubt that the pressure in government institutions, though intense throughout the system, accumulated most at the bottom of the hierarchy where those with no one beneath them could not gain merit by motivating inferiors but could merely save themselves from unemployment by submitting their own bodies to the operating table. Of the people interviewed in Welcome, all the men with more than two children who were working in the MCD—a mixture of sweepers, water-supply men, demolition workers, construction workers, carpenters, and gardeners—were sterilized (or occasionally had their wives sterilized) under the threat of losing their jobs. The same was true for all those with two or more children employed by the DDA and DESU (Delhi Electricity Supply Undertaking).[10] But the fact that the pressure dug deepest into the bodies of the unskilled labor force should not deceive one into thinking that its members did not actively participate in the very system of motivations and rewards that oppressed them. For the pressure to motivate others for sterilization extended into every domain, both inside and outside the workplace and at every level of the socioeconomic strata. So too did the system of rewards and deprivations. And it was when these "incentives" and "disincentives" became framed in terms of land and property that the family planning program and the DDA housing schemes joined hands.

URBAN DEVELOPMENT AND THE DDA DURING THE EMERGENCY

Urban development policies in Delhi during the Emergency were built around the notion of clearing, beautifying, and imposing order on the city. These objectives were to be obtained by three major plans of action: demolition, resettlement, and planting trees. Unauthorized property all over the city succumbed to DDA and MCD bulldozers, leaving more than half a million people displaced.[11] The vast majority of these were either *jhuggi* (slum shack) dwellers or residents of congested areas in the heart of the old city previously known as Shahjahanabad, which had earlier been classified as a "notified slum" and scheduled for massive clearance and redevelopment. The displaced were shifted in trucks to resettlement colonies on the outskirts of the city, where most were allocated small plots on which they were entitled to build new homes. As vast sections of the urban poor found themselves relocated on the edges of the metropolis, their demolished territories were either leveled for new development or converted into park land and planted with trees. Where there was insufficient space for such ecological imperatives, the remaining buildings were spruced up, and the area declared beautified.

The parallels between the sterilization drive and the demolition drive, both of which seemed to function to remove the urban poor, if not obliterate them from the city center, are impossible to ignore, but we must also recognize that the two policies initially functioned independently, with the latter taking the lead. This meant that during the first ten months of the Emergency all of the people whose homes were demolished had the right to a DDA plot without having to prove their participation in family planning. By the summer of 1976 the situation had changed. The DDA, having already accumulated sterilization cases from among its staff, began to extend its family planning objectives into the public domain by making family planning, and in particular sterilization, a criterion for the right to DDA housing. Flats, plots, tenements, and loans were officially denied to those with more than two children who were not sterilized, while those with less than two children had to sign a declaration promising to limit their off-spring to two. To those already living in DDA property who had more than two children, the DDA announced its plans for eviction, while to those who got themselves voluntarily sterilized, the DDA offered priority allotments of new or existing housing facilities (Dayal and Bose 1977: 212–15). An order issued by the Delhi Administration on 15 May 1976 clarifies the objectives. Under the heading "Provisions for the General Public" it reads, "Allotment of houses flats, tenements, shops, and plots in all income groups . . . will be made only to "eligible persons" or eligible couples. An ineligible person can become eligible on production of the sterilization certificate in respect of him/her or his wife or her husband from the prescribed authority" (223).

By incorporating the family planning policy into its housing policies, the DDA had effectively trapped thousands of Delhi citizens into sterilization. This trap was deepest for those citizens whose homes were being demol-ished on the outskirts of the city. As summer temperatures gave way to the hostile monsoon months,[12] the need to have some form of shelter was obvi-ous, but with demolition squads all over the city, it became increasingly difficult to squat temporarily on unauthorized land. Some of the displaced citizens from inner-city areas were still able to obtain plots purely on the basis of demolition slips, while others took shelter with relatives to tide them over for this harrowing period, but for *jhuggi* dwellers living in and around resettlement colonies, the situation was more difficult. Their relatives were either in their villages of origin or, like them, displaced from demolished *jhuggi*s. For them, the only official way of remaining in Delhi was by getting sterilized through the rapidly emerging DDA family planning motivation camps. It was essentially a choice between sterilization or homelessness. Through examining the reactions of those who obtained plots in Welcome, we can gain insight into how people coped with and, to some extent, cir-cumvented this choice.

WELCOME:
A RESETTLEMENT COLONY UNDER THE EMERGENCY REGIME

Although Welcome was to take its current shape during the Emergency, it is not a direct product of the Emergency period.[13] It was initially developed under the Jhuggi Jhompri Removal Scheme (JJRS) in the 1960s when evicted slum dwellers were allocated plots on a leasehold basis in exchange for their demolished *jhuggi*s.[14] To be entitled to a plot, families had to be in possession of a DDA or MCD "demolition slip" and "allotment slip" (some-times combined), which served as proof of their authenticity and entitle-ment. What they got in return was a temporary "camping plot" (twenty-five square yards) or a "commercial plot" (twelve square yards), for which they

were charged a nominal license fee.[15] Some wealthier residents soon transferred to built-up tenements on a rental basis, but the majority either made
do with simple plots or left the colony. By the mid-1970s there were 2,551
residential plots in Welcome, of which approximately 75 percent were in
the hands of the original allottees, with the remaining 25 percent either
abandoned, rented, squatted, or purchased by newcomers.

How did the DDA's Emergency policies affect the development of the
colony? The most obvious effect was that an additional 1,483 plots were provided for incoming residents. They were people whose homes had been
destroyed in the new demolition drives throughout the city[16] as well as tenants from nearby areas and people transferring from other resettlement
colonies further afield. Those who were "fortunate" enough to have their
homes demolished in 1975 were allocated plots on the simple basis of
demolition slips, but for many of those entering the colony in 1976, as well
as those already living in the colony without allotment slips, the situation
was more complicated. They soon found themselves trapped in the new
double bind initiated by the DDA's intensive participation in the family
planning scheme. What this actually meant varied considerably according to
a person's particular situation, but the main thrust was that without a sterilization certificate, a family risked losing its right to both property and space:
those whose homes had been or were being demolished in and around
Welcome were barred from getting new plots, whereas those who had purchased or rented accommodation in the colony were threatened with eviction. By contrast, those who produced a sterilization certificate could obtain
plots, regularize unauthorized structures, transfer from other colonies,
obtain loans, transform residential into commercial plots, and do all manner of things which were usually impossible. But the one problem was that
in order to do these things, a person had to get sterilized. Or so it at first
appeared from the DDA statement that a person must produce a sterilization certificate "in respect of him/her or his wife or her husband." Further
scrutiny reveals an ambiguity in the wording of the document, however,
which was to offer the seekers and savers of plots an alternative path. When
the document states that the certificate should be "in respect" of the husband or wife, we need to ask what this actually means. Does it mean that it
is the husband or wife who must get sterilized and produce their own
certificates, or does it mean that as long as either the husband or wife reg-
isters a sterilization certificate then the transaction is valid? If in theory it
meant only the former, in practice it clearly meant the latter too. This gave
vulnerable people two alternatives to homelessness: either they could get
sterilized and submit their own certificates, or they could produce someone
else's certificate as proof that they had "motivated" the latter. It was, of
course, an extension of the system practiced in government institutions,
where the motivators rather than the motivated reaped the choicest

rewards. And it was this possibility of motivating the other that was to invite the process of co-victimization as many chose to transfer the pressure for sterilization onto those more vulnerable than themselves. As one man in the colony recently put it, "It was like sacrificing others to get benefits for yourself."

Before turning to the personal experiences of people in the colony, it is helpful to get an idea of the number of people involved. Of the 3,459 personal files available concerning plots in Welcome,[17] a total of 975 (28.1 percent) contain a document called the "DDA Family Planning Centre Allotment Order." These orders bear witness to 1,098 operations, of which 506 (46.1 percent) were "motivated," 486 (44.3 percent) were "self," and 106 (9.6 percent) remain unspecified. The number of operations exceeds the number of allotment orders because in some cases the DDA extracted more than one case per plot out of the motivators. These figures do, of course, represent only property-related cases. To obtain the total number of operations performed on the residents of Welcome, one would probably have to double, if not triple, these amounts.

The DDA Family Planning Centre Allotment Order is a small slip of paper containing a matter-of-fact list of required information: the applicant's name, father's name, age, number of children, address, "date of voluntary sterilization," and "nature of assistance claimed." Flicking through hundreds of such orders in file after dusty file in the offices of the Slum and JJ Department, one gets a picture not so much of violent abuse but of a frighteningly mechanical bureaucracy whose very efficiency seems to mask the fact that it is dealing not in lottery tickets but in human infertility. Under point 5, demanding the date of the "voluntary sterilization," the DDA official notes either "self-sterilization" or "motivated case." In the former instance he fills in the applicant's name, sterilization number, and date of operation; in the latter case he includes the same details with regard to the motivated person or persons. This leads to point 6, "nature of the assistance claimed," opposite which the DDA officer generally writes one of the following: "allocation of residential plot," "regularization of residential plot," "regularization of commercial plot," "transfer of plot in applicant's name" or "transfer from colony," and so forth. Occasionally one comes across an unusual case, such as a Hindu woman regularizing an unauthorized temple by getting herself sterilized, but even this is made to seem unremarkable through the starkness of the statement: "regularization of religious plot." Finally the order is signed or thumb-printed by the applicant concerned and handed over to the local DDA Executive Officer, then Mr. K. K. Nayar, who personally signed and dated every order. Once processed, the slips are slashed in blue ink and a comment added to the effect that the incentive has now been used up. This was to prevent the same allotment order being used twice.

It is not difficult to draw a profile of the people who submitted their own bodies for self-sterilization. They were, on the whole, the poorest of the colony, who could not afford to motivate others but wanted either to save their homes from confiscation or to obtain a plot. As one old man put it, "We would not have got sterilized ourselves if we had had the money to purchase cases [i.e., motivate others]." In spite of having listened to many of their accounts as to how they came to have the operation, my aim here is to focus, not on their experiences, but on the predicament of those who decided, for whatever reason, to motivate others. For it is they who, by transferring the burden of sterilization onto friends, neighbors, and total strangers, became co-victims of the Emergency regime. Through their experiences we can trace the process by which the family planning program developed into a warped but profitable trade which lured ordinary citizens into active participation. We can also get a clearer sense of the logic and reasoning that enabled these participants to perceive this blatantly abnormal trade as acceptable and, at times, even desirable.

BECOMING A MOTIVATOR

Let us begin by tracing how people in Welcome set about trying to motivate others. It certainly was not through convincing them of the benefits of family planning. Since both the motivators and the motivated were almost unanimously opposed to the operation,[18] the terms of persuasion had to lie elsewhere. Some turned to their immediate families, where loyalty and sacrifice were easiest to find. In Welcome there were a few cases of husbands motivating wives, wives motivating husbands, brothers motivating brothers, sons motivating mothers and fathers. It is likely that these were not monetary transactions but cases of family members pulling together to help each other either to increase or to save their collective property. The most common permutation is that of sons motivating their fathers. In this case a recently married young man living in a joint family could succeed in obtaining a separate plot for himself, his wife, and child by persuading his father to get sterilized. Since it was the son who was the motivator, it was he who claimed the reward, while at the same time retaining his own fertility. Meanwhile his father, who was probably nearing the end of his child-producing years, did not lose too much by having the operation. Similarly in cases where a family had already spread its territory through purchasing a second plot, this same technique could be used to save the purchasers from eviction. Since no one was entitled to have more than one plot registered in his or her name, the system of motivations provided a useful means by which a family could expand and legitimize its right to more property. This could, of course, be considered a form of "family planning" but one which had very little to do with birth control. It throws light on the fact that for those registering cases with the DDA, sterilization had much more to do with property rights than with trying to limit the size of the family.

As long as motivators persuaded people from their own families, the system of motivations retained a personal element. But such cases were comparatively few. Of the motivated cases documented in the files in Welcome, only eleven record motivations within the nuclear family. Even bearing in mind that when a man motivated his married sister, as I was told sometimes happened, it was not recorded as a family matter, we can still conclude that motivations within the immediate family were relatively rare. This meant that it was necessary to find one's victim among more distant friends and relatives, but since they too were probably in need of sterilization certificates, they were not necessarily ready to comply. Furthermore there was something awkward about persuading one's own relatives to face the knife, particularly for Muslims, most of whom considered sterilization a grave sin.[19] For some families, the motivation option may well have provided a means of establishing or resolving long-standing family debts. But conversations with people in Welcome suggest that the vast majority preferred to find their victims elsewhere. Once the search began outside one's own friends and relatives, the choice of victims was greater but the motivational factor was no longer sympathy or emotional blackmail but cash.

FROM MOTIVATION STRUCTURE TO MARKET STRUCTURE

The government was offering various incentives: tins of ghee, electric clocks, radios, and between 75 and 90 rupees to those undergoing the operation. This meant that a potential motivator had to be prepared to offer considerably more. For private employers, there was a simple solution; they could motivate their staff under threat of dismissal. But the majority of people in Welcome did not have any staff and had to find their victims among people as poor or even poorer than themselves. A few such candidates could be found within the colony, living mostly in those 1960s blocks that were inhabited mainly by people classified as scheduled caste.[20] Here it was possible to find people who were willing to undergo the operation in exchange for offers of cash. Being too poor to raise permanent constructions on their existing plots, they were not interested in obtaining more land and were therefore more attracted by offers of money than plots. But such people were in a minority, and finding them directly was a difficult and awkward process involving much searching and bargaining. Furthermore it was a process which must have soured relationships within the colony as each scanned his or her neighbor's *gali* in search of a potential victim. An ironing man who found that his authorized 1960s plot had been regularized in the name of a squatter who had taken it by force during his absence told me of the many difficulties he had faced in trying to find someone to motivate. Having three small children and full financial responsibility for his family, he was frightened of getting sterilized himself lest he should be weakened by the operation. On the other hand he needed a plot to replace the one that had been seized from him by force. Scanning the colony, he was apparently unable to find anyone willing to be motivated for less than one thousand rupees, which was way beyond his meager capacity (probably at least four times his monthly income). In the end he had to abandon the search altogether and has been living in a rented place ever since, while his original plot has remained in the hands of the impostor who got himself sterilized in order to transfer the leasehold into his own name.

But there was a simple way to avoid the sordid and embarrassing necessity of finding a person willing to submit to sterilization, and that was by obtaining the potential victim indirectly through a *dalal* (broker). Such *dalal*s were easy to find, since they hung around in droves outside the Family Planning camps, and sometimes even came door to door offering their services. They found their victims mainly outside the colony among pavement dwellers, beggars, laborers, rickshaw pullers, and villagers. Once outside the vicinity, they were in a good position to obtain cheap sterilizations and to sell them at competitive rates back in Welcome. For the motivators, not only were the cases they purchased through *dalal*s as cheap if not cheaper than directly motivated cases, but they had the added advantage of reducing the human contact, since all the arrangements and financial transactions were accomplished by the *dalal*. The motivator would simply accompany the victim to the hospital in order to be sure that he did not escape or try to run off with the sterilization certificate.

In order to comprehend the circumstances that led people to approach such *dalal*s, let us examine the predicament of a *kabadi* (second hand/junk) wood merchant in the colony. He had been allocated a plot after the demolition of his *jhuggi* in Matka Pir, New Delhi, in 1972. He had since purchased a second plot in the colony, and he stood to lose that plot during the Emergency. Government officials accompanied by local *goondas* (ruffians) came to his door giving him an ultimatum: either he was to hand over the documents of purchase, or else he was to get sterilized, or "give a case." As a practicing Muslim, he considered sterilization a sin against God and was also convinced of its negative effects on the body. This left him with only two options: either he was to hand over his documents, thereby losing both the plot and the structure he had raised on it, or else he could pay a *dalal* about five hundred rupees to purchase a case on his behalf. Had he himself been faced with the direct task of finding a person for sterilization, the *kabadi wala* may well have hesitated or even chosen to renounce his plot. But with a *dalal* to do all the intermediary work, the choice of action seemed obvious: of course it made sense to pay for a case and save his property. Like many other "motivated" people, the *kabadi* man's victim was a villager who had fled to

Delhi to escape sterilization in his village. The *kabadi* man, speaking nine-teen years later, recalls, "The person who got sterilized for me had escaped from a village called Mehwad in U.P.[21] His buffaloes had been captured by the *patwari* and *amin* (local-level officials) with the help of the local police, and he was told that if he didn't get sterilized, his land and house would be confiscated too. So he ran away from his village and came to Delhi, thinking that if he had to get sterilized, he would rather do it here where the doctors were better and where he could earn some money for having the opera-tion." Asked about the victim's age and whether he had children, the *kabadi* man answered, "He was a young man. . . . I think he must have had chil-dren, but I can't say for sure." Then, with an ironic laugh, as if suddenly struck by the brutality of his own vagueness, he added, "You only thought of yourself at that time!" The money he had paid went directly into the hands of the *dalal,* and the *kabadi* man never knew how much of it was seen by the person who got sterilized. Neither did he need to think too much about it. The victim had disappeared out of his life on the same day he had entered it, and the *kabadi* man did not have to see or hear of him again. There are many people in Welcome who, like the *kabadi* man, accepted the services of *dalal*s either to save their purchased or rented plots or to obtain a plot to replace their demolished *jhuggi*s.

The personal contact may have been reduced by *dalal*s finding victims outside the colony and bringing them to purchasers inside the colony, but it had not been eliminated altogether. There was still that awkward moment when the motivators had to meet their victims in person and accompany them to the hospital. The fact that two decades after the event, the *kabadi* man can still remember details of the villager he "motivated" suggests that he had not been able to ignore the poor man's plight altogether. But the risk of rousing uncomfortable emotions in the minds of motivators could be minimized yet further by *dalal*s offering sterilization certificates directly for sale. Once a motivated person had been taken to the hospital by the *dalal* and made to renounce his certificate, there was no need for the motivator to suffer seeing him at all. So by eliminating awkward factors such as the age, identity, and situation of the victim, the *dalal* was able to reduce the transaction to a purely monetary affair. The motivator need not worry whether his victim was unmarried or not; he was simply purchasing a piece of paper for which he would bargain as best he could. This left *dalal*s free to obtain the valuable certificates by whatever means they could, whether directly from victims or from other agents such as shopkeepers, other *dalal*s, and the local police. The elimination of the human element was therefore liberating both for the motivator and for the *dalal,* making the sterilization certificate just one more commodity on the black market. And like all black market products, sterilization certificates had histories which were best left buried as they passed from one person's hands to another.

To get an idea of the dubious means by which such certificates were sometimes obtained, I turn to the account of a factory worker who was living in Old Delhi until he got sterilized for a plot in Welcome. He gave a description of how shopkeepers in Old Delhi used to connive with members of the local police in order to extract cases in the area where he worked: "It happened like this; the shopkeepers would give information to the police concerning local laborers, telling them who were the ones who were homeless or slept outside in the streets since these were the easiest targets. The police would then arrest these people and keep them in the police station overnight. The next day, the shopkeepers would go to the station and offer to bail the laborers out if they agreed to get sterilized. Once there, it was not difficult to make them get sterilized, since they wanted to escape from the police and were frightened of going to jail. . . . For every forty cases bailed out by the shopkeepers, the police could keep ten sterilization slips for themselves." Obviously victims trapped in such tenacious sterilization networks were not in a position to ask for money. Rather, they had to be grateful to the shopkeepers for bailing them out. Meanwhile their sterilization certificates were siphoned off by both shopkeepers and police and entered local markets through *dalal*s who sold them to individual clients. Divorced of the circumstances under which they were obtained, these certificates appeared to their purchasers not as evidence of blackmail but as passports to security in the struggle over DDA plots. Concentrating more on their own plight than on that of the people they "motivated," these purchasers were apt to believe the *dalal*s when the latter told them the certificates had been obtained without any use of force.

While it is easy to be critical of the position of the purchaser, it must also be recognized that such purchasers, trapped between family planning and DDA policies, were often in desperate positions themselves.[22] Take for example the DESU worker who managed to escape sterilization at work on the grounds that he had only one child, but who then found his *jhuggi* demolished, only to learn that he could not get a new plot without producing a sterilization certificate. Technically a couple with only one child was "eligible" for a DDA plot without a certificate, but since priority always went to people with certificates, those without (usually the childless, the widows, the aged, people with only one or two children) stood little chance. For this reason quite a number of people who produced "motivated" cases rather than self-sterilizations in Welcome were those with less than three children. Feeling themselves unable to have the operation on the grounds that they wanted more children, they were more or less obliged to purchase cases. A notable example is that of a young woman laborer who was working on a building site and paying rent for a *jhuggi* at the time of the Emergency. Despite being only seventeen and having only one child, she had initially decided to get sterilized herself in a desperate attempt to save her family from the burden of paying rent. But her husband and mother had forbidden her to have the operation and even pulled her out of a government jeep that was heading for the hospital. Poor though they were, they decided that their only option if they wanted a plot was to motivate others. When they contacted a relevant official, they were told to produce five sterilization certificates, a figure which was later reduced to three. In the desperation of the moment the couple's attention was focused more on how to raise the money than on whose certificates to purchase. Selling all her wedding jewelry, the woman was able to raise enough to purchase three cases for a record low of 150 rupees each. After much difficulty, including sexual harassment from a dubious agent, she was able to register her cases and obtain a plot. Speaking twenty years later, the couple are adamant that there was no force used in the family planning program in Delhi (even though one of their own relatives had allegedly died following the operation in Uttar Pradesh). They claim that the people who got sterilized and sold their certificates to *dalals* did so because they wanted the monetary benefits. This might be true for some of the "motivated," but in this particular instance the couple had paid only 150 rupees per case to the *dalal*. One wonders, then, what possible benefits the victims could have enjoyed. Perhaps they got only the official 75–90 rupees or an electric clock or some ghee from the government. Or perhaps, like the laborers duped by the police and shopkeepers in Old Delhi, they did not receive even this. The point is that when people purchased sterilization certificates in the open market, they did not know the history of the "motivated," and it is no doubt this very ignorance that enabled them to ignore the more sordid aspects of the trade. Some even seem to have inverted their potential guilt by turning against the invisible victims, accusing the latter of abnormal levels of greed. Such reasoning left some motivators free to look back on the Emergency as a positive time of opportunity for all. The woman above even stated that she wished another such opportunity would arise so that other poor *jhuggi* dwellers and homeless people could obtain a plot, although she did qualify her statement by saying that the sterilization should be voluntary.

THE MULTIPLICATION OF MOTIVATIONS

How was it that the cost of sterilization certificates varied so dramatically, with one person claiming to have paid 150 rupees per case, another 1,200 rupees, and the majority between 400 and 500 rupees?[23] These fluctuations seem to have occurred according to how difficult it was to persuade someone to get sterilized, how many cases were required per plot, how many plots were available from the DDA, and whether the *dalal*'s profit was made on the proportion of cases per plot turned over to the DDA or on the sale of a single case to a client. The price also depended upon the victim's willingness to sell and the purchaser's capacity to buy. Since some victims came more expensively than others, the *dalals* would, it seems, sell the expensive certificates to the wealthier purchasers while reserving the certificates they had obtained for nothing for their poorer clients. There were no doubt also some forged certificates circulating on the black market, although it is difficult to know their number.[24] No one interviewed in Welcome could tell me anything about this trade, and most seemed to be ignorant of it. Since purchasers were anxious to secure legitimate rights to land, it seems they needed to assume there was a genuine sterilized body behind the certificates they purchased, and besides, many had actually accompanied the motivated to the hospital and were therefore left without doubt.[25]

Another factor that influenced the price of certificates was the decreasing availability of people to be sterilized. As one man put it, "As the time went on, it became more and more difficult to find people who had not already been sterilized. So the rate increased, and some people paid up to 1,000–1,200 rupees for a case. Before that the price had depended on how easily the people could be persuaded. Now it depended on how difficult it was to find someone still eligible for the operation." All of these factors help to explain why some residents in Welcome seem to have paid considerably less than others, but they do not explain why some residents gave two or three cases for a single plot, while others gave only one. There are various possible reasons for this. One is that the DDA was running out of plots in the colony and was therefore raising the premium for the remaining plots.[26] But this does not explain why only certain types of people seem to have been told to produce more than one case per plot. Examining the personal files in Welcome, it appears that most of the givers of two or three cases were either young couples with one, two, or no children, or else they were Muslims (occasionally they were both). What childless couples and Muslims shared in common was their violent opposition to self-sterilization, the former on reproductive grounds and the latter on religious grounds. This raises the possibility that the DDA and/or individual officers within it were deliberately exploiting the reluctance of these groups to get sterilized by using them as agents to extract the maximum number of certificates from others. If such a hypothesis is true, it would certainly help to explain how in the wood market and the iron market, both of which are run by Muslims, the maximum proportion of cases per plot were accumulated. It would also help to explain how the woman laborer above, who had only one child, and her neighbor, who was childless at the time, were both expected to give three cases for their plots.

How the DDA officials justified their extraction of extra cases varied according to context. In some instances they simply claimed that the cost of a plot was high from the start. The laborer and her neighbor had initially been told to produce five certificates until the number was later reduced to three. Since they were from outside the colony, they did not know that others had obtained plots with only one certificate. While the former had to sell her jewelry to raise the money, the latter, who had no jewelry, had to resort to selling the family's cooking vessels. Their accounts provide ample proof that wealth was not the criterion for establishing the number of cases a person had to give. In other instances the DDA officials would begin by demanding one case but later raise the demand to two or three by producing some convenient excuse. This was the technique employed in the wood market. In situations where a wood merchant produced a sterilization certificate by motivating his craftsman, he would be told by intermediaries that only sterilizations within the family could be accepted. But in situations where a family member did get sterilized, the merchant would be informed that his first certificate had been mislaid, and he would have to produce another. How many of these extra certificates went into the pockets of *dalals* and how many were used for official purposes is not clear, but at least nine files concerning plots in the wood market contain evidence of two motivated cases per plot.

The accumulation of cases through the scrap iron merchants was even more systematic and excessive. Unlike the wood merchants, the scrap iron merchants were trying to enter the colony for the first time, because their existing *kabadi* market on the Grand Trunk road was due for demolition. The fact that the existing market of thirty shops was authorized by the DDA gave the merchants the bargaining power to negotiate for fifty-square-yard plots in Welcome. Initially they were told that allotment slips would be issued at the time of demolition, but as time went on, the executive officer told them it was impossible to allocate the plots without their producing one sterilization certificate per plot. This was agreed to by the *pradhan* (head) of the Market Association, who decided to take personal responsibility for finding the cases. Acting as a *dalal,* he and some "assistants" scanned streets and railway stations at night in search of possible candidates for sterilization. When he found them, he brought them back to the traders, each of whom paid to have a case registered in his name. But by the time they had accompanied thirty men to the hospital for sterilization, the DDA demand had increased. The *pradhan* recalls, "At first they demanded thirty cases. But then they kept on increasing the amount. When we gave thirty cases, they said, What is thirty cases? That's nothing! Give us thirty more! And when we gave them sixty cases, they said, We want another thirty! . . . We paid around 400 to 500 rupees per case. The highest it went up to was 700." The DDA executive officer justified these demands on the grounds that his superiors were trying to get the market moved to a less convenient location. Only by producing more certificates could the *kabadi* merchants be shifted to Welcome, which was the colony they most favored. Just what personal rewards the *pradhan* reaped from organizing the ninety sterilizations is not clear, but it is certain that he would have benefited for his labors.

By trying to extract the maximum density of cases out of Muslims, the government was, it seems, hoping to compensate for the general reluctance of Muslims to participate in the family planning scheme. The fact that the Head Imam of the Jama Masjid had announced the denial of last rites to all Muslims who got sterilized had strengthened the popular Islamic view that sterilization was a sin against God. Trapped between threats from the government if they did not get sterilized and threats from their own religious leaders if they did, Muslims were presented with a particularly difficult dilemma. Giving a motivated case, though also considered a sin by some, was the only way of minimizing potential losses on both sides. Cases found outside the community at least saved Muslims from having to lead other Muslims down the path of sin. But at times the government did not even allow this option, specifying instead that only Muslim sterilization certificates would be accepted from Muslim applicants. This had the effect of inviting people to turn not only against their own religious doctrine, but also against their community in the struggle for survival. A Muslim toolmaker found himself faced with just such an invitation when the government demolished his shop near the Jama Masjid and allocated him a commercial plot in Welcome. Since his home was still in Old Delhi and most other toolmakers were obtaining plots in the newly constructed Meena bazaar near the Jama Masjid, this toolmaker tried to get a transfer. But a senior government officer told him he could only transfer if he produced ten cases—and not just any old cases: "He told me, 'Give me Muslim cases! I don't want any purchased cases from you, I want only the cases of your own close relatives.'" Unable to promise to betray his own relatives into committing the sin of sterilization, and unwilling to get sterilized himself, the toolmaker had to resign himself to remaining in Welcome. But there were some Muslims who were willing to impose the operation on other poorer members of their own community. The *pradhan* of the iron market, for example, had been ready to motivate ninety people, most of whom were, he claims, Muslim villagers who had fled to Delhi in fear of being forcibly sterilized at the hands of the local police. Meanwhile the *pradhan* retains the view that sterilization is a sin against god and that he himself would never undergo the operation.

These last examples raise the question of whether the family planning policy also became a vehicle for systematic religious discrimination—an accusation which was often raised in the literature published immediately after the Emergency. Muslims in Welcome do not seem to favor such an interpretation.[27] They emphasize, as do most Hindus, that the pressure was on every poor man to get sterilized at the time and that if the pressure was greatest on Muslims, that was only because their resistance was greatest— something of which most Muslims are proud. Both Hindus and Muslims are in agreement that the former were sterilized more than the latter, a fact which some Hindus resent.

TURNING A POLICY ON ITS HEAD

Most of the cases presented so far have involved people trapped between government policies. They participated in the family planning scheme in order to lessen the crushing impact of the DDA scheme, which threatened them either with eviction or homelessness. They can therefore be identified as victims who, driven by circumstances, took on the role of agent. But there were others whose motivations were clearly more opportunistic. Instead of stopping short at using the Family Planning Scheme to alleviate the effects of DDA policies, they went one step further and used the scheme as a convenient means of obtaining more and more plots. In the process they reversed their victimhood entirely and converted family planning objectives into an instrument with which to dupe the DDA. One such category of people were those *jhuggi* dwellers who, after obtaining plots through self-sterilization, sold the plots and returned to settle in *jhuggis*, knowing that the DDA would demolish their *jhuggis* a second time, so enabling them to obtain another plot in a different colony. Having already gotten sterilized themselves, they would take the opportunity of giving a motivated case the second time round. This was not difficult, since they had cash available from the sale of their original plots and were still able to retain some profit after purchasing a sterilization certificate. The immense scale of DDA demolitions made it impossible for officials in different colonies to keep tabs on the thousands of names filling their files, so such cases generally went unnoticed. Although no one likes to confess openly to having adopted this strategy, there are many in the colony who claim to have witnessed it firsthand. The frequency with which such behavior is described suggests that it was not uncommon. One man estimates that at least a quarter of the inhabitants of his particular block have sold their plots and settled in *jhuggis*, many during the Emergency period.

For wealthier members of the colony, there was another strategy which proved even more lucrative. They would first obtain a plot, either through self-sterilization or through giving a motivated case. As long as this plot remained registered in their name, it would be difficult for them to register a second plot in the same colony, so they had to find an alternative solution. What they did was find an indirect method of motivating others, offering them five hundred rupees, not for the operation but for handing over their plots after the operation. The motivated man would register his case with the DDA as if it were self-sterilization. But once allocated a plot, he would be under obligation to sell it to the unofficial motivator with whom he had previously made a deal. Some of these unofficial motivators did this in order to obtain two adjacent plots, enabling them to have twice the amount of space as their neighbors. But others made a veritable business out of it and would go on to sell the plots they accumulated, thereby entering the lucrative property market by using sterilization certificates as a cheap means of obtaining plots. A survey conducted in 1989 bears witness to the fact that some plots were immediately sold after their allocation in 1976. It is likely that these were the plots obtained by the unofficial motivators. Since Welcome was relatively well situated by comparison to many resettlement colonies, there was no shortage of buyers for plots accumulated in this way.

Most of those who entered the property market were relatively prosperous men who had enough capital and political weight to motivate more than one person for sterilization. Since the majority of people in the colony had difficulty motivating even one person, there probably were not many who made a full-scale business out of the trade in plots. Nonetheless, some poor women apparently found an alternative means of entering the market. Their strategy was to obtain sterilization certificates through sleeping with *dalal*s. For them prostitution was a means of paying for the certificate which, for most people, cost more than their monthly earnings. While some poor women seem to have slept with *dalal*s out of sheer desperation, others apparently did so professionally in order to accumulate successive plots for sale. Such manipulations may not have been common, but they demonstrate the extent to which individuals could subvert the system, turning oppressive policies to their own gain.

In focusing on the active victims of the Emergency and on those who modified their victim status by aggressively exploiting DDA policies, my aim has been to highlight the existence of co-victimization at the bottom level of the socioeconomic strata. This is not to deny the state's responsibility for much of what went on during the Emergency, nor to underestimate the trials of those who unwillingly perpetuated state policy, but rather to reverse the imbalances found in the literature on the Emergency, which tends to portray the intellectual as the emotional sufferer, the bureaucrat as the active participant, and the poor as either passive victim or noble resistor. Such stereotypes are dangerous, for they seem to mask the most frightening aspect of the Emergency regime, which was its ability to draw all kinds of people, through fear or greed, into participation. To ignore the active role of the thousands of men and women who competed for plots in the resettlement colonies of Delhi is tantamount to denying the generality and diffuseness of the power of the state as it seeped into the corners of everyday life, inviting individual responses. For just as disturbing as the blatant force by which some victims were sterilized is the ease with which other victims imposed that burden on others.

MEMORIES IN PERSPECTIVE

As an anthropologist who had not set out to work on the Emergency, I found much in the DDA files and the experiences of the people of Welcome to be, at first, disconcerting.[28] When the above material was presented in the context of an anthropology seminar in London, it was clear that there were others who had a similar reaction. Part of this unease seemed to stem around our general reverence for the body as a domain which is deeply personal, almost to the extent of being sacred. This makes us reluctant to accept the apparent ease with which it was commodified during the Emergency. It is disturbing to find that receipts for sterilization are not much different from coupons for bargains in the supermarket, or to discover that the residents of Welcome talk about their experiences in casual, undramatic tones, sometimes even with humor and a flourish. The *pradhan* of the iron market, for example, had displayed a sense of amusement and fun when he spoke of how the DDA had raised the requirement from thirty sterilization certificates to sixty and finally ninety. The tale was told, not to highlight the sense of oppression, but rather to evoke something of the challenge of those days and the ultimate heroism of the *pradhan*.

The sense of unease seems to increase the deeper we wade into the gray zone of complicity where comfortable moral categories no longer seem clear-cut. For with the institution of the motivator, we enter "the space which separates the victims from the persecutors," a space which we like to perceive as empty, but which is generally filled (Lévi 1988: 25–26). Once in the gray zone, it becomes difficult to distinguish not only where victimhood ends and opportunism begins but also how judgment is possible. The suspension of judgment in this paper seemed particularly disturbing to some Western researchers who felt the need for categorical distinctions between right and wrong.

Yet both the feeling of unease and the desire to condemn seem less appropriate when the accounts of the people of Welcome are situated within the broader context of their life histories and narratives. After all, their accounts of the past are located within a present which is punctuated by its own difficult moments. Struggles of the present and recent past help to dilute earlier experiences, pushing them back in time and intensity and making the casual nature of Emergency reminiscences more comprehensible. Today, it is fresher wounds that are recounted with a sense of pain. In particular the "communal riots" of December 1992 stand out as a scar which is yet to be healed in the colony.[29] During my research from 1995–97, conversations about the Emergency often included reference to this recent violence, particularly in the Muslim-dominated section of the colony, where some thirty people had allegedly lost their lives, and where homes, shops, mosques, and markets had been violated. The "riots" surfaced in people's narratives not only as a time of trauma but also as an event which carried severe social and economic consequences from which people are only now recovering. The high profile of the violence in Welcome gave the colony a bad reputation, so that even after the fighting and curfew were over, it became difficult to renew business relationships. Furthermore, the lack of trust between Hindus and Muslims has resulted in the redrawing of spatial boundaries, with Muslims leaving the Hindu-dominated area, and Hindus leaving the Muslim-dominated area. Welcome is now more clearly divided on religious grounds than ever before, with each community knowing that the actual enemy of the past and potential enemy of the future is accumulating collective potential just a few streets away.

Supplementing the trauma of this violence was the experience of the Delhi assembly polls in 1993. When they went to vote, many families discovered that their names had been deleted from the electoral role.[30] They were then issued official notification stating that they were Bangladeshi unless proved otherwise. Most residents of Welcome could prove otherwise, tracing papers from their natal villages and providing evidence that their names had been in earlier census lists. This meant that they qualified for the newly introduced identity card. But all of this took time. The result was that the vast majority of Muslim families and a few Hindus could not vote in the 1993 local elections. Such events in the present form a frame for recounting and remembering experiences of the past. Viewed through this frame, the specificity of the Emergency becomes less clear. The importance of the sterilization certificate, for example, no longer seems so exceptional when compared to the importance of the new identity card. As one man put it, "The time was such [during the Emergency] that you had to produce that *nasbandi* card wherever you went if you wanted any work of yours to be done. If you went to the hospital for some treatment, they wouldn't treat you unless you had that *nasbandi* card. It was exactly like it is now with Seshan's[31] identity card. That *nasbandi* card was needed at every place and in all Government offices." Here the sterilization certificate becomes just one in a series of important papers that have always been necessary as proof of one's credentials, whether it is the ration card, the sterilization certificate, or the new identity card.

So, viewed from the present, which is built both through perceptions of the past and anticipations of the future, the Emergency becomes just one in a sequence of disruptive events which people deal with as best they can. And if it has been superseded by more recent troubles, it has also been preceded by other experiences, more or less traumatic. Take, for example, the slum clearance program which was so prominent in written and judicial critiques of the Emergency after the event. Viewed from the perspective of the average resident of Welcome, it is difficult to see why Emergency demolitions should have been singled out as being so exceptional. At least two-thirds of the residents had already gone through the experience of demolition before the Emergency and no one had made a major public issue of it at that time. Those whose homes were destroyed during the Emergency may have been given less warning than most others, but their experience was not qualitatively different. And besides, at least during the Emergency there were more opportunities for obtaining plots. Some had not been so fortunate on earlier occasions.

To view the Emergency from their perspective, we turn to the experiences of the residents of block QX.[32] In the early 1950s and 1960s they had been living in Jamuna Bridge, an undeveloped area along the river bank which has always attracted *jhuggi* dwellers and continues to attract them today, despite numerous government attempts to eradicate them. During the war with Pakistan in 1965 the bridge was perceived as a primary target for bombardment, with the result that the *jhuggi* dwellers beneath it were suddenly removed. Again, it was a time of emergency—an "external emergency" this time as opposed to the "internal emergency" of 1975–77. To the person experiencing sudden demolition and displacement, the distinction is hardly important. But the disadvantage of being displaced during the 1965 emergency was that people were not given plots. Instead they were dumped on what was then barren wasteland in the Welcome area, where they built new *jhuggis* in the hope that the official plots promised by the government would one day materialize. Some two years after their arrival there was an outbreak of Hindu-Muslim violence in the area precipitated by the issue of garbage dumping. The DDA reacted by demolishing the new *jhuggis* and offering plots in the more distant resettlement colony of Seemapuri. Many families took up the offer, but some refused to move and simply rebuilt *jhuggis* in another part of Welcome, hoping that one day they would be able to secure property rights there. This they finally did during the Emergency of 1975–77 when the demolition squads moved in for a third time. But this time there was the new possibility of securing land rights through getting sterilized or "giving a case." It is hardly surprising that for families who had already experienced demolition twice before and who wanted to make Welcome their official home, the Emergency appears as an opportunity of sorts in their narratives.

The tale of the residents of block QX not only locates the Emergency experience within a broader sequence of events but also reveals the internal dynamics of the relationship between policy and practice. On the one hand it shows how, with each major disturbance, whether local (communal tensions), national (Emergency 1975–77), or international (war with Pakistan), the conditions of existence seem to change for people situated at the bottom of the socioeconomic ladder in Delhi. Yet it also reveals how these same people develop strategies for coping with such changes and, in some cases, turn them to their advantage. Such a dynamic is by no means unique to the Emergency. Ever since its inception, in 1958, the Jhuggi Jhompri Removal Scheme has been plagued by the fact that many use it as a quick and efficient means of acquiring land. On the one hand there are those who come to the city and build *jhuggis* at the time of demolitions precisely in order to get resettled. On the other hand there are those who get resettled in order to sell their plots and return to *jhuggis*, thereby waiting for the next round of demolition and resettlement. Each policy creates its own winners and losers, and there are some who are capable of winning out on all fronts, just as others are capable of losing almost everything.

Returning to the experiences of those who once inhabited the slums of Jamuna Bridge, one can see how some were able to exploit the situation with considerably more success than others. Those who followed the simple pattern of demolition at Jamuna Bridge followed by demolition at Welcome and resettlement in Seemapuri conformed to the behavior charted out for them by government policy. But some chose to interpret the fact that they had initially been dumped in Welcome as proof of their entitlement to a plot there. They remained, eventually using the family planning policy as a means of securing plots during the Emergency. Of the forty-two families who managed to remain in Welcome, some were considerably more successful that others. As one woman explained, "The people who were really astute were the ones who accepted plots in Seemapuri, but who then sold them and returned to Welcome, where they built *jhuggis* and later got plots through sterilization." By contrast the victims of the situation were the six families who got sterilized or motivated cases towards the end of the Emergency period, only to find that the policy had changed, and they were no longer entitled to plots. But although such people cannot be described as winners, they refuse to fit the profile of losers either. They have dealt pragmatically with the situation by building houses in Welcome anyway. One such woman, who still keeps her sterilization certificate in the hope that it might one day fulfill the purpose for which it was intended, explained her situation thus: "We have occupied this piece of land here in the hope that when they demolish our home, they will have to provide us a suitable alternative." Protecting such families is the local *pradhan,* whose countenance resembles that of a heavyweight boxer and whose power extends over four blocks in the colony. His letters concerning the issue, written back in 1977, still lie in the DDA records, accompanied by supporting letters from a member of Parliament, written on Lok Sabha paper. The six remaining families still live in unauthorized circumstances today, but given the nature of the links between *pradhans*, local *goondas*, and politicians, the *pradhan* is no doubt serious when he states, "If the Government officers ever want to start causing problems over this, then they will have to get my permission first."

What this suggests is that the power relationships and social dynamics that surfaced during the Emergency were by no means unique to it. Rather, what happened during the Emergency was an intensification of dynamics and relationships already in existence, with some individuals changing places in the balance of power. This is clearly evident when one looks at the question of who motivated whom for sterilization. At one level we find a straightforward restatement of many of the classic inequalities in Indian society as the rich turn to the poor; the educated to the uneducated; the city dweller to the villager; the government official to his or her subordinates; the village authorities to the landless laborer or peasant; the employer to the employee. On the other hand we find that people are internally differentiated within the main target group, with some accepting the role of victim, while others reverse their victim status by manipulating the system from below. Where, as was usually the case in Welcome, brute force was avoided, the market interceded through the familiar figure of the *dalal,* who offered something for everybody, thereby converting family planning into a trade like any other. As one man put it, "No one ever has a fixed business in India. It keeps on changing all the time. A man who is selling *angithis* (handmade ovens) one day will start selling stoves the next. They change their business according to what is profitable at the time. The *dalals* [of the Emergency] were no different. They came into this business because they felt they could make good money out of it. . . . No one can say specifically who they were." In some accounts, not only the role of the trader but also the nature of the trade appears as something unremarkable. On at least three occasions the sterilization trade was explained by reference to the contemporary trade in blood and kidneys. Hence a worker in a sock factory explained, "It was just one type of business, which even today is still going on. If you go to Irwin hospital you will find people lined up on the pavement to give blood or to sell a kidney for money. What is the difference?"

Yet, despite its similarity to other moments, the Emergency *was* different. It was the first time that the entire administrative structure of the northern states, as well as a number of civic bodies, were reduced to instruments of bribery and coercion which threatened to invade the bodies of ordinary citizens on a mass scale. Its particularity as a "critical event" has been immortalized by the people of Welcome through the renaming and remembering of the Emergency as *nasbandi ka vakt.* This was the time when all young men from poor families lived in dread of the knife, not of the local *goonda* (hooligan) but of the government doctor—a person who is supposed to incarnate education, respectability, and, above all, responsibility. This is not to say that coercive sterilization of the type described here was entirely new in India. On the contrary the target-orientated policy, the monetary incentives, the networks of "motivators," and public-sector doctors were all in place before the Emergency and are only now being called into question.[33] But it was only under the conditions of extreme authoritarianism imposed during the Emergency that the trade in infertile bodies became inserted at the very center of the social, political, and economic functioning of the country. This makes it different from the trade in blood and kidneys, which occupies a comparatively marginal niche in contemporary Indian affairs.

What is most chilling in the narratives of people from Welcome is the fact that in spite of regarding the sterilization trade as blatantly "wrong," they nonetheless participated in it. Viewed from this perspective, the Emergency ceases to be just one more disruptive moment. It becomes instead a time of intense and unnatural oppression, the horror of which lies precisely in the way it became so rapidly normalized and routinized through the structures of everyday life. For it is in the ordinary phenomenon of the market that black and white merge into many shades of gray and notions of responsibility seem to become forgotten. Most people in Welcome blame, not Indira Gandhi, nor even Sanjay Gandhi, for what they underwent, but the *dalals* and petty bureaucrats who "subverted policies" and "put temptation in people's way." Few seem to reflect upon their own role in perpetuating the state regime through participating in the market. But occasionally one comes across an alternative interpretation. Asked whose responsibility the family planning program was, an ironing man replied acerbically, "What responsibility? Everyone was responsible for this. You were responsible, and I was responsible. The Government started the program, but it depended on the person whether he accepted it or not."

NOTES

I am grateful to Denis Vidal, Dhirubhai Sheth, Kit Davies, Veena Das, Helen Lambert, Patricia Jeffery, and Arthur Kleinman for their comments and to Rajender Singh Negi for his assistance throughout the period of research. The paper is based on fieldwork and archival research conducted in Delhi at various intervals from 1995 to 1997. An earlier and shorter version was presented at the South Asia Anthropology Group (SAAG) conference entitled "Hegemony and Dissent" at London School of Economics (LSE) in September 1995 and was published in *Economic and Political Weekly* 30, no. 46 (November 1995). The research was conducted in affiliation with the Centre for the Study of Social Systems, JNU (Delhi), and the Department of Anthropology, LSE. I am grateful to the Economic and Social Research Council (ESRC) of Great Britain for funding the research.

1. The Emergency was justified by the claim that India's security was threatened by internal forces. Technically it lasted for a period of twenty-one months, although many Emergency measures were slackened after nineteen months when Indira Gandhi announced plans for a general election. Mass arrests, the banning of trade unions, press censorship, slum clearance, and coercive sterilization were amongst the issues that mobilized the Indian electorate to vote against the Emergency government in what became a massive defeat for Indira Gandhi and the Congress party in March 1977.

2. Colonies which provide plots of land and occasionally apartments on a lease-hold basis mainly to people evicted and displaced from newly demolished "slums."

3. There are currently forty-six resettlement colonies in Delhi. The collective population of official residents is thought to be around 216,000 households. The actual population is likely to be much higher, owing to the development of unauthorized *jhuggi* clusters (shanty towns) within resettlement colonies (Ali 1995).

4. It is named after the old Welcome Hair Oil factory, which used to be located there but has long since closed down.

5. The Ministry of Health and Family Planning's attempt to get family planning added as the twenty-first point to Indira Gandhi's twenty-point program was rejected one month later on the grounds that such a measure was not necessary. This was presumably because Sanjay Gandhi's four points (later expanded to five) were to be treated with equal validity as the official twenty points (Shah Commission 1978: 163–64).

6. A National Population Policy Statement issued by the government on 16 April 1976 clearly stated that sterilization was to be the main plank of the program, (Mehta 1978: 118). That this was the case is evidenced by the fact that the achievement of national sterilization targets reached 190 percent in the year 1976–77, while achievement in regard to other forms of contraception fell far short of targets set for the same period (Shah Commission 1978: 154)

7. The committee was set up by the Lt. Governor of Delhi, Kishan Chand, in late December 1975 with Mrs. Vidya Ben Shah taking the role of chairperson (Mehta 1978: 116). Its primary function was to motivate the top bosses of Delhi's civic organizations to take active responsibility in the vigorous new wave of family planning. Its most infamous unofficial member was Ruksana Singh (otherwise known as Ruksana Sultana), who took charge of the controversial family planning camp in the Muslim area of Dujana House in Old Delhi.

8. In fact such was the level of centralized authority and intimidation emanating from Delhi, that physical proximity to the capital became one of the key factors in explaining the "performance" of different states in the sterilization race (Gwatkin 1979: 42 and notes 24 and 25).

9. This target was in fact raised to one hundred thousand by the Lt. Governor of Delhi in April 1976. The indiscriminate raising of targets by different state Governments is considered one of the major causes of the family planning excesses which followed. In his statement before the official commission set up to look into Emergency abuses after the event, the former Union Minister of Health and Family Planning, Dr. Karan Singh, attributed this target-raising to the fact that Chief Ministers were anxious to win favor with Sanjay Gandhi, referred to indirectly as "an extra-constitutional centre of power." (Shah Commission 1978: 199, 206).

10. Out of those I interviewed, the only people with more than two children who managed to retain their government jobs during the Emergency without being sterilized were working for the railway authorities. One worked as a coolie, and the other two worked in the parcel department at Old Delhi Railway station, where their superintendent was apparently antisterilization on the grounds that it would incapacitate his workforce. This superintendent was later "transferred" and replaced by a stricter man who managed to motivate a number of sterilizations, but it still seems to have been possible to avoid the operation. Of the three railway employees I interviewed, one avoided sterilization altogether, one motivated a case of sterilization, and the other's wife got sterilized. These sterilizations were undergone not in order to save jobs but in order to obtain plots.

11. It is difficult to know the precise number of people resettled during the Emergency. Jagmohan, then Vice Chairman of the DDA, states that 145,000 residential plots and 10,000 commercial plots were developed at the time. He talks in terms of the resettlement of 120,000 families, involving a population of around 700,000 (Jagmohan 1978). That demolitions and tree planting were directly proportional is suggested by a DDA publication during the Emergency which apparently boasted the

resettling of half a million people and the planting of half a million trees (Dayal and Bose 1977 :109).

12. The monsoon rains of 1976 were particularly heavy, causing floods and cyclones in ten states. In Delhi the Jamuna was reported to have risen 90 cm above the danger mark, leading to the evacuation of some areas (*India Today,* 1–15 Sept. 1976, p. 11). The resettlement colonies in the trans-Jamuna were particularly badly affected owing to their location on low-lying territory, originally designated as "green land" in the Master Plan.

13. I am grateful to the Director of the Slum and JJ Department of the MCD and to the staff of the Slum and JJ Department, East Zone B for their kind cooperation in allowing me access to DDA and MCD files.

14. The JJRS was initiated in 1958 on the recommendation of the Advisory Committee set up by the Ministry of Home Affairs, Government of India. It was approved in 1960, and its implementation was entrusted to the Municipal Corporation of Delhi (MCD). Over the years it has undergone frequent changes and modifications, with responsibility for its implementation being passed back and forth between the MCD and the DDA (Ali 1990: 76–82). The majority of the early settlers who came to Welcome were removed from slums in BN Nagri (1963); Delhi Gate (1963, 1964, and 1965); Rajghat (1964); Central Power House (1964); behind the Red Fort (1964); Sher Shah Road (1965); Jhandewalan (1964); Dairy Kisan Chand (1965); and Jamuna Bazar (1965, 1967, 1968, 1969).

15. The official 25-square-yard plot includes space for the front gutter. The actual space available for building a house is therefore 22.5 square yards. In the earliest resettlement colonies of Delhi the government had begun by issuing plots of 80 square yards. The size was later reduced to 50 square yards and then to 25 square yards. The usual explanation given for this reduction is that large numbers of resettled people were selling their substantial plots and returning to *jhuggis* while others found themselves unable to pay the necessary monthly installments (Ali 1990: chap. 5). By 1963, when Welcome was established, the size had already been reduced to 25 square yards.

16. They were mainly from Bapu Dham (1975); Laxmi Nagar (1975); British School (1975); Janta Manta road (1975); Jamuna Bazar (1975); Defence Colony (1975); Khyala (1975); I. N. A. (1976); R. K. Purum (1976); and areas around the Jama Masjid, including Dujana House (1975), Kalan Mahal (1975), and Urdu Park (1976). Others were from demolished *jhuggis* in Welcome (1976) and nearby resettlement colonies (1976).

17. Welcome contains 4,034 residential plots and 198 commercial plots, making a total of 4,232 plots. The above statistics are based on an analysis of the contents of 3,459 files. The remaining 773 files were reported missing.

18. Both men and women tended to link vasectomy to the notion of impotence and, at times, castration. None of the men interviewed who underwent the operation during the Emergency claimed to have wanted it. The same is true of the women who underwent tubectomy. All felt pressured by forces which had nothing to do with family planning: saving jobs; getting children admitted in school; preventing evictions; obtaining plots; and so forth (Tarlo, forthcoming, chap. 5). Two decades later, some are in favor of family planning, but they resent the way it was forced on them at the time.

19. Most Muslims interviewed in Welcome were opposed to sterilization, considering it an unnatural interference with Allah's will. Although some prominent Mus-

lims did take an active role in promoting family planning during the Emergency, they tend to be remembered more as traitors to the community than as leaders worthy of respect.

20. An official category introduced in 1935 to refer to groups previously considered "untouchable."

21. Uttar Pradesh, a poor state east of Delhi.

22. By focusing on the dilemmas of the urban poor, I do not wish to imply that the process of co-victimization was specific to them. Rather, I would argue that it characterized the structure of the family planning policy in general. Teachers, for example, were told to produce five sterilization certificates and threatened with the withdrawal of their salaries if they failed to comply. Many motivated their pupils' parents with reluctance, while others purchased certificates from *dalals*. They too were co-victims of the system, but for those with neither power, education, money, nor influence, the situation was even harsher.

23. I have no way of checking whether the prices quoted for motivations in this article correspond to the actual prices of the time. On the one hand the figures given by people in Welcome often exceed those quoted in the literature published immediately after the Emergency, which suggests that people may have elaborated the cost over time. On the other hand the majority of people quote a similar figure of around 400–500 rupees per sterilization, which suggests that this may well have been the actual amount. Information on this is difficult to ascertain, since the market for sterilizations was unofficial even if encouraged by the nature and structure of the family planning policy. The DDA records do, however, sometimes record the salaries of the resettled, which mostly varied between 100 and 400 rupees a month, with a large number earning between 150 and 250 rupees per month in the year 1975–76. Today a low-level government employee earns around 1,000 rupees a month.

24. Mehta speaks of the proliferation of the black market and recalls the arrest of a gang of forgers in Delhi who claimed they had recently switched from forging university certificates to forging sterilization certificates (Mehta 1978: 123–24).

25. There is an interesting discrepancy here between the attitudes of the poor and those of the educated elite. The latter, when discussing this issue, are likely to emphasize both the production of forged certificates and the trumped-up nature of figures quoted for sterilization achievements. The most plausible explanation for this is that it was the elite, especially high- and middle-ranking government servants, including doctors and teachers, who relied on purchasing forged certificates and who had access to the forgers, who were probably mainly located within government institutions. One disturbing consequence of the elite emphasis on corrupt practices in family planning during the Emergency is the implication that not that many people actually were sterilized. This notion is blatantly false, as the experiences of the people of Welcome show. If reproductive rates did not decrease as much as expected after the Emergency, this was partly because many of the people sterilized were those reaching the end of their fertile life.

26. There certainly were more people applying for plots in Welcome than plots available. As a result, some families have sterilization certificates from the Emergency period but never secured plots.

27. This is perhaps surprising, given the communalist nature of many interpretations of the past in contemporary India. Patricia Jeffrey, who has worked in Uttar Pradesh, informs me that there is a tendency for Muslims there to link partition in

1947, sterilization in 1976, and the demolition of the Babri Masjid in 1992 into a narrative sequence demonstrating the persistent persecution of Muslims over the years.

28. My interest in the Emergency came about through my accidentally stumbling across sterilization documents in the DDA files of Welcome, which I was consulting for background information about the area.

29. The destruction of the ancient mosque at Ayodhya by right-wing Hindu fundamentalists in December 1992 sparked widespread Hindu-Muslim violence throughout India. Welcome, which houses Hindus and Muslims in more or less equal proportion, was one of the worst-hit areas of the capital. The term *riot* generally used to describe this episode belies the fact that much of the violence was more organized than spontaneous.

30. According to a newspaper article, over fifteen hundred names were deleted from the electoral role in Seelampur (*Amrita Bazar Patrika,* 22 December 1993).

31. T. N. Seshan was the Election Commissioner responsible for introducing identity cards in 1992 against considerable opposition from the state governments.

32. To protect residents, the actual name of the block has not been given.

33. Tracing the history of the family planning policy before the Emergency, Marika Vicziany demonstrates convincingly that the Indian birth-control program was never genuinely voluntary in character and that many of those who were sterilized in the pre-Emergency period did so under coercion of one form or another (Vicziany 1982–83: 373–402, 557–92.) Given the level of criticism that Emergency abuses provoked, it is astounding that the Indian government continued to pursue a target-oriented program after the Emergency when the emphasis shifted from vasectomy to tubectomy. It is only now, in the last half of the 1990s that serious efforts are being made to find other methods of encouraging birth control. Early experiments show that family planning staff in India are so used to working to targets and for monetary incentives that they are finding it extremely difficult to change their approach.

REFERENCES

Ali, Sabir. 1990. *Slums within Slums: A Study of Resettlement Colonies in Delhi.* Delhi: Vikas.

————. 1995. "Typology of Delhi Slums." Working paper presented at the Delhi Seminar at the CSDS, Delhi, 18 April.

Dayal, John, and Ajoy Bose. 1997. *For Reasons of State: Delhi Under Emergency.* Delhi: Ess Ess Publications.

Gwatkin, Davidson R. 1979. "Political Will and Family Planning: The Implications of India's Emergency Experience." *Population and Development Review* 5, no. 1: 29–59.

Jagmohan. 1978. *Island of Truth.* Delhi: Vikas.

Lévi, Primo. 1988. *The Drowned and the Saved.* London: Abacus.

Mehta, Vinod. 1978. *The Sanjay Story.* Bombay: Jaico Publishing House.

Ministry of Health and Family Planning. 1975–1977. *Annual Reports of the Ministry of Health and Family Planning, 1975–1977.* Delhi: Government of India Publications.

Shah Commission. 1978. *Shah Commission of Inquiry: Third and Final Report. Delhi:* Government of India Publications.

Tarlo, Emma. Forthcoming. *Unsettling Memories: Narratives of the Emergency in Delhi.* London: C. Hurst.

Vicziany, Marika. 1982–83. "Coercion in a Soft State: The Family-Planning Program of India." *Pacific Affairs* 55, pt. 1, no. 3: 373–402, and pt. 2, no. 4: 557–92.

The Quest for Human Organs and the Violence of Zeal

Margaret Lock

The answer to all questions of "What for?" is "More."
PHILIP RIEFF,
The Triumph of the Therapeutic

The history of medicine, despite its ultimate objective of healing, is replete with violence—violence usually justified in the name of improved medical practice. Vivisection of humans and animals carried out by Herophilus in fourth century B.C. Alexandria earned him a lasting reputation as the "father of scientific anatomy" (Potter: 1976, 45). Eighteenth-century London was home to numerous charitable hospitals where the destitute purportedly ended up for treatment, but the historian Ruth Richardson (1988) argues that they were made into unknowing experimental subjects, the majority of whom died, and their corpses were then commodified. The Japanese in their "factories of death" in Manchuria during the Second World War conducted gross human experimentation and vivisection on Chinese prisoners, the results of which the American government, in its haste to advance the cause of "science," procured at the price of obtaining immunity for the perpetrators of those crimes (Harris: 1994). The Tuskegee experiments conducted for nearly forty years in Alabama, in which black patients suffering from secondary syphilis were deliberately left untreated (Jones: 1981), provides yet another notorious example of experimentation carried out in the name of medical science. These examples, together with numerous others where physicians have participated in human rights abuses, many of which are documented in *Medicine Betrayed*, published by the British Medical Association (1992), are testimony to a checkered history in the name of medical progress. Despite the drawing up of international codes of ethics for experimentation, blatant abuse of African children in connection with efforts to develop an AIDS vaccine has recently come to light (Culliton: 1991). A good portion of the colossal sacrifice of animal life can also be placed on the balance when passing judgment about medical experimentation.

If we make what I take to be a reasonable assumption, namely that medical knowledge should not stagnate, then an inherent tension between the desire for improved knowledge through experimentation and the best possible care of patients is unavoidable. We read almost daily about the results of tests carried out with new drugs, for example, but the newspaper reports rarely remind us that this knowledge is available because patients have been subjected to controlled clinical trials. It is only recently that the fate of those patients dying with breast cancer and AIDS who are assigned to the placebo group in such trials has been questioned (Elliott and Weijer: 1995). The logic of scientific experimentation in connection with drug promotion and usage entails an unusual type of structural violence, one in which a number of patients are deliberately selected to be left untreated in order to meet the currently required scientific specifications for accuracy (of course, experimentation with new drugs is never without danger, and it may well be that both groups in a clinical trial, those who receive the drug and those who do not, are placed at higher risk than if they had refused to participate in the experiment, but this serves only to conflate the original doubtful ethical maneuver justified as scientifically essential).

In this paper I elaborate on a specific case of this unavoidable tension between knowledge production and patient care. My focus is primarily on the management of two classes of people who have been brought to our attention over the course of the past thirty years, and who are situated in a peculiarly fraught relationship to one another, namely, potential organ donors and potential organ recipients. With the institutionalization of the organ transplant enterprise in tertiary care hospitals around the world, increasing complexity has been inserted into the knowledge/care tension, for living human body parts are now put to use in "saving" the lives of other patients.

A potential conflict of interest arises within the research world itself, between those concerned with the advancement of basic scientific knowledge and expertise in connection with transplantation, and those working in the field of traumatology striving to avert the deaths of potential donors. This tension is manifested in the hostility which so often surfaces between those clinicians caring for patients designated as potential organ recipients while they wait, clinging precariously to life, for an organ to become available, and "intensivists" in charge of traumatology units. Intensivists, neurologists, and neurosurgeons are often described by those interested in procuring more organs, on the basis of little or no evidence, as "uncooperative" and actually working to obstruct the transplant enterprise by electing not to approach families of dying patients to ask if donation would be possible (Prottas: 1994). In a similar vein, the staff of an intensive care unit in a

Canadian hospital, who approach many families and succeed quite often in securing organ donors, were recently chastised in writing by the local transplant procurement organization for not obtaining sufficient organs for transplant. In the United States, a pediatric surgeon in charge of an intensive care unit in the midwest informed me that he had been forced to evict transplant surgeons who were "trolling" his unit.

The trope which currently overrides this competing network of interests is that of a "shortage of organs," a perceived scarcity which has been described as a "public health crisis" (Randall: 1991, 1223). It is a trope in which the pressures of both time "passing" and the timing of events are exquisitely acute, and it will be my starting point for creating a critical argument with respect to the fostering of practices in connection with organ donation as though they are unequivocally benevolent—resembling deeds in the world of Hinayana Buddhism that accumulate merit for one in the afterlife. My position is that violence, both visceral and structural, is unavoidable when performing transplant technologies, and that this violence has been largely masked to date by the powerful rhetoric associated with the "gift of life."

There is no argument that organ transplants are often extremely successful and significantly prolong the lives of numerous patients, many of whom return to full participation in social life for many years (sometimes for more than twenty) after surgery. However, recognition of the violence associated with this technology, largely ignored thus far by the medical profession, is becoming increasingly urgent. The question of how the bodies of certain individuals are designated as donors, and the prolonged arguments, scientific and philosophical, as to how to negotiate the process of dying in order to "increase the supply" of organs for transplantation, has not to date captured the imagination of either the media or the public in North America (although in parts of both Europe and Asia this subject has received considerable media attention). Similarly, the tension between the advancement of scientific knowledge in this field and the fine line between experimentation and routinized care is rarely discussed. As Fox and Swazey (1992) note, a barely disguised agenda when discussing transplants in America has been the question of payment for treatment. If transplants are deemed experimental, then third-party payments will not be made for these procedures. There is, therefore, considerable pressure to routinize this technology and to evaluate new procedures and medications as part of routine practice rather than by introducing them only after extensive experimentation.

Discussion often takes place within medical circles these days about what is designated as "futile treatment" for those patients whose continued existence is either said to cause them unbearable suffering or is described as no longer "meaningful." Among these patients are those marked as potential organ donors. The danger is very real that in the increasingly utilitarian climate of our times, we will all too readily define certain patients as having lives which are without meaning, especially if we perceive ways in which their bodies can be made "useful" to the medical enterprise, and thus indirectly to society. This is particularly likely to happen given the pressure to reduce expenditures that all medical systems are now under. A rationalization of procedures which free up hospital beds, and which serve at the same time to assist indirectly in "restoring" health to other patients whose beds too will be liberated, can sound very persuasive in a climate where fiscal restraint is dominant.

AN INSATIABLE DEMAND

The case of seventeen-year-old Terry Urquhart, which made front-page news in Canadian newspapers a few years ago, encapsulates many of the contradictions that abound in the transplant world. Terry, a patient with a fatal lung disease who also has Down's syndrome, will probably live, it is agreed by all concerned, at most for another five years. Nevertheless, his parents applied to an Alberta hospital to have their son placed on the waiting list for a lung transplant, not in the expectation that it would "save" his life, but, in the words of a newspaper reporter because, "the medical miracle of a new lung means simply the chance to live out his last few years without gasping for air." Because Terry did not meet the program's written criteria of "satisfactory intelligence," his application was initially turned down. His parents went public with their story, causing the hospital to hastily rewrite its policy and then place Terry on the waiting list.

In response to this case, phone calls flooded into the hospital accusing it of "wasting" organs; hundreds of callers threatened to tear up their donor cards if mentally disabled individuals were routinely to receive transplants. Other callers, fewer in number, agreed with Terry's parents that to be denied a transplant on the grounds of intellectual criteria amounted to discrimination. That a concept of "satisfactory intelligence" caused public polarization is predictable (incidentally, no other transplant programs in Canada have such a requirement). Perhaps equally predictable was that none of the public furor was concerned with the enterprise of transplant technology itself—the squabble was essentially reduced to an argument about who, among many potential patients, should be granted the "miracle of life."

In 1995 at the time of this dispute, less than thirty single-lung transplants were done in Canada each year, and of those who undergo this operation, about 14 percent of patients die within thirty days, and only about half of those who survive the initial onslaught remain alive three years later. Terry is now eligible to undergo six weeks of assessment, after which, if he decides to go ahead with a transplant, he may have to wait for an agonizing couple of years for a suitable donor. Then he faces between one and three months in hospital, and for the remainder of his short life will take powerful immunosuppressants daily, together with other types of medication producing unpleasant and possibly life-threatening side-effects. The hospital's transplant program, which must demonstrate "success" in order to survive, is likely to intervene aggressively so that Terry's statistic does not produce a downward turn in its "survival curve." Meantime, we are told, someone else will die "waiting" for a lung.

More than eight hundred organ transplantation programs are currently operating in the United States alone, and in 1992 almost 10,000 kidneys, 2,100 hearts, 3,000 livers, 500 pancreases, and 450 other vascularized organs (mostly lungs) were transplanted. Eighty percent of recipients of heart, liver, and kidney transplants have a survival rate of one year or more, but beyond five years this rate drops quite dramatically. For recipients of kidneys there is a 60 percent rejection rate of the transplant after five years (which means a return to dialysis, and consideration for a second transplant), and a much higher risk of rejection of livers and hearts, in which case the patient dies unless another organ can be found exceedingly quickly. Yet this is a technology which is no longer considered to be experimental because the techniques of perfusing, "harvesting," and inserting donated organs into recipients are routinized and, in the case of kidneys and hearts, considered to be a "piece of cake" by most involved surgeons. Failure is usually attributed to the quality of the donated organ, immunological rejection of the organ by the recipient, or death of the patient due to "co-morbidity" (that is, from causes other than those relating directly to the transplant). The quality of life of organ recipients is very rarely assessed in the medical literature. Nevertheless, for the large numbers of patients in whom the transplant is successful and causes few long-term problems, this technology is clearly life-saving, and for "straightforward" cases the survival rates and quality of life are improving year by year with the accumulated experience of physicians and surgeons and more effective immunosuppressants.

Because transplantation has been routinized, the numbers of patients accepted to waiting lists to receive organs has increased. In the United States between 1988 and 1991, for example, potential patients increased by 55 percent and by the end of 1993 roughly 30,000 hopeful patients were waiting for a suitable organ to be found for them (Arnold et al.: 1995, 1). During the same period the number of donated organs increased by only 16 percent, and at present, in the States, just over 4,000 are procured each year (Prottas: 1994). However, the number of organs procured from brain-dead donors has dropped rather dramatically over the past ten years from approximately 20,000 to approximately 10,000, due primarily to improved automobile safety (Arnold et al.: 1995, 1). There is no argument that as transplantation has become more "successful," sicker and older patients receive transplants; moreover, second, third, and occasionally further repeat transplants are being carried out when previous ones fail. Thus, with perceived improvements in the surgical techniques associated with transplants, the criteria for selection of patients are loosened, and failure of organs to "take" in the recipient's body are usually located, not in any deficiency on the part of the selection committee who picked out the patient as an appropriate candidate, nor in the surgeon, but in weaknesses in the transplanted organ, or the recipient's constitution, or a lack of compliance.

"SAVING" LIVES, AT WHAT COST?

In theory the donation and reception of organs are contingent upon the informed consent of involved patients and families. A recent Canadian case suggests, however, that the wishes of families may not always be respected. The parents of an infant with biliary atresia, a fatal disease, were informed that a liver transplant was the only means by which their son's life might be saved. The parents made extensive inquiries of relevant medical personnel, did an exhaustive search of the literature in connection with pediatric liver transplantations, and visited two families where children had undergone such transplants. After agonizing over their decision, they decided on the basis of the suffering that they believed their baby would have to endure, the extremely high risk that the child would die from simple infectious diseases such as chicken pox after the transplant, due to the medications he would have to take, the increased risk he would incur of contracting cancer and other deadly diseases, and the damning statistics on the long-term survival rates, that they did not want their son to undergo transplantation surgery. The physician in charge of the case sought an order to make the infant a ward of the court so that he might arrange for the surgery without parental consent. The couple, fearing that their baby would be taken from them, fled to an adjacent province. The parents spent most of the final weeks of their son's life in court, where the case was eventually decided in their favor. The baby died before the family could complete the long journey back home. There has been one other similar case in England where the ruling was also in favor of the parents.

Another case, from the American midwest, raises further troubling questions about the motives behind certain decisions about transplant surgery. In this instance, a young woman had received a lung transplant which her body rejected shortly after surgery, followed by a second which was also unsuccessful. The possibility for a successful outcome decreases with the number of attempted transplants, and lung transplants do not, in any case, have good outcomes. The involved physicians nevertheless seriously contemplated a third attempt. However, after considerable discussion, they eventually decided to inform the patient that no further surgery would be carried out. Shortly after this decision one member of the surgical team, who was leaving to establish his own unit in another hospital, approached the dying patient and offered her a third transplant, provided that she had herself moved to the second hospital. The interpretation of the anthropologist directly involved in this case is that competitiveness among physicians and a chance to practice surgical techniques were the driving motives behind this offer, which the patient ultimately turned down after a time of extremely painful reflection (Marshall et al.: 1996).

The transplant industry is riddled with inflammatory issues, the most contentious of which is about the inequitable distribution of organs. In America, for example, although transplant surgery is covered by insurance, low-income patients experience discrimination because they are unlikely to be referred for placement on waiting lists (Caplan: 1992), and the one-third of the American population just above the poverty level who cannot afford health insurance are also clearly ineligible for financial reasons, nor would they be able to buy the expensive medication that they must take for the rest of their lives should they undergo the surgery. In most European countries, Canada, and Australasia, organ allocation appears to be reasonably fair, but in countries without a socialized health care system, or without something approaching democratic ideals, clearly this technology will only be made available for the wealthy.

The buying of organs, especially kidneys, from live donors has caused considerable concern in India, the Philippines, and other Asian countries. Almost without exception, organs are taken from impoverished individuals and transplanted into the wealthy, some of whom reside outside India. The Indian government has recently made the selling of organs illegal, but it is apparent that infractions regularly take place (*India Today:* 1990). It is claimed that many Indian donors who have sold their kidneys can avail themselves of free medical care for several years after surgery should any complication arise, and also that they usually receive valuable presents from the recipients of their organs (Marshall et al.: 1996). Even if this is the case, however, the potential for abuse not only of donors but of potential recipients is enormous (Kandela: 1991). It has been argued that if autonomous individuals perceive that the selling of a kidney will alleviate the living conditions of their family or themselves, then they should be free to exercise this right (Dworkin: 1993; Radcliffe-Richards: 1996). Abstract moral reasoning permits such a conclusion, but this raises questions which cannot be answered in the abstract, namely, those concerning the means by which coercion would be ruled out, the implementation of regulations in connection with the control of organ sales and with transplantation practices, and the virtual elimination of bribery and gross exploitation. Clearly, brokers for the sale of organs must be disposed of, and sales should be made to some form of neutral, nonprofit organization; but even so it appears extremely unlikely that sales of organs procured from living individuals could ever be practiced without abuses of one kind or another. The matter is not as straightforward as it might appear, however, because, as Radcliffe-Richards argues, on what grounds can we rule that under no circumstances should someone be permitted to sell organs if it is the only means they have to feed their families or themselves, or obtain urgently needed medical treatment?

Use of executed prisoners in China as a source of organs has been roundly criticized (Guttmann: 1992). Chinese officials have argued that sales of organs to foreign buyers permits them to meet public health expenditures. A different kind of argument has been made when discussing the possibility of American prisoners on death row donating organs, namely, that such individuals might actively wish to donate as a means of redemption for their crimes. Once again, adept reasoning could probably create an argument in which, in principle, no moral justification can be found to ban the sale or donation of organs from executed prisoners. In practice, however, well-documented cases of gross abuse exist (*Human Rights Watch/Asia:* 1994), and it seems highly unlikely that impeccable regulatory bodies, independent of government, medical, and drug-company interests, could be put in place to oversee the treatment of prisoners around the world.

The *possible* murders of children and mentally ill patients in Latin America for purposes of organ retrieval (Raymond: 1989) are among the most egregious practices which have been uncovered to date in connection with organ retrieval. With the notable exception of a handful of politically active surgeons, little concern has been shown on the part of the transplant industry as a whole about the sources of organs for transplant. It is as though nature provides this "harvest" for the taking.

The so-called shortage of organs for transplant has encouraged experimentation with animal donors—xenotransplants raise another set of issues concerning, first, animal rights; second, possible infection of recipients with nonhuman viruses, which could have repercussions reaching well beyond individual cases; and third, the fact that this type of surgery is purely experimental and has so far been entirely unsuccessful (Fox and Swazey: 1992). Guidelines have recently been put out for xenotransplantation, but a recent report argues that enormous risk to both individuals and populations remains in connection with this technology, a risk that most guidelines have failed to address adequately (Allan: 1996).

In summary, violence is unavoidable in the procurement of organs. At a minimum, family grieving is severely disrupted while the body is taken away for organ retrieval, a process that necessarily involves mutilation of the body. When prisoners are "volunteered" as organ donors, and the method of their extermination is specifically orchestrated so that vital organs will remain in good condition, gross violence is coupled with gross injustice. However, aside from a little discussion in the tight circle of the transplant world, and among a few commentators in the field of bioethics, very little general discussion has as yet taken place on questions of morality and justice associated with organ procurement. Nevertheless, transplantation proceeds apace, and the "shortage" of organs which will, by definition, always remain greater than the supply (because of ever-widening parameters created within the medical world as to who is eligible to receive an organ), grows ever more acute.

Since the end of the 1960s, in parallel to the routinization and expansion of organ transplant programs, a relatively quiet but rather sinister discussion has ensued over definitions of death. By far the majority of solid organs are presently obtained from donors diagnosed as "brain dead." In the remainder of this paper I will discuss the creation of this concept and consider some of the debate that has taken place over the past thirty years in connection with it, followed by an analysis of arguments involving suggestions for further revisions regarding which persons might be considered as good as dead and from whom organs could therefore be extracted. These maneuvers, which inevitably insert acts of violence into the process of dying, are intimately associated with the perceived "needs" of the transplant industry.

LOCATING THE MOMENT OF DEATH

Doubts about false declaration of death and premature burial are not a recent phenomenon. Pernick, in an article entitled "Back from the Grave," has shown that a concern about ascertaining the time of death correctly has been revived repeatedly throughout history, most often in the wake of "new medical discoveries" in connection with experimental physiology, resuscitation, and suspended animation (1988, 17). As late as 1940, an article in *Scientific American* stated that "frequent" errors in diagnosing death remained the cause of cases of premature burial (Newman: 1940). Despite this concern, pronouncing death did not *usually* pose a problem; dying usually took place rather gradually, and whether in hospital or, as was usually the case, at home, the final moments were often unremarkable. Until the late 1960s, the precise time of death was of little consequence, unless foul play was suspected.

Matters became complicated with the introduction in the late 1950s of the artificial respirator or ventilator, by means of which patients who were no longer breathing independently could be kept alive. Many patients are "weaned" off the ventilator to a partial or full recovery, but others never regain consciousness or the ability to breathe for themselves and become, in Willard Gaylin's heavy-handed neologism, "neomorts"—no longer living, but sustained as though alive by artificial means (1974). The existence of brain-dead patients did not initially produce much of a stir in the medical community, no doubt because, until very recently, a body that has sustained massive brain damage, even when kept functioning artificially, nevertheless degenerates badly, usually in the space of a few days or weeks, and the ventilator is then unplugged (but see Shrader: 1986). However, from 1968 on, when transplant surgeons started to make use of patients who had what they determined was irreversible brain damage as a source of human organs, the situation changed drastically. It became imperative for the first time to agree upon a diagnosis of death which could be clearly pinpointed in time, as an event, rather than as an indeterminate process. Such a death had to be recognized as expediently as possible so that vital organs could be removed legally and while they remained in good condition. Such a diagnosis would have to be based on a lack of brain function, rather than on the condition of the heart and lungs, as had been the case since the nineteenth century.

When the necessity of redefining death was brought up for discussion, from the start, it was fear of repercussions from an anxious public that would refuse to cooperate with organ donation that was uppermost in the minds of many transplant surgeons (Shapiro: 1969, 50; Schmeck: 1969; Paton: 1971, 163). Above all, it was agreed, the public had to understand that potential donors would be protected from an untimely death—from "a snatch" of their organs (Reeves: 1969, 406).

Throughout this century, animal experimentation, the usual testing ground for developing therapies suitable for human use, has been carried out in connection with vital organ transplants. Nevertheless, when human kidney transplants were first performed in the 1950s, followed by liver and then heart transplants in the late 1960s, a debate was still raging as to whether these procedures were experimental or therapeutic (Fox and Swazey: 1992). Contrary to popular knowledge, physicians at a Mississippi hospital claim that they, and not Christiaan Barnard in South Africa, were the first to conduct a human heart transplant. In 1964 these physicians sacrificed a chimpanzee and placed its heart into a sixty-eight-year-old man with severe myocardial disease, in a state of "preterminal" shock at the time of the surgery, who was expected to die during the course of the next day or two. In the publication that followed this experiment we are given a graphic account of the removal of the primate heart, its care after removal, its treatment once placed inside the recipient, and also of the state of the diseased heart removed from the recipient. Readers are not informed that the patient died but are simply told that the transplanted heart "ceased to function two hours after stabilization in the recipient." The experiment was described as having "far-reaching significance" because it enabled the researchers to establish that a heart could be kept functioning by perfusion alone for at least an hour independently of either primate or human body. The physicians lamented that the human donor they had hoped to make use of had not died speedily enough, and therefore they were forced to use a primate heart which was not sufficiently large, and secondly that the recipient was so sick that he was "perhaps the major factor in eventual failure of the transplant" (Hardy and Chavez: 1968, 777).

In 1967 Christiaan Barnard carried out what was to be internationally recognized as the first human heart transplant. Despite the fact that the recipient experienced acute rejection and lived for only eighteen days after the surgery, many other attempts rapidly followed suit. Fifteen months later, 118 heart transplants had been performed in eighteen different countries, with a surgical mortality rate of 50 percent (that is, 50 percent of the patients died up to thirty days after surgery) and a cumulative six-month mortality rate of 88 percent (Cooper and Mitchell: 1969).

Although Barnard's first heart transplant was initially acclaimed triumphantly in the media, doubts and criticism followed hard on its heels. There was a call from some quarters for Barnard to be disbarred permanently from medical practice (Schmeck: 1969). Furthermore, although considerable critical attention was given to possible mistreatment of organ recipients, equal concern was initially expressed about the fate of the donor. One American senator apparently believed that all dying patients on ventilators were now vulnerable to having their lives peremptorily extinguished in order to retrieve their organs (Schmeck: 1969, 672). The *Nation* published an article headed "The Heart Market" in which they asked rhetorically if someone was playing God, and asserted that a "shocking international heart transplant race" was under way. This article also reminded its readers about the forgotten half of the transplant equation—the donor—and added, "contrary to the general impression, few doctors can predict the so-called 'moment of death' with certainty" (*Nation:* 1968, 720). The article went on to point out that of a group of 120 head-injury patients at Cambridge University Hospital in England who were unconscious for more than a month, 63 survived. "As the need for donors grows larger, the definition of death must be carefully redefined. When are you dead *enough* to be deprived of your heart?" asked the *Nation* (1968: 721). *Time* (1967) and *Saturday Review* (1968) were equally scathing, particularly of Christiaan Barnard himself, while *Ebony* cautioned, "It is doubtful . . . that the transplant of a Colored heart into a white man will have any positive effect upon the rigidly segregated life of South Africa" (1968, 118).

In May 1968 an editorial appeared in the *Journal of the American Medical Association* in which the dilemma posed by vital organ transplants was clearly formulated for the first time: "It is obvious that if . . . organs [such as the liver and heart] are taken long after death, their chance of survival in another person is minimized. On the other hand, if they are removed before death can be said to have occurred by the strictest criteria that one can employ, murder has been done." The editorial went on to state that it is therefore "mandatory that the moment of death be defined as precisely as possible," and concluded as follows: "When all is said and done, it seems ironic that the end point of existence, which ought to be as clear and sharp as in a chemical titration, should so defy the power of words to describe it and the power of men to say with certainty, 'It is here'" (*JAMA:* 1968, 220). One month later, in August 1968, an Ad Hoc Committee composed primarily of physicians called together by the Harvard Medical School published the findings of their meetings in the *Journal of the American Medical Association.* The committee agreed that "'irreversible coma' must be substituted for 'cessation of vital functions' as the criterion for death." Two reasons were given as to why there was a need for this new definition: first, improvements in resuscitative and supportive measures had led to increased efforts to save desperately injured individuals, sometimes with only partial success, so that a patient with irreversible brain damage might continue to have a beating heart. It was argued that the burden of such patients was great on families, hospitals, and those in need of beds. The second reason given was that "obsolete criteria for the definition of death can lead to controversy in obtaining organs for transplantation" (*JAMA:* 1968, 337). The report noted that the first problem for the committee was to determine the "characteristics of a *permanently* nonfunctioning brain." It was emphasized that a decision to declare irreversible coma must be made only by the physician-in-charge, in consultation with one or more physicians directly responsible for the case (implying that transplant surgeons should not be involved). The report continued, "it is unsound and undesirable to force the family to make the decision."

A legal commentary which followed this statement corroborated that judgment of death was solely a medical issue and that the patient be declared dead before any effort is made to take "him off a respirator," otherwise the physicians would be "turning off the respirator on a person who is, under the present strict, technical application of law, still alive" (*JAMA:* 1968, 362). The article also noted that Pope Pious XII had, in 1957, stated that it is "not within the competence of the Church" to determine death in cases where there is overwhelming brain damage, and that verification of death can be determined "if at all" only by a physician (362). In what seems to be, in retrospect, a surprising oversight, the impression is given in this article that from now on *all* death will be determined by the condition of the brain.

PLUGGING UP THE LOOPHOLES

The concept of "brain death syndrome" was challenged in the courts during the early 1970s in North America. In one landmark case in Virginia, in 1972, the jury ruled against the donor's family, who claimed that the transplant surgeons had been responsible for the death of their relative. Other court cases followed, including several involving homicide victims, but none resulted in the prosecution of a doctor (Simmons et al.: 1987). At the same time a debate about medical practice was under way in the medical world itself, in particular as to which tests, if any, could be relied upon to confirm an individual doctor's opinion about brain death, and secondly as to who would act as "gatekeepers" to protect physicians from malpractice suits (Black: 1978).

By 1981 it was recognized that public policy in connection with defining death had become an urgent matter, and accordingly a Uniform Determination of Death Act was proposed after extensive debate among the members of a special President's Commission, less than half of whom were physicians. This Act was immediately supported by the American Medical Association and the American Bar Association, and subsequently adopted over the years by the majority of state legislatures.

The President's Commission, in opposition to the position taken by a good number of individual physicians, philosophers, and theologians, opted to further rationalize and update what they characterized as "obsolete" diagnostic criteria present in the Harvard statement, and to enshrine a definition of death in law, something which thus far had not been the case (Annas: 1988, 621). The commission's report stated at the outset that their mandate was to produce "clear and principled guidance" for determining whether bodies which breathe only through artificial means and have no capacity for integration of bodily functions, no consciousness, and no capacity for other human experience are alive or dead (President's Commission: 1981, 3). The report stressed that it was the death of a human being, "not the 'death' of cells, tissues, and organs," about which they were concerned. Although it was recognized that functional cessation of vital bodily systems can be used as a standard to judge whether biological death has occurred, the importance of such findings, it was asserted, lies in what they reveal about "the status of the person," rather than about the body physical (58).

The report was explicit that the "meaning" of death should not be radically changed, and thus its focus was on independent breathing or a lack thereof, and the rapid effects a lack of oxygen has on brain function, together with the relationship of these observations to the person as a whole. There was concern, above all, to establish a single set of standards which would be accepted throughout the United States. (These standards were also recognized in Canada. To this day, Great Britain uses a different set of standards, and in Sweden and Denmark it was only relatively recently that brain death was legally recognized.) The difficulties of transporting bodies across state lines for the purposes of "treatment" was raised as a major stumbling block unless a clear public policy was set in place. It was also emphasized that physicians must know as early as possible when a mechanically supported patient's brain ceases to function, so that they could adequately take care of those organs designated for transplant. It was explicitly stated that in a brain-dead patient, even when on a respirator, internal organs undergo changes which make them less fit for transplants unless they are carefully perfused and certain medications avoided.

With these points in mind, the commission recommended that a concept of "whole-brain death," equated with an "irreversible loss of all brain function," be adopted. This condition was carefully distinguished in the report from a "persistent vegetative state," as exemplified by patients such as Karen Ann Quinlan and Nancy Beth Cruzan, whose brain stems continued to function despite an irreversible loss of higher brain function. The earlier definition of "irreversible coma" left room for doubt as to whether patients such as these could be taken for dead, and the concept of whole-brain death was designed specifically to clarify this point (President's Commission: 1981, 24).

Despite this effort to establish uniformity, a good number of publications appeared shortly after the Act was passed in which medical professionals, philosophers, and social scientists pointed out the numerous ways in which the wording of the Act remained ambiguous, particularly so because *two* criteria were recognized as acceptable in the determination of death: irreversible cessation of circulatory and respiratory functions *or* irreversible cessation of all functions of the entire brain, including the brain stem. Their interest in the state of potential organs for transplant ensured that the commission sought to establish as early as possible along the continuum of the process that death was indeed taking place—in other words, that an *irreversible* situation had set in. If it could be agreed that the brain was no longer functioning in an integrated fashion, and that this situation could only get worse, then it would "naturally" follow that the *person* no longer existed. Even though many of the cells of the body remained active after brain death, it was assumed that few people would argue against the concept of whole-brain death, because the brain and therefore the person was clearly damaged beyond hope of recovery.

The bioethicist Tristram Engelhardt, who wrote as early as 1975 that a definition of death as irreversible coma is a "conservative definition," is one such person. He asserts that "it takes more to be a person than reaction to pain, spontaneous respiration, and reflex activity" (1981, 364). Engelhardt, rigorously following a mind/body dichotomy, believes that an "intellectual decision" has been made by defining death in terms of the brain, namely that "human biological life is not the same as human personal life. An otherwise intact and alive, but brain-dead, person is not a human person. We who have grown up since the development of modern neurology and neurophysiology take for granted the assertion that to be a mind in this world is to 'have' an intact functioning brain" (365). Engelhardt then pursues the argument to what for him is a logical conclusion, namely, that lack of upper brain function alone signals death and that therefore patients in a persistent vegetative state are dead. For this bioethicist, "The brain-oriented concept of death offers medicine a way of distinguishing between patients, i.e., the persons to whom medicine has obligations, and the collection of human organs (i.e., mere human biological life), which can be used to help persons still alive" (366). Since there are no obligations to organs, no ethical quandary exists about the removal of organs from those defined as non-persons.

Twenty years later doubts persist as to whether or not we are on an ethical slippery slope, and as to what actually constitutes death (Arnold and Youngner: 1993; Veatch: 1993). In some segments of the intellectual and medical worlds we clearly remain, in Kuhn's terms, in a paradigm crisis, striving for commensurability but unable to achieve it.

LOCATING THE PERSON

The President's Commission which culminated in the Uniform Determination of Death Act stated clearly that for death to be diagnosed, all brain function must have ceased, including the reflexes controlled by the brain stem. At this point a lack of "neurological integration" exists, and what is left is "no longer a functional or *organic* unity, but merely a *mechanical* complex" (Bernat et al.: 1981, 391). Zaner, a bioethicist, has pointed out that, for whole-brain advocates, "it is the biological organism (or, more specifically, the physiological/anatomical nervous system) which is definitive for life and death, not the *person* whose organism (or nervous system) it is" (1988, 7). Zaner believes that the commission put the cart before the horse when it tried to develop a concept of death out of a set of standardized medical tests while evading the central issue of just *who* had died. In order for there to be a uniform statutory definition of human death, there must be first of all, according to Zaner, a general consensus regarding what constitutes "personhood" or "personal identity" (1988, 5).

The commission acknowledged that no such consensus exists, pointed out that the issue has been debated for centuries, and explicitly sought to circumvent the problem by making a biological argument in which rationally conceived operational criteria and medical tests provided the answer, something with which not only the scientists, but also the lawyers on the Commission were apparently comfortable. Critics of the findings of the commission argue that neither operational criteria nor valid tests can be created unless an agreed-upon working definition is first established—namely, a concept of what it *means* to die (Bartlett and Youngner: 1988). Such a definition has to be "societal" and not biological, the philosopher and psychiatrist team of Bartlett and Youngner argued, since it is the permanent loss of personhood which is of central concern, rather than the demise of the body physical.

Definitions of death grounded in the idea of a loss of personhood have been characterized as "ontological" and contrasted with what are taken to be narrowly defined scientific definitions based on the state of brain function (Gervais: 1987). Lamb, a philosopher, has expressed grave reservations about ontological definitions of death. He states that those who argue for yet another redefinition of death based on ontological criteria are in actuality appealing to the idea that a loss of higher brain function alone, and not the whole brain, is what ultimately counts. What has come to be known as "neocortical death"—conditions where there is an irreversible loss of consciousness and cognitive function, but an intact brain stem—is simply, according to Lamb, a rewording in scientific terms of a definition based on a loss of personhood (1990). Lamb cites one of the papers in the Zaner collection where the author, a lawyer, argues that neocortical death has already been legally recognized, since life support has on occasion been removed from patients in a persistent vegetative state, that is, from patients who have undergone "neocortical death." This author is explicit that medical recognition of neocortical death would be invaluable in the increased procurement of organs for transplants:

> A neocortical death standard could significantly increase availability and access to transplants because patients . . . declared dead under a neocortical definition could be biologically maintained for years as opposed to a few hours or days, as in the case of whole-brain death. Under the present Uniform Anatomical Gift Act, this raises the possibility that neocortically dead bodies or parts could be donated and maintained for long-term research, as organ banks, or for other purposes such as drug testing or manufacturing biological compounds. (Smith: 1988, 129)

Lamb points out that those who make such arguments are concerned only with criteria that assist in describing "the minimum necessary qualities for personhood, defined in terms of psychological abilities" (1990, 44).

Gervais has in turn criticized Lamb for placing too much reliance on a biological definition; Lamb, she states, sees death as "a fact awaiting discovery" (Gervais: 1987, 155), and characterizes the ontological approach, in contrast, as based in ethical reflection. Lamb has countered this rebuttal by claiming that whole-brain death is an "ethically superior formulation" to neocortical death because "in matters of life and death, objective, testable criteria concerning presence or absence of vital functions are more reliable than indeterminant assessments concerning the quality of residual life, or speculations regarding personhood, or utilitarian requirements for transplant organs" (Lamb: 1990, 46). Lamb is clearly concerned that overriding interests about the supposed crisis precipitated by an "organ shortage" will seize the day and send us on our way down the slippery slope to redefining death in response to a perceived need. Thus he is adamantly opposed to Green and Wikler (1981), for example, who argue for the importance of a "psychological continuity" equated with higher brain function as necessary for the preservation of personal identity and hence life. For psychological advocates such as these authors, Lamb states, "personal identity" appears to be "the measure of human life" (1990, 46). He adds that the whole-brain death formulation does not dispute that all capacity for integrated mental activity is lost, but he believes that the "essence" of personal identity is an elusive concept which in any case resides in a different logical space than the cessation of vital functions, and is certainly not one on which doctors should rely in making decisions about death. Personal identity, after all, does not have any specific, anatomical location, claims Lamb, but is a quality akin to "spirit," "will," or "soul," with religious, legal, and political associations.

As early as the 1970s Hans Jonas detected the classical "soul-body dualism" of Enlightenment philosophy at work in recent reformulations of death in North America and Europe.

> [In] its new apparition . . . the dualism of the brain and body . . . holds that the true human person rests in (or is represented by) the brain, of which the rest of the body is a mere subservient tool. Thus when the brain dies, it is as when the soul departed: what is left are "mortal remains." Now nobody will deny that the cerebral aspect is decisive for the human quality of life of the organism. . . . The position I advance acknowledges just this . . . [but] the extracerebral body [has] its share of the identity of the person. The body is uniquely the body of this brain and no other, as the brain is uniquely the brain of this body and no other. What is under the brain's central control, the bodily total, is as individual, as much "myself," as singular to my identity (fingerprints!), as noninterchangeable, as the controlling (and reciprocally controlled) brain itself. My identity is the identity of the whole organism, even if the higher functions of personhood are seated in the brain. (Jonas: 1974, 139)

Lamb, in agreement with Jonas asks, "If patients in a persistent vegetative state are to be considered dead, then how much neocortical damage would be necessary for a patient to be labeled as vegetative?" (1990, 53). He points out that there is no "clinical homogeneity" in vegetative patients and no firm criteria for defining just what such a state is. Diagnosis can be difficult (Beresford: 1978), and is particularly so in children; absence of consciousness and self-awareness is not at all easy to define or establish, and cases of significant recovery from this condition have been reported in reputable journals (Dougherty et al.: 1981, 997; Rosenberg et al.: 1977, 167–68)

In summarizing this contentious debate as it stood at the end of the 1980s, Fost argued that the problem with utilitarian justifications for redefining death, including the Uniform Determination of Death, is that they invite constant redefinition whenever utility requires it, creating "not only instability, but the perception and possibility that unwanted persons can be defined out of existence [whenever] it serves the greater good" (1988, 7).

Recently the philosopher Veatch, taking up this contentious issue once again, has argued that the "definition of death debate is actually a debate over the moral status of human beings. It is a debate over when humans should be treated as full members of the human community. When humans are living, full moral and legal rights accrue" (1993, 21). Thus, Veatch believes, science cannot solve the problem, nor are we likely to reach an easy agreement in a pluralistic society, since the issue is basically one of morals, philosophy, and religion. Veatch claims that diversity of beliefs should be tolerated, and therefore individuals should be free to choose their own definition of death; however, such choices would have to "avoid violating the rights of others and avoid creating insurmountable social problems for the rest of society" (22). Veatch then argues that people would not be able to pick a definition of death that "required society to treat them as dead even though they retained cardiac, respiratory, mental, and neurologically integrated functions. Likewise, I assume that people would not be permitted to pick a definition that would insist that they be treated as alive when all these functions were absent" (22). In practice, Veatch concludes, individuals should be able to choose among "heart-, whole-brain, and higher-brain-oriented definitions," and he would like to see a definition of "irreversible cessation of the capacity for consciousness" written into law as a third option for death. However, Veatch himself believes that a whole-brain orientation to death is "old fashioned" and is becoming increasingly less plausible: "To me, the principle is that for human life to be present— that is, for the human to be treated as a member in full standing of the human moral community—there must be integrated functioning of mind and body. That means some version of a higher-brain-oriented formulation" (24).

THE SLIPPERY SLOPE OF TRUTH

Although it is frequently reiterated that debates about the concept of death must be kept entirely separate from the organ-procurement enterprise, it is evident that in reality this is extremely hard to do. Probing reveals quite quickly that concern about organ retrieval drives the debate no matter whether it is couched as a moral, legal, or scientific argument. For some participants, notable among them neuroscientists, the concern is primarily over accuracy of diagnosis and mismanagement of clinical care of the dying should the guidelines be loosened or radically altered. An overwhelming consensus holds that the diagnosis of brain death as it is presently determined is exceedingly accurate and leaves no room for error (provided, of course the required protocol is correctly followed), but that should a neocortical or upper-brain definition of death be recognized, then the specter of uncertainty will loom large. Among participants in this debate, in contrast to the caution exhibited by neuroscientists, those who are not responsible for clinical care of patients suffering from trauma appear rather cavalier at times in their eagerness to remake death for the sake of organ procurement. The current argument is tending toward general agreement that a consensus about a conclusive definition of death will never be reached. In order to make more human organs available for transplant, one alternative to pursuing a standardization of death is to move ahead and create classes of patients who may be counted as good as dead, including those whose upper brains alone are no longer functioning and from whom organs can be extracted, even though most of these patients breathe unaided.

Patients who have been diagnosed as persistently vegetative for more than twelve months are known as "permanently vegetative." Recently the criteria for making this diagnosis have been clarified and refined (*New England Journal of Medicine:* 1994), and despite the fact that one or two cases of partial recovery have been documented in patients who have been in a vegetative state for over a year, an argument has been made for discussion as to whether such patients, if prior consent had been given, could be considered as organ donors (Hoffenberg et al.: 1997).

Virtually unnoticed by the public, two more sources of organs are already being made use of. Prior to the institution of brain death, organs were usually obtained from living related donors or from donors whose hearts had already stopped beating. The great disadvantage of this second type of procurement is that the organs are very likely to be damaged due to a lack of blood flow during their retrieval from the donor. It is now recognized that if a patient is perfused with specially prepared cold fluids immediately prior to and/or after cardiac arrest then the organs remain in reasonably good condition, even after cardio-pulmonary death, and can be removed for transplantation. The difficulty with this approach, known as "uncontrolled donation" because death is unexpected, is that only on very rare occasions has consent been obtained ahead of time to remove organs, and hence body cooling usually takes place as though donation will proceed, often before the next of kin have been located. A second, equally troubling feature, is the question of whether every effort is made to carry out resuscitation prior to declaring death.

"Controlled donation" from patients whose hearts have stopped beating takes place when patients and their families opt to donate organs after such terminally ill patients have decided to forgo life-sustaining treatment. Usually the patient is taken to the operating room, where treatment is stopped, and the waiting surgical team removes the organs immediately after death has been declared. It comes as no surprise that the first implementation of these practices was carried out at Pittsburgh University

Hospital which, it is widely agreed, has the most aggressive transplant program in the United States. Weisbard, in commenting critically on these practices, as several other authors have done (Arnold et al.: 1995), states that

> In its rawest form, the Pittsburgh protocol envisions wheeling a . . . still-living prospective donor into the O.R., prepping the individual's body for subsequent removal of organs, presiding over a series of events . . . hopefully culminating in the individual's death (or, at least, the individual's being "declared" dead by a new and scientifically unvalidated set of criteria), and finally removing the individual's organs for transplant—all this unless something goes dreadfully wrong, and the patient survives . . . enormous pains are taken to characterize events as an allowing to die, rather than a killing, and as a series of stepwise "adjustments" of respiratory support and pain medication, each portrayed as "intended" to respond solely to the patient's needs of the moment. The protocol has the secondary or "unintended" (if foreseen) effect of bringing about the patient's (desired) death. (Weisbard: 1995, 147)

In another move to obtain more organs for transplant, after years of debate, the Council on Ethical and Judicial Affairs of the American Medical Association has recently reversed an earlier decision and now states that it is morally permissible to consider the anencephalic neonate, although alive according to current definitions of death, as a potential organ donor. Two-thirds of surveyed bioethicists and medical experts agreed with this decision (*JAMA:* 1995). Arnold and Youngner (1993) point out that to date society has assured itself that potential donors will be protected from harm because of what is known informally as the "dead donor" rule (Robertson: 1988). Clearly we have quietly subverted the intent of this rule and are now embarked on the process of "allowing patients to die," "hastening the process of death," and, further, are keen to count other people with brain damage as good as dead, in order that their organs can be retrieved as expediently as possible. Against this, the suffering of potential organ recipients must be kept in mind, and their plight alleviated if this is reasonably possible. The inherent tension between these two classes of people can never be resolved while organs from dying patients or those whose brains are irreparably damaged are commodified for the benefit of those in need of transplants. The point is not that commodification is necessarily wrong, but that violence is unavoidable, and every aspect of this enterprise, the procurement of organs as well as the heroics of transplantation, must be openly discussed and debated.

SYMBOLIC VIOLENCE AND THE "SAVING OF LIVES"

Bourdieu has described the concept of symbolic power as "a power of creating things with words" (1990, 138); symbolic power represents the possibility of imposing on other minds a vision enforced indirectly, one that is effectively disguised because a selective repression or concealment of knowledge and information is involved. This type of power, symbolic or euphemized violence, is folded seamlessly into institutional, legal, and governmental activity, and appears as a natural and inevitable part of daily life. With government backing, citizens are encouraged to make a charitable donation of their organs; at the same time they are encouraged to believe that they have a right to receive donated organs should they need them and, furthermore, that the "giving of organs" is a simple and uncomplicated life-saving activity, with an approximately 80 percent success rate for transplant recipients. This iconic figure is cited very widely in the rhetoric that accompanies organ transplants, but stops short of presenting a more complete picture, namely, that for adults the *one-year* survival rate is 80 percent, after which it drops off considerably, depending upon what type of organ is involved, and with young children the picture is much more bleak. Furthermore, because of lifelong medication, organ recipients are placed in great danger of contracting cancer and other diseases, as well as of experiencing iatrogenic side effects on a long-term basis, in addition to which many patients go though cycles of organ rejection for which they must be hospitalized. Lifelong medical surveillance is necessary for all patients, and immunosuppressant medication is extremely expensive. The mother of the infant who needed a transplant whose case was described above found that even after repeated questioning, the transplant surgeon did not give a fair picture of the uncertainty and risk involved with the procedure; media reporting about organ transplants tends to focus on stories that appear to have successful outcomes, although none of these stories are followed up for more than a day or two. I am not suggesting that a deliberate, self-conscious concealment is customary; both the violence and the heroics associated with transplants are normalized and rationalized through a rhetoric of progress, one in which the source of human organs is studiously ignored almost all of the time.

An undivided pursuit of scientific knowledge, surgical experience, and successful outcomes for transplant patients drives the transplant industry, but this professional interest is largely hidden from public view and constituted instead as a moral obligation on the part of the public to cooperate fully in a life-saving humanistic endeavor. Although there is a constant lament about a shortage of organs, there is a tendency to talk rather complacently about how well the United Organ Sharing Organization (UNOS) functions in the United States, and the Canadian provinces proclaim equity in the distribution of organs as the basis for their success in obtaining cooperation with donations from the public. However, the transplant industry is unavoidably part of the global economy; exploitation and abuse of the poor in many countries so that this industry can flourish cannot be set to one side—Euro/America is not hermetically sealed; further, without multinational drug companies, transplants would not take place, nor would the showy international meetings on which the scientific advances of this industry thrive—actual and symbolic violence flourish in every aspect of the enterprise.

The inherent tension present in the pursuit of medical knowledge cannot be avoided, as I suggested at the outset of the paper. There is no argument that we must experiment, often on animals and humans, and we have established codes of conduct for such purposes. However, too often ethics is reduced to individual rights and interests, and questions of autonomy. This is in itself one form of symbolic violence, in my opinion, because by so doing medical practices and their associated ethics are individualized, and social, political, and economic aspects of problems are silenced. The court case in connection with the parents who refused a transplant for their infant was set up as a case of the rights of the infant versus the interests of the parents, and the parents only won the case because it was decided that there was no assurance that a liver transplant was in the best interest of the infant. Similarly, the Down's syndrome case was set up as a case of the rights of the individual patient. These are iconic cases, and the legal judgments are important, but their political ramifications remain understated. Obviously many patients benefit enormously from receiving donated organs, but this industry will be tainted until such time as the silence—the violence—associated with organ procurement is fully discussed and debated.

REFERENCES

Allan, Jonathan S. 1996. "Xenotransplantation at a Crossroads: Prevention Versus Progress." *Nature Medicine* 2, no. 1: 1820.

Annas, George J. 1988. "Brain Death and Organ Donation: You Can Have One without the Other." *Hastings Center Report* 18: 2830.

Arnold, Robert, and Stuart Youngner. 1993. "Back to the Future: Obtaining Organs from Non-Heart-Beating Cadavers." *Kennedy Institute of Ethics Journal* 3: 103–11.

Arnold, Robert, Stuart Youngner, Renie Shapiro, and Carol Mason Spice, eds. 1995. *Procuring Organs for Transplant: The Debate over Non-Heart-Beating Cadaver Protocols*. Baltimore: The Johns Hopkins University Press.

Bartlett, Edward T., and Stuart J. Youngner. 1988. "Human Death and the Destruction of the Neocortex." In *Death: Beyond Whole-Brain Criteria*, ed. R. Zaner, 199–216. Dordrecht: Kluwer Academic Publishers.

Beresford, H. R. 1978. "Cognitive Death: Differential Problems and Legal Overtones." *Annals of the New York Academy of Sciences* 315: 339–48.

Bernat, James L., et al. 1981. "On the Definition and Criterion of Death." *Annals of Internal Medicine* 94: 389–91.

Black, Peter. 1978. "Brain Death." *New England Journal of Medicine* 229: 338–44.

Bourdieu, Pierre. 1990. *In Other Words: Essays Towards a Reflexive Sociology.* Stanford: Stanford University Press.

British Medical Association. 1992. *Medicine Betrayed: The Participation of Doctors in Human Rights Abuses.* London: Zed Books.

Caplan, Arthur. 1992. *If I Were a Rich Man, Could I Buy a Pancreas?* Bloomington: Indiana University Press.

Cooper, Theodore, and Sheila C. Mitchell. 1969. "Cardiac Transplantation: Current Status." *Transplantation Proceedings* 1, no. 2: 755–57.

Culliton, Barbara J. 1991. "AIDS Trials Questioned." *Nature* 350 (28 March): 263.

Dougherty, John Jr., F. Rawlinson, David E. Levy, and Fred Plum. 1981. "Hypoxic-Ischemic Brain Injury and the Vegetative State: Clinical and Neuropathologic Correlation." *Neurology* 31 (August): 991–97.

Dworkin, Gerald. 1993. "Markets and Morals: The Case for Organ Sales." *Mount Sinai Journal of Medicine* 60, no. 1: 66–69.

Ebony. 1968. "The Telltale Heart." 23 (March): 118–19.

Elliott, Carl and Charles Weijer. 1995. "Cruel and Unusual Treatment." *Saturday Night* (December): 31–34.

Engelhardt, Tristram. 1981. "Defining Death: A Philosophical Problem for Medicine and Law." In *Biomedical Ethics,* ed. T. A. Mappes and V. S. Zembaty, 363–66. New York: McGraw-Hill. Reprinted from *American Review of Respiratory Disease* 112 (1975): 587–90.

Fost, Norman. 1988. "Organs from Anencephalic Infants: An Idea Whose Time Has Not Yet Come." *Hastings Center Report* 18: 5,10.

Fox, Renée C., and Judith P. Swazey. 1992. *Spare Parts: Organ Replacement in American Society.* New York: Oxford University Press.

Gaylin, Willard. 1974. "Harvesting the Dead." *Harper's* 52: 23–30.

Gervais, Karen G. 1987. *Redefining Death.* New Haven: Yale University Press.

Green, Michael B., and Daniel Wikler. 1981. "Brain Death and Personal Identity." In *Medicine and Moral Philosophy,* ed. Marshall Cohen, Thomas Nagel, and Thomas Scanlon, 49–77. Princeton, NJ: Princeton University Press.

Guttmann, Ronald D. 1992. "On the Use of Organs from Executed Prisoners." *Transplantation Reviews* 6: 189–93.

Hardy, James D., and Carlos M. Chavez. 1968. "The First Heart Transplant in Man: Developmental Animal Investigations with Analysis of the 1964 Case in the Light of Current Clinical Experience." *American Journal of Cardiology* 22: 772–81.

Harris, Sheldon. 1994. *Factories of Death: Japanese Biological Warfare, 1932–45, and the American Cover Up.* New York: Routledge Press.

Hoffenberg, Raymond, Margaret Lock, Nicholas Tilney, Carlos Casabona, Abdullah S. Daar, Ronald D. Guttmann, Ian Kennedy, Samarin Nundy, Janet Radcliffe-Richards, and Robert A. Sells. 1997. "Should Organs from Patients in Permanent Vegetative State Be Used for Transplantation?" *Lancet* 350 (1 November): 1320–21.

Human Rights Watch/Asia. "China: Organ Procurement and Judicial Execution in China." Vol. 6, no. 9: 1–42.

India Today. 1990. "The Organs Bazaar." 30 July: 60–67.

JAMA. 1968. "What and When Is Death." Vol. 204, no. 6: 219–20.

———. 1995. "The Use of Anencephalic Neonates as Organ Donors." 273: 1614–18.

Jonas, Hans. 1974. *Philosophical Essays: From Ancient Creed to Technological Man.* Englewood Cliffs, NJ: Prentice Hall.

Jones, James. 1995. *Bad Blood.* New York: Free Press.

Kandela, Peter. 1991. "India: Kidney Bazar." *Lancet* 337 (22 June): 15–34.

Lamb, David. 1990. *Organ Transplants and Ethics.* London: Routledge.

Marshall, Patricia A., David C. Thomasma, and Abdullah S. Daar. 1996. "Marketing Human Organs: The Autonomy Paradox." *Theoretical Medicine* 17: 1–18.

Nation. 1968. "Someone Playing God." 30 December: 720.

New England Journal of Medicine. 1994. "Medical Aspects of the Persistent Vegetative State." 330: 1499–1508 (Part 1) and 1572–79 (Part 2).

Newman, B. M. 1940. "What Is Death?" *Scientific American* 162 (June): 336–37.

Paton, Alec. 1971. "Life and Death: Moral and Ethical Aspects of Transplantation." *Seminars in Psychiatry* 3, no. 1: 161–68.

Pernick, M. 1988. "Back from the Grave: Recurring Controversies over Defining and Diagnosing Death in History." In *Death: Beyond Whole-Brain Criteria,* ed. R. Zaner, 17–74. Dordrecht: Kluwer Academic Publishers.

Potter, P. 1976. "Herophilus of Chalcedon: An Assessment of His Place in the History of Anatomy." *Bulletin of the History of Medicine* 50: 45–60.

President's Commission for the Study of Ethical Problems in Medicine and Biomedical and Behavioral Research. 1981. *Defining Death: Medical, Legal, and Ethical Issues in the Determination of Death.* Washington, DC: U.S. Government Printing Office.

Prottas, J. M. *1994. The Most Useful Gift: Altruism and the Public Policy of Organ Transplants.* San Francisco: Jossey-Bass.

Radcliffe-Richards, Janet. 1996. "Nepharious Goings-On: Kidney Sales and Moral Arguments." *Journal of Medical Philosophy* 21: 375–416.

Randall, T. 1991. "Too Few Human Organs for Transplantation, Too Many in Need . . . and the Gap Widens." *Journal of the American Medical Association* 265 (13 March): 1223–27.

Raymond, Janice. 1989. "Children for Organ Export?" *Social Science and Medicine* 2: 237–45.

Reeves, Robert B. Jr. 1969. "The Ethics of Cardiac Transplantation in Man." *Bulletin of the New York Academy of Medicine* 45, no. 5: 404–11.

Richardson, Ruth. 1988. *Death, Dissection, and the Destitute.* London: Penguin.

Rieff, Philip. 1966. *The Triumph of the Therapeutic: Uses of Faith after Freud.* New York: Harper and Row.

Robertson, John. 1988. "Relaxing the Death Standard for Organ Donation in Pediatric Situations." In *Organ Substitution Technology: Ethical, Legal, and Public Policy Issues,* ed. D. Malthieu, 69–76. Boulder, CO: Westview Press.

Rosenberg, G. A., S. F. Johnson, and R. P. Brenner. 1977. "Recovery of Cognition After Prolonged Vegetative State." *Annals of Neurology* 2: 167–68.

Saturday Review/Research. 1968. "A Realistic Look at Heart Transplants." 3 February.

Schmeck, Harold. 1969. "Transplantation of Organs and Attitudes: The Public's Attitude Toward Clinical Transplantation." *Transplantation Proceedings* 1, no. 1: 670–74.

Shapiro, Hillel, ed. 1969. "Experience with Human Heart Transplantation." *Proceedings of the Cape Town Symposium, 13–16 July, 1968.* Durban: Butterworths.

Shrader, Douglas. 1986. "On Dying More Than One Death." *Hastings Center Report* 16, no. 1: 12–17.

Simmons, Roberta G., Susan Klein Marine, and Richard L. Simmons. 1987. *Gift of Life: The Effect of Organ Transplantation on Individual, Family, and Societal Dynamics.* New Brunswick, NJ: Transaction.

Smith, David Randolph. 1988. "Legal Issues Leading to the Notion of Neocortical Death." In *Death: Beyond Whole-Brain Criteria,* ed. Richard M. Zaner, 111–44. Dordrecht: Kluwer Academic Publishers.

Time. 1967. "Surgery: The Ultimate Operation." 15 December.

Veatch, Robert M. 1993. "The Impending Collapse of the Whole-Brain Definition of Death." *Hastings Center Report* 23, no. 4: 18–24.

Weisbard, Alan. 1995. "A Polemic on Principles: Reflections on the Pittsburgh Protocol." In *Procuring Organs for Transplant: The Debate over Non-Heart-Beating Cadaver Protocols,* ed. Robert Arnold, Stuart Youngner, Renie Shapiro, and Carol Mason Spicer, 141–54. Baltimore: The Johns Hopkins University Press.

Zaner, Richard M. 1988. "Introduction." In *Death: Beyond Whole-Brain Criteria,* ed. R. Zaner, 1–14. Dordrecht: Kluwer Academic Publishers.

Mayan Multiculturalism
and the Violence of Memories

Kay B. Warren

Mayan Indians in Guatemala face many dilemmas as they reassert their cultural presence in a political environment where mass killings from the counterinsurgency war of 1978–85 have abated, yet military repression continued through the early 1990s.[1] A central issue is how different groups of Mayans made sense of violence as the country moved from active warfare to low-intensity peace. The constant in this process was a militarized environment that distrusted social criticism. In the past, Mayans expressed their social analysis in the veiled language of community religion (Warren 1989); now Mayan journalists and publishing houses openly circulate social commentary produced by the newly emerging field of Mayan Studies to wider publics. This essay seeks to understand the layering of politics and meaning early in the transition to democracy by examining key essays produced by the indigenous social commentator Enrique Sam Colop in the early 1990s and the place of his work in the development of Guatemala's Pan-Mayan social movement. At that point, after almost three decades of military rule, few would have guessed that this marginalized movement would soon set the terms for a rethinking of Guatemala as a multicultural nation.

Scarry's description of torture as an "unmaking of the world" through fragmentation, the creation of divided selves, and physical destruction strikes anthropologists and others as appropriate for situations of state terrorism. For her, a crucial act of resistance to the militarization of civilian life becomes the representation of pain—a devastating and elusive yet crucial experience to communicate.[2] Echoing these concerns, the Pan-Mayan scholar-activists who emerged publicly in the late 1980s to press for indigenous rights have rewoven the story of internal warfare and "unmaking" into a narrative of cultural resurgence in writings on history, resistance, and cultural rights (Warren 1993, 1994, 1998). Seeing this social movement as an attempt to use culture to heal and remake the world does not seem far off the mark (Scarry 1985: 15).

Sam Colop[3] is the author of a widely distributed 1991 essay which directly confronted Guatemalan racism and articulated a Mayan critique of colonialism and signs of its persistence. He argued that racism and assimilationist policies are foundational forms of political violence, that cultural imperialism within Guatemala is just as important to combat as imperialism without. His work reflects the Mayan practice of trespassing disciplinary boundaries and divisions of knowledge in Western research. Enrique Sam Colop served as the director of the Maya archives at CEDIM in 1992–93, earned a Ph.D. in Maya linguistics at SUNY-Buffalo in 1994 after studying at the University of Iowa, and consults for the Academy of Mayan Languages, UNICEF, the Center of Regional Investigations of Mesoamerica (CIRMA), and for a variety of legal reforms projects associated with Guatemala's peace process. His arguments, which reflect the thinking of many Pan-Mayanists, have been used in forums and adult education programs throughout the country.

It should not be surprising that Mayan commentators find a tortured past and room for a veiled presentism in their revisionist histories. Mayan historical sensibilities have been shaped not only by their experience of marginalization—that is, by "not being taken into account," as was the frustration twenty-five years ago—but also by the internal war, which introduced the threat of being labeled "a subversive" by the military or "a collaborator" by the guerrillas and, therefore, deserving of torture and death (see Warren 1993). This stigmatizing language has long been publicly used by the military to stifle social critique.

Democracy in Guatemala is fragile, and the military continues to play a key role in governmental affairs. In his 1993 dictatorial takeover, President Serrano Elias instituted media censorship and attempted to disestablish Congress, the Supreme Court, and the Constitution. This unsuccessful move toward formal authoritarianism once again reminded Guatemalans of the tentativeness of democracy, reestablished in a very contingent way in 1986 after twenty years of repressive military rule. A surprising alliance of business elites, union groups, students, and indigenous leaders convinced the army that the internal coup lacked international and national legitimacy. The takeover's failure demonstrated the powerful fluidity of interests and factions in Guatemala and growing citizen involvement in national politics. The subsequent selection of Ramiro de León Carpio, the national human-rights advocate, as president sparked hopefulness; but public confidence that he would be successful in dealing with the grave economic problems faced by the country was soon eroded. By 1994, he had become an apologist for counterinsurgency as a continuing national military policy, despite (or perhaps precisely because of) strong evidence that guerrillas were no more than a minor political presence in the countryside. As the 1995 elections neared, national violence increased, as many expected.

In the volatile political environment of the early 1990s, when Sam Colop published his most important essay, it was extremely dangerous for Guatemalan commentators to write about contemporary political violence in any detail. For example, shortly before the takeover imposed media censorship, national newspapers printed reminders of powerful political intolerance, including interviews with military officials who targeted civilians critical of government policies. Newspapers covered the trial and conviction of the soldiers who brutally killed Myrna Mack, a Ladina anthropologist on the left who was writing about internal refugees at the time of her death. Even as the newly democratized courts exposed past human-rights violations, the military used the national press to threaten its critics. They denounced Ricardo Falla, a Ladino priest from one of Guatemala's elite families, who, as an anthropologist, had written on indigenous resistance and most recently on human-rights abuses in the highlands (1978, 1992). After falsely accusing Falla of being a guerrilla leader, the military confiscated his fieldnotes and marriage and baptism records. In addition, the Mayan leadership of CONAVIGUA—the widows' group mobilized by class-based organizing during the earlier period of violence and active in exposing forced military recruitment—were branded as guerrillas by military officials. Although calling someone a communist had lost its sting in much of the rest of the world, this was not the case in Guatemala. The practice continued of threats and violence to neutralize social criticism and punish activists. Military authorities were quoted in the national press as asserting, "As subversives, [these critics] deserve whatever comes their way" (see *Siglo Veintiuno,* 7 March 1993; Schirmer 1998).

In this climate, Mayan scholars formulated their own applied social science, committed to the collective empowerment of Mayans as a people (*nación*). The emerging scholarship forms a diverse, paradigm-rejecting field of cultural studies. Through research and educational centers all over the country, Pan-Mayanists are working to unify Mayans across language groups and localized ethnicities in order to build a national movement. Their strategy is to erode internal divisions and localized identifications to create an encompassing "imagined community."[4] A Pan-Mayan identification, however, would not displace the "diversity within unity" of the twenty Mayan language groups; nevertheless, it would allow for new routes of cultural and political expression for indigenous peoples who constitute 60 percent of the national population. Significantly, history has become a vital element of this project, a tool for identity transformation.

This essay illustrates the development of Mayan Studies as a field of study by Mayans for Mayans. Mayan scholars and students at universities in Guatemala, the United States, and Europe assert a uniquely Mayan way of knowing: a subject position no one else can occupy and political interests no one else needs to defend. They argue an essentialist position—in tension with Gayatri Spivak (1988), Renato Rosaldo (1990), and Gloria Anzaldúa (1990)—to claim unique authority as social critics. Their goals are clear. They seek to undermine the authoritativeness of accounts by Guatemalan Ladinos or foreigners, which until the last decade monopolized the published representations of Mayan culture.[5]

THE PROJECT OF RECAPTURING THE RACIST PAST

The public intellectuals who promote Mayan resurgence are well aware of the ways the past has been used to legitimize current social arrangements in Guatemala. "Official" national histories published by cultural elites, foreign scholars, and (interestingly enough) the Guatemalan military reappear in school texts, newspaper articles, and advertisements. Mayan teachers, parents, and community leaders on the periphery of the revitalization movement—not to speak of those directly involved—angrily complain about the national obsession with the indigenous defeat at the Spanish conquest and the virtual erasure of indigenous peoples as historical agents after their subjugation. Just mentioning Tecún Umán, the tragic hero in national mythology, makes many Mayans livid.

Mayan culturalists resent their commodification and folklorization in national popular culture, that their civilization is admired as Mayan "ruins" and their culture transformed into a timeless tradition of colorful handwoven dress. Exalting Mayan culture for the benefit of entrepreneurs and tourists—who feel no particular responsibility to channel proceeds to local communities—is made all the more possible by their absence from the historical time of nation building and modernization.

Given this situation, it was not surprising that Mayans concerned with revitalization were beginning to formulate their own histories. One genre was the contemporary essay, gaining its energy and authority not from focused archival work but rather from a telling juxtaposition of historical materials with current scholarship, journalism, and national policy to produce a collage that detailed the fragmented persistence of corrosive racism in event and commentator. The Mayan essayist took the position advanced by Benjamin of "piling wreckage upon wreckage" (1986: 257) to condemn history's effect.

Enrique Sam Colop published his programmatic essay "Jub'aqtun Omay Kuchum K'aslemal: Cinco Siglos de Encubrimiento" in monograph form for national and international distribution by the Mayan press Cholsamaj. It was timed for release at the 1991 intercontinental meetings in Guatemala which brought together indigenous and grassroots activists from throughout the New World.[6] Sam Colop sought to identify arguments that negate the humanity of specific segments of the country's population and thus act to legitimize violent political action against them. He made the case for Guatemalan racism as an accumulation of the historical discourses of "muting," "invasion," "the Indian," and "twentieth-century colonialism."

Following the lead of Eduardo Galeano (1986: 115–16) and Beatriz Pastor (1988: 4–64), Sam Colop replaced the heroic language of the "discovery" of the New World with a discussion of the muting of indigenous culture by Spaniards who, because of their own compelling worldviews, were quick to condemn but unable to understand New World cultures in their own right. Muting captures the marginalization of indigenous communities but rejects arguments that European culture replaced local culture through forced assimilation. Rather, this language suggests that in resisting domination, indigenous peoples employed strategic assimilation—for example, participation in decentralized forms of Catholicism—to buffer their cultural systems from the full weight of Spanish control. These writers argue that words such as *discovery* and *encounter* only obscure the effects of European expansionism. They criticize the language of *conquest* for its totalizing implication that denies indigenous culture and resistance. The term these Latin American scholars prefer is *invasion,* which conjures an image of territorial violation instead of the heroism of total conquest and gives the outcome critical indeterminacy. Sam Colop's essay created space for a public reassessment of racism as violence. He drew on the literary critics Tzvetan Todorov (1984) and Beatriz Pastor (1988), who reveal the ideological nature of the sixteenth-century Spanish chronicles that recounted the initial European-indigenous contact in the New World. These authors emphasized the disempowering language of the Spanish chronicles: *"If Columbus recognizes that the natives have language, then he refuses to accept it as different; if he recognizes that it is different, then he refuses to accept it as language"* (Sam Colop 1991: 12; emphasis mine). This paradigm justified violence to civilize the barbarous and to enforce Spanish terms of economic and moral exchange. Sam Colop explained the implications of this reasoning for New World populations in the following terms:

> Columbus also perceives the natives with ambiguity: on one hand, he considers them equal and identical to himself and for this reason believes he understands their languages. In this respect, Columbus argues that the natives do not know how to speak their own languages well (Pastor 1988: 77–88). The perception of equals permits Columbus to propose a politics of assimilation that for him implies an "interchange" in which "the Spaniards give religion and take gold" (Todorov 1984: 45). The other perception considers them different and, in consequence, inferior. This permits him to propose his later objective. When Columbus becomes aware that gold is not abundant, he articulates a discourse that justifies slavery: dividing the natives into innocents and idolaters, into peaceful and warlike. The innocent and peaceful are subject to

his power and the others to slavery. Columbus suggests that ships bringing live-
stock to America return to Spain full of slaves. (Sam Colop 1991: 11)

Sam Colop's 1991 essay sought to undermine the authoritativeness of
accounts based on first-person observation. A key revelation is the constructed or fictional quality of Spanish chronicles—a quality that has been
accessible to all close readers of such colonial observers as Christopher
Columbus, Hernán Cortés, Bernal Díaz, Francisco López de Gómara,
Bartolomé de las Casas, and Pedro de Alvarado. He noted omissions, addi-
tions, and distortions, and showed how accounts created *post hoc*
justifications of Spanish violence. His analysis highlighted the self-interested
subjectivity of the chroniclers. Citing the studies of Ramón Iglesia (1942),
Lesley Byrd Simpson (1966), and Pastor (1988), Sam Colop illustrated how
competitiveness, personal animosities, and individual biases colored first-
person accounts as writers attempted to enhance their own prestige and dis-
credit other observers.

Sam Colop wondered not only about the motives behind the original
authorship of the Spanish chronicles but also about the reasons for their
use in more recent histories. What, he asked, would cause scholars in the
present to continue to promote the dissemination of these chronicles as
neutral windows for viewing the national past when they are clearly not
transparent or disinterested renditions of reality? In Guatemala, major
twentieth-century Ladino research centers and historians—such as the
Guatemalan Society for Geography and History (cf. Díaz del Castillo 1933),
Luis Cardoza y Aragón (1965), and Francis Polo Sifontes (1986)—have
treated these representations of the past as historical truth. They have
republished colonial accounts with admiring introductions, excerpted them
in their own writings, and justified colonial prejudices or left them unchal-
lenged. As a result, sixteenth-century descriptions of indigenous people by
López de Gómara as "stupid, savages, lacking feelings, vice ridden,
sodomites, liars, ingrates, tale tellers, drunks"; Díaz's obsession with their
"cannibalism"; Oviedo y Valdes's treatment of them as inanimate objects;
and Ortiz's judgment that they were "stupid, . . . ungrateful, unable to
learn, . . . beardless, . . . and lacking art or industry" live on in the twentieth
century (Sam Colop 1991: 14, 17, 23). Outside Guatemala, such epithets
are routinely subject to scrutiny and examined for the political interests
embedded in their constructions of "self" and "other" during periods of
Western expansion and colonialism.

The theme central to twentieth-century versions of colonialist discourse
is national unity to be achieved through hispanization, *mestizaje* (biological
blending), and homogenization. "*If Mayans are the 'other,' then they are inferior;
if they are not the 'other,' then they can be assimilated*" (Sam Colop 1991: 36) is
the modern echo of Columbus. Sam Colop noted that today's journalists,

historians, and politicians still employ this logic to argue that national history should tell the story of that fusion:

> In 1990, *La Hora* newspaper (Aug. 11: 3, 29) argued against primary school instruction in Mayan languages, based on what David Vela said: that these languages "are stuck in the middle of the sixteenth century and are *relatively poor* in expressing contexts and present values. There are many languages, and they are not mutually intelligible." Likewise, David Vela warned that one should "not carry enthusiasm for indigenous languages too far, even less be interested in studying them, because this is a *dangerous political game against national unity and is also bad for the destiny of our Indians.*" The *La Hora* columnist continued from there: "The esteemed teacher sticks his finger in the sore. Unfortunately or fortunately, in reality *our Indians* were very backward when the Spaniards came; . . . [many] wanted to cheat *our Indians* and take advantage of them, flattering them with the fiction they had superior culture." (1991: 35; emphasis Sam Colop)

Sam Colop's analysis of this column continued as follows:

> First, these statements show the continuing *encomienda*[7] spirit. They think of Mayans as property that must be protected. Second, the idea that instruction in Mayan languages is "harmful" for the speakers is evidence of the sixteenth-century thought that Indians only have those rights the colonizer deems convenient to give them. Third, the concept of "national unity" is what Carlos Fuentes calls the Legal *Patria* but not the Real *Patria*. The Legal *Patria* denies Mayans their rights to language, culture, and self-determination—collective rights recognized by the Universal Declaration of Human Rights and international pacts through the United Nations. (1991: 35–36)

These racist constructions justify Ladino resistance to government programs for the rural poor that might slow assimilation, such as bilingual education for Mayan-speaking children, on the grounds that they undermine the nation-state. In this social imaginary, people who maintain their cultural distinctiveness despite the pressure to assimilate become folkloric exemplars of another time rather than modern citizens expected to exercise individual rights in contemporary civil society. Thus, nation building, the quintessence of modernity, cannot recognize the contemporary relevance of cultural difference. This political logic produces a double bind that denies Mayans and their culture a *political* future (Sam Colop 1991: 29–35).

Sam Colop concluded his 1991 essay with a discussion of resistance, rights, and alternatives to colonialist ideology: "For Native Nations of the Continent, 1992 signifies 500 Gregorian years of physical, cultural, and political resistance. Physical resistance is manifested in the survival of the Native Nations; resistance against cultural domination is manifested in the maintenance of Amerindian cultures and languages. Resistance against colonial domination is manifested by the struggle for the legitimate recovery of political, economic, cultural, and social rights" (1991: 36–37).

In his view, the sixteenth-century Spanish priest Bartolomé de las Casas, who denounced colonial violence against indigenous people, offered an interesting model: a plural society in which the only necessary relation between culturally distinctive groups would be the diplomatic-administrative machinery of the state (1991: 37).

With purposeful irony, Sam Colop's essay argued that Spain is the modern exemplar of the successful multicultural state: "The Real *Patria* can only be pluralist. Today Spain serves as an example of this process; it has not disappeared as a political entity with the recognition of its autonomous communities or its bilingual regions" (1991: 36).

By evoking the Universal Declaration of Human Rights and UN proposals, Sam Colop added the contemporary language of transcendent rights and self-determination for cultural minorities to his critique. He observed that Germany, Russia, and the Vatican admitted responsibility for past violence in other areas of the world, and in some instances even offered indemnification to survivors.[8] The *nunca más* for Guatemala would involve an international discussion of complicity—including Spaniards, North Americans, and others—and indemnification through Mayanist organizations working to actualize revitalization.

What is striking in Sam Colop's essay is his synthesis of the languages of rights and pluralism from international sources and from his legal training in Guatemala. His goal is to reveal the power relations and paternalism ingrained in Guatemalan political practice: rights are accorded to Mayans as Ladino society wishes rather than seen as inherently belonging to individuals who will exercise them according to their own wishes. This is the explicit legacy of the past, the liberal moral of his analysis.

But additional dimensions of this analysis are muted if we only pay attention to the universalizing language of rights.

RELEVANCE OF COLONIALIST STRUCTURES
OF REPRESENTATION FOR THE PRESENT

Sam Colop's project parallels recent multiculturalist challenges to U.S. educational and research establishments. In this sense, he is part of a transnational movement which has challenged established canons by questioning how the production of knowledge in education, government, and mass media politically marginalizes certain sectors of the population. Multicultural historical critiques fight a presentist battle (see Rajasingham 1993). They hope to lay the groundwork for transformations in the way nations represent and conceive of themselves. In education, for instance, reforms inspired by these critiques would not only assert the liberal goal of widening impoverished communities' access to education but would also question the veiled prejudices children are taught as authoritative knowledge and the limits they are given for legitimate claims on national society. Moreover, the current question here and elsewhere is, "Access to what?" In Guatemala, the substance of school curriculums and languages of public instruction are at issue (see Warren 1994).

It would be a mistake, however, not to see Sam Colop's analysis as firmly grounded in Guatemalan culture and politics. His analysis interrogated the invasion's savagery and discussed the genocidal decimation of an estimated 70 million of the 80 million inhabitants of the New World in the sixteenth century. One of Sam Colop's major sources, Todorov (1984: 133–45), excerpted jarring descriptions of Spanish cruelty from colonial chronicles and judged the invaders responsible for the consequences of their actions—as they viciously murdered and enslaved indigenous people, exploited them through heartless labor conditions, demanded crushing amounts of tribute from struggling communities, and understood epidemics of European diseases as effective weapons against the infidels.

To drive his case home, Sam Colop drew on early indigenous accounts of the invasion. The Florentine Codex narrated Alvarado's colonial slaughter of unsuspecting Aztec soldiers during a celebration at the Main Temple:

[The Spaniards] ran in among the dancers, forcing their way to the place where the drums were played. They attacked the man who was drumming and cut off his arms. They cut off his head, and it rolled across the floor.

They attacked all the celebrants, stabbing them, spearing them, striking them with their swords. They attacked some of them from behind, and these fell instantly to the ground with their entrails hanging out. Others they beheaded: they cut off their heads, or split their heads into pieces.

They struck others in the shoulders, and their arms were torn from their bodies. They wounded some in the thigh and some in the calf. They slashed others in the abdomen, and their entrails all spilled to the ground. Some attempted to run away, but their intestines dragged as they ran; they seemed to tangle their feet in their own entrails. No matter how they tried to save themselves, they could find no escape. (Léon-Portilla 1962: 74–76, as quoted in Sam Colop 1991: 25)

In retelling rather than debunking the Black Legend, Sam Colop would seem to be writing against the grain of current scholarship[9] and in tension with Guatemalan historians such as Francis Polo Sifontes (1986: 57), who argued for historical relativism in the case of the sixteenth-century European treatment of indigenous peoples. A closer look at his analysis, however, reveals a different goal for Sam Colop's historical project: the unmasking and critique of colonial structures of representation of "self" and "other." His 1991 commentary pursued a specific angle: Alvarado's violence toward indigenous populations when the Spanish invaded Guatemala in 1524 and the displacement of blame for their deaths onto the indigenous leaders themselves. Alvarado's letters which recounted victories over the K'iche' were used by Cortés in reports to the Spanish Crown:

> And seeing that by fire and sword I might bring these people to the service of His Majesty, *I determined to burn the chiefs who, at the time that I wanted to burn them, told me, as it will appear in their confessions, that they were the ones who had ordered the war against me and were the ones also who made it.* They told me about the way they were to do so, to burn me in the city, and that with this thought (in their minds) they had brought me there, and that they had ordered their vassals not to come and give obedience to our Lord the Emperor, nor help us, nor do anything else that was right. And as I knew them to have such a bad disposition towards the service of His Majesty, and to insure the good and peace of this land, I burnt them, and sent to burn the town and to destroy it, for it is a very strong and dangerous place, that more resembles a robber's stronghold than a city. (translation by Mackie 1924: 62–63; emphasis mine; cf. Sam Colop 1991: 19–20)

Sam Colop singled out Alvarado as "the cruel and ruthless prototype of the 'conqueror'" for his actions in Mexico and Guatemala (1991: 19). According to sixteenth-century accounts authored by his countrymen, he massacred unarmed populations and torched towns; raped, kidnapped, and intimidated those from whom he demanded tribute; and executed other Mayan leaders *(ajpopi')* by hanging. His policy was one of "*tierra arrasada con sangre y fuego*" (scorched earth by blood and fire; 1991: 19–21).

The fact of Alvarado's cruelty is not the only issue that stands out. Just as significant for Sam Colop was the driving logic of his brutality:

> There is an elaboration of certain materials in Alvarado's discourse. Note three key elements: (1) Alvarado's determination to burn the rulers alive, (2) the rulers' confessions under Alvarado's compulsion, and (3) the confessions as justification for the burning to death of the *ajpopi'*. Alvarado manipulates these elements so that the K'iche' leaders are responsible for their own misfortune, for not wanting to submit themselves. In this way, Alvarado's responsibility is less important than the victims' guilt. This framing of the discourse goes beyond the facts. Alvarado, according to Recinos (1952: 77), has the common practice of "bringing up other people's *possible intentions* and imposing punishment before an offense takes material form." (Sam Colop 1991: 21)

The striking connection for me is with Elaine Scarry's (1985) theorizing of the archetypal torturer who sets the stage so that the blame falls on the victim, who therefore merits punishment, rather than on the instigator of violence. A variety of historical themes in Sam Colop's writings resonate with this preoccupation: the forced confessions of the Mayan rulers that could not alter the inevitable, the power of language to stigmatize, the concern with collective dehumanization, and the legitimation of violence as redemptive. Scarry saw torture as a crisis of power, language, and communication: "The physical pain [of torture] is so incontestably real that it seems to confer its quality of 'uncontestable reality' on that power that has brought it into being. It is, of course, precisely because the reality of that power is so highly contestable, the regime so unstable, that torture is being used" (1985: 27). Sam Colop cited Spanish and Mayan chronicles of the invasion precisely to document the new regime of power and its brutality/vulnerability.

The unmaking of the Mayan world involved the tragedy of coerced (or imputed) confessions in which the victim "shifts into being the agent of his own annihilation" (Scarry 1985: 47). Although coerced confessions inevitably raise the specter of the victim's betrayal of others, the stripping of "all control over, and therefore responsibility for his world, his words, and his body" (47) calls into question any such judgment. The Spanish torturer sought the displacement of blame in order to deny responsibility for physical violence. As Scarry observed, "It is not merely that his power makes him blind, nor that his power is accompanied by blindness, nor even that his power required blindness; it is, instead, quite simply that his blindness, his willed amorality, *is* his power, or a large part of it" (1985: 57). Sam Colop's extensive quotations from Mayan chronicles focused on Spanish brutality—on agency and damage—to represent the experience of pain.

From an anthropological point of view, Scarry offers many insights into colonial structures of representation even as her striking imagery reduces torture to a unitary discourse of power and pain, the product of the interpersonal relationship of the torturer and tortured. One must step outside the torture chamber to see the wider cultural context of violence and to discover that the unmaking and making of the world is a continual issue for subordinates in repressive regimes. Sam Colop's style—his strategic pause after describing Spanish and Mayan accounts of torture and executions—purposefully leaves to the reader the task of contemplating the pain of violent physical extinction for the Mayan rulers. His analytical work shifts to another issue: the political psychology of domination and racism.

POLITICAL CONTEXTS FOR MAKING A TORTURED HISTORY

Concealed, yet waiting to be discovered in Sam Colop's essay, is an important lesson about the logic of terror that blamed its early victims in the sixteenth century. In Guatemala, as elsewhere, virulent hate speech—whether blatant or veiled—has often rendered violence logical, appropriate, and just. Sam Colop attunes the reader to the language of reciprocity and morality, asserted *and* negated in accounts of Alvarado's execution/slaughter of Mayan leaders. The focus on torture-confession-punishment signals reverberations between the sixteenth and twentieth centuries which Mayans found especially important as the counterinsurgency war of the 1980s wound down. In fact, torture and execution were common practices during Guatemala's civil war, when an estimated one hundred thousand civilians were killed. As documented by the Commission for Historical Clarification, the army committed 93 percent of the violence; guerrillas, 3 percent; and the rest is unattributed. An estimated 83 percent of the fully identified victims were Mayans versus the 17 percent who were Ladinos (CEH 1999). Thus, the blame for wartime atrocities has been unequivocally placed at the feet of the army. Yet those in structural positions of power—be they Spanish invaders, Guatemalan military officers, or the insurgency—found ways of evading responsibility for their violence against others.

Mayan historical commentaries constitute a presentism that challenges the civic nationalism and authoritativeness of official histories. Sam Colop's work argues that racism operates through transforming analogies of sameness and difference. The creation of counterhistories involves a multiculturalist rereading of accounts of the past and an appraisal of the existential dilemmas that continue in the often turbulent present. As I have suggested, his work can be read on several levels for its analysis of domination and the scope of effective resistance.

SELECTIVE APPROPRIATIONS OF LATIN AMERICAN SOCIAL CRITICISM

There are diverse others in this history making. Sam Colop drew inspiration from European and Latin American literary critics and social commentators. But his appropriations were cautious, given the nature of his project. Eduardo Galeano—an anti-imperialist social critic who has lived in Uruguay, Argentina, and Spain and is best known for *The Open Veins of Latin America* (1973)—is useful for his discussion of the conquest as concealment. In *El Descubrimiento de América que Todavía no Fue y Otros Escritos* (1986), he wrote with special intensity about indigenous struggles, human-rights abuses, and government censorship of free expression and Latin American writers. Interestingly, he concluded the book with a ray of hope: that Spain, after having confronted the cultural violence of its authoritarian past, has been able to rediscover its own internal cultural and linguistic pluralism as it currently struggles for democracy. Suddenly, instead of "the Spaniards," readers hear of Castilians, Basques, Catalans, Andalusians, and Galicians. Galeano's lesson from his years of exile in Spain was a more nuanced colonial critique that acknowledged the dialectics of identity construction for both indigenous peoples and Europeans.

Sam Colop made a place for this complicating irony when he dealt with contemporary Spain as a multicultural society in his earlier writings (1983). Clearly, the colonizing other does not have to be frozen in history to play the role of the European dominator and the progenitor of the Ladino. These observations parallel the recent wave of revaluing European cultural and linguistic pluralism that has accompanied the creation of the European Community in the 1990s (Rajasingham 1993; see also *New York Times*, 3 May 1993). In the Pan-Mayan movement, two catalysts for multicultural identification have emerged: ties with the originating peoples of the New World and with linguistic minorities such as the Basques in Europe.

Sam Colop also drew inspiration from the Latin American literary critic Beatriz Pastor, who provided a detailed analysis of the "mythification" of New World cultures by the Spanish explorers in *Discurso Narrativo de la Conquista de América* (1988). In her own work, Pastor detailed the breakdown of heroic domination evident in the wider corpus of the Spanish chronicles. These accounts described Spanish vulnerability and stark failure in the face of the untamed natural world that threatened the invaders with disease, starvation, and economic ruin. They also depicted Spanish rebellions against Crown representatives who were denounced as deceitful, corrupt, and dishonorable when expeditions suffered heavy losses and failed to find promised wealth. In Pastor's view, the process eroded and blurred the hierarchies Spaniard/native, and civilized/barbarous.

Pastor's narrative, however, culminated in the genesis of a unique New World culture, born of a Hispanic-American consciousness that celebrates marginality, the paradoxes of its dual origin, and a critical view of its own past (1988: 439). The physical and cultural amalgamation—a *mestizo* melting pot—displaces (through idealization or erasure) historical antecedents, indigenous and European alike. By focusing on the ethnogenesis of the *mestizo* through the fusion of Spaniards, their New World descendants, and diverse indigenous peoples, Pastor reaffirmed a modernist trajectory for Mexican history and naturalized the dominance of the *mestizo* mainstream.

As one would expect, Sam Colop was very selective in his appropriation of Pastor. He rejected any solution to the riddle of domination-and-resistance that implies the cultural and physical merging of the colonized "self" and "other" through *mestizaje*. Mayan fusion into the Other's mainstream is unacceptable. Interestingly enough, Pastor apologized for ignoring indigenous chronicles and peoples in her analysis. But that is the point: the New World became a *sui generis* creation in her view. The obvious problem in her narrative is the bracketing and marginalization of substantial New World populations who have continued to count themselves as indigenous.[10]

INTERACTIVE REMEMBERING

In his 1991 essay, Sam Colop urged the critical study of history to unlock the terms and tenacity of prejudice in the present, and to clarify current existential dilemmas by deploying them in the past. Continuities in racism—

which subvert narratives of national progress and modernization—are the overt message of his essay. The Benjaminian moment of danger—in this case, the reverberation of terror across centuries—is a connection left to individuals to make, perhaps half-consciously as they read the essay. It is foreshadowed by the use of *"tierra arrasada con sangre y fuego"* (scorched earth by blood and fire) to sum up the horror of the sixteenth-century invasion. No one has to point out to Guatemalan audiences that this was the language of government counterinsurgency policies aimed at Mayan communities in the late 1970s and early 1980s.

Connective flashes are not one-way temporal insights, the simple intrusion of the past into the present. Rather, given the Mayan use of history to understand the political-psychology of violence and domination, these flashes represent the reflection of present violence and racism in a past of which the present is a part. Thus, the Mayan historical project is strikingly different from Ladino nationalist histories, from new university projects in municipal archives, from quincentenary revisionism that seeks to be fair to the Spaniards, and from historically compartmentalized studies of resistance. The echo of a cycle in the present's relation to the past is not, I suspect, accidental. It marks the historicizing cyclicity of Mayan constructions of time, so often misunderstood by those structuralists who see Mayans as deterministically driven by their elaborate calendrics.

Sam Colop's work challenges nationalist histories that focus on the development of the modern state and materialist histories that see foreign imperialism and class conflict as the only driving issues. Sam Colop sees reality as a consequence of power relations wherever they are manifested. To this end, his analysis draws the reader into the realm of political psychology, colonialism, and racism, which are related but not reducible to class exploitation. Sam Colop's strategic essentialism is creative, unstable, and self-contradictory, at once essentializing the other as the racist outsider, selectively appropriating foreign research, and collaborating with North Americans.[11] The overriding rationale for his essentialism is an ideological one: the forging of a unified Mayan consciousness.

Is there an inevitable divergence between the academic quest for history beyond orientalism and Mayan activists' efforts to spur the revitalization of Mayan culture, challenge racism, and combat internalized prejudice? For the postcolonial world, Prakash argues that nationalists' attempts to create a romanticized cultural essence for themselves and a dismissive condemnation of Western society as repressive run the risk of muting other struggles and heterogeneities within the subaltern and the metropole. In the case of the Pan-Mayan movement, for example, culturalists have suppressed the discussion of gender as a legitimate heterogeneity within the movement and rejected calls by women activists for wider self-criticism and for a consideration of political interests beyond the consensus on cultural autonomy. At worst, Prakash argues that romanticization fortifies the West/Rest contrast and the power relations that anticolonial studies seek to challenge. He warns, "Essentialism carries an enormous risk, even when it takes the self-canceling form," as in subaltern studies (1992: 373).

Darini Rajasingham suggested to me that essentialism and reverse orientalism (cf. al-'Azm 1991) may characterize the first wave of anticolonial, subaltern, indigenous authors. Following Gyan Prakash (1992), a subsequent post-orientalist wave would acknowledge its historical debt but find reasons to move beyond the subaltern critique by dealing with the dialectics of identity construction on all sides: not only with the colonizer and colonized in all their heterogeneity but also with the transcultural flow of individuals, institutions, and signs that elude or subvert national boundaries. The appropriation of ideas for rethinking politics and culture is a global phenomenon.

It is important, however, to remain skeptical of any universalizing framework, certainly of one that suggests global stages in political consciousness.[12] As in the past, Mayans now transform what they borrow—indigenous rights discourses (COMG 1991; CECMA 1994; Cojtí 1994), African-American multiculturalism, European literary criticism, and Latin American anti-imperialism—and make it their own in ways that reflect and reshape their particular concerns and circumstances. In the process, multiculturalist strategies become Mayan strategies for social critique. An interweaving of political voices, rather than discrete stages leading to a transcendent post-orientalism, best captures the Mayan movement. Current land conflicts and simmering controversies over women's voice in politics remind activists of issues that need to be addressed *within* and *among* Mayan communities, among the fragments they see as building blocks for a wider movement.

Finally, it is important to follow the dynamics and scope of Mayan Studies as it defines its mission in practice—to get back to the local grounding of Mayan programs for cultural resurgence—rather than to freeze the emerging field in any characteristic mode of analysis. At present, the field both condemns "the other" as racist by definition and finds continual exceptions to this rule, as in the cases of Las Casas, modern Spanish policies toward the nation's pluralism, and foreign intellectual collaborators.

Sam Colop's enduring contributions range from a penetrating analysis of racism and violence to discussions of politics and epistemology. He radically questions established works that are treated as authoritative in Guatemalan schools, universities, and public culture. He arms Mayan readers with important critical tools by demonstrating that first-person accounts—whether written by the observer or recycled in others' works—should never be taken at face value but rather seen as motivated and shaped by a flux of intentions suppressed by their creators and appropriators. And he shows that not all foreigners are the same or need to be appropriated wholesale.

Sam Colop's major insight has been to question the political and personal stakes involved in portraying the past.

In bringing this essay to a close, I must confront the limits of the interpretive schemes I have used even as they have, hopefully, generated some measure of insight. Universalizing readings of Scarry and Prakash and the text-based literary analysis I have used in this essay—no matter how much these strategies attempted to mirror Sam Colop's collage and its abstract distancing language—run the risk of muting precisely what we are trying to understand: Mayan movements for community-building and cultural self-determination as distinctive socially and historically constituted forms of agency. Thus, a wider portrayal of this movement would create something more than a genealogy of knowledge for the emergence of Mayan Studies. The way out of this dilemma is to locate the sources of inspiration for Mayan discourse that lie outside the realm of published texts and to trace the effects of this emerging discourse in practical affairs (Warren 1998). This is where anthropology, literary criticism, subaltern studies, and history often part ways. Rather than accepting the silences publicly imposed on published social commentary as the end of the story, it is critical to deal with Mayan experiences of contemporary violence and the practical sites where history and culture are taught by Mayan educators as part of their decentralized efforts to forge a national movement.

NOTES

1. This essay was presented at the 1995 Conference entitled "Violence, Political Agency, and the Construction of the Self," held in Delhi, India, and sponsored by the SSRC and Rajiv Gandhi Foundation. Fieldwork for the ongoing project has been supported by the John Simon Guggenheim Foundation, the Institute for Advanced Studies, the MacArthur Foundation, the Wenner Gren Foundation, the Princeton Latin American Studies Program, the Princeton Committee on Research in the Humanities and Social Sciences, and the David Rockefeller Center for Latin American Studies at Harvard. In addition to the stimulating feedback from colleagues at the Delhi conference, it is a pleasure to recognize the following colleagues for their responses to earlier drafts of this essay: Enrique Sam Colop, Irma Otzoy, Demetrio Cojtí, Vincanne Adams, Quetzil Castañeda, Darini Rajasingham, Judith Maxwell, and Ted Fischer. As always, I alone assume responsibility for the final argument. For the wider project, see Warren (1998). All translations are my own unless otherwise noted.

2. See Warren (1993, 1998) on the issue of silence and nonrealist representations of violence in Guatemala.

3. Originally from the activist agrarian hamlet Xecam outside the municipal center of Cantel, Sam Colop joined other young students who had exhausted local educational opportunities. They commuted on crowded public buses to Quetzaltenango, Guatemala's second largest city, which had a long history of Mayan

commerce and activism. While finishing his law degree at the University of San Carlos in the early 1980s, he wrote a thesis on national education policy and Mayan nationhood.

4. Benedict Anderson (1991) gives us this language, and the Mayans remind us of how diversified the grassroots process is.

5. See Warren (1998) for a fuller accounting of the movement and its politics. Although there is overlap in personnel and issues, the culturalist emphasis on revitalization contrasts with national class-based movements on the left, which involve Mayas and Ladinos in such organizations as CUC, CONAVIGUA, and Majawil Q'ij, and concentrate on mass mobilization and political protest. Culturalists work with non-Mayans within and outside Guatemala, but their principal goal remains to foster Mayan literacy, leadership in local and national affairs, and a collective sense of nation.

6. That these titles are multilingual is a measure of Sam Colop's linguistic abilities and, as this essay argues, of the important role of transculturalism in ethnic resurgence. As of 1993, versions of the essays had been published in Spanish, English, and Italian. To further illustrate his argument, he wrote "1992 y El Discurso de Encubrimiento: Five Hundred Years of Guatemalan Mayan Resistance, A Dialogue between Mayan and Non-Mayan Scholars" for a collection of indigenous writings in the journal *Global Justice* in 1992. A condensed version of his argument appears in English in Sam Colop 1996.

7. For their service to the Crown, Spaniards were rewarded with *encomiendas*, trusteeships that gave them the right to extract tribute and labor from a given regional population.

8. Of course, subsequent history has revealed Germany's ambivalence and reluctance. Moreover, Germany and Russia have been transformed into new entities since 1989. I note this to underscore the volatility of such claims and the reasons why, although Mayans use comparative observations to make the case for alternative possibilities, they also look to organizations such as the UN for trans-state leverage.

9. See, for example, Klor de Alva (forthcoming) and Maltby (1968).

10. Sam Colop also selected aspects of Todorov useful for his argument about continuities in the political psychology of violence and racism. The rest of Todorov's argument—especially the problematic thesis of Aztec vulnerability to the superior Spanish capacity to improvise contingent political moves and his argument about the suppressed individuality in Aztec society—is ignored.

11. See Prakash (1992: 372) and Spivak (1988: 372–45) on essentialism.

12. I am not suggesting that the sequences or periodicities of Latin American and South Asian historiography mirror each other. Their colonial histories are distinctive, with different regimes of power, patterns of differentiation between the colonized and colonizer, experiences of nationalism, and reactions to internal heterogeneity. In India, nationalism was part of a twentieth-century challenge to European colonizers. By contrast the nineteenth-century struggle for independence was waged in Latin America among political groups which were New World cultural, ethnic, and political formations. Although there was no European national/racial group to eject, there were heterogeneous populations constructed as being outside the mainstream of emerging nation-states.

REFERENCES

al–'Azm, Sadik Jalal. 1991. "Orientalism and Orientalism in Reverse." *Khamsin:* 5–25.

Anderson, Benedict. 1991. *Imagined Communities: Reflections on the Origin and Spread of Nationalism.* London: Verso.

Anzaldúa, Gloria, ed. 1990. *Making Face, Making Soul, Haciendo Caras: Creative and Critical Perspectives by Feminists of Color.* San Francisco: Aunt Lute Press.

Benjamin, Walter. 1986. *Illuminations: Essays and Reflections.* Edited and with an introduction by Hannah Arendt. New York: Schocken Books.

Cardoza y Aragón, Luis. 1965. *Guatemala, las Líneas de Su Mano.* Segunda edición. Mexico: Fondo de Cultura Económica.

Carmack, Robert, ed. 1988. *Harvest of Violence: The Maya Indians and the Guatemalan Crisis.* Norman: University of Oklahoma Press.

CECMA. 1994. *Derecho Indígena: Sistema Jurídico de los Pueblos Originarios de América.* Guatemala City: Serviprensa.

CEH (Guatemalan Commission for Historical Clarification). 1999. Guatemala: Memory of Silence Tz'inil Na'tab'al. Internet: hrdata.aaas.org/ceh/report

Cojtí Cuxil, Demetrio. 1994. *Políticas para la Reivindicación de los Mayas de Hoy.* Guatemala: Cholsamaj.

COMG (Consejo de Organizaciones Mayas de Guatemala). 1991. "Derechos Específicos del Pueblo Maya: Rujunamil Ri Mayab' Amaq'." Guatemala: Cholsamaj.

Díaz del Castillo, Bernal. 1933. *Verdadera y Notable Relación del Descubrimiento y Conquista de la Nueva España y Guatemala.* Guatemala: Biblioteca de Goathemala de la Sociedad de Geografía e Historia.

Falla, Ricardo. 1978. *Quiché Rebelde: Estudio de un Movimento de Conversión Religiosa, Rebelde a las Creencias Tradicionales, en San Antonio Ilotenango, Quiché (1948–1970).* Guatemala: Editorial Universitaria de Guatemala.

———. 1992. *Masacres de la Selva: Ixcán, Guatemala (1975–1982).* Guatemala: Editorial Universitaria.

Galeano, Eduardo. 1973. *The Open Veins of Latin America.* New York: Monthly Review Press.

———. 1986. *El Descubrimiento de América que Todavía no Fue y Otros Escritos.* Barcelona: Editorial Laia.

Iglesia, Ramón. 1942. *Cronistas e Historiadores de la Conquista de México.* Mexico: Fondo de Cultura Económica.

Klor de Alva, Jorge. Forthcoming ms. "Aztec Confessions: On the Invention of Colonialism, Anthropology, and Modernity."

Las Casas, Bartolomé de. 1951. *Historia de Indias.* Vol. 3. Mexico: Fondo de Cultura Económica.

———. 1975. *Apologia.* Madrid: Editoral Nacional.

Mackie, Sedley J., ed. 1924. *An Account of the Conquest of Guatemala in 1524 by Pedro de Alvarado.* New York: The Cortes Society.

Maltby, William S. 1968. *The Black Legend in England: The Development of Anti-Spanish Sentiment, 1558–1660.* Durham: Duke University Press.

Martínez Peláez, Severo. 1980. *La Patria del Criollo: Ensayo de Interpretación de la Realidad Colonial Guatemalteca.* Guatemala: Editorial Universitaria.

Pastor, Beatriz. 1988. *Discurso Narrativo de la Conquista de América.* Guatemala: Casa de las Americas.

Polo Sifontes, Francis. 1986. *Los Cakchiqueles en la Conquista de Guatemala.* Guatemala: CENALTEX.

Prakash, Gyan. 1992. "Writing Post-Orientalist Histories of the Third World: Indian Historiography Is Good to Think." In *Colonialism and Culture,* ed. Nicholas B. Dirks, 353–88. Ann Arbor: University of Michigan Press.

Rajasingham, Darini. 1993. "The Afterlife of Empire: Immigrants and the Imagination in Post/colonial Britain." Unpublished Ph.D. diss., Department of Anthropology, Princeton University.

Rosaldo, Renato. 1989. *Culture and Truth: The Remaking of Social Analysis.* Boston: Beacon Press.

Sam Colop, Enrique. 1983. "Hacia una Propuesta de Ley de Educación Bilingüe." Unpublished thesis for the Licenciatura en Ciencias Jurídicas y Sociales, Universidad Rafael Landívar, Guatemala.

———. 1991. "Jub'aqtun Omay Kuchum K'aslemal: Cinco Siglos de Encubrimiento." Seminario Permanente de Estudios Mayas, Cuaderno no. 1. Guatemala: Editorial Cholsamaj.

———. 1992. "1991 y El Discurso de Encubrimiento." *Global Justice* 3, nos. 2 and 3: 33–38.

———. 1994. *Maya Poetics.* Ph.D. diss., State University of New York at Buffalo.

———. 1996. "The Discourse of Concealment and 1992." In *Maya Cultural Activism in Guatemala,* ed. R. McKenna Brown and Edward Fischer. Austin: University of Texas Press.

Scarry, Elaine. 1985. *The Body in Pain: The Making and Unmaking of the World.* New York: Oxford University Press.

Schirmer, Jennifer. 1998. *The Guatemalan Military Project: A Violence Called Democracy.* Philadelphia: University of Pennsylvania Press.

Simpson, Lesley Byrd. 1966. *Cortés, the Life of the Conqueror [Istoria de la Conquista de México].* Trans. Francisco López de Gómara. Berkeley: University of California Press.

Spivak, Gayatri. 1988. "Subaltern Studies: Deconstructing Historiography." In *Selected Subaltern Studies,* ed. Ranajit Guha and Gayatri Chakravorty Spivak, 3–32. New York: Oxford University Press.

Todorov, Tzvetan. 1984. *The Conquest of America.* Trans. Richard Howard. New York: Harper.

Warren, Kay B. 1989. *The Symbolism of Subordination: Indian Identity in a Guatemalan Town.* Austin: University of Texas Press.

———. 1993. "Interpreting *la Violencia* in Guatemala: Shapes of Kaqchikel Resistance and Silence." In *The Violence Within: Cultural and Political Opposition in Divided Nations,* ed. Kay B. Warren, 25–56. Boulder: Westview.

———. 1994. "Language and the Politics of Self-Expression: Mayan Revitalization in Guatemala." *Cultural Survival Quarterly* (summer/fall): 81–86.

———. 1998. *Indigenous Movements and Their Critics: Pan-Mayan Activism in Guatemala.* Princeton: Princeton University Press.

Reconciliation and Memory
in Postwar Nigeria

Murray Last

INTRODUCTION

The Nigerian civil war and Biafra's attempted secession have a more than local significance on account of two important decisions: the decision to implement a policy of postwar reconciliation that minimized the public memorializing of the conflict and restored a semblance of the status quo; and, second, the decision of some First World aid agencies to take upon themselves for the first time the right to override the government of the country concerned and to give help to rebels in the name of saving life, despite recognizing that such help might also, in prolonging the war, cost even more lives. This latter dimension of the conflict is not the main concern here, although the humanitarians' claim to a right-to-intervene has had repercussions worldwide and is still hotly contested today. The processes of reconciliation, however, are important and more complex than they appeared at first sight; thirty years on, it is possible to look back and reexamine those processes and their long-term implications.

The decision to adopt a policy of reconciliation was not inevitable. It was not the only, nor the obvious, policy that the Nigerian government might have tried. To put it simply, the Biafran leadership under Emeka Ojukwu was guilty of treason; their armed forces had to be forced militarily into surrendering without conditions. There was good reason for those in the federal government and in the armed forces to be very angry at the needless loss of lives and the huge expense incurred because of the war, especially since before the fighting started the Aburi accords had given Ojukwu everything he had been demanding. At stake, too, was the cultural ethos then in Nigeria of punishing political wrongdoing severely; furthermore it was a military regime that was in power, and discipline (if nothing else) is the hall-

315

mark of the military. There was concern as well that a bad precedent would be set: was any future secessionist to expect a pardon if he failed—and were his supporters to get their jobs back as if nothing had happened? In short, the case for putting the Biafran leadership on trial, whether that led to imprisonment or even to execution, was strong. And there were plenty of precedents in history elsewhere to make such action legitimate. The fact that the Biafran leader, Ojukwu, flew off to Côte d'Ivoire before the war ended and took refuge there relieved the government of putting him on trial or offering him reconciliation; as the Nigerian leader at the time, Yakubu Gowon, has since said, it would have been difficult not to have charged Ojukwu for treason; he was too much the focus of great bitterness. However, in 1983 he was allowed to return and went back to his home town amidst considerable publicity, to resume life as a national politician. A chapter of Nigerian history seemed closed.

Reconciliation was a policy primarily of government, initially announced along with other measures midway through the war as an inducement to get an early end to the fighting and to counter the scare stories of the diehards within Biafra. Its grassroots popularity as a policy varied widely. Near the front line, for some the enmities died hard (if at all), the atrocities rankled, abandoned properties were not returned, and individual vendettas were carried over into the peace. For others, especially Igbos and others inclined to the federal government's side, it gave their opposition to Biafra a particular moral standing. For many people in Hausaland, however, far from the battles, the policy of reconciliation was seen as an act of exceptional generosity towards a community that had done serious wrong. The wrongdoers, in this view, had suffered enough, first in the massacres and then in losing the war. They had been punished. Such views, though, were expressed privately; in public there was discreet silence. Only much later was there open debate, though even then some strongly urged that old wounds were better left untouched.

In retrospect, reconciliation at the popular level was initially not so much about canceling hurts as about not allowing those hurts to stand in the way of everyday life. People were asked to cancel not the memory of injury but its mention. Hurt was shifted out of the public domain and became a dimension of private memory. Reconciliation required neither creating friendship where none existed before, nor putting aside the differences that underlie social divisions. It was simply about being able to work together, to live as neighbors as and when necessary. The success of reconciliation at this level depended on distinguishing clearly between the public and private domains; it meant a compromise in which personal pursuit of justice was foregone in the interests of the wider good. There was no public judgment on what had been suffered, no reparations, no apology; almost no one was held to be accountable for what they had done. Nor were any medals awarded.

The practical effect of having reconciliation in public while shifting the whole subject of hurt into the private domain was to give more space to widely discrepant interpretations of the war and its causes. Both sides of the conflict saw only the justice of their own position and admitted to no wrong. In particular, the government's policy of reconciliation focused on Biafra's attempted secession and the ensuing civil war, whereas for many Biafrans the crucial issue was the earlier massacre of civilians in northern towns and the exodus that the riots provoked. For them, secession was forced upon Biafra—it was not their choice. Since it is arguable whether reconciliation would have been possible had these radical differences been brought to the fore, the reconciliation that was achieved could only be partial. It seemed enough at the time.

Reconciliation allowed the process of memory and recovery to go on within local communities undisturbed by wider public debate. "Private" did not mean "secret": experience of war and flight were not matters of shame, to be hidden unshared with others; the private domain of church, town union, and family network offered air enough for mending hurts collectively, making good the losses over time and inflicting punishment on those who had transgressed the moral code. There were costs, however, in keeping it out of the public domain: the sense of ambivalence was left unresolved, the scale of anger and resentment still felt could not be assessed nor its location identified. Even today the success or failure of reconciliation cannot be fully judged. This essay is a first step towards that private domain of memory and recovery.

A SUMMARY OF EVENTS

On the night of 15 January 1966, the federal prime minister, the northern and western premiers, the federal finance minister, and some senior commanding officers were murdered. The coup leaders were Igbo and Yoruba; the victims were Hausa and Yoruba; no Igbo was killed, no Hausa was involved among the conspirators. The coup leaders were arrested, General Aguiyi-Ironsi (an Igbo) was made president. In May 1966, the president decreed the existing regions would be abolished and the country unified— anyone could get a job anywhere; anyone could obtain land anywhere; the quota system that gave preference to locals over migrants would be outlawed (thus putting into effect the program of the initial coup-makers). Anger suddenly erupted with rioting in several northern towns; hundreds of Igbos were killed, and their properties burnt. At the end of July, a coup killed Ironsi and forty-seven other Igbo officers. At the end of September and into October, riots were sparked off by a radio report of Hausa being killed in the eastern region; the result was the massacre of at least seven thousand Igbos who lived in the north, this time in the smaller towns all over the region. Many of the rioters were non-Hausa—Tiv were notably involved—and trainloads of Igbo refugees were attacked as they passed through on their way to the east. The ferocity and the suffering were appalling. A million or so refugees arrived in the eastern region, looking for shelter and the start of a new life, adding to the existing population of about seven million Igbo and five million non-Igbo in the former eastern region. There had already been talk of splitting up the federation, initially in the north (*a raba;* "split!"), where northern officials had to tour the region to calm passions after the initial coup and stifle calls for violent retaliation. In 1967, it was now the Igbos who were talking of secession—but a secession that would include all the eastern region, not just the Igbo areas within it. Igboland by itself was not viable.

The areas that could be identified as "Igbo" were not those that produced either the bulk of the food (grains, meat, or salt) or the bulk of the crude oil; furthermore, it was land-locked, and surrounded by neighbors who felt threatened by Igbo hegemony. The key to success had therefore to be (1) international recognition and aid, and (2) a willingness of non-Igbo minorities within the eastern region to accept Igbo hegemony—and that willingness would presumably be affected by the economic success that an autonomous Biafra could achieve. The federal Nigerian strategy was to give those minority groups within the former eastern region/Biafra their autonomy in a newly created state system. As anglophone Cameroon had explicitly voted, when given its chance in a referendum in 1961, not to remain under eastern Nigerian control, there was always the possibility that other parts of eastern Nigeria would similarly opt out. The perceived threat from the proposed Biafra was not just political or about exclusion from the "pork-barrel" spoils system. The success of the Igbo economic network lay in its ability to work closely together in exclusive "unions" that tended to take over markets; while non-Igbo traders were apt to become paranoid about the competition in their home marketplaces, local consumers in rural areas also resented the very high interest they had to pay for goods on credit.

The crucial ally Biafra needed was the Yoruba-dominated western region of Nigeria or even the more pluralist midwestern region (which had a large Igbo minority). Wole Soyinka was involved, as is well known, in secret talks aimed at getting one or both regions to join Biafra; many Biafrans indeed fought in the belief the Yoruba would join them. The failure of the Yoruba to go along with secession added betrayal to the idioms of a political and economic rivalry which still bedevils reconciliation.

If local support for an autonomous Biafra was in doubt, the campaign for international support was strenuous and able. There was, above all, the humanitarian card, with its appeals to Catholic unity (Eire, the Holy See) in the face of Muslim aggression; Scandinavian churches financially (and Tanzania diplomatically) responded to appeals over genocide through famine and the ghettoization of Igbos (the "Jews of Nigeria," in Azikiwe's phrase). De Gaulle was seriously interested in Biafra (oil?), but was unable to persuade Nigeria's francophone neighbors, Cameroon or Dahomey, to join it in recognizing Biafra (staunchly francophile Côte d'Ivoire and Gabon did so, however). Otherwise it was left to Portugal (and South Africa, Rhodesia?) to support secession; like France but for different reasons, they saw no advantages in a strong Nigeria.

With inadequate support and resources, Biafra had a disastrous first year (September 1967–September 1968) of independence; for most of the second year, the fighting lapsed, leaving famine, propaganda, and diplomacy to carry on the conflict.

WAR'S END

Amnesty does not mean amnesia
POPULAR SLOGAN PARAPHRASING A. U. ASIKA

After two and a half years of warfare the attempt of Biafra to secede from the Nigerian Federation came to a sudden end. Biafra's leader flew out to Côte d'Ivoire on Saturday, the armies stopped fighting on Monday; the formal surrender ceremony took place on Thursday (15 January 1970). As soon as war ended, the Nigerian troops (on the western front) were seen to be fully occupied setting up camp on the hills away from the villages; the massacres predicted by the Biafran directorate for propaganda did not take place, and the following week the roads were packed as people trekked back home. Thousands were on the move. There were indeed some rapes, some shooting, some looting, some beatings. But the policy of a general amnesty, first publicly proclaimed in the middle of the war, was repeatedly broadcast—"No victors, no vanquished" was a common slogan (some added "only losers"); another was the three Rs, "reconciliation, rehabilitation, reconstruction." The fierce talk of guerrilla warfare, of genocide, of resistance to the bitter end ("The blades of grass will fight when there are no people left"), of marauding Muslim soldiers dipping the flag of jihad in the sea—talk fanned by and for humanitarians and churchmen—gave way to the language of "healing the nation's wounds": "I solemnly repeat our guarantees of a general amnesty for those misled into rebellion, . . . reconciliation in full equality, . . . no second-class citizens." In short, the ordinary enemy were not criminals; being an ordinary rebel was not a crime. Hence, those who had left their jobs were free to return to their old posts; those who had abandoned their properties anywhere in the federation were to get them back. Biafran currency notes were to be exchanged for Nigerian notes.

In practice, such policies were not always easy to implement. Jobs in the regional civil services were the least problematic; in the federal civil service and the parastatals, abandoned posts had been readily filled by others, and these could not be sacked. Returnees might be reemployed, but the status quo ante simply could not be restored after three years. Overmanning was therefore inevitable, as was some loss of rank or power for some of the returnees. In the army and the police, some half of the Biafran officer corps was reintegrated (none over the rank of major). A tribunal was held to sort out who should or should not be reinstated; but no war-crimes tribunal was held, nor was Ojukwu tried in his absence. In the northern region, abandoned properties had been sealed and listed; these were relatively easy to return, some with their accrued rents. Less easy were buildings in the areas that had been temporarily under Biafran control—for example, the city of Port Harcourt—and had been liberated early in the war: those who had suffered at the hands of the Biafrans were reluctant to let them back in to retake commercial (let alone political) control of areas that were not considered as originally Igbo. The exchange of Biafran currency was also problematic: in the end, every Biafran head of a household was given 20 Nigerian pounds, simply as a lump sum, but in fact not everyone collected it, while some collected several times over. The middle class who had managed to save or profit from the war thus lost their savings if these were in Biafran notes; but some well-connected Biafrans had U.S. dollars, while others had ensured they had Nigerian currency via the trade across the front line.

Reconstruction involved making good the material damage to buildings, roads, and bridges; it involved stopping the erosion that had been accelerated by the need to grow food absolutely everywhere, and clearing the mines from farmland and paths. Land had not been taken over by migrants during the war, so that most people's farms were intact and needed only to be cleared for planting (once seed was available; food shortages had meant what was usually saved for seed had been eaten). Above all, it meant reweaving a social fabric, repatterning trust, within an old framework that had been tensed and transformed by war.

WHO WERE THE VICTIMS?

The Scale of the Losses

The number of lives lost in the war will never be known; records were not kept. But realistic estimates put the maximum at a million, with six hundred thousand being the figure offered by St. Jorre, one of the most thorough historians of the war.[1] Not all of these casualties, of course, were Igbo or Biafran. A calculation of the losses in Rivers State suggests the high figure of one hundred thousand; other fought-over minorities, such as the Annang, may have suffered as badly. What is clear is that "genocide" did not occur, and figures given out in 1968 at the height of the war-for-aid, such as the death of 40 percent of children between two and four, were exaggerations.

As Harneit-Sievers points out, in East Central State primary school enroll-
ments were 914,037 in 1970 and rose to 1,170,310 in 1972 (in 1964, the
numbers had been 757,968); similarly, tax registrations in 1971 were
817,000, compared with 808,000 in 1965.[2] Symbolically, however, the losses
that occurred not in the war but in the prewar riots and in the massacres of
evacuees en route were the worst of all. It was the manner of their dying
rather than the numbers that shocked, and still shocks. The images of flight,
of being perpetual refugees—with the implication that this is not truly one's
own land—sustain for many even now a specifically "Biafran" sensibility.

We must remember, too, that large numbers of Igbos, especially those in
western and midwestern Nigeria, had never fled to Biafra—and had kept
their positions in Nigeria all through the war; some, like the former Ibadan
lecturer A. U. Asika, who was put in charge of East Central State, supported
the idea of a federal Nigeria. Others, such as the veteran politician Azikiwe,
lived quietly either in London or Nigeria. Reintegration, then, was not of
"the Igbos" tout court, but primarily of those who had identified themselves
with Biafra or, driven by the riots, had left their homes outside Igboland to
join the cause. Excellent propaganda had fostered that identification (and
fear of the alternative) among Igboland's existing population whose lives
and livelihood were not otherwise threatened until secession. In time, war-
weariness and the fraternization during lulls in the fighting had sapped
enthusiasm. Many, in short, were ready to be "reintegrated."

The Survivors

The traders and craftsmen who normally held jobs in parts of the federation
outside their homeland had suffered enormously, first as refugees and survivors of the riots in northern towns, then as refugees within Biafra, especially once war had started. For them, war's end meant claiming back their
properties and restarting trading. Given the credit-based system of distrib-
uting and selling imported goods, they did not require their own stock-in-
trade. So long as their safety was guaranteed and their old trade contacts
were willing to welcome them back, return to their previous niches was
quite feasible. They may have lost their dominant position in the marketplace, and in the war years competition from local traders for the middle-
man role had grown—but they had a future.

Another category of survivors were the farmers and others who make
their living in eastern Nigeria and constitute the bulk of Igbo society. The
damage to them was mainly material and left the infrastructure of their
economy badly dislocated. In fact, some areas of Biafra had been relatively
un-damaged, particularly the core areas around Nnewi, Ojukwu's home
town; these areas recovered faster than others, and were earlier in rebuilding a substantial industrial base. Other areas that had specialized prewar in
overseas trading also suffered less long-term damage, as they were able to

draw upon external resources; again, a community like Abiriba was able to establish an industrial economy quite quickly. Within ten years, these two areas were offering employment and profits that were as good as, if not better than, anywhere else in Nigeria. Other areas, liberated early in the war, had a head start in the process of rebuilding.

A third category is the Biafran elite—whether commercial, administrative, or intellectual—who had been part of the broad Nigerian bourgeoisie. In so far as they had been the brains that had led the Biafran quest for autonomy, they had lost. No one could be said to have "misled" them; they had miscalculated (in retrospect, the miscalculation is surprising). Some even questioned whether the amnesty referred to them, or only to those "*misled* into rebellion," that is, to the rank and file. Their hurt was as much moral as physical—and their "wounds" remain the most sore. At least the men have the knowledge that they tried, and that even in defeat there are in retrospect the elements of a "heroic failure."

Within the Igbo/Biafra milieu there were also others more subtly hurt by the war. The fear of dissent within Biafra affected more than the non-Igbo areas of eastern Nigeria. The term *saboteur* was used of anyone that might be thought to be disillusioned or dismayed at what was going on in the name of "Biafra." There was tension between the regular army and the enthusiastic militia; between the existing civil service and the new, efficient, and effective directorates that ran the special emergency programs. Individuals of rank were locked up; some were executed; others escaped through the lines. Alongside the enthusiasm and voluntary sacrifice for the community, distrust too was commonplace; some people, as always, were unscrupulous in racketeering, conning the fearful and the vulnerable out of what they had. The sense of wartime injustice remains.

Given the threat to Biafra of secession by minorities within its own sphere, Biafran policy took a hard line towards its own minorities. They were disarmed, kept under close surveillance, and were liable to have "mob action" launched against them. As a result, the most bitter aftermath of the war has been in these doubly burnt-over regions—regions that were neither victors nor vanquished but simply victims. The classic instance is the Ogoni people, who were herded by the retreating Biafrans out of their homelands and then dismally treated as refugees. Postwar, they have once again been dismally treated, by Shell-BP and by the federal and local governments, as well as being subjected to massacres whenever they resist. Other groups, particularly on the eastern front, were treated notoriously badly by Biafra; women and children were penned as refugees in concentration camps and deprived of food (the overseas aid meant for them was diverted), while an Igbo jibe against them was that they were the target of a Biafran "operation wipe-out."

The very fact that the Biafrans for political reasons had to be reintegrated rapidly and restored to their former positions overshadowed people's awareness of the effects of the war upon other groups. The Biafrans had the solidarity of a people who had fought against the odds and lost. They were able to use that solidarity in defeat to rebuild cooperatively their shattered economy. But other groups, on the margins, were not even united: some had supported Biafra, some Nigeria—the split communities were embittered by a sense of betrayal. My argument is that the victims of war were not necessarily the vanquished, not those to whom the hand of reconciliation was extended, but the powerless, those too weak both to fight and to demand the three Rs of reconciliation, rehabilitation, and reconstruction.

RECONCILIATION

Everyone agrees that the postwar recovery was remarkable. The disagreement is over who (or what) was responsible for the recovery, and over whether the recovery should not have been greater. By and large it was the middle classes who felt most aggrieved by any shortfall in the restoration of their prewar position on the national stage. For this, they blame the Yoruba elite, Awolowo in particular, for "stealing" what should have been the Igbo share of prizes: for example, when foreign companies had to sell or transfer equity to Nigerians under the Indigenisation Decree of 1972 (foreign merchants were not allowed to become Nigerians), the main beneficiaries were Yoruba businessmen and politicians; the Igbo middle class, so soon after the war, were in no position to buy into companies when shares were absurdly cheap, nor did they have the same scale of required collateral to get the necessary bank loans.

The causes of the recovery are usually laid at the door of Igbo social structure and the 1970s economic growth based upon oil, growth that became spectacular after the oil price rises of September 1973. The latter made it possible to overman the civil service and the army, as well as making the Federation a place worth belonging to, since the Igbo traders were able to operate in a buoyant market. Had the Nigerian economy been destroyed by the war, there might well have been much less willingness to let former "rebels" take a share in scarce resources. The ability of Igbo communities to run local savings schemes and self-help projects, to emphasize the dignity of hard work, and to give everyone no matter how disabled a job to do, along with the readiness of Igbo entrepreneurs to invest in strictly local enterprises (rather than risk their capital again in investments in non-Igbo towns)—all this gave a dynamism to the recovery that no amount of external or government aid could generate on its own. In fact, one of the complaints about the period of reconciliation is that not enough aid was pumped by the federal government into the economies of war-torn communities. Again this is sometimes phrased as a Yoruba move to keep down commercial competition.

Amidst this reconciliation and oil-based boom, what of the minorities, who were apparently the main victims of the war in the long term? On a political level, autonomy in the form of further new states has channeled the flow of funds into areas that had seen themselves as losers. But it is not at the level of communities that I suspect the hurts are most often felt. The very success of the recovery in the 1970s and 1980s only accentuated inequalities, as individuals who were in no position after the war to catch the economic tide found themselves stranded. Familiarity with weapons and their ready availability increased levels of violence, while the war had broken down taboos against acts of sadism and other excesses. Thus one of the main casualties has been the normal moral code on which social trust is based. The dead too have been largely forgotten. There are no formal days of remembrance, no cemeteries, no graves marked, nor monuments—not even lists of the fallen. Indeed, there is in some areas a strong feeling that the soil remains polluted by the blood spilt and is still uncleansed; that the community is not yet put to rights. The mainstream churches have all lost out as a result of the war. New congregations, independent and often charismatic, have multiplied in areas "burnt" by the war. Furthermore since the main churches during the war were seen to use their access to overseas famine relief as a means of poaching congregations, their claims to moral standing as well as their humanitarian credentials were called into question.

WATCHING VIOLENCE

The Problem

I want to distinguish between the watchers of violence and bystanders. By the latter I am referring to a phenomenon much reported now—how an act of violence can occur in a public place yet not be "seen" (or "heard") by those around. At issue is the refusal of aid, the refusal even to recognize or be recognized as even an accidental witness to a violent act. The alternatives are either intervening as an ally or a mediator, or—especially when it comes to riots and crowds in action—immediately leaving the scene of violence. In a society as unconfrontational as Hausaland, staying away (like removing yourself from the field of battle) is a decisive act. So, too, is a refusal to speak; turning the head away is perhaps the strongest of social statements, much stronger than loudly arguing back. Silence = consent is not a Hausa equation. But when in the riots there was little attempt to stop the violence (although there were notable exceptions), it seemed to many like an act of collusion—as indeed it may have been.

By contrast, watchers of violence are traumatized by what they are witnessing even from afar. As with exiles, their feelings of ineffectiveness only add to the hurt (and to the fierceness of their anger). In the generation of riots or civil war, the watchers play a key part, acting on behalf of victims (or in the case of Kano's riots, of leaders who were humiliated): they create the agenda for the violence to come. Biafra's secession, for example, was declared and the war fought ostensibly for the refugees who had fled the massacres—to give them a safe homeland. But they were already safe and at home in eastern Nigeria (and to a lesser extent in western and midwestern Nigeria too); what they needed, more than a Biafra at war, was a safe Nigeria where they could live and trade. Ojukwu and his colleagues, justly aroused by the appalling stories of the refugees, nonetheless interpreted their suffering and responded in a way that promised less to the refugees than to the Biafran elite-to-be.

Reconciliation has also to be aimed at the watchers, the interpreters, the co-victims—yet often they are more resistant to reconciliation than the victims, making unattainable demands and lacking insight into the realities of actually making a living in the aftermath of confrontation. The kinds of compromise that enable life to be patched up and made to last do not come easily after an injustice has been done, but at a distance, uncompromising justice can become a matter of dogma, and failure to achieve such justice may itself be judged and turned into a hurt.

Among the watchers I count historians (such as myself) who dwell upon the hurts of others. Like many other Europeans, I am obsessed with the past, interpreting the present by reference to what has been before. Hausa colleagues trained in the traditional sciences reject that hyperconcern for the past as irrelevant—or at least of limited, political relevance—and treat history as a trivial matter unfit for the real scholar. Indeed "peoples without history" may not want to have a history (but European scholars will give them one anyway); it is those with a history who suffer. By contrast, what lies ahead is what is important; the past sins of all but the dyed-in-the-wool sinner do not rule out reform. Promise outweighs the past; youths become adults, eventually. Indeed, history is the story of only the "outer layer" both of society and of the individual; the inner core has a different truth to it ("myth"?), with other, larger forces at work shaping its destiny. The fact that there are these forces makes your actions yesterday not fully your responsibility: you can be absolved of them. "Possession" by forces beyond your control impelled you perhaps into acts that seem out of character. Crowds in particular are susceptible: spirits, for example, congregate in markets—especially on the western boundary, by the butchers' slabs where there is blood—and can send people on the rampage (and cause butchers to be prone to violence). Hence, they suggest, a line *can* and should be drawn under the past.

Historians and other watchers of violence seek to cross that line. They can apportion blame. Diviners and Muslim scholars cross it too, therapeutically or as "lawyers" pursuing for a client the spiritual causes of a crisis. Their purpose, though, is to close a case finally, not reopen it: the aim is to appease, not to confront. Watchers of violence, in interpreting suffering unasked, are therefore seen as trespassing into territory that is either past or private (or both). If they were coming as allies, that might be different; their agenda would be political, and not claimed as moral or neutral.

The War and Its Literature

The Nigerian civil war was notable for the attention it attracted from the international community. That attention has been much analyzed as diplomatic history, and I will not dwell upon it here. I should point out, however, that by treating Biafra as a humanitarian and not a political issue, the good intentions were, from the Biafran perspective, politically counterproductive; pressures for a cease-fire were aimed at keeping children from dying of starvation, not at giving recognition to Biafra as a sovereign state.

In addition, the various interventions prolonged the fighting. A calculus—of lives saved through aid versus lives lost by a longer war—is impossible, even with hindsight. Given the way sanctions had created shortages of all kinds of necessities in Biafra, much of the aid was inevitably siphoned off by those with arms; vastly more aid was needed if looting was to be made unnecessary and the thousand or so refugee camps were to be adequately maintained. Indeed aid-workers returning from Biafra told me at the time that if there was any "genocide" it was in their view being experienced by the minority groups held in camps within Biafra. Once the war was over, international attention largely ceased. France quickly mended fences with federal Nigeria; Côte d'Ivoire was willing to subscribe to Gowon's West African economic community (ECOWAS). The policy of reconciliation was widely praised: it enabled those who had backed Biafra to change sides, and those who had supported Nigeria to regain the moral high ground, saying how right they were after all.

It is not, however, the international watchers of violence that concern me here. Their role in the longer processes of reconciliation was minimal. More significant are those who, as Nigerians, watched the violence and wrote up their reactions in novels or analyses. There seem to be four phases to the literature on the war. First, instant analyses were produced by authors with ready access to publishers in Europe and to the European market. Second, there was a period of comparative silence as the European market moved on to other interests, and those Nigerians most involved came to terms with their experiences and rebuilt their lives. A third phase of writing is dominated by the memoirs of the major participants in the conflict,[3] and these give rise to a fourth phase in which countermemoirs lay out the uglier sides of the war. In this literature it is particularly noticeable how women writers who experienced the war first-hand offer a much less heroic account of events. One woman writer, however, whose fighting apparently took place mainly in Trafalgar Square, does reiterate the male line about the glory in warfare; is hers a typical watcher's tale?

Perhaps the greatest obstacle to reconciliation has been the persistence of competing myths about what actually happened. The propaganda of both sides lives on as different truths. For example, figures of casualties vary hugely—even the same author has used widely different numbers. Terms like *genocide, holocaust,* even "Masada" continue to be used to draw a parallel between Igbos and the Jews; atrocities and the effects of bombing are held up for recognition. An attempt was made by a panel of academic historians to arrive at a kind of consensus about the meaning of the civil war and its implications for social and governmental institutions, but that was an isolated effort. It has been published, however, and would scarcely appeal to the passionate. How exactly the history of Biafra is being taught, in schools or in homes, to the children of today has yet to be researched (a project is being planned, with funding promised); it is there that we may find the interpreters who are determining the ultimate success or failure of reconciliation.

PERPETRATORS OF VIOLENCE

Finally, there is the question of how any society could consider legitimate the massacre of defenseless fellow-citizens on the scale and with the ferocity of the rioting in northern towns. If reconciliation is, on one side, about forgiving the secessionist war, is it possible for the other side to forgive a massacre? Is reconciliation a kind of trade-off? Or has the policy of reconciliation, by focusing primarily on the war, succeeded in drawing a curtain over the core problem? The return of abandoned properties was a fine gesture, but has it diverted attention from the real grievance—the unreturnable loss of lives? Will reconciliation ever be possible when there cannot be an open acknowledgment that the killings were fundamentally evil? Or will it come about only when no one truly is a "second-class citizen" in any part of Nigeria?

There is no simple answer, but the following comments may be of help in understanding the role of violence in a society which, like Hausaland, normally puts great value on self-restraint and order. It is important to understand the victors' concepts if only because it is alongside them that the vanquished and the victims of violence have, in the real world of everyday life, to rebuild their lives and, if they can, get the victors to alter their concepts in the very different climate of Nigeria postwar, under its various military governments. The threat of violence and rioting, however, remains despite the changes, and calls into question how successful has been the policy of reconciliation as it has been practiced in Nigeria these past thirty years.

First there is, I suggest, in Hausa society the conviction that collective action (or rioting) is the only possible form of popular punishment available to the community when a government fails to act against wrongdoers.

Whether it is "the market" *(kasuwa)*, or the congregation of Muslims *(jama'a)* after Friday mosque or the 'Id prayer, the crowd is considered to act collectively on behalf of the community. A thief is chased and killed; an insult to Islam or to the Muslim *jama'a* is set right. Whereas a brawl or brief disturbance is labeled *rikici*, the term for prolonged collective violence is the more euphemistic *tashin hankali*, implying that the people have taken leave of their senses and their habitual calm; the crowd is "possessed," beyond blame, beyond control too, perhaps. Such acts, so long as they are on behalf of the community, are seen as just and beyond everyday law.

Secondly, there is general agreement that severe punishment is just, and that justice is the key characteristic of good government. Preachers and poets alike stress hell and the severity of Allah's judgment; historians praise the strong ruler and contrast the disasters that people suffer when the emir is gentle. Teachers and adults generally are not expected to spare the rod (or the leg-irons) on the young. Dissidents, whether against colonial or pre-colonial regimes, have always been treated with little mercy. Punishment, in short, is physical and harsh; and the rioting seems appropriate punishment.

Thirdly, targets for attack are often symbolic or indirect. The standing of any important man lies in his ability to protect his own people wherever they are. Failure to do so effectively proves he is, after all, a person of no real substance. To kill a leader's defenseless, dependent women and children is to strike where he is most vulnerable, and to inflict on him maximum hurt. Such targets are easy, but that is only part of the point: their very easiness is important symbolically—their weakness is his weakness. To attack them is not seen necessarily as immoral.

The massacres of Igbo residents in the northern towns conformed to this pattern of "legitimate" communal violence. It was claimed that they were justified as "punishing" the coup-makers and their associates for the murder of the northern region's political leader and the violent overthrow of their elected government. The riots were expressions of a social anger that had been kept damped down for several months. At the time, just before the first riots, the bitterness was explosive, even in a cosmopolitan city like Zaria. Daily I was told and retold tales of arrogance in the marketplace, of insults that could not be answered. A magazine article purporting to be an interview with the Sardauna (pictured as a corpse in hell, apologizing for his political errors) was passed around. Attempts that I knew of by the administration in Zaria and in another smaller town (Jalingo) to defuse the tension and prevent violence were ineffective despite days of talks. There was, it seemed, no other way of giving expression to pent-up public fury except through violence; and to many this seemed legitimate, even against the defenseless. The violence served other ends, too: it was a "war" fought in defense of jobs, land, and market-share; it met the interests of dispossessed politicians and rallied otherwise discredited factions. It offered loot; it provided excitement—the "madness" spread as town copied town, with rumor and news intermixed. To my knowledge, a few brave individuals stood out against the violence, turning away mobs or hiding refugees, and there were no doubt others whose stories are not recorded. If nothing else, they prove that "collective" acts are not necessarily as culturally compelling as their apologists claim.

CONCLUSION

Reconciliation is, ultimately, about restoring sociality, about establishing the trust necessary not just to tolerate but to cooperate in partnerships that can survive even the threat of failure. How that is done is the perennial problem. There does seem to be a common pattern of response—first of silence, then (often ten years later) writings or new religious expressions, in which interpretations deepen with distance, and the tragedy is stripped both of its heroics and its total despair. Finally, the episode of trauma is transformed into history. Whether that transformation in its turn brings on another bout of violence—or whether society has been immunized by experience ("Never again!")—is only seen in hindsight; political scientists, though, have not ceased to dream and scheme how to forecast civil conflict. My interest here is not in such large-scale modeling but in how a social group, seen as a field of force, might recharge itself without destroying the particles within it or their coherence.

The underlying premise here is that the healing of postwar trauma can be done socially, and that the practice of such social healing takes place at the level of the community. A further assumption is that, while some communities manage to recover rapidly with their own resources, others are more vulnerable, more structurally "sick" even—and still are suffering in some form from the after-effects of war. A general agenda for social healing might focus on the following four main areas:

1. How to establish a framework of *security* in which there can be some confidence that, should a crisis arise again, there can be recourse to help and justice ("social defense" is one possible model being tried out; protection through a patronage system, however undemocratic, is another)
2. How to reopen the pathways of *exchange* . . . enabling people once more to hear regular news of each other, to visit kin . . . setting up regular border fairs (tax-free!) and market places
3. How to *cleanse* the land, lay the ghosts of the unburied war dead, purify the community, and rid the individual of the pollution incurred under duress (this may mean new roles, as healers for example, for those whose experience in war has damaged their ability to function ordinarily within society)

4. How to offer credible grounds for adults to have *hope* for the future, by providing schooling or school fees for their children, by enabling their sons and daughters to marry and start families

In the Nigerian context, in the core areas of the former Biafra, these basic aspects of sociality began to reappear soon after the war ended. The areas where this has not happened, or happened only amidst much inequality, are those where the problems of armed robbery, underemployment, political in-fighting, and quests for a new faith seem to persist. In the northern areas of Nigeria, new solutions are tried: there has been increased marriage between Hausa and Igbo elites (especially in Kaduna); there have been Igbo conversions to Islam (in Kano); parts of the *bariki* are now armed and the Sabon Gari in Kano has been proved defensible against riots (but rents there have in consequence risen sharply). The army has now become so intermarried that the old regional divisions are no longer clear-cut; and soldiers have entered the new religions in a way that makes a simple Muslim/Christian schism within the military seem no longer so dangerous. Finally, in a recent crisis, Igbo elders took out advertisements in national newspapers warning Yoruba separatists not to expect Igbos to join them in a second civil war: "Never again," they said. And never again it may well be, despite the alarms.

In this essay I have used the case of the Nigerian civil war to suggest more generally how, if reconciliation is to be achieved, we must understand the concepts of violence among the "victors," and to identify the victims (and not just the "vanquished"); we need, too, to recognize the role of the interpreters of such violence. Although almost all of the essay has focused on the past, yet future (if not the present) levels of violence will depend on how successfully the process of reconciliation can be carried over into the new generation of Nigerians whose knowledge of the horrors of civil war comes through history and not through experience. In that sense, "Biafra" is not the past but part of the future, a half-heard commentary on the realities of violence.

NOTES

I am deeply indebted to all the (unrecorded) conversations I have had in Nigeria both during and after the war. As a graduate of the University of Ibadan (1961–64) I was privileged to have close friends who subsequently came to be on opposite sides of the war; at the start of the political crisis, and then after the war, I was carrying out research at Ahmadu Bello University. In all those years the tragedy of the social violence and the fighting was a stark reality, only a fragment of which I witnessed first-hand but which, secondhand, underlies this essay.

1. As a chronicle of the Nigerian civil war I have mainly relied on the account by

John de St. Jorre, which is generally acknowledged to be the best researched as well as impartial. I have also used the more partial work of Suzanne Cronje. For retrospective analyses, I have used the papers of the 1983 Zaria conference on Nigeria since independence edited by J. A. Atanda and others (1985), as well as the more substantial and focused *The Civil War Years,* edited by Tekena Tamuno and S. C. Ukpabi (1989), and Siyan Oyeweso's two studies published in 1992.

2. On the effects of the war on the states of eastern Nigeria, I have had the great benefit of reading the paper of the Berlin scholar, Axel Harneit-Sievers, "No Victors, No Vanquished? Reconstruction and Reintegration after the Nigerian Civil War," a paper he gave in Chicago in November 1994 and kindly sent to me. On this subject I have consulted Tom Forrest (1994) for data on Igbo firms postwar, as well as Herbert Ekwe-Ekwe's more general work (1992). On the literature of the war, there are a number of accounts—one that was particularly useful was by Jane Bryce (1991).

3. Over the years I have read a large number of memoirs of the war, but the ones most used here are Rose Njoku's *Withstand the Storm,* Jeremiah Essien's *In the Shadow of Death,* Ken Saro-Wiwa's *On a Darkling Plain,* and more recently, Dympna Ugwu-Oju's *What Will My Mother Say?* Of the various novels and short stories written after the war or set in the postwar period, I have used Eddie Iroh's thriller, *The Siren in the Night,* as well as the collected stories of Flora Nwapa and Chinua Achebe.

REFERENCES

Achebe, Chinua. 1972. *Girls at War, and Other Stories.* London: Heinemann.

Atanda, J. A., A. Y. Aliyu, M. O. Kayode, and Y. B. Usman, eds. 1985. *Proceedings of the National Conference on Nigeria since Independence, Zaria, March 1983.* 2 vols. Zaria: Nigeria since Independence History Project.

Bryce, Jane. 1991. "Conflict and Contradiction in Women's Writing on the Nigerian Civil War." *African Languages and Cultures* 4, no. 1: 29–42.

Cronje, Suzanne. 1972. *The World and Nigeria.* London: Sidgwick & Jackson.

Ekwe-Ekwe, Herbert. 1992. *The Biafra War: Nigeria and the Aftermath.* Lampeter: Mellen Press.

Essien, Jeremiah. 1987. *In the Shadow of Death.* Ibadan: Heinemann.

Forrest, Tom. 1994. *The Advance of African Capital.* Edinburgh: Edinburgh University Press for the International African Institute.

Harneit-Sievers, Axel. 1994. "No Victors, No Vanquished? Reconstruction and Reintegration after the Nigerian Civil War." Working paper. Chicago.

Iroh, Eddie. 1982. *The Siren in the Night.* Ibadan: Heinemann.

Njoku, Rose. 1986. *Withstand the Storm: War Memoirs of a Housewife.* Ibadan: Heinemann.

Nwapa, Flora. 1975. *Never Again.* Enugu: Nwamife Publishers.

———. 1980. *Wives at War, and Other Stories.* Ogui-Enugu: Tana Press.

Oyeweso, Siyan. 1992a. *Perspectives on the Nigerian Civil War.* Lagos: OAP Publications.

———. 1992b. *The Post-Gowon accounts of the Civil War 1975–1990.* Lagos: African Peace Research Institute.

St. Jorre, John de. 1972. *The Nigerian Civil War.* London: Hodder & Stoughton.

Saro-Wiwa, Ken. 1989. *On a Darkling Plain: An Account of the Nigerian Civil War.* Port Harcourt: Saros.

Tamuno, Tekena, and S. C. Ukpabi. 1989. *The Civil War Years.* Volume 6 of the series *Nigeria Since Independence: the First 25 years.* Ibadan: Heinemann.

Ugwu-Oju, Dympna. 1995. *What Will My Mother Say? A Tribal African Girl Comes of Age in America.* Chicago: Bonus Books.

Mood, Moment, and Mind

E. Valentine Daniel

The future, which [the mind] expects, passes through the present, to
which it attends, into the past, which it remembers.

PAUL RICOEUR,
Time and Narrative

The future is available in the present through a feeling of "struggle over
what shall be" (Peirce 5.462).[1] The present is thus the "Nascent State of
the Actual" (Peirce 5.462), that is, the locus where reality becomes actualized and moves towards the determined status of the past.

ROBERT S. CORRINGTON,
An Introduction to C. S. Peirce

Mood, moment, and mind—the themes of this chapter[2]—are intended to
correspond to Peirce's phenomenological categories of Firstness, Secondness, and Thirdness, respectively, a triad that has been more expansively
illustrated and employed elsewhere (see Daniel 1984: ch. 7, 1996: 81–83;
Parker 1998: ch. 5). Firstness is the phenomenological category of the possible; Secondness is the category of actual instantiations of certain possibilities; and Thirdness is the tendency of the universe—including human-
kind—to adopt and adapt to an evolving "lawfulness" among human beings
and between humans and their environment. There is, of course, nothing
that is a pure First, a pure Second, or a pure Third, but in certain experiences one category or another might predominate. In considering mood as
a relative First, then, I think of its connotations of a state of feeling—usually
vague, diffuse, and enduring, a disposition toward the world at any particular time yet with a timeless quality to it. Some of the connotations I wish to
associate with "moment" may be drawn from the *Oxford English Dictionary:* a
small particle, a moment of time too brief for its duration to be taken into
account (I see "taking into account" as an act that gives meaning to something that lacks meaning), a determining argument, the smallest detail, and
a turning point in a course or event. The "moment," like the category of
Secondness under which I have presented it, entails a sense of a unique fact

or event, a here-and-nowness, a selective narrowing of possibilities to just one actuality. Reported facts of violence—especially when the informant relives the experience during the telling—are momentous in this sense, with the then-and-there being radically transformed into the here-and-now. "Mind" I bring under the covering category of Thirdness: the tendency to generalize, to reason, to take habit. If a moment, an event, a violent act, say, is a given—to the eye or the ear—it is also a "taken." Taking is a mindful act, a phenomenon of Thirdness. But every "taking" of a perceptual fact (a Second) is dependent on its abduction from an indeterminate continuum that arises in humans interacting among themselves and with their environment, providing a "primitive epistemological [and ontological] feel of continuity [that is experienced] as a duration [in contrast to a momentary] present" (Rosenthal 1994: 60). This "feel of continuity" experienced as a durational present is a mood, a relative Firstness. To name a mood is to be too specific, to convert a First into a Third. In the case of Sri Lanka, this mood—a primitive feel of continuity—hangs over like a fog of which neither the beginning nor the end can be fathomed. This gray mood has tarried longest with its brooding over the Estate Tamils. How does an anthropographer represent this mood?

THE CHALLENGE:
REPRESENTING THE MOOD, MOMENT, AND MIND IN VIOLENCE

More than ten years have gone by since the responsibility of writing an anthropography of violence pierced,[3] like a shriek in the dark, my world of other preoccupations. I distinctly remember the moment of my commission. A daughter who had witnessed her father's murdered body being dragged away by the army Jeep to which it was tied said at one point in her interview with me, "You are a man who has seen the world, please take this story and tell the world of what they did to my father, how they treated him." And at another point, in the same interview, she pleaded, "Please don't tell anyone else this story. My father is such a dignified man. He never comes to dinner without bathing and without wearing a clean white shirt. I don't want anyone to remember him the way I see him, with his clothes torn off his body." Two aspects of this woman's statements are significant to this chapter. The first I shall only mention now and return to later. This concerns her constant and easy drift back into the present or the present continuous while speaking of an event that happened in the past. The second has two parts. One is her construction of me as a "man who has seen the world," presumably a world where the difference between good and evil still holds, but also a world that needs to be told and must not be allowed to forget. The other concerns the ambivalence of her charge to me, to tell and yet not to tell. This same ambivalence was to be expressed by other survivors and witnesses at other moments, in other ways, and for other reasons. Over these twelve years this charge has been further compounded; the task has become one of not only deciding what story to tell and what not to tell, but how to and how not to tell a story. How to tell the truth? With Lacan, I am obliged to say that "I always speak the truth. Not the whole truth, because there is no way to say it all. Saying the whole truth is materially impossible: words fail. Yet it's through this very impossibility that the truth holds onto the real"[4] (1990: 3).

Only the extraordinarily gifted or the excessively unmindful (mindless?) can write a book or a chapter on violence without being troubled by the particular challenge the representational form of writing poses for the task at hand, even if this task be described in the words of my pleading informant, as "a story." Poets, novelists, and literarily talented writers in general have the privilege of not having to account for why and how they choose to represent their subjects in the written form. They, as the cliché goes, "just do it." It is left to the literary critic or reader to determine how well it has been done. For very different reasons, for most social scientists—including, until recently, anthropologists—"writing" was something that we did not have to wrestle with; or if we did, we could not, in deference to protocol and good taste, openly discuss it. In its most "scientistic" form, writing was seen as a medium that, when judiciously employed, provided transparency between writer/reader and reality. To that extent, if there was a problem in writing, it was perceived as being limited to the finding of an objective, neutral vocabulary and analytic framework. More recently, anthropologists have come to acknowledge the fact that ethnography is, among other things, also a literary form. To say that it is a literary form is to admit not only to its aesthetic and rhetorical liabilities but to its political ones as well (see Daniel and Peck 1995).

There may come a day when the admission of ethnography's inherent literary burden, and by extension its rhetorical and political ones, will be so commonplace as to warrant neither special comment nor special pleading. That day is not here as yet. Should we, until such a day, belabor the point of such an admission at every possible occasion of writing an ethnography or an anthropography? Heaven forbid! But there are times when and reasons why such a belaboring may be warranted. Writing about violence is such a time, and theorizing about modes of writing provides such a reason. As far as theorizing about writing goes, anthropologists have yet to say much. At the end of this chapter, I shall suggest in prolegomena fashion—and no more—theoretical directions with respect to writing that are worthy of our contemplation. I shall conclude by admitting to a mode of writing as well as a theory of (re)presentation toward which the subject matter of the book from which this chapter was drawn, especially as my writing of it progressed, has made me increasingly partial. As I hope to make clear, this partiality has been prompted by the perdurance of the presence (the fact or condition of being present) of violence in the lives of a people among whom I have lived and learned over a great part of my life: Sri Lankans generally, but Estate Tamils in particular.

THE PRESENCE OF VIOLENCE

Greater than the challenge that violence in general poses to writing is the one posed by the presence of violence. My task would have been easier had the violence been a thing of the past, a done deed, or if the future and its hopes, in being attended upon by the present, had better survived the latter's relentless and deforming scourge. Relatively independent of the present, the past and the future are easier to fathom because they can be conceptually seized and positioned for a still-life representation, a representation hovered over by the protective shadow of a coherent narrative.[5] The Sri Lankan experience is overburdened with the present, a present "under (traumatic) erasure," besmudged before the ink on the page is dry. The anthropography at hand is both present-driven and present-stifled. Where the present dominates, the future and the past, because they have to pass through the present, are shaken even as they partake of the present's impermanence. Friends whom one considered to be unshakably likeminded change their opinions on vital matters. Today's good cause turns out to be tomorrow's evil. Yesterday's liberators become today's torturers. Last month's confidants become next month's informers. This week's promise becomes next week's betrayal. There are shifts in the other direction as well, from worse to better. Bigots turn into ardent nondiscriminators, murderers into penitent helpers, avengers into *satyagrahis* (nonviolent activists), hatemongers into compassionate human beings, raving extremists into rational mediators, chauvinists into humanists. Social scientists want the world to hold still or, better yet, to follow the course of their predictions. The world moves on regardless. The Buddhist doctrine of *anicca* (the doctrine of the impermanence of all being) holds.

When the present looms large in this manner, both memory and hope become either emaciated or bloated. In either case, it is the present that determines the past, making the past a mere simulacrum of the present.[6] The future, thanks to the capriciousness of the present, is uncertain and bleak. Neither the vision of a united Sri Lanka nor that of a separate Tamil Eelam is clearly defined. In 1990, I spoke with Kamalam in a refugee camp in India. Having lost her son in an army raid five years earlier, and having lost every last photograph of him with her house—it went up in flames when a helicopter gunship dropped a gasoline bomb on it—she confessed that she could no longer remember what her son's face looked like. His features had become vague and confused. She remembered his gait, his school uniform, even his bicycle, but she could not recall his face. All the albums containing his photographs had been burned with the house. This did not prevent her from seeing her son in the face of every young man who came to the camp. Some of them were pacifists, some were seasoned fighters, some were terrorists, some were politicians, some were entrepreneurs, and some were just boys. But traces of her son's face appeared and disappeared in all of them. The more they ruffled the clarity of her memory, the more she longed to be able to see her son again, clearly; but the ever-changing faces of the present got in the way of her enframing the face of her son, in memory or in expectation. In my interview with her in her refugee camp at Mandapam, she complained of her eyesight, blaming it for her inability to recall her son's face clearly. Instead of projecting her loss onto her missing son, she introjected the loss of her son to the loss of eyesight. She had just turned thirty-five. As for why her eyes had dimmed, she blamed the sea by which she sat from sunrise to sundown. I asked her why she stared at the sea. She said that at first she did so because she had been told that Jaffna was only twenty miles away and that on a clear day she might be able to see it. When some of her fellow refugees found out what she was doing, they disabused her of that hope. Some other refugees reminded her that even if she could see the shores of Jaffna, her home was not in Jaffna but in Vavuniya, which was farther south. This had reminded her that her home was not even in Vavuniya, for she was born in the hills of the tea country, in the south-central highlands of Sri Lanka.

> May the woman who tells me that I could see Jaffna perish. May those who tell me that I cannot see Jaffna perish. Let them make fun of me. "You are not from Jaffna," they tell me. "You are from Vavuniya." I tell them, "Look here, I am not even from Vavuniya but one who was born on the tea estates." The biggest mistake my father made was to take us to Vavuniya. "Yes," I say, "I am a *tōṭṭakkāṭṭān*."[7] "She is an Indian Tamil!" they say; as if they have seen a ghost. "But the camp authorities think she is Sri Lankan," says one of the *kaṅkāṇis*.[8] "Look here," I say, "you are here in Mandapam. This is the same camp from which *my* ancestors left for the tea estates one hundred years ago." He shut his mouth.

And thus she presents the past. She is angry and stares even more determinedly, expecting the tall mountains of the tea country to make their appearance over the horizon and vindicate her anger. She says that, of course, she knows that that is not going to happen. "But anger does strange things to your mind. I know that the distance is too far and what is gone is gone, but I don't have to think," she says. Occasionally a wave from the distant past rolls toward her. But most of the time she lives thinking, "What happened, what will happen, who knows." Then she poignantly adds, "I don't say, 'Tomorrow my son might come.' I say, 'Here he comes. Here I see his face.' That is the way I see. That is how my life is."

The vision of and for the future of the nation has undergone a fate sim-

ilar to this mother's vision of her son's face. Prior to 1983, and even immediately after that summer, both separatists and nonseparatists were able to
define the contours of their future nation, as they saw it, with clarity. It is not
so today. The moment a glimmer of a clear outline begins to take form, the
present, with a bomb, a betrayal, an ambush, or an assassination, shatters
the outline and scatters the bits of the nascent image. Scholars gather in
person or in their writings, sometimes pooling their thoughts in conferences or edited volumes, attempting to rechart their own visions for the
future. It all seems contrived and even hopeless. Only the naive and the
innocent pose the straightforward question: "What is the solution?" An
embarrassed hush falls upon a room filled with the seasoned, to be broken,
after a trying pause, by someone who is willing to offer a polite, even if
painfully inadequate, response. There are no clear answers, no clear visions.
Bold visions like those of Vijay Kumaratunga and Rajani Thiranagama are
few.[9] This lack, however, we are not supposed to admit, and certainly not as
social scientists. It is our calling to offer answers, to offer hope, to make the
present submit to a (better) future, even if this endeavor calls for a radical
remaking of the past.

THE PRESENCE OF THE PAST: THE CASE OF THE ESTATE TAMILS

That the present bears heavily upon all Sri Lankans today is a truism; and
the frantic effort to recover the past either as heritage or as history, by
Tamils and by Sinhalas, is but a symptom of the overwhelming presence of
the present in their lives. But whereas most Sri Lankans experience the present acutely, the experience of the heaviness of the present by Estate Tamils
may be best described as an enduring condition. "How can we think of the
future when we don't even know who we are or where we will be tomorrow?"
asks a plantation worker, pondering his situation. "We have known nothing
else," remarks another. Not only has the existence of these workers been a
hand-to-mouth one, but their citizenship in a world of nation-states has
been equally uncertain. Sri Lankans call them Indians and Indians call
them Sri Lankans. "Aliens" in Sri Lanka, they are unwelcome in India.
Bilaterally agreed-upon repatriation schemes notwithstanding, on the
Indian side those who have been repatriated, and who thought they were
"returning to their motherland," are called—much to the displeasure of the
repatriates—"refugees." They wish to be called *tāyakam tirumpinōr* (the ones
who have returned to the motherland). Most repatriates, especially those
who are middle-aged and older, would like to keep the distinction clear
because, among many other reasons, they resent being identified with the
very group that had held them in such contempt for so long during their
sojourn in Sri Lanka, the Jaffna Tamils, who are today the true seekers of
refuge in India and elsewhere. Impelled by a certain vindictiveness, they feel

that it is time for Jaffna Tamils to be held in contempt for a change, a contempt from which they would for once be excluded. It has not turned out that way, however. The Tamils of South India—those who never left their motherland—call them Sri Lankans and, by extension, refugees.

While the quasi-theoretical focus of this chapter is on representation in writing, the ethnographic focus is on a group of Estate Tamils who were repatriated to India from 1960 onward. Being unwelcome in their ancestral villages is but one fate among several—mostly dismal ones—that may await Selvi and others who have begun to leave the island of their birth. In working with these and other groups of persons displaced from the plantations, one is struck by the burgeoning of the present in their lives. To be sure, neither past nor future is completely extinguished, but they often do appear to be. The group of repatriates of whom I have chosen to write in this chapter are paradigmatic of the burgeoning present that I have just mentioned. The quality of their life seems nothing but an assemblage of instances, disruption their source of possibility, interruption their only reverie, shock their only trance, surprise the basis for their openness to the world, the recalcitrant other the only route to their inner selves, chaos their only community, brute force the main impress of power, action the only manifestation of their feelings, doubt the mark of their innocence, contiguity the ground of their freedom, the timbre of tokens the tone of their lives, suspicion their principal trope, and the moment the determinant of their mood.

In *Charred Lullabies,* I presented, in the form of composite oral histories, the deep grievance that Estate Tamils bore against the Sinhala majority and a deeper one against the fully enfranchised northern and eastern "Jaffna" Tamils. The power over their lives seemed to rest in the hands of others: their supervisors, their (mainly) European overlords, the Sinhalas or the Jaffna Tamils, and now the Tamils of southern India. No wonder, then, that their lives are torqued by distrust.

The story of the present chapter begins in 1949–1950, when by two consecutive acts of Parliament—recounted in chapters 1 and 3 of *Charred Lullabies*—a majority of the Estate Tamils (estimated at nearly a million persons) are disenfranchised and made stateless.[10] The Estate Tamil leadership in the late forties and early fifties is made up of two trade unions, the Ceylon Workers' Congress (CWC) and the Democratic Workers' Congress (DWC), and is caught by surprise, without a plan. The government decrees that anyone wishing to lay claim to Ceylonese citizenship has to formally apply to the assigned government agency, which would then determine whether or not the applicant qualifies for citizenship. The criteria for qualification are so stringent as to lead one parliamentarian, Mr. Pieter Keuneman, to observe that "even Dudley Senanayake, who was later to become the prime minister of Ceylon, could not comply with the clauses [of the Citizenship Acts of 1948 and 1949] because according to his own admission in the House of

Representatives he could not trace his father's birth certificate" (Devaraj 1985: 212). Pieter Keuneman's position is no different from Dudley Senanayake's, because the practice of registering births was not current when his father was born.

Ninety-five percent of the vulnerable are plantation workers. The leaders of the trade unions to which these workers belong issue conflicting instructions to members. At first they are instructed not to apply for citizenship so as to collectively undermine the moral, if not the legal, basis of the new decree. Those Sri Lankans of recent Indian origin who are not estate workers, but who belong to a largely successful mercantile class located in the major cities, go ahead and apply for citizenship. Where birth certificates of fathers and grandfathers are unavailable—and this is generally the case— sworn affidavits from leading bona fide citizens and (noncitizen!) Britons, stragglers of the departing empire, are accepted by the appropriately empowered magistrates. Some of Colombo's leading merchants of Indian descent—mainly Borahs and Parsis, but also a few Tamils—whose abiding interests are not in Ceylon but in India, enlist the very same politicians who help pass the Citizenship Act of 1949 in vouching for their qualifying pedigree. Many of the schoolteachers and white-collar workers on the plantations also submit their applications; so do several leaders of the trade unions, even if secretly. Word gets out, and at the.eleventh hour instructions spread through rumor and word of mouth that all should apply, only to be contradicted by other rumors that the latest rumor was just that, a rumor. In the confusion, a few more apply for citizenship, but most do not. Even among those plantation workers who do request the appropriate application forms, most report that they either never received any or received them after the application deadline had passed. Those who fail to receive the requested forms suspect sabotage by the postal service. Some claim that the highest authorities of government ordered postmasters to delay or entirely refrain from delivering envelopes originating from the government department in question, while others maintain that postmasters made such decisions on their own. Most postmasters who work in the small hill-country towns near the tea estates are Jaffna Tamils, as are a high proportion of all civil servants of the period. This fact makes the charge against postmasters part of a broader suspicion directed against Jaffna Tamils who, it is believed, are against the enfranchisement of Tamils of recent Indian origin. Those estates that happen to fall within the distributive area of post offices manned by Sinhala postmasters, it is claimed, have received their applications without delay or loss. (I had neither the time nor the resources to verify such charges and claims, except to note a pattern in which when and wherever a Sinhala was pitted against a Jaffna Tamil vis-à-vis the interests of the Estate Tamils, justifiably or not, the Sinhala came out the nobler—if more naive— of the two in the opinion of Estate Tamils.)

Mr. Sivaprakasam, a Jaffna Tamil, who had served both as a postal clerk between 1949 and 1953 in one of the post offices of these hill-country towns and, later, as a clerk in a tea-estate office, remembers this period somewhat differently. He does not recall any screening of or tampering with mail destined for the tea estates. "The fact is," said Mr. Sivaprakasam,

> very few estate laborers received any mail. They were illiterate. Their relatives in India were illiterate. The only thing they received were wedding cards. These they did not have to read. It was news they already knew, before the cards came. News traveled through messengers. The *ka[nd]kāṇis* and a few laborers with money used to come to the post office to send money orders to their relatives in India. That was the only business they ever had with the post office, other than mailing marriage announcements.

In his account, Mr. Sivaprakasam believes that most instances of letters lost, misdirected, or delayed were the result of petty acts of power exercised by the estate office clerks and other white-collar workers on plantations—the literate few, over the mass of laborers, the illiterate many. The laborers depended on those who could read and write well enough to request, receive, and recognize application forms, inform the addressees of their arrival, fill them out, and send them back to the appropriate address. Such favors were rarely done for money in those days, but payment was extracted in the form of labor, loyalty, and acknowledgment of one's lowliness. Who were these empowered literates? Mostly educated Tamils and Malayalees from India, followed by Jaffna Tamils, and a scattering of Sinhalas and Muslims. Many laborers were either incapable or deemed incapable of providing this kind of payment and had their forms sabotaged. In most of their cases their attempt to obtain Sri Lankan citizenship never went beyond the first step of merely having obtained the application forms. Once again, there is no way of verifying Mr. Sivaprakasam's account, but there is reason to believe that there was some truth to it.

Mr. Thomas, a Syrian Christian from Kerala, himself a retired clerk of a tea estate, begs to differ with Mr. Sivaprakasam on several points. His reading of estate intrigue, though at odds with Mr. Sivaprakasam's, is equally insightful:

> Two things were not possible [on plantations]. First, it was not possible to refuse outright, to say no, I cannot, I will not help you by filling out those forms. Because the laborer can always go to someone [else]. And when that happens? Yes. You will lose respect. You lose authority. Someone else has authority over him, not you. Of course if he is a lazy and useless blackguard, you can tell him to go fishing. But in that case he is the type that everyone he goes to for help will say the same thing. So no loss for you. No loss for anybody. But otherwise we oblige. Any clerk or conductor or tea maker, when asked, helped. Now, sabotaging the forms, misfiling the forms, et cetera, is also not possible. That is too risky. Every clerk watches what the other clerk is doing. If

anything is wrong, he will not report it right away. He will save it up and use it at the right time. Because Tamils, all Tamils, especially laborers, never trust. Do you know of a Tamil who asks how to go to someplace from one man only, and believes only that man's advice? No. He will ask again and again, from many people, many times. My own father—he did not know to read or write English very well—used to have me fill out some form or write some letter for him. Then he would slowly take it to my brother, to have him check it to see if it was all right, then to next-door person, to the tea maker, to the school-teacher. By the time he finished, the whole estate knew everything in his let-ter. He never trusted one person. Not even his son. So no saboteur of forms could have escaped. Unless several people got together in a plan. But Estate Tamils, unlike Jaffna Tamils, were very bad [at] conspiracy. Secrets are like cash. They don't know how to invest. They only know to spend. That was true then. It is true now. That is why the Jaffna Tamil succeeded in those days, and that is the secret for the Tigers' success today.

While these accounts differ as to what might have taken place in the early part of the 1950s and why, we get a general picture of a climate of suspicion, duplicity, and circumstances in which the illiterate among the plantations' workers feel vulnerable. The net effect on their aspirations for citizenship is disastrous. Most plantation workers are condemned to statelessness. The two estate workers' trade unions subsequently do get their acts together and make citizenship for their workers a plank in their platforms. But on the whole these trade unions have little effect on the policies of the govern-ment, and they lack the will and the means to bring the appropriate pres-sure to bear on the tea industry, given the island's dependence on it, so as to push through their wishes on the citizenship question.

There are many incidents that occasion distrust between the two Tamil groups, but the singularly poignant one occurs when Mr. G. G. Ponnambalam condones the Citizenship Act by accepting a ministry in the United National Party government that has just succeeded in disenfran-chising a million Tamil plantation workers. Mr. G. G. Ponnambalam is a Jaffna Tamil, a gifted lawyer and orator, and the founder and head of the Tamil Congress, a party that was formed in 1944, in response to the early signs of Sinhala-Buddhist hegemony. Estate Tamils see G. G. not only as an opportunist who sold the Tamil side for a mess of political pottage but also as the forensic mind behind the two infamous parliamentary acts that ren-dered these Tamils voteless and stateless. However, this moment of betrayal and rift between the two Tamil groups also yields an opportunity for trust and unity in the figure of another Jaffna Tamil lawyer-politician who soon displaces G. G. from his position of leadership of the Tamils of Ceylon. This is Mr. S. J. V. Chelvanayakam, who becomes the leader of the Federal Party, the party that breaks away from the Tamil Congress in 1949. The fact that G. G. is a Hindu and Mr. Chelvanayakam a Christian does not matter one bit to the Tamil electorates of the north and east. Mr. Chelvanayakam's slow and deliberate speech stands in stark contrast to the specious fluency of G. G. and comes to stand for the contrast between a principled man and an opportunist. One of the reasons for his split with G. G. is the latter's betrayal of the Tamils of the plantations. Most Estate Tamils only vaguely appreciate the stand the Federal Party has taken on their behalf. Rather, the only message of the Federal Party that reaches them loud and clear is its demand for a federated state wherein the predominantly Tamil provinces of the north and the east (not the central highlands where the Estate Tamils live) would be guaranteed a modicum of autonomy and protection from Sinhala-Buddhist majoritarianism. The Estate Tamils, situated as they are in the middle of Sinhala country and with neither vote nor citizenship, see little of interest for them in this prominent item of the Federal Party's platform. They are preoccupied with the politics of the two trade unions, the Ceylon Workers Congress and the Democratic Workers Congress, the one led by a Hindu, Mr. S. Thondaman, and the other by a Muslim, Mr. Aziz. Here again it is noteworthy that religion does not matter at all. (Those were the days!) Ironically, seven years later, when the very article in the Federal Party's platform that contains the potential for the restoration of trust and unity between the two Tamil groups was brought to the Estate Tamils' attention, that potential was shattered in an apparent act of betrayal. This time the betrayal centers on the Bandaranaike-Chelvanayakam Pact of 1957. A year earlier, Mr. S. W. R. D. Bandaranaike has been elected prime minister on the promise that he would make Sinhala the official language within twenty-four hours of his election. His election confirms all the fears entertained by the Tamils—the Jaffna Tamils, in particular—of their systematic demotion to the status of second-class citizens, contravening all earlier assurances, constitutional and otherwise. Those Tamils who engage in acts of civil disobedience and nonviolent protest are set upon by crudely armed Sinhala mobs. As bloodied and wounded parliamentarians, including Mr. S. J. V. Chelvanayakam, arrive at the parliament building, seeking first aid, from the neighboring Galle Face Green where they have been carrying out their nonviolent protests, the pipe-puffing prime minister is supposed to have been garrulous with cruel wit and flippant invectives at the expense of the injured. A senior Tamil politician who had known Mr. Bandaranaike quite well was emphatic in assuring me of Mr. Bandaranaike's racism. A racist Bandaranaike was not. Neither was he even a Sinhala-Buddhist chauvinist. He was a pragmatic politician. On an interpersonal level he is said to have been at greater ease with Tamil politicians of his own class and with similar prestigious high school and university pedigrees than with most of the Sinhala politicians of his party who lacked such pedigrees. When I ask this politician how the prime minister could then have allowed his Tamil friends ("fellow diners and winers," as he called them) to be bloodied up in the

Galle Face Green, he replies, "I think the prime minister looked at it more like a ragging in Oxford than an attack by hooligans."

The following year (1957), this pragmatic politician, recognizing his inability to govern without the support and citizenship of a crucial minority, and realizing that the game has taken a far more serious turn than he had thought it would, chooses to be more conciliatory. He invites the leader of the Federal Party to his private residence for deal making. Mr. Chelvanayakam enters the prime minister's residence with four concerns: (1) the recognition of Tamil as an official language and its unimpeded use for official purposes in the predominantly Tamil northern and eastern parts of the country; (2) the reversal of government-promoted Sinhala settlements in areas with Tamil majorities aimed at gradually tipping the balance in favor of the Sinhalas; (3) the creation of regional councils that would result in greater autonomy of the predominantly Tamil regions of the north and the east; and (4) the restoration of citizenship and voting rights to the Tamils of the plantations. After many hours of deliberation he emerges from the prime minister's office with a pact. The pact accommodates the first three of Mr. Chelvanayakam's concerns; the fourth—the one that means most to the Tamils of the plantations, the one that could restore intra-Tamil trust—is sacrificed to politics, the art of the possible. As it turns out, even this pact, such as it is, is dramatically torn up by the prime minister within a year, under the pressuring protests of Buddhist monks and in their full view.

The trade unions, for lack of trust or political will and perspicuity, fail to exert any pressure on the Federal Party, the only party that was inclined by virtue of ethnic and linguistic propinquity to represent the interests of these "other Tamils." As things turn out, the Estate Tamils are, as a whole, so thoroughly excluded from the political process that even as late as 1964, when the prime minister of India, Mr. Lal Bhadhur Shastri, and the prime minister of Sri Lanka, Mrs. Sirimavo Bandaranaike, conclude their own pact on the citizenship question, none of the leaders of the Estate Tamils, trade unionists or otherwise, are consulted.

By the terms of the Sirimavo-Shastri Pact, 525,000 of the stateless persons are to be repatriated to India within fifteen years. The fate of 150,000 more and their progeny is to be decided at a later date. This later date comes around in 1974 when a second pact, known as the Sirimavo-Indira Pact, is agreed upon, by which 75,000 are marked for deportation to India. And yet by mid-1984 only 445,588 persons in all have been repatriated to India, most of them against their will. Most of the nearly 112,000 families thus repatriated are, to use the normalizing though ironic terminology of the state, "settled" in their "home state"—another normalizing term—of Tamil Nadu. Of course, the 1983 anti-Tamil riots were to suddenly and dramatically alter this state of affairs, and Estate Tamils flooded the Indian High Commissions in Colombo and Kandy to obtain their entry papers to "return" to India. But we are getting ahead of our story. For what I wish to do next is to go back and look at the lives of those Estate Tamils who do opt to return to India well before the trickle turned into the post-1983 flood. Of special interest are those "repatriates" who return to India in the 1970s, for the conditions into which they fall are the most relevant ones against which to measure and understand the hopes and disappointments of post-1983 émigrés like Selvi. On the whole it cannot be said of most of those who return to India as a result of the various Indo-Sri Lankan accords that they settle successfully in the land of their ancestors. True, the earlier ones fare better than the later ones. That they have had more time to adjust to their new country only partly explains their relative success. But the resettlement of those who go to India in the 1970s is by far the most distressing. In the following section I wish to focus on one group of these repatriates, a group that ends up in the hills of Kodaikanal, in the vicinity of one of South India's most popular hill resorts.

In the summer of 1987 my own interest descends on one of the most unsettled of the settlements, on an episode that is paradigmatic of the whole story of this immigrant people. I am referring to the three hundred-odd families who live in a state of bondage, confined to what are known as "coupes," in the hills of Kodaikanal. The term *coupe*, as understood in the official records, refers to an area of work demarcated by the Forest Department for the commercial purpose of felling, barking, stacking, and transporting forest trees, and where the laborers are settled in temporary sheds. These sheds, or huts, are also called coupes. The details of bondage in these coupes have been not so much concealed as deemed irrelevant to the Indian government's democratic concerns for almost twenty years. The whole matter becomes relevant to the various agencies of the government with the "liberation" of forty-four families, brought about by an extraordinary conjunction of events and persons: the accidental discovery of a coupe by a high school class from the local "International School" during a social studies field trip; the presence of a maverick subcollector who happens to be a Sikh (and therefore an outsider in the state of Tamil Nadu); the timely vacation of his boss, the district collector,[11] who doubles as a lackey of a minister in the state government (a vacation that frees the subcollector to push through some papers and petitions beyond the point of retraction); two determined Jesuit priests; an investigative reporter from Poona who manages to convince his southern newspaper colleagues that the story is, if nothing else, potentially sensational; a Supreme Court that is willing to entertain a writ petition filed against two contractors working for Tan India and South India Viscose; and the ambushing of these two giant national corporations when their "what's-so-wrong-about-that" attitude regarding the use of bonded labor is rudely jostled by a series of moves that lands them before the Supreme Court.

The episode develops as follows: The Indian Supreme Court orders the payment of unpaid wages to the heads of the forty-four families in this coupe, that they be liberated, and that they be rehabilitated. Neither Tan India nor South India Viscose is punished, except for being forced to pick up the tab on what it cost the Court Appointed Commission to research and write up its report. As for the contractors who had not paid the laborers, some for as long as fifteen years, their being forced to cough up back pay is deemed punishment enough. A man with "Rajiv Gandhi connections" is appointed to oversee the families' rehabilitation on land made available by the state of Tamil Nadu. At the time of my fieldwork (June 1987), eighteen months have passed since this man was appointed to the job. Over these eighteen months, he visits the "liberated" coupe once and the designated site twice, acquires a Jeep after the first month, a Maruti[12] after the second, and builds himself a two-story bungalow by the tenth. His assistant acquires only a Maruti, but he also buys some real estate in Kodaikanal, the nearby hill resort, and takes to gossiping about how his boss is becoming very rich on the rehabilitation project. The forty-four families are allowed to stay in their shacks until the land has been surveyed and appropriately partitioned. They do not understand why surveying and allocation has to take so long, especially since there are no ecological or potential economic differences among the plots. They are given rice rations and an allowance by the state and are told by the assistant not to try their "*bandhs* (political demonstrations) and such nonsense" with him around.

On the fourth occasion of my collecting narratives of emigration from a middle-aged couple inside one of the coupes, the assistant happens to visit this settlement. "I will have the police skin you alive," I hear him say. A small crowd gathers. I see him from inside the dark coupe, which is lit only by the daylight that comes through the solitary door—now partially obstructed by my informant who has stepped out to see what is happening—and by the light from the fickle flames of the hearth upon which a pot of water has been set to boil for some tea. The assistant cannot see me. His *vēṣṭi*[13] is folded up so as to expose his blue boxer shorts. He arcs an oyster of phlegm, which lands in a puddle of water near the doorway of the dark coupe wherein I squat and watch. As the assistant continues to thunder with threats and abuse, one of the men, cupping his hand behind his ear with an exaggerated gesture signaling deafness shouts, "What did you say?" He has a bark-peeling knife tucked in his waistband. A silence falls upon the crowd. The assistant gently drops his "miniskirt" to the respectful ankle length, acting like a man who for once has been caught without a pose. The women take note. An older member of the coupe, a man with a fatherly manner, gently leads the assistant away and intones in a soothing drone the words, "Now you go along. Go and screw your mother." It is hard to tell whether this advice was intended to fuel or foil the assistant's temper.

No sooner does the assistant leave than I emerge from the darkness and take the shortcut down the hill to intercept his Jeep and hitch a ride to the hill resort town, Kodaikanal. He takes me for a rich tourist from Bombay. But he is even more pleased to know that I am from the United States and that my ancestral village is near the South Indian town of Thenkasi. "An N.R.I.!"[14] he observes with pleasure, and obliges with oily amiability. He considers it quite unwise of me to walk around these parts and tells me that I should have taken the next bus out of the last town even if I had to wait a few hours. "There are Sri Lankans around here. Dangerous people," he warns. He calls them "refugees." I cautiously offer that I have met some "coolies" carrying bundles of wattle along the way. "That's them, that's them," he jumpily interjects. "Dangerous, very dangerous," he keeps repeating. It is obvious that he has been rattled by his recent encounter with the coupe-dwellers, and he proceeds to tell me his version of what has happened: he went to supervise the distribution of payment and food to these refugees and was threatened with a knife for not coming with more. That was the sum of his version. "Refugees! What kind of refugees!" I do not ask him if he thinks there is a difference between Sri Lankan Tamil refugees and the Estate Tamil repatriates who never tire of insisting that they are "returnees to their motherland and not refugees." But I do wedge open the possibility of a retraction, or qualification, or amendment by remarking that in my conversation with the "coolies" I had heard them speak Indian Tamil and not Sri Lankan ("Jaffna") dialect of the refugees. "The mostly Sri Lankan Tamil refugees I have met speak such a distinctly different dialect," I observe. "They are all refugees," he insists, and then adds, "They are also Tigers."

On our way we pass the oncoming Jeep of the inspector of police. The assistant stops him to report the impertinence he has just experienced, omitting the bit about taking food and wages to the refugees. He also does me the favor of introducing me to the inspector of police, adding his own elaboration that I am an N.R.I. tourist who likes hiking through the mountains and forests and was on my way to Kodaikanal from Kerala and had misjudged the distance to Kodaikanal from the last town nearest to where he had picked me up, and, thanks to him, I have been saved from the dacoity of the Sri Lankan Tamil refugees. He wants the inspector of police to go to the coupe and give them a good thrashing. The inspector of police tells the assistant to ignore them, that they are dangerous and mad. "These refugees' cheek knows no limit. The more they get, the more they want." Once again, in the South Indian dialect of Tamil, I remark to the inspector that the "coolies" I have met along the road, whom the assistant calls "refugees," did not speak the dialect of Jaffna Tamils. "They are refugees from the tea estates of Ceylon," he observes. "You don't mean those who went from India as laborers and who have been sent back?" I query. "They are all the same.

Refugees. The only difference is that those in camps are the ones who have some education and money and connections. These animals here have none. Animals, sir, animals. Just animals."

The laborers I met worry about the 290 other families that are still in bondage. But the contractors of Tan India and South India Viscose have taken measures to assure the silence of these other bonded laborers by infecting the labor force with better-paid, Indian-born laborers who double as informers. The courageous young subcollector receives transfer orders moving him to a safer and lesser position, getting him out of the way, so that the Supreme Court's orders will get lost and remain unenforced in the deep forests of the Kodai hills. The subcollector finds legal means of resisting the transfer and is reinstated. His brother comes to Tamil Nadu to visit the subcollector but is arrested and tortured under charges of being a Sikh terrorist. Unable to bear the harassment and the plight of his brother, the subcollector gives up the battle and moves out. His brother is released after three years in a maximum security prison; no charges whatsoever have been brought against him. When released, he is insane. The press has moved on to other matters of interest, such as the Liberation Tigers of Tamil Eelam and the state of the chief minister's kidneys.[15] One of the biggest shareholders of the two giant companies happens to be the president of the Republic of India. Alagammal, a "liberated woman," calls him the *Periya Kaṅkāṇi* of *Periya Kaṅkāṇis* (an allusion I shall return to below). She asks me, "Who is this *ācārya* of the Kanchi Maṭam?[16] Why does he run away in the stealth of the night from his *maṭam?*" And she also wants to know why President Venkataraman has personally gotten involved in the search for His Holiness, why the president's wife herself is so worried about the *ācārya*'s whereabouts, and finally, why she or anyone else should care, even though the story about this *ācārya* has been appropriating the front pages of the local newspapers for weeks.

What she wants to know (and does not say) is why and how their own story, which had its brief moment of glory in the attention of the press, got displaced; why the color photographs that had deservedly made the front page of the glossy newsmagazine *Front Line* are not there anymore. Instead, there are pictures of this "holy man" who chose to disappear, abdicating his position of leadership at a famous South Indian "monastery," and pictures of other VIPs, who have been profoundly and visibly affected, in ways quite mysterious to her, by this "holy man's" willful disappearance. "They [the reporters] took so many pictures of us," she says. "Where are the other pictures?" Neither she nor most of the other residents of the coupe understand or care for the written word, and that the latter no longer embodies their story in the press is something she does not mind. But the photographs she understood and now misses. She turns to me to accuse me of belonging to the "same *jāti* (genus) as those educated people with cameras, pens, and

notebooks, who forget us with the first belly-filling meal in their bungalows."
Like the woman who told me to tell and yet not to tell of the manner of her
father's death, and who constructed me as "a man who has seen the world,"
Alagammal too sees me as a man who had not only seen a wider world but
belonged to it. Alagammal, however, is not sanguine about that world's
being one in which good and evil could be told apart. She had been in Sri
Lanka, the land of her birth, and now is in India, the land of her ancestors,
and has seen only a little of both these countries, never being able to drift
too far away from her place of labor. In neither country is she impressed by
its people's ability to tell the difference between good and evil. The even
wider world that she glimpses through the few issues of *Front Line* gives her
no reason to believe that matters are any different elsewhere. Her narrative
of events and sketches of her life are never straightforward narratives about
her life or events. No narrative, for that matter—mine included—is a
straightforward representation, made up of transparently decodable con-
statives. Alagammal's is not a mere telling; it is a performative. It constructs
me as a possible belly-filler, a forgetter, but also as a potential messenger,
even as she admonishes me not to forget.

This story that I have chosen to tell you foregrounds the phenomenological moment of Peircean Secondness, albeit in an extended form, as an
amplified moment of discordance. This moment is overwhelmed by "the
present," the *hic et nunc,* in its capricious, and at times shocking, brutality.
The protagonists of this story experience life as a series of interruptions.
Power, mostly in its primitive form of force that is neither subtle (as in
Foucault's capillary power), reasonable (as in Gramsci's hegemony), nor
productive (as in Wartenberg's "coercive power"),[17] raids their lives with frequent irregularity. The moment of discordance, in its sheer momentous-
ness, extends its shock waves into all possible moods and meanings of the
lived experience of these displaced and dispossessed people. The here and
the now overwhelm and deeply affect mood and meaning. Academic discourse in general and ethnography in particular (whether it is called interpretive or not) tend to privilege what Peirce called Thirdness. In Thirdness,
understandings abound, explanations appease, reason holds court, and
concordance is king. Such a "concordance is characterized by three features: completeness, wholeness, and an appropriate magnitude" (Ricoeur
1984, 1: 38). In writing about a people whose lives have been anything but
whole or complete, how does one even determine the appropriate magnitude of one's representation of their lives, let alone presume the possibility
of concordance among representations and the correspondence of one's
representation with the represented? And yet the anthropologist is asked to
tell the world the story. How, in whose voice, or rather, in which of the many
available voices, ought an anthropologist to tell such stories? And what does
he tell when the most poignant parts of their voices are their silences?

BEING HUMAN: BEING IN ANTHROPOSEMEIOSIS

Anthroposemeiosis is such a cumbersome word. But none other better describes what it is to be human: why it is that the young woman who sees her father being dragged by an army Jeep—and many like her—want their "story" to be told to "the world," and why Alagammal fears that the words she tells me would be forgotten by me and lost to "the world"; why silence is so disconcerting. The universe is perfused with signs, and the activity of signs is what we call semeiosis—with a nod of deference to the Greek *semeion,* "sign." Semeiosis describes the activity of the giving, the receiving, the transforming, and the disseminating of signs. What differentiates anthroposemeiosis from semeiosis in general is that it involves human beings' knowledge or awareness of the relations of signification (Deely 1994: 51). In fact, it defines what it is to be human. It is this awareness that separates out anthroposemeiosis from within the larger semeiosic networks of zoösemeiosis, phytosemeiosis, or even the physiosemeiosis that sustains it. "Unlike other animals, we not only know; we know that we know" (Bauman 1992: 12). And that is why silence, especially silence that resists its incorporation into semeiosis, is so fundamentally threatening of humanity.

Consider the following excerpt from a dialogue between a sympathetic official from the fact-finding committee appointed by the Indian Supreme Court and a member of the coupe described above:

OFFICIAL   Tell! Tell (me) about your situation.

LABORER   How can I describe it? It won't even come into my mouth (It does not conform to words).

OFFICIAL (after much coaxing by the officer and stubborn silence on the part of the laborer)   If you don't say it, it will mean that nothing was the matter.

Throughout Sri Lanka and elsewhere, among Tamil and Sinhala victims of violence, the lasting effect that one often witnesses is a sort of stunned repose settled upon individuals and groups. Whereas silence or speechlessness is one of the main and pervasive effects of violence, the juridical legal apparatus demands words (or other signs) so that justice may be done. The ethnographer, in her turn and in her own way, has come to rely on words (or other signs) so that her ethnography may be done. But in the sympathetic official, whom I later came to know, and his urging the coupe-dwellers to speak, we find not only a desire for justice as an end in itself but also the desire to reestablish the flow of life, human life, in the anthroposemeiosic process. The same would hold true for the sympathetic fieldworker, where the ethnography ought not to be an end in itself, an end to a semeiosic activity begun in the field. Consider again a statement of a laborer from the 22 Beats Coupe—the name given to this particular coupe—as recorded in the

Supreme Court Commission's report, who anticipates such a consequence when he observes, "If the condition of our life goes on this way, then we might soon lose the faculty of speech."

Consider for the last time the struggle of the poet Stefan George, whom Heidegger cites (cited in Connolly 1987: 143):

> So I renounced and sadly see:
> where the word breaks off
> no thing may be.

In all these instances, however, there is either an implicit or an explicit acknowledgment that language is essential for the being of things, but also for being human. The impasse experienced by all of these persons, where the word struggles to articulate with "the thing," also brings to light the mystery of language, even its essence. At the same time it must be noted that in all these examples (especially in the poem of Stefan George quoted by Heidegger quoted by Connolly—itself a transmission metaphoric of the flow of semeiosis) there is the unwarranted danger of construing language too narrowly. For what defines language is not solely the use of words, or even that of conventional signs; it is the use of any sign whatsoever as involving the knowledge or awareness of the relation of signification. Anthroposemeiosis entails practices that contain an interpretation of what it is to be a human being, to belong to a discursive community, a community with a more or less shared horizon. Thus the act of cutting off the arm of a white overseer by an angry young man (Daniel 1996: ch. 3) indicates as forcefully an awareness of the relation of signification as does the reflexive poet who writes the origin myth of Estate Tamils (Daniel 1996: ch. 1). And we know through signs or, more precisely, through the activity of signs or semeiosis.

Silence or, rather, the unwillingness or inability to partake in anthroposemeiosis of any kind could signify several things. For one, such semeiosic abstinence might conceal a knowledge of its significance. It could be motivated by the desire to bring about a breach between sign and object, words and their customary referents and interpretants, thereby forcing, even shocking, the "world" into taking notice. But it could also, more ominously, indicate the withdrawal from all anthroposemeiosis, as much refusing to be fully human as rejecting others' humanity. Being human is being part of the process of the reception, transformation, and production of meanings, shared and sharable by an indefinitely open community. Silence could spell the cessation of that process. And that would be truly tragic.

BEING HUMAN: BEING IN TIME

The highest form of sharing—human sharing—also entails caring. When Alagammal wonders whether I too, like the rest of the photographers and journalists, will forget her people with the first belly-filling meal, she wants to discern whether I care. She wishes to know whether her particular tribulations fall within the compass of things I care about, whether they belong— to be more precise—to my "care structure."[18] In Heidegger's ontological sense, the "care structure" is the "structure of disclosedness." Our world, our environment, is disclosed to us by virtue of our familiarity not with particulars but with its referential whole. On so many occasions, after giving me accounts of their trials, victims of violence would say, in despair, "What do they in America care about what happens to us!" or wonder, "Would they understand what is being done?" Questions or rhetorical assertions such as these are the performatives of those whose participation in the ongoing process of being human has been stifled by the threat of silence, by semeiosic paralysis, and by the inescapable presence of violence, and who want to be free again. Such performatives are uttered as a means to move the world, even if only by a sort of magical hope, to incorporate their particular condition into the care-structure of a larger humanity and a wider horizon of disclosedness. For it is only within the horizon of our disclosedness that we can *care* about what our fellow human beings care about. And it is through the spread of signs, especially symbols—the carriers of so many of our lives' meanings—that sharing and caring are possible. "Symbols grow and spread among the people. In use and in experience [their] meanings grow" (Peirce 2.302). Furthermore, "for every symbol is a living thing, in a very strict sense that is no figure of speech. The body of the symbol changes slowly, but its meaning inevitably grows, incorporates new elements and throws off old ones" (Peirce 2.222). To belong to this growth and this spreading of symbols, to belong to anthroposemeiosis, is to be human.

Growth, however, is a process in time. This is especially true of the growth of signs. Thus, in the words of Santaella Braga, "Where there is a sign, there is a temporal process seeing that the action of the sign is to develop itself in time" (1992: 313). And growth, especially the growth and spread of symbols, like time, is characterized by continuity. But even though, ontologically, time is continuous, "more like a moving tide rather than a series of discrete atomic moments" (Corrington 1993: 182), its continuity is not uniform in its three familiar modes: the past, the present, and the future. This is because the three modes of time are qualitatively different. It is this difference that makes the unfolding of time uneven; and in this "unevening" of time, it is the present that plays the principal agitating role.

In and of itself, the past is closed, and "not a realm of possibility" (Corrington 1993: 182). "The Past consists of the sum of *fait accomplis,* and this Accomplishment is the Existential mode of Time" (Peirce 5.459). "It acts upon us in the present as if it were a brute existent" (Corrington 1993: 57), and to that extent it is actualized in the present. To illustrate the actualization of the past in the present, let me turn to the story of Palanisamy as an example that is culturally embedded and far more pertinent than the one about the stellar nova given to us by Peirce.[19] Palanisamy is a former estate worker whom I find in the hills of Kodaikanal one evening huddled in his shack in pain, near a dying fire. He is unable to move his arms. The long hours of scraping wattle off trees for Tan India and South India Viscose have almost paralyzed them. He has also fallen and hurt his back. I suspect a pinched nerve at best or a far more serious spinal injury. But he has a different explanation.

His great-great-great-grandfather was the one who left India for Sri Lanka almost 150 years ago. This ancestor's son was born with stumps for hands. His grandson had lost his in a factory accident. His great-grandson, Palanisamy's grandfather, had his arms broken by the police (who were in the estate superintendent's pay) for having dared to write a petition to the police captain against the superintendent regarding his brutality toward laborers on the estate. The punishment, as Palanisamy's wife interjects, was more for his flaunting of his literacy than for the petition itself. His father, who had remarried when Palanisamy's mother died, returned to India with his new family in the early 1950s and died there of leprosy. He, Palanisamy presumes, lost his limbs to leprosy, "as all lepers do." When Palanisamy was repatriated to India, he first went to his ancestral village, the village that his great-great-great-grandfather had left. To his surprise, he was not welcome. He was told why. The pioneer ancestor was a teenager when he left. It so happened that his young sister was pounding rice paddy in a *ural* (mortar) with an *ulakkai* (pestle). The wooden mortar was about two and a half feet tall and the heavy wooden pestle was about five feet long. His sister, who was barely four feet tall herself, found it difficult to raise the pestle high enough before dropping it onto the grain in the hollow of the mortar. Deciding to make it easier for herself, she climbed onto the rim of the mortar and began pounding the grain from this more comfortable height. Her elder brother, Palanisamy's pioneer ancestor, seeing his sister desecrate the mortar—considered sacred by Tamils—in this manner, grabbed the pestle from her hand and struck her with it on her back. The little girl's back broke and she died. As punishment, the elders of the village banished him and his parents, forbidding them or their progeny ever to return; they then came to Sri Lanka for refuge and labor. "It is that act of murder that keeps coming back," said Palanisamy. "But my karma is over. I have no sons. My arms are the last to go. What has happened, has finally happened [i.e., the past is finally past]."

When the past facts return in memory and in experience only to reactualize themselves, the past does not enter the flow of time in the full sense. The past is repeated but is not continuous in and as time. The past's continuity in and as time depends on the possibilities and the generalizability of the future. Expanding on the nature of the future, Peirce wrote, "Future facts are the only facts that we can, in a certain measure, control" (5.461). What did he mean by this assertion, and what are its implications? To begin with, a fact is something that one believes to be true. And beliefs are arrived at inferentially, mostly unconsciously. Our—inferentially arrived at—beliefs also determine our conduct, about which Peirce observes that "the only controllable conduct is future conduct" (5.461). Accomplished facts of the closed past that are *actualized* in the present can be *realized* through beliefs generated by habits and habit-taking, these based on inferences that determine how we would conduct ourselves with respect to those facts in the future—what our comportment would be given our belief that certain things are true. Thus we find that continuity is fully realized only in the temporal mode of the future. And the temporal mode of the future is brought into play via elementary forms of inference, be they induction, deduction, or, most important, abduction. Thus even "the 'percept,' that is, the unitary element at the base of experience, is a vague something that is immediately given shape by a perceptual judgment." And "a perceptual judgment, while unconscious and automatic, functions as a kind of primitive abduction" (Corrington 1993: 59–60), a mode of inference that disposes one to act toward the world, even if only hypothetically, so as to reduce surprise and shock. To be able to have some control over what would happen (future subjunctive) is to be part of the movement of signs in time, to be part of anthroposemeiosis, to be part of the project of being human. When the future is so uncertain as to be nonexistent, semeiosis is essentially choked off; so is "human" life. For the bonded laborers of the coupes, there seems to be no future, but only a present that serves as the repository of a deadening past.

It is the presence of violence that concerns us most in this chapter. But what is the present? Working through and with Peirce on his struggle with the present does shed light on our own understanding of the presence of violence and of those whose lives are trapped in the violent present. If Peirce was clear about the ontological status of the past and the future, the present turned out to be far more inscrutable. Hence he wonders "whether no skeptic has attacked its reality." And he continues, "I can fancy one of them dipping his pen in his blackest ink to commence the assault and then suddenly reflecting that his entire life is in the Present—the 'living present,' as we say, that instant when all hopes and fears concerning it come to their end, this Living Death in which we are born anew. It is plainly that nascent state between the Determinate and the Indeterminate" (5.459). And further on, while discussing the nature of introspection too as being wholly a matter of inference, he writes: "One is immediately conscious of his Feelings, no doubt; but not that they are feelings of an *ego*. The *self* is only inferred." And then comes the startling addition: "There is no time in the present for any inference at all, least of all for inference concerning that very instant" (5.462). But if semeiosis is a series of inferences, and inferences are possible only in time, how can the absolute present even be a mode of time rather than a mere breach in time? In other words, it would be impossible to tell a percept apart from a perceptual judgment because the percept without a perceptual judgment is not *about* anything; that is, it does *not stand for* anything but itself. In the context of torture, for instance, pain becomes an end in itself, a percept that stands for nothing but itself. It signifies nothing itself (See Daniel 1996: ch. 6). It is the perceptual judgment that makes introspection and—more generally—inference possible. "Percepts are brought into the structure of time by their mediating judgments. Consequently, Thirdness, as ingredient in all perceptual judgments, makes full temporality actual for the realm of percepts" (Corrington 1993: 111). The word that Peirce uses for the combined reality of the percept and the perceptual judgment is "percipiuum." Once the percipiuum is born, the present has already lost its unique presence, its characteristic innocence, if you will. Thus Peirce observes that "in a perceptual judgment the mind professes to tell the mind's future self what the character of the present percept is. The percept, on the contrary, stands on its own two legs and makes no professions of any kind" (7.630). "The consciousness of the present is then that of a struggle over what shall be; and thus we emerge from the study with a confirmed belief that it is the Nascent State of the Actual" (5.462). The present qua present is like a tiny bubble in the tide of continuity that, however fleetingly, is an isolated monad, imprisoned in itself, lodged in the heart of time and yet not part of time.

Hidebound with time, semeiosis in general, but anthroposemeiosis in particular, does not always unfold or evolve evenly or smoothly (5.462). And it should be clear now why I said above that it was the present that played the principal agitating role in making the flow of time "uneven." Depending on the agitation of and in the present, time may move tremulously, stochastically, convulsively, and at times even cataclysmically. Life in its everydayness is made unremarkable by the smooth, semeiosic activity that bears time along. Strictly speaking, of course, the present qua present, as we have analyzed it, by being only at the threshold of time and not part of it, cannot introduce discontinuities into time. That is, the metaphor of the wave used to describe the flow of time should hold regardless of the present's presence in its conative externality. However, what I wish to argue is that the degree of trauma in the present, within the isolated bubbles that remain unbroken in the midst of the breakers they cause, and the manner of these bubbles' eventual explosion, have a bearing on the shape of time.

To return to our victims of violence, the arrhythmia, the tremors, the convulsions, the cataclysms in their lives are indicative of the continuing presence of the present in their lives, a present that has yet to be inferentially appropriated into the flow of time, a present that—if only it could be redeemed from its self-imprisonment—could play a nonstochastic part in determining future conduct, conduct guided by purpose. The repeated use of or drift into the trauma of violence I take to be an indication of the persistence of the effects of the presence of violence in their lives, an indication that the foaming, eddying presence of the past has yet to be fully delivered from the present into the flow of the future.

In this chapter, in deference to the presence of violence and the persistence of its effects in the here and now, and in deference to the sustained and predominant use of the present tense to indicate the presence of the not-yet-past in my interviewees' speech and life, I too resort to the rhetorical device of favoring the present tense. I employ, if you will, an iconicity of style. But this rhetorical device alone would fail to do justice, I believe, not only to the stories my informants have told me but, more specifically, to the great number of my informants who are multiply alienated from the master narrative of those in power. Let me explain. What I have called the "iconicity of style" is still, in a certain measure, tethered to the concerns of representation. To that extent, I am more attuned to the concerns of those who either have or wish to possess the master narrative. The master narrative is primarily representational in its presumptions. In other words, its conceit is in its claim that it represents the truth or reality. Even though other functions emerge from or accrue to the master narrative, as those who narrate it see matters, the narrative's main claim is its claim to representational truth. This indeed is the mode of the narrative of "modern history." Those who are multiply distanced or alienated from such narratives teach us not so much that the representational function is only partial and needs to be supplemented and complemented by other functions as that the representational function is not the only function.[20] This compels us to go further, beyond the appropriate tensing of language in the representational spirit, and to attend to the manner of representation's use and the effectiveness of its claims. In order to do this, let us return to Stefan George's problem, expressed in representational terms, as to how language and reality articulate, how "word and thing" come together.

FOUR WAYS OF REPRESENTING

I shall, adapting a scheme put forth by the political theorist William Connolly, address this problem by reviewing four major modes of relating reality to language. The most common view is that language represents. This view provides the raison d'être of the Supreme Court Commission's report, the newspapermen's stories, and the writ petitions. It stresses the aboutness of the language. This representational view of language, in its naive form, has been rightly taken to task by language philosophers, among others. It would be wrong, however, to assert that language is totally unrepresentative. Language does represent whatever object it claims to represent (and more), but only in some respects and not in others, in some capacities and not in others, and to somebody or something and not to others. This modified representational view flows into a second theory of language-object relationship that has been posited. This may be called the constitutive theory of language. Whereas the first affords primacy to the object, the thing referred to, the second vests constitutive powers in the subject or, in the more sophisticated version, in the intersubjective discursive patterns, in a consensual community, or in the system of shared meanings. Some of us call the latter culture.

There is a third theory of language, which, following Charles Taylor, I shall call the expressive theory of language. In this theory is contained the essential critique of the earlier two forms. To quote Taylor, "Our most expressive creations, hence those where we are closest to deploying our expressive power at the fullest, are not self-expressions; . . . they have the power to move us because they manifest our expressive power itself AND its relation to our world. In this kind of expression we are responding to the ways things are, rather than JUST exteriorizing our feelings" (1985: 239). This formulation is a corrective to the extreme forms of both representationalism and constitutivism. It brings together, much as Peirce did some one hundred years ago, epistemological idealism and ontological realism in the coconstruction of reality; consensus and correspondence strive toward unity. The consensus is no longer limited to the concordance between what I think and what my fellow human beings think, but extends to the concordance between what we think and feel and the world that is independent of our fancies yet can be known only relative to our fancies.

This theory is very seductive. In my own work on Hindu village India (1984) I have celebrated the cultural value placed on equilibrium and equipoise, the hope that concordance is achievable because it is there to be achieved. My belief is that this concordance should extend to the way of doing ethnography, that the optimal mode for doing such an ethnography is something akin to the expressive mode advocated by Taylor. My own choice of the present tense to be in harmony with the voices of my informants is a form of acquiescing to this theory. There will be, according to this view of the world, a day in the indefinite future when word and object will be perfectly articulated in the *OM*, when event and description will be perfectly attuned. But herein lies the danger: in the seduction, the hope, the illusion that someday there will be the perfect closure. The perfect click in the possible "long run" deafens one to the cacophony of the actual "short run." Connolly highlights the danger thus:

> The rhetoric of articulation, attunement, expression, responsiveness, faithfulness, depth, and self realization is designed to carry us through interpretation to a closer harmony with the world. But these terms insert a social ontology into discourse which itself might be interrogated. We are led to ask: does the pursuit of attunement draw us to an order in which we can be more at home in the

world, or does it insinuate a fictional ideal into discourse which can be actualized only through containment of that which deviates from it? (1987: 151).

In other words, the expressive theory of language shares with its representational and constitutive counterparts a vantage point that "consistently
gives hegemony to integration" (151). Such a rhetoric may be theoretical,
as formulated by the academic and intellectual; it may be commonsensical-
juridical, as in the case of the official who wanted the coupe laborer to
match words to experience because only such a matching would make his
words and his experience real; or it may be cultural, as celebrated in Hindu
cultural nondualism. But regardless of which form it takes, it conceals the
violence done to life when the recalcitrantly ambiguous character of lived
experience is downplayed or swallowed up by ever higher forms of compul-
sive ordering, an activity at which we intellectuals, in particular, excel.

This brings me to my fourth alternative way of viewing the relationship
between word and object. Connolly, with a bow to Nietzsche, calls it the
genealogical model. At the very outset let me admit that even though in this
chapter I favor the last and fourth view, it is not my intention to deny the
appropriateness of the other three in different proportions under conditions of different interests. In this chapter, I make a case for the fourth
because (1) this view is in general an excommunicant in the social scientific
discourse and denied (though ever-present) in commonsensical discourse,
and (2) the story of my concern is embedded in a larger social and historical context of discordance, to which this view is most appropriate, not
because of its purported consonance with such dissonance, but because it
privileges voices that are not in sympathetic vibration with the major channels of history, culture, and power. The representational and the constitutive views of concordance tend to be cognitive and mechanical; this is the
view of language that was made and then unmade in the earlier and later
Wittgenstein respectively. The expressivist sees this bringing together of
word and object as an affective coming together—a coming home, so to
speak, with hope and longing, much like the beguiled Sri Lankan tea-estate
worker who comes to his motherland of India and home state of Tamil
Nadu. In contrast to all three, the genealogist does not presuppose either
the possibility or the inevitability of concordance. Connolly's, and presumably Nietzsche's, genealogist assumes the world to be fundamentally indifferent to us, the world here being either internal or external nature. My
genealogist, if one might still call her that, is too Peircean to go that far.
"Peirce ties the meaning of truth and reality to the practices of inquiry in
the long run" (Joswick 1995: 880). At best, I can only be agnostic about the
"long run" and its possibilities for concordance. The states of violence in
which and with which one works, the sheer hopelessness this spawns, makes
the Nietzschean picture hold, at least in the "short run." My own position on

the appropriate stance to take, shaken as it is by the caprice of the present and, at best, by the hopelessness of the "short run," is to strive for congruence—a notion which I oppose by convention to that of coherence (Derrida 1978: 57).

The genealogist does not seek "attunement with higher unities," be it God, the state, or the world. For Alagammal, the state's symbolic head, the president of the republic, is a *kaṅkāṇi*, the biggest of them. And who is a *kaṅkāṇi*? The *kaṅkāṇi* was the recruiter of labor in the villages of India in the nineteenth and early part of the twentieth centuries. As a fellow villager, he was their self-appointed leader, their proctor and protector, supervisor and solicitor, and often their patriarch and provider. Such was the script. But he works overtime, mostly overtime, and then outside the script. He steals their wages; he squeezes every possible drop of toil out of them; he rapes their daughters and weeps when their sons die; he holds them in bondage; he sells their labor to the white man and builds himself bungalows and buys himself estates; he builds temples and feeds Brahmins; his wife is invariably pious and hankers for holy men. The *kaṅkāṇi* is that enduring note of discordance in the lives of these immigrant workers, a repository of caprice. The older man who led the assistant away with the words, "Now go along and screw your mother," is, according to Alagammal's daughter, also a *kaṅkāṇi*. The characterization is part facetious, part earnest. "We are all *kaṅkāṇis*," Alagammal adds. "This *kaṅkāṇi*-mentality is born with us and dies with us."

If this were true, then these laborers' agony would be as much the oppression from without as the will to domination from within. Indeed, genealogy does seek out attunement to such discordances within the self. Not just within the individual Cartesian or Jamesian self, that self contained in a "box of flesh and blood" (Peirce 7.591; cf. Colapietro 1989: 27–118.), but within the selfhood of a class, a community, a people. Normalizing, discursive practices, practices that employ vocabularies dispensed by the state, welfare organizations, and even trade unions, need to be interrogated by those assertions and asides coming out of the mouths of those like Alagammal, which are ordinarily "deflected, ignored, subordinated, excluded, or destroyed by (normalizing) discursive formations" (Connolly 1987: 155).

On a plantation in Sri Lanka, I was once instructed on why the white superintendent was a good man.[21] "He was good because we could laugh at his Tamil." The Sinhala superintendent who took the white man's place when the plantations were nationalized was also seen as good, better than the *kaṅkāṇi*. Why? "Because though he is like us (brown), he tries to be like the white man. He makes himself different. He is a dissembler (*veśakkāran*). We laugh at him." To be able to laugh at someone is to bring him down to size. He is your perfect mimic man (see Bhabha 1984): the brown sahib on a motorbike with pith helmet, khaki shorts, boots, and woolen stockings, who speaks Tamil with a cockney accent and English with exaggerated diphthongs and Sinhala syntax. Different and therefore not dangerous.

A *kaṅkāṇi,* by contrast, is one of them. He is each one of them: their history, their psychic geography, their political economy. He is a Tamil, a recalcitrant force, the embodiment of the "moment," the lord of caprice, not to be laughed at. A genealogical account, then, seeks attunement not with concordance but with its opposite: with the discordance that obtains between the self and the identities established for it by the civil state, civil religion, and civil psychiatry, "between personal identity and the dictates of social identification" (Connolly 1987: 155), between metaphors that usher in confluence and those that disrupt and disturb flow.

How then ought the story to be told in the genealogical mode? In its vocabulary and rhetoric, its own ambiguity must be made overt so as to caution those who read or hear to be wary of doctrines that glorify normalization. This also returns us to the choice of voice. Normalization at its best must be treated as an ambiguous good to be qualified, countered, and politicized. And politics, at its best, calls into question settlements sedimented into moral consensus, economic rationality, psychiatric judgment, academic habit, and ontological necessity. All these are *triangulations* of the moment and mood in meaning, in Thirdness, in semeiosis. But there is a danger in finding meaning before the full effects of discordance are appreciated. For while meanings grow, they are also predisposed to sink into petrified habits, into thinking that the job has been done and questions answered, into solving and forgetting. To be true to discordance, the discordance one detects in the tremulous present tense of Selvi's, Alagammal's, and Kamalam's speech (see also Daniel 1996: ch. 7), one must suspend, not merely hasten to solve; and the triangulation that an ethnography of that discordance must resort to is not one in which meaning dominates but one in which meaning yields to the moment, underwritten by a mood of suspicion turned against readily available normalizing ontologies. It would appear that I contradict myself. If I do, let me do so productively. First, I argued that to be human is to be in anthroposemeiosis. Then I claimed that anthroposemeiosis, the activity of signs in the lives of signifiers who know their significance, is an inferential activity. Third, that inference delivers the past and the present into the future. In the successful appropriation of past, present, and future in semeiosis, the necessary triangulation of Firstness, Secondness, and Thirdness, of mood, moment, and mind, is achieved. But now I seem to caution against triangulations of this sort. The caution is against preemptive triangulations of recalcitrant experience, against the premature acceptance of meanings that culture has to offer, or the ready-made solution the social scientist comes up with. The moment cannot be sacrificed to a mind or meaning that will only reproduce the same mood.

With the progression of this chapter, I have drifted toward a mode of writing that I call the genealogical mode. Despite the singular number in which "mode" and "method" are mentioned, there is no unitary genealogical method or mode. Most specifically, it does not concern the by now tired old distinction between the relative propriety of the first-person (reflexive?) account and the third-person (nonreflexive?) one—or, as Professor Michael Silverstein once punned over dinner, between "I(eye)-ing" the "it" and "(h)it-(t)ing" the "I(eye)." But genealogy is suspiciously alert to the voice of coherent narratives and their concerns and equally—but sympathetically—alert to those voices that are not in concordance with such narratives and are, at times, in direct discordance with them. This is no claim to questing after a truer "hidden transcript" in the deep recesses of the subaltern (Scott 1990). Nor is it even intended to identify master narratives with centers of power and institutions exclusively. It is to urge the anthropologist fieldworker, who in this one respect has an advantage over his or her fellow social scientists, the economist and political scientist in particular, to tune her ear in the field to statements, claims, accounts, and stories that—in the words of a political scientist friend of mine with whom I shared a sampling from my fieldnotes—"have nothing to do with anything." My friend was at that time working in Colombo with her taped interviews of several leading Sri Lankan politicians; what she meant by her assessment of my gleanings was that there was no way of relating such "fragments" to the master narratives of history, the state, welfare organizations, international relations, international aid organizations, the law, or trade unions. Typically, removed from the centers of power and opinion making, the anthropologist fieldworker is more likely to encounter the "outlandish" and thereby subjects his or her own power and opinion, garnered in the academy and the metropolises, to trial and erosion.

Anthropology and fieldwork notwithstanding, the ideal of writing genealogically is one thing, its realization quite another. True, I chose one of the most marginalized of the ethnic subgroups in Sri Lanka whose perspective I was going to privilege; and among them, true, I turned my attention to the voices of women and children; and true, genealogical writers such as Nietzsche, Foucault, and—more to the point of the task at hand—Allen Feldman (1991) have helped me tune my ear to the genealogical in general. But the gap between my ideal and my achievement is in itself a testimony to the enormity of the challenge of overriding and writing over coherent narratives in general and master narratives in particular. For one, there is, as always, the "background" that needs to be told. It is only natural that the reader who is uninitiated into Sri Lankan matters expects such a telling; equally naturally, the initiated reader also wants it to be told so as to measure the divergences between this telling and the one he or she might have chosen to tell. Background also establishes common ground. And it is the master narrative that serves as the readily available source for such a common ground of understanding, agreement, and disagreement. It makes available prefabricated questions: What is Sri Lanka? Where is Sri Lanka? Who are the Tamils? Who are the Sinhalas? When did the ethnic troubles start? What caused them? Are the Sinhala Buddhists chauvinists? Are the Tamil Tigers terrorists? Who do you think will win this civil war? How do you explain this violence? Does America have anything to do with what is going on? To all these and more, it also has a supply of answers from which one may choose. For another, even the "stateless" plantation worker is a (sovereign) subject of the hegemony of master narratives. The stories that plantation workers tell about themselves and others, about the country of their ancestors and the country of their birth, about goodness and evil, about bad men and kind men, all draw heavily from the text of master narratives, prepared in advance. There is a significant difference, however. Estate Tamils' experience is further removed from the concerns of these master narratives than are those of the Jaffna Tamils and the majority Sinhalas. This distance manifests itself in slippages, contradictions, and lacunae revealed by their stories that serve as potential spaces for genealogical prying. To be sure, such slippages, contradictions, and lacunae appear as such only for those who are at home in little else besides in the unfolding of coherent master narratives. At times Estate Tamil variations of a story are simply wrong. An example would be when a particular member of Parliament is named as having voted against their interest on a major issue when in fact he had voted in its favor. It is easy for me, as a scholar who has access to the facts in the parliamentary Hansards, to say that on this point the master narrative which cites the Hansard to back up its story is correct and the plantation workers' account is incorrect. My task would not be to stop there but to find out the conditions that make the refractory transformation of the "fact" both possible and necessary. The answers may not always be profound; but then again, sometimes they are. And violence, when examined at close range, interrupts the coherence of a master narrative. But to deny the coherence of violence is not the same thing as appreciating the challenge posed by its congruence with time, with semeiosis, and with our responsibility of writing an anthropography.

As indicated in the introduction to my book, *Charred Lullabies,* my visit to Sri Lanka in 1983 was motivated by a quest to find narratives that were alternatives to the master narrative: narratives contained in the songs of female tea plantation workers. Violence revealed far more than I had expected to find. Not only was I inundated by narratives that were alternatives to the expected alternative to the master narrative, but I also found the master narrative itself to be neither singular nor secure but plural and thoroughly vulnerable to the fires it had ignited and then had tried to tame. Although one might be tempted to deem the official story the master narrative, in the context of violence this story was master neither of its own narrative nor of those to whom the story was narrated. There were as many masters as there were narratives, the official source being but one of them. Some masters' narratives were never master narratives, and other masters' narratives were only master narratives some of the time. Violence undermined the narrativity of the master as well as the mastery of the narrative. I was also to realize that the subalterns have their own master narratives, narratives that are—as in the case of E P. Thompson's English working class (1966)—capable of frustrating the official narrative's mastery of itself. The politically dominant institution does not have full control over the master narrative, especially in the context of violence. The *kaṅkāṇi*'s narrative is a subaltern master narrative in its own right, but only to be undermined by the narratives of such persons as Alagammal and Kamalam, narratives that are as disturbing as they are fleeting.

Postscript

In the summer of 1994 I attempted to track down Kamalam. The camp by the sea was being dismantled. Kamalam's batch of refugees had long since left—escaped, died, or returned to Sri Lanka to live or die. Arrangements for the remaining refugees to be sent back to Sri Lanka were well under way. Where Kamalam had stood the last time I saw her, a russet-colored dog kept watch. The only one to remember Kamalam was an Indian fisherman. According to him, the hours that Kamalam spent looking at the sea began earlier and earlier and lasted later and later, until toward the end she spent all night and day by the ocean's edge. She did not know one day from the next. She said that she was waiting for her ancestors who had left to work on the hills of the tea estates. Not for her son—she never mentioned her son—but for her great-grandfather and great-grandmother. "They went for *peraṭṭu*,"[22] she would say. "Behold, they will come! (*Itō vantiruvāṅka*)." For her, neither death nor distance had consumed them. People who knew her had tried to take her with them when they left, but she had refused to go. "Then," continued the fisherman, "one day, she was gone. Some say soldiers took her away. Some say she went to the hills of Kodaikanal to work on the new potato farms. Others say she went with the sea. My wife thinks she is still around. I think she'll come back." As for me, I still see her

> . . . listening
> to the surf as it falls.
> the power and inexhaustible freshness of the sea,
> the suck and inner boom
> as a wave tears free and crashes back
> in overlapping thunders going away down the beach
> It is the most we know of time
> and it is our undermusic of eternity.
>
> Galway Kinnell

NOTES

1. In the conventional manner of citing from the works of Charles Sanders Peirce, the number to the left of the decimal point indicates the volume, and the number to the right indicates the paragraph.

2. This chapter was previously published in a slightly different form in my book, *Charred Lullabies* (Daniel 1996). It served as a transitional chapter that attempted to make explicit the effort that had in the previous three chapters of the book been implicit: to wit, the effort of writing about violence. To mark this transition, I began by posing the tacit question in the manner of an open query:

> To what shall I compare the writing of this book? I shall compare it to the lowering of a tetrahedron held by a string attached to its base into a liquid so that the point of the inverted pyramid, where the planes of three triangles meet, enters the liquid first. [The analogy derives from Peirce (5.263) where he presents the illustration of an inverted triangle dipping into a liquid in order to argue against the belief in a "first cognition." Cognition arises, he argues, as a *process* of beginning.] Alas, an individual "point" of contact is only an illusion. From its very first moment of contact, it is a contact with three sides, each side with three triangular planes. The three corners of the first of these planes are writing, violence, and time; of the second, representation, object, and interpretant; of the third, mood, moment, and mind. (Daniel 1996: 104)

3. For an explanation for the use of *anthropography,* see Daniel 1996: 7–9.

4. As a note of caution to the reader who is aware of the difference, I must stress that my understanding of the "real" is Peircean rather than Lacanian. Thus I render the "real" in the quotation from Lacan in Peircean terms.

5. I am making no claim here regarding whether or not the ontological experience of time in the manner of my treatment of it here is universal. I write only for South Asia and invoke Western notions of time to the extent that they do not contradict South Asian experiences of time.

6. Determination is active, whereas representation is passive. By "determination" Peirce meant the "delimitation of the possible" rather than "cause" (Peirce 8.177).

7. *Tōṭṭakkāṭṭān* is a derogatory term used by non-Estate Tamils of Sri Lanka to refer to Estate Tamils. It denotes one who labors on plantations and connotes one who is uncivilized and ill-mannered.

8. In this context, the man she refers to is not a real *kaṅkāṇi*—that is, one who was a labor leader on the plantations and is of Indian Tamil origin—but a Jaffna Tamil man who acts like one. *Kaṅkāṇi* in this context is somewhat like the facetious use of the term *boss*.

9. Both Vijay Kumaratunga (a popular movie star of the Sinhala screen and the late husband of the current president, Chandrika Badaranaike, who campaigned for a truce and an open and unconditional dialogue with the Tamil separatists) and Rajani Thiranagama (a professor of anatomy who kept the conscience of the Tamil people alive by documenting human rights abuses on all sides) were assassinated in the prime of their political activity.

10. For reasons that will become clear, in this chapter I shall favor the use of the present tense in my narrative. In the translation of interviews I have paid special attention to preserving the tenses used by the interviewee at every point of the interview. This is significant.

11. A collector is an appointee of the Central Government, a man (usually) who,

from the position's inception in the colonial days on, has wielded considerable power and prestige. He is the most powerful government official in a district. His office is comparable to that of the French "prefect."

12. At that time the most fashionable, "sporty," Indian-made car.

13. Men's unstitched lower garment that is tied at the waist and hangs to the ankle.

14. A Non-Resident Indian—that is, an Indian who has settled in the West—commands a certain measure of respect that the resident Indian does not.

15. The late Mr. M. G. Ramachandran, the chief minister of the state of Tamil Nadu, was recuperating from surgery in the United States.

16. An *ācārya* is, in this context, a kind of Hindu prelate. A *maṭam* is a monastery. The story that dominated the headlines of all the major newspapers and magazines of Tamil Nadu during this time was about a young Hindu prelate's leaving his *maṭam*. Ironically, the story had little or no interest for most non-Brahmin Tamils, who constitute 98 percent of the state's population. A story of interest to only 2 percent of the population had taken over the newspapers.

17. Wartenberg observes that force is "predominantly negative in that it can keep an agent from performing certain actions but cannot get an agent to *do* anything. Unlike force, coercive power actually functions by getting an agent to *do* something" (1990: 10).

18. For more on the ontology of care, see Heidegger (1962: 225–73).

19. "For instance, when a *Nova Stella* bursts out in the heavens, it acts upon one's eyes just as a light struck in the dark by one's own hands would; and yet it is an event which happened before the Pyramids were built. . . . The instance (certainly a commonplace enough fact), proves conclusively that the mode of the Past is that of Actuality" (Peirce 5.459).

20. I must thank Webb Keane, who helped me appreciate this point (personal communication).

21. Before the tea plantations of Sri Lanka were nationalized in the early 1970s, most plantation managers, "superintendents," as they were called, were Britons. Since nationalization, the Sinhalas have dominated the rank of planters.

22. From the English "parade," meant to describe the "parade" of workers to the field.

REFERENCES

Bauman, Zygmunt. 1992. *Mortality, Immortality, and Other Life Strategies.* Cambridge: Polity Press.

Bhabha, Homi. 1984. "Of Mimicry and Man: The Ambivalence of Colonial Discourse." *October* 28: 125–133.

Colapietro, Vincent. 1989. *Peirce's Approach to the Self: A Semiotic Perspective on Human Subjectivity.* Albany: State University of New York Press.

Connolly, William E. 1987. *Politics and Ambiguity.* Madison: University of Wisconsin Press.

Corrington, Robert S. 1993. *An Introduction to C. S. Peirce: Philosopher, Semiotician, and Ecstatic Naturalist.* Lanham, MD: Rowman and Littlefield.

Daniel, E. Valentine. 1984. *Fluid Signs: Being a Person the Tamil Way.* Berkeley: University of California Press.

———. 1996. *Charred Lullabies: Chapters in an Anthropography of Violence.* Princeton: Princeton University Press.

Daniel, E. Valentine, and Jeffrey Peck, eds. 1995. *Culture/Contexture: Explorations in Anthropology and Literary Study.* Berkeley: University of California Press.

Deely, John N. 1994. *New Beginnings: Early Modern Philosophy and Postmodern Thought.* Toronto and Buffalo: University of Toronto Press.

Derrida, Jacques. 1978. *Spurs: Nietzsche's Styles.* Chicago: University of Chicago Press.

Devaraj, P. 1985. "Indian Tamils of Sri Lanka." In *Ethnicity and Social Change in Sri Lanka,* 200–19. Colombo, Sri Lanka: Social Scientists' Association.

Feldman, Allen. 1991. *Formations of Violence.* Chicago: University of Chicago Press.

Heidegger, Martin. 1962. *Being and Time.* New York: Harper & Row.

Joswick, Hugh. 1995. "Charles Peirce's Pragmatic Pluralism by Sandra B. Rosenthal: A Review" *Transactions of the C. S. Peirce Society* 31, no. 4: 875–86.

Lacan, Jacques. 1990. *Television: A Challenge to the Psychoanalytic Establishment.* Trans. Joan Copjec. New York: W. W. Norton.

Parker, Kelly. 1998. *The Continuity of Peirce's Thought.* Nashville: Vanderbilt University Press.

Peirce, Charles S. 1932. *Collected Papers.* Vols. 1–6. Ed. C. Hartshorne and P. Weiss. Cambridge: Harvard University Press.

———. 1958. *Collected Papers.* Vols. 7–8. Ed. A. Burks. Cambridge: Harvard University Press.

Ricoeur, Paul. 1984. *Time and Narrative.* 3 vols. Chicago: University of Chicago Press.

Rosenthal, Sandra. 1994. *Charles Peirce's Pragmatic Pluralism.* Albany: State University of New York Press.

Santaella Braga, Lucia. 1992. "Time as the Logical Process of the Sign." *Semiotica* 88, nos. 3/4: 309–26.

Scott, James C. 1990. *Domination and the Arts of Resistance: Hidden Transcripts.* New Haven: Yale University Press.

Taylor, Charles. 1985. "Language and Human Nature." In *Philosophical Papers.* Vol. 1: 215–47. Cambridge: Cambridge University Press, 1985.

Thompson. E. P. 1966. *The Making of the English Working Class.* New York: Vintage.

Wartenburg, Thomas E. 1990. *The Forms of Power.* Philadelphia: Temple University Press.

CONTRIBUTORS

E. VALENTINE DANIEL, Professor in the Department of Anthropology, Columbia University

VEENA DAS, Professor in the Department of Sociology, University of Delhi, and Professor in the Department of Anthropology, New School University, New York

ALLEN FELDMAN, National Development and Research Institutes, New York, NY

ARTHUR KLEINMAN, Professor in the Departments of Anthropology and Social Medicine, Harvard University

MURRAY LAST, Professor in the Department of Anthropology, University College, London

PATRICIA LAWRENCE, Professor in the Department of Anthropology, University of Colorado

MARGARET LOCK, Professor in the Department of Social Studies of Medicine, McGill University

DEEPAK MEHTA, Lecturer in Department of Sociology, University of Delhi, India

MAMPHELA RAMPHELE, Vice Chancellor, University of Cape Town, South Africa

PAMELA REYNOLDS, Professor in the Department of Anthropology, University of Cape Town, South Africa

JONATHAN SPENCER, Senior Lecturer in the Department of Social Anthropology, University of Edinburgh

EMMA TARLO, Lecturer in the Department of Anthropology, Goldsmiths College, University of London

KAY B. WARREN, Professor in the Department of Anthropology, Harvard University

SUSAN L. WOODWARD, Senior Research Fellow, Centre for Defence Studies, King's College, University of London

INDEX

abuse, child, 103, 231, 271, 291; human rights, 271, 298; physician participation in, 271; sexual, 103

accords, Indo-Sri Lankan, 345

agency, 4, 5, 16–17, 20, 120, 121, 133, 136, 169, 180, 187, 199, 239; body and, 136; collective, 123, 196, 197; displaced, 129; embodying, 186, 200; naturalization of, 239; political, 42, 136; violence and, 16

agent, 125; indigenous as, 299; victim as, 306; of violence, 183

aggressors, gendering of, 62

AIDS, 272; economic abuses fostering, 226; hemophilia patients and, 226, 235–37, 240nn2, 3; stigmatized space for, 236; vaccine against, and African children, 271

Alvarado, Pedro de, 301, 304, 305, 306

American Medical Association, Council on Ethics and Judicial Affairs of, 290; Uniform Determination of Death Act and, 283

anamorphosis, figures exhibiting, 70

Anderson, Benedict, 133–34

animal imagery, 67, 68, 69, 96

anthroposemiosis, 350–51, 352, 355

Antigone, Lacan on, 206–07, 219

Anzaldúa, Gloria, 299

apartheid: children and, 141, 147; family and, 7, 155; kinship and, 7; legacy of, 103, 105, 108, 115; manhood and, 114; patriarchs and, 113; struggle against,

10, 141. *See also* family; manhood; masculinity

apology, 316; examples of, 17n1; sincerity and, 14

Appadurai, Arjun, 8, 9, 59

Apter, Emily, 59

assimilation, forced, 300–301, 302

Atget, Eugene, 60

atrocities, 17, 20

Babari Masjid, demolition of, 98n5, 99n8, 269n27

Baker, James, 37

Balkanization, 20

Balkans, 20–22, 32, 43n1

Bandaranaike, Sirimavo W. R. D., 124, 343–44

Barnard, Christiaan, heart transplant by, 280–81

beliefs, 196, 354

Benjamin, Walter, 75n25, 299

Biafra, healing in, 329–30; independence for, 319, 322; minorities in, 322; recognition for, 319, 322, 326; secession of, 315, 325; support for, 318–19; survival in, 321–23; teaching history of, 327

bioethics, 279, 285, 290

body, 47, 50, 53, 63, 65, 86–87, 92, 95, 97, 113–14, 136, 214, 217, 220, 222, 234, 251; as bestial, 79, 94–98; circumcision and, 79–80, 89, 239; derealization of, 71; disappearance of, 90–92; ethno-

Text:	10/12 Baskerville
Display:	Baskerville
Composition:	BookMatters
Printing and binding:	Friesens